# Joined in
# Discipleship

REVISED AND EXPANDED

# Joined in Discipleship

## THE SHAPING OF CONTEMPORARY DISCIPLES IDENTITY

### MARK G. TOULOUSE

Chalice Press

ST. LOUIS, MISSOURI

Cover design: Michael Domínguez
Cover illustration: Will Hardin

10  9  8  7  6  5  4  3  2  1                97  98  99  00  01  02

**Library of Congress Cataloging–in–Publication Data**
Toulouse, Mark G., 1952-
    Joined in discipleship : the shaping of contemporary Disciples
    identity / Mark G. Toulouse.
    Includes bibliographical references and index.
    ISBN0-8272-1710-2
    1. Christian Church (Disciples of Christ)   I. Title.
    BX7321.2.T68  1997                                286.6'3

Printed in the United States of America

To
*Joshua, Marcie,* and *Cara*
Three Toulouse children
who, in their own unique ways,
represent the faith, spirit, and
discipleship of the church
in future years

91415

# CONTENTS

# PREFACE

Writing books, in some ways, resembles raising children. You give them your very best attention and relate to them with the grandest of intentions. You try to develop within them the expression of particular values, and hope that others who encounter them will see those values expressed in the lives they assume once they have left the family environs where the home fires are brightly burning. But the bottom line is always the same. Once they leave your oversight, and usually before, they will assume a life all their own. Their futures are outside your "parental" control. People will meet them and respond to them in any way they see appropriate. As parent (or author) you want to protect them from those who will understand them in ways different from your own, but the truth is, you simply cannot. Books, like children, will always end up saying things you never intended for them to say.

The perceptions of those whose lives they eventually encounter help books (and children) to form new identities. That is not really a bad thing either, for it enriches the conversation in the familial and familiar places that matter to us most. The conversation represented by this book has already been enriched at many points and by many people. There were, for example, many "godparents" for this book. I am most thankful to twelve years of seminary students in Disciples history classes at Phillips Graduate Seminary and at Brite Divinity School whose joys and concerns regarding our denomination have influenced immeasurably the raising of this particular offspring. I am especially grateful for the work done by my student assistant of some years back, Holly Stovall, who worked so diligently on the index of this book during a time when she was frantically attempting to finish simultaneously her semester's course work at Brite and her final preparations for her two-year assignment with the Division of Overseas Ministries in Argentina. As well, I am indebted to others outside the classroom who took the time to read and comment on this text, among them people like Ken Teegarden, Bert Cartwright, Kay Bessler Northcutt, James Duke, Clark Gilpin, Joey Jeter, and Gene Boring. The critical commentary provided by these people was always to the point and greatly appreciated. Any blame related to the final shape of the text, of course, must not be placed at their feet.

ix

Various congregations and areas of the church have also contributed in their own ways to the development of this book. First Christian Church of Beaumont, South Hills Christian Church of Fort Worth, First Christian Church of Fort Worth, First Christian Church of Amarillo, Central Christian Church of Nocona, First Christian Church of Denton, First Christian Church of Tyler, the Trinity Brazos Area Leadership Education and Development program, the Tres Rios Derrick Cluster of congregations, the SNOASIS Youth Event in Bentonville, Arkansas, the Dallas Area Disciples Ministers, the Disciples Ministerial Fellowship of Fort Worth, and the District 9 Ministers in Oklahoma—all of these groups over the years have heard portions of this material in some form or another and offered valuable response that has served to enrich the whole of this text.

The library staff at the Disciples Historical Society in Nashville was, as always, very accommodating whenever I called for help. Brite Divinity School and Texas Christian University have supported this project in ways too numerous to mention comprehensively. Much of this book was written while on a university and divinity school funded research leave from teaching and committee responsibilities. During this time period, the university library granted me the use of a study carrel which I have utilized rather heavily for this and other research purposes. My secretary at Brite, Robin Gray, has provided expert aid in helping me complete the seemingly endless stream of details that always accompanies the final production of most any book.

My association with Chalice Press, especially working with editor David Polk, has been a good one. I am pleased that Disciples have a press and staff so deeply committed to the publication of books that address the past, present, and future dimensions of our life together as a Christian people consciously seeking to live in ecumenical dialogue with all other Christian peoples.

As is always the case, writing, in combination with teaching and research, involves time commitments that extend beyond some mythically typical 8:00 a.m. to 5:00 p.m. workday on Mondays through Fridays. Therefore, family members often are affected by the writing commitments of a spouse or a parent. My wife, Jeffica, and all three children are very supportive of my bent toward spending some of my late evening and weekend hours in the study. They also solidly surround me with the best dimensions of what it means to be a family.

So, with publication, this "book-child" takes on its own life. My hope for it is not that everyone will understand it in precisely the same way I do, for such a wish, if fulfilled, could ultimately limit its ability to speak beyond my own very limited intentions for it. As people read these pages, my hope is that new conversations will emerge, between reader and book, and between readers and readers. The first conversation will no doubt be enriched by the concerns and hopes brought to the text by each individual reader. The second conversation, likewise, should produce insights far more important than the limited ones presented within the book itself. If such possibilities materialize, then I just might happily indulge myself by assuming a small measure of the pride that so often finds a resting place among parents whose children ultimately participate in accomplishments that obviously exceed the inherited limitations specific to the genetic pool of their origin.

Mark G. Toulouse
Brite Divinity School
Fort Worth, Texas

# INTRODUCTION

---

*We rejoice in God, maker of heaven and earth, and in the covenant of love which binds us to God and one another. Through baptism into Christ we enter into newness of life and are made one with the whole people of God. In the communion of the Holy Spirit we are joined together in discipleship and in obedience to Christ.*

From the Preamble to
The Design for the Christian Church
(Disciples of Christ)

---

Søren Kierkegaard relates a story about a Swedish peasant who came into a small and unexpected sum of money. Anxious to spend his newfound fortune, he traveled by foot to the nearby capital city. After he purchased a much needed new pair of shoes and stockings, he discovered he had enough money remaining to get drunk, something he had been unable to afford for years. Later, drunk, and stumbling down the road toward home, he became so tired that he lay down right in the middle of the road and fell asleep. After a short period of time, a wagon appeared. The driver of the wagon shouted down at the peasant, "You had better move your legs or I will run over them." The peasant awoke from his drunken stupor long enough to look down at his legs. Because they were dressed in new shoes and stockings, he did not recognize them. He looked up at the driver and, with a wave of his arm, said, "Drive on; they are not my legs."[1]

1

As is often the case, the tragic resides just under the surface of the comic. The peasant's story acts as a metaphor for many who define their identity by reference to superficial things. The self is never truly defined by the outer dress. The drunk peasant, like so many Americans even today, defined himself by reference to external matters. Yet beneath those new shoes and stockings existed the man who failed to recognize himself. The core of the person was made up of something more substantial than mere outer trappings. He had commitments and beliefs. He possessed loves and hates. His life contained centers of faith and pockets of disbelief. All of these inward attributes defined the real person.

As I reread that story recently, while the pages of this book were fresh on my mind, I could not help but wonder if Disciples from earlier days, sober though they always were, would recognize those of us today who, dressed in new shoes and stockings, still identify ourselves as members of the same body of Christians they organized some two hundred years ago on the American frontier. Or would they look up at the driver of the wagon and exclaim, "Drive on; they have no relationship to me"? In many ways, we would certainly look strange to them. At first glance, because of the change wrought by time and circumstance, as well as by conscious theological and pragmatic choices made over time and in response to circumstances, early Disciples likely would not easily recognize us. Further, in today's postdenominational context, where Christians move easily from one Christian tradition to another, it is not easy to find much conscious continuity with our respective denominational pasts. Yet one can hope that in us and in our work, early Disciples would recognize pieces of themselves. For, in many ways, we are who we are because of who they were. If they looked closely enough, beneath the outer trappings of change wrought by time and culture, they would most likely catch a glimpse of their own commitments, their own centers of faith, living on in us.

## *Joined in Discipleship*

In a very real sense, we are "joined in discipleship" with our denominational ancestors. Our stories carry on the narratives of their stories. What they began resides in us and moves unsteadily toward the future, even as it did in their own time. From out of their future and our past, we still find inspiration to proclaim the essence of the church's unity and to express our despair over the reality of the church's fragmentation. We serve the same God they served. We are enlivened by the same Spirit. We acknowledge the same saving grace of God revealed in the same Christ.

To recognize continuity is not to deny change. We ask the same questions today, but we do not always come up with the same answers. We have changed. Our world is different from their world. The frontier is long gone; it had begun to disappear before Disciples had fulfilled the days of their youth. Today, tall skyscrapers occupy our landscapes; indeed, even some of our church properties. In many ways, our faith has taken on new dimensions of meaning and expression. Faith has found new voices, some of them outside the range of experience known by Disciples of the early nineteenth century. Theology has found new forms, some of them frightening to those who are most comfortable with more traditional understandings. Most would agree, however, that the reality of change is a part of human existence. Christian witness, as it moves across the stage of human history, had best take notice of it.

Change cannot negate the very real connections present-day Disciples could explore between ourselves and those who have gone before us. As Disciples, we do share a rich heritage. The problem, however, is that the more important of these connections are often below the surface, beneath the outer dress that so often captivates our attention. As a result, some connections are lost among those of us who concentrate only on the outer trappings of faith. As a people, we do not possess a strong history of reflection about what it means to be Disciples. We are proud of our freedom in Christ. But does freedom in Christ have to mean fuzziness in the expression of our faith? Is diversity truly the most important mark of our identity? Is it an appropriate posture to proclaim that "you can believe anything you want and still be a member of the Disciples of Christ"?

The passion running through Disciples heritage contradicts such a posture. Though early Disciples affirmed diversity, they did not shy away from commitment. They were excited by the gospel. The gospel of Jesus Christ provided a new way of seeing the world. Disciples preached it with conviction. Alexander Campbell and other Disciples like him were equally committed to the rational expression of their faith. In other words, they engaged wholeheartedly in the theological enterprise. They opposed "theology" whenever it appeared in their midst as "dogma." Most of the theology they saw around them they condemned as static and dead, as something imposed by authorities instead of being generated by a living faith. But they never condemned theological reflection. On the contrary, they embraced and exemplified it. They thought through the implications of their faith, and they sought to provide a vital and rational witness that would speak powerfully to their times.

Clark Williamson has pointed out that "theology is a *critical* discipline that reviews the witness of the churches and asks whether that witness is appropriate and true."[2] Such a task is impossible among those who have no convictions, who claim nothing in particular to be true and worthy of belief. Theology seeks to define Christian identity and attempts to speak to what it means to be Christian. Where there is no Christian identity, there can be no Christian witness. Theology asserts that the

things we believe about God make a difference in the way we see ourselves and in the way we live. We cannot say that God is a God who
loves each and every human being and then refuse to participate in what
the love of God means for the world. We cannot say that Christ revealed
a God who seeks justice for each and every human being and not be
moved to act out the meaning of God's justice for our world.[3] Our theological claims must be revealed by who we are; otherwise, they mean
nothing. For Christians, business can never proceed as usual, as it does
with the rest of the world. These claims about God's love and justice, as
revealed in Christ, are continuing theological claims. They continue to
guide our theological reflection.

But theology itself is not a static discipline. It emerges from the ever-
present interaction between God's redemptive activity in the world and
our own contemporary human life. Since we are human beings, we realize our theological understandings can be wrong. Theology is an active
reflection, not a settled dogma. Early Disciples realized that static theology meant static faith. It meant an affirmation of God's activity in the
past but a denial of God's activity in the present. Vibrant theology evolves
from the continuing human experience of what it means to affirm God is
at work in our world: in our history, in our present, and in our future.
Living theology seeks to express the wholeness of creation, and the wholeness of God's activity in the midst of creation. No time or place is ever
isolated from God's presence or God's activity. The present, therefore, is
inextricably bound up with the past and the future in the reality of God's
activity in the world.

To say we are "joined in discipleship" with Christians from our past,
therefore, is to say something very important. Their task, Christian
discipleship, is also our task. We do not ask what early Disciples believed
and practiced so that we can believe and practice exactly the same things
in exactly the same ways. We are not out to establish a nineteenth-
century congregational life and witness in a world about to enter the
twenty-first century. To do so would be to fall prey to the temptation of
relying upon past human opinion for our present life and work and to
turn theology into a static enterprise. Nineteenth-century Disciples
criticized the church of their day at precisely these points.

Early Disciples sought to be faithful to apostolic faith but did not
attempt to confine God's activities to some distant past. Rather, they
were concerned with living a life of faithfulness to the gospel that could
testify powerfully to the meaning of God's activity in their own present.
Open also to the newest developments in human understanding and
scientific knowledge, their leaders sought to understand faith, not by
denying the capabilities of human reason, but rather by exploring those
capabilities to their fullest extent. For them, Christian discipleship reflected a contemporary, active, and reasonable task. The biblical witness

of God's activity in the world revealed that human life could be whole, coherent, and ordered. In God's relationship with Israel and in the Christ event, the meaning of human life became clear. Discipleship seeks an ordering of contemporary life to reflect that meaning. Early Disciples of Christ were dedicated to the task. Present-day Disciples, like those who have gone before us, must seek to live a life of discipleship that speaks appropriately to the time in which we live.

As we do so, we are joined in discipleship not only with our particular Disciples ancestors but with all Christians past, present, and future. For the life of discipleship is not limited to any one time or any one place. Though the forms of Christian life may change with time and location, the meaning of the gospel and the task of discipleship remain the same. All Christians seek to live in their present as those who recognize the meaning of God's gospel for human existence. Human witness to God's activity continues across time. Our present and future become somebody else's past. The narrative of our stories, of our successes and our failures, may provide inspiration for future Disciples, for future Christians who face different problems in different cultural contexts. All of us, all Christians through time, are joined in discipleship, in providing the content that some day, in God's time, will constitute the comprehensive story of Christian discipleship. It will be a story of Christians who, for their own times and places, sought to witness to God's love and God's justice in a world filled with difficulty and possibility, with despair and hope.

## An American Religious Movement

W. E. Garrison, the Disciples' first professional church historian, used the title of his second book on denominational history to describe Disciples as "an American religious movement."[4] Yet his belief that Disciples had to be understood in the context of their American surroundings appeared clearly in his first book on Disciples history, *Religion Follows the Frontier*, as well. Within the pages of that book, Garrison described the birth of Disciples as

> a typical case of a group originating on the frontier, embodying in its first period the intellectual and cultural characteristics of the frontier, and gradually undergoing modifications of attitude, structure, and interests with the passing of the frontier stage, the developing economic, social, and cultural life of its environment, and the urbanization and sophistication of what had been a simple and rural society.[5]

Most Disciples historians since Garrison have recognized the American character of the Disciples movement. Most books since his have attempted to place the social and institutional development of Disciples within the general American context.

This book, like those of other authors, takes seriously the social context of early Disciples. This book, however, is different in at least two respects. Ever since Oliver Read Whitley's 1959 interpretation of Disciples history, an analysis heavily dependent upon Garrison's frontier analysis, most informed Disciples have viewed their history through the rubric of the movement from sect to denomination.[6] Whitley argued that this change "was due largely to what was happening in American society and culture."[7] I believe it is time to question the accuracy of the wholesale depiction of early Disciples history as "sectarian." The rich theological heritage of the early days of the movement, dedicated as it was to the wholeness of the church and the importance of apostolic faith for that wholeness, seems to call at least some aspects of the sectarian analysis into question. I believe it is more accurate to understand the commitments of early Disciples as part and parcel of a struggle toward wholeness in church life, one lacking in maturity and often naive, one often affected by the fluctuations of American culture, but nevertheless one that was inclusive in intent and, therefore, hardly sectarian.

Secondly, this book differs from previous treatments of Disciples history in its attempt to present the theological heritage of Disciples of Christ from within the context of both the impact of American culture and that of the larger ecumenical community. The histories of our denomination have largely concentrated on the social and institutional development of Disciples life. They represent a style of "institutional" history more than "theological" history.[8] Every church needs such histories. Yet the particular approach of these histories has left the door open for more theological treatments to emerge. I believe the time to address theological issues in our heritage is long overdue. This book hopes to stimulate more work in this area.

The first chapter of this book describes the contextual background against which the emergence of this "American religious movement" took place. The major focus of this book is upon the Disciples of Christ in North America. This focus should not be interpreted as a devaluing of the lively existence of Christians related to the work of Disciples of Christ in Australia, Zaire, Kenya, Japan, the Philippines, and other locations throughout the world. Rather, this book is more narrowly focused on Disciples of Christ in North America in order to help these Disciples become more conversant with the historical, cultural, and theological roots of their own denominational identity. Part of the story, however, includes the development of a Disciples identity that has become increasingly aware of the importance of God's work in other locations of the world.

## History and the Contemporary

I am not a proponent of progressive history. I do not believe that older is automatically wiser. Nor do I believe that things are automatically better today than they were yesterday. Indeed, one of the great ways to abuse history is to use present standards to judge past actions, as if everything in the present is automatically superior to everything in the past. When people approach history from this perspective, they are bound to reinforce personal biases and prejudices. They may find justification for their own self-righteousness, but they most certainly will not learn anything from history or understand what it truly has to offer them as a check against their own parochialism.

There is an opposite temptation that often results in a similar abuse of history. That temptation resides in the belief that everything in the past is better than everything in the present. This perspective tends to view history as *automatically bad*, rather than automatically good. History, in other words, is naturally heading for worse times than we face today. The world only gets worse and worse until such time that the end comes. From this perspective, many judge everything in the present from the perspective of life in the past. Anything that smacks of the "modern" should be avoided at all costs. Wisdom only resides in the past, and only in people who repudiated the developments of their own time in favor of the wisdom of the ages.

Though such a posture might avoid some dimensions of the parochialism of present culture, it is, nevertheless, held captive to the parochialisms of past cultures. It is, therefore, not immune from the same devastating self-righteousness found among people who think history is automatically getting better. The meaning of the struggles and hopes of the past, struggles that were contemporary for those who lived through them, are lost to anyone who views history from such a perspective. [9]

As we think about Disciples identity, we must avoid the connotations associated with believing either Disciples are automatically getting better or automatically getting worse. The process of developing an identity does signify acquiring certain habits, traits, attitudes, and commitments. To have an identity means to develop a memory, both conscious and unconscious, both individual and collective. Over the past two hundred years, Disciples of Christ have developed a memory. Much of that memory lies unexamined for many in the life of the church. Norman F. Cantor, a scholar of medieval history, described the danger associated with such a position when he wrote, "The unexamined memory of the past is...prejudice, and however influential...prejudice may be in conditioning social action, [it is] error and not truth."[10]

This book attempts to examine the memory of the Disciples of Christ. Its chapters examine the development of the habits, traits, attitudes, and commitments that have guided Disciples life through time. Some of these qualities have developed in self-conscious ways; others have had a more surreptitious history. Some have improved with age; others have not. The aging of Disciples, therefore, has included both reflective and unreflective elements, both positive and negative dimensions. One enduring aspect of this process of aging, however, has included an ever-increasing appreciation for, and application of, a wider, more inclusive understanding of the notion of what it means to be church. Disciples began with a commitment to the universality of church and, through time, have come to express that commitment in more meaningful ways, both institutionally and theologically.

In this book, I have made my best effort to tell the Disciples story honestly, and to probe it carefully, in order to uncover a path to a type of denominational self-knowledge that might speak to the conditions of our present life. Yet, as a historian, I also must admit there is no such thing as an entirely objective history. Historians make judgments in the selection and handling of their materials. Such an admission, however, should never discourage us from trying to understand our present in light of our past. The knowledge of our past is essential to our ability to face the future with hope. The times we live in demand our ability to give an accounting of the faith that is within us, and to do so with intelligence *and* passion. In my inaugural address at Brite Divinity School, I put it this way:

> Church history acting as a partner in dialogue leads us to a more meaningful vision of our Christian identity, not only by exposing the relativity of our own claims, but also by leading us to a clearer understanding of the transcendent and more normative aspects of our life and faith. We come to an understanding of our connectedness with the whole community of humanity, not only the international community of which we are only a part, but also with the community of humanity in all times and in all places. This is the transcendent message of the gospel that lies at the heart of our Christian identity....Together, as we come to a greater appropriation of our Christian identity, we can better bear the burden of carrying the message of redemption to a hurt and broken world.[11]

## *A Disciples Identity*

The chapters of this book are topical. The Table of Contents provides the reader with a quick summary of what I regard as the essential aspects of the Disciples memory, and, therefore, of a contemporary Disciples identity. History has had its effect on each of these aspects of our identity. Each of the following chapters investigates a particular dimension of Disciples life. The first three chapters deal with what most Disciples theologians and historians have accepted as the foundational principles of early Disciples identity. These include the early Disciples emphases upon freedom of biblical interpretation, restorationism, and church unity.[12]

Scholars from the three contemporary movements tracing their origin to early Disciples have traditionally argued about which of these three commitments had priority. Disciples have tended to argue that unity was prior to everything else and guided Disciples life more directly than the other two commitments. Churches of Christ and the Independents have generally emphasized restorationism as the primary mark of early identity, with freedom of biblical interpretation running a close second. Part of the reason for these arguments stems from the fact that these principles seem to contemporary Christians to be so incompatible with one another. Most interpretations point out that the early divisions of Disciples life stem, in part at least, from the recognition that these principles created such severe tension that different groups of Disciples began to emphasize one of these principles above the others. As they did so, various Disciples advocates of these principles discovered they were unable to live with one another.

Regardless of the truth of these interpretations of later developments and divisions, one can state with certainty that early leaders of the movement viewed these three principles as completely complementary. They would probably have been unable to choose one above any of the others. Instead, they viewed all three as absolutely essential to the nature of the Christian enterprise. Their cultural context made freedom of biblical interpretation extremely important to them. They could not have imagined life without it. Many of the problems of church life, so evident all around them, had, in their view, resulted from the attempt of church authorities to control the messages of the Bible by imposing particular interpretations on Christians. The political context in which they lived respected the voice and understanding of the common person. The church could do no less.

God's revelation, according to biblical witness, had been provided for all human beings. The Disciples nineteenth-century view of the propositional nature of that revelation (that God communicated truth in clear and infallible declarative sentences) did not enable them to understand how any church could justify a belief that God had made the message too hard for the common person to understand without the aid of some authoritative interpretation.

As they exercised their God-given right to read and interpret the Bible for themselves, early leaders became convinced that God had provided a precise guide to the ordering of church life within its pages. Further, their experiences on the frontier brought them face-to-face with what they perceived as dramatic examples of blatant disregard for the self-evident biblical norms pertaining to church life. Obscure interpretations had obstructed the clear meaning of scripture. Such examples of hierarchical interpretation served only to reinforce the necessity of an individual's right to approach the Bible without the aid of an intervening authority. No one needed help to interpret what God had already seen fit to reveal. The context of the frontier in America, under the umbrella of religious freedom, offered the perfect opportunity to return the church's life to the picture of it presented in the biblical witness. Disciples leaders seized that opportunity and inaugurated what they referred to as the "reformation" of the nineteenth-century church.

Was concern for unity the driving force in this effort? Did Disciples begin with a theological recognition that the church was one and then hit upon freedom of biblical interpretation and restorationism as two primary ways to restore that unity? One can claim that unity, from the beginning of the movement's history, served as a formative goal. Yet early Disciples sought to set the unity of the church within the context of certain parameters. Unity, even if it was the prior principle, seems never to have existed independently of these other two principles. Early leaders consistently viewed it from within the context of biblical interpretation and the scriptural witness of the early church. The Bible set the conditions by which this unity should reach fulfillment and expression.

We are left where we began. There seems no simple solution as to which of these three principles had priority. It seems best to conclude that dedication to the unity of the church arose within the context of certain presuppositions about the nature of scripture. These included at least a commitment to the Bible's clarity and ultimate accessibility, and to its authoritative status as a source for the ordering of church life. Without the context provided by these two principles, the Disciples concern for unity might have expressed itself quite differently. Among contemporary Disciples, therefore, it is important to understand the historical developments affecting these two areas of our life before turning to the topic of unity. For this reason, chapters on biblical interpretation and restorationism precede the discussion of the enduring Disciples commitment to unity.

Chapter five is new to this book, arriving with this second edition. Few Disciples today, if asked to outline the beliefs shaping early Disciples identity, would talk much about eschatology. Few Disciples historians and theologians have examined this theme in any detail. There has been, however, a recent interest in the eschatological beliefs of the earliest Disciples.[13] My own reading in early Disciples sources these past few years, since the original publication of this book, has convinced me that the "eschatological principle" influenced earliest Disciples identity as much as any one of the three principles we have talked about to this point. As one historian of the movement put it, "Campbell's ultimate concern was for the kingdom of God, the millennium on earth....Campbell's millennial dream was one of the constant factors upon which his other, penultimate commitments shifted and changed."[14] This ultimate concern is illustrated by how Campbell named his journal, a title he chose "because of [the journal's] devotion to the principles which all christendom admits must spread before the millennium commence and triumph in that happy period."[15] Perhaps it is time to add a fourth "principle" to our understanding of Disciples identity at the beginning of our movement's history. This chapter makes that argument and attempts to emphasize the theological insights Campbell and other early Disciples derived from this aspect of their faith.

Chapters six through nine address the evolving commitments of early Disciples life. There is a logic followed in the order of these particular chapters. Disciples life, from its very beginning, proved to be dynamic. Its willingness to challenge traditional understandings of church life, based upon its four foundational principles (including the eschatological principle), eventually led to an equal willingness to examine its own life and thought and, as necessary, to affirm the need to change and reform its own understandings. The nature of this willingness to change and adapt is clearly evident in the chapters dealing with the foundational principles. These next four chapters describe the development of Disciples understandings in four essential areas of church life (sacraments, ministry, mission, and the meaning of "church"). The order of these chapters is determined by the chronological progression and accompanying social circumstances of eventual development in each of these four areas.

One of the earliest changes in identity among Disciples of Christ resulted from a new understanding of the importance of believers' baptism. When, in 1812, Disciples began to make this particular form of baptism important to the construction of their church life, they embarked on a new course, one that has had a profound effect upon the maturing of their life from that point forward. Change also emerged with regard to the Lord's Supper. Though Disciples had practiced a weekly Lord's Supper from the beginning, the Christians associated with Barton Stone had not. When, in 1832, the movements of Barton Stone and Alexander Campbell began to discover a common life, they simultaneously came to new understandings of the importance and meaning of the Lord's Supper. These two subjects, considered from a theological perspective, form the heart of the sixth chapter.

The story of the Disciples concept of ministry also reveals significant development through Disciples history and is found in chapter seven. After 1835, the Disciples struggle to cultivate and empower ministers dominated Disciples life. Social circumstances and incredibly rapid growth conspired to divert Disciples attention to this very important area of their church life. The effort to define Disciples ministry has continued to the present day, but the years from 1830 to 1870 introduced the factors demanding a more comprehensive approach to the development of a working and effective ministry for the life of their expanding group of congregations.

The years after 1870 witnessed a fresh engagement between the developing ministry of Disciples and the world missionary effort of the church. Beginning with the work of the women of the Christian Woman's Board of Missions in 1874, Disciples launched a comprehensive effort to meet the broadening demands of their emerging understanding of the Christian ministry. During these years, they woke up to the needs of global evangelism and sought to assume their responsibilities in that area. Though Disciples had possessed a strong sense of mission from their very beginnings, they reached a maturing sense of what that meant as a community only after their communal identity began to solidify.

Had it not been for the disruptive cultural atmosphere occasioned by events leading to the Civil War, this identity might have emerged sooner than it did. As it was, Disciples had to wait until after the war to begin to fulfill their responsibilities in world mission. They were transformed by the resulting experience. Chapter eight describes how the Disciples involvement in missions after 1870 led Disciples to deeper fulfillment of their ecumenical commitments and to a serious theological reconstruction of what the mission of the church in the world ultimately means.

As Disciples moved through the twentieth century, heavily invested in both missions and the ecumenical movement, they slowly arrived at a more inclusive and universal sense of church life. Theological reflection led them to a renewed understanding of the practical implications of viewing the nature of the church in terms of its identity as the "Body of Christ." Beginning in 1960, Disciples began the process of putting their renewed sense of the unity of the church into practice. Chapter nine describes this development. As the "Christian Churches" became the "Christian Church," the historical saga of Disciples identity reached yet another important turning point.

Chapter ten is also a new addition to this book. It addresses several features of the changing social context of contemporary church life in America since the late 1960s. Just as Disciples officially joined, in a self-conscious way, the ranks of the American denominations, American culture took an anti-denominational turn. American pluralism in this modern world has led today to the "cultural disestablishment" of the mainline denominations. What does it mean to be a denomination in a post-denominational age? This chapter makes the argument that, in an ironic sort of way, a reaffirmation of, and renewed concern for, contemporary Disciples identity may be the most important response we can make to this social context. Is it possible that attention given to the question of what it means to be a denomination can be an appropriate initiative in a post-denominational context?

Biblical interpretation and unity: these principles retain their importance for Disciples today. The restoration and eschatological principles have left a legacy of residual identity largely divorced today from the specifics of the original beliefs of the founders. But these latter two principles contain theological insights deserving of our renewed consideration as we think about contemporary Disciples identity. Sacraments, ministry, mission, church: these aspects of Disciples communal life continue to find meaningful expression in our midst. Commitments related to all these areas have weathered the historical process and remain with us still, important elements in the memory that defines our Disciples identity today. None of these areas remains precisely as it was in the beginning. Each of them has changed in some significant way, some more dramatically than others. None of them has ever stood alone. Each of them has played upon the others, and in some way or another, has been transformed by the process. None of them has been immune to the influence of the culture. Nor has any of them been overtaken by it. As the story that follows reveals, these various threads of Disciples life continue to weave a fascinating tapestry. Perhaps they can help contemporary Disciples deal with the ebb and flow of living as a denomination in a post-denominational age.

## *Questions for Reflection and Discussion*

1. What is Disciples identity? How is it primarily defined among us: is it defined according to external matters (like the celebration of communion every Sunday) or the internal beliefs and commitments of Disciples (what do Disciples understand communion to mean as they celebrate it every Sunday)? How does the concept of *memory* enter into an understanding of Disciples identity? What do you find helpful in the Introduction that might aid your attempt to define the identity of Disciples?

2. How could Disciples work to bring practice and belief to fuller partnership in all they do? How is theology (things we believe about God) related to Christian practice (the way we live our lives and act our faith)? In what ways do these two things, theology and practice, in dialogue with the memory we share, constitute the substance of our discipleship, both as individuals and as a community of faith?

3. In our time, can you think of examples of how faith has been expressed by "new voices, some of them outside the range of experience known by Disciples of the early 19th century?" Why are new voices or new forms so threatening to those of us who hold to more traditional views? How might we be open to change while, at the same time, we are concerned with faithfulness to the gospel? Can you name some examples

of how we might confuse "gospel" with other things (certain dogmas, forms, or voices of our own)?

4. What does it mean to be "joined in discipleship?"

## Notes

[1]Søren Kierkegaard, *Fear and Trembling* and *The Sickness unto Death*, translated with introductions and notes by Walter Lowrie (Garden City, New York: Doubleday Anchor Books, 1954), p. 187.

[2]Williamson, "Good Stewards of God's Varied Grace: Theological Reflections on Stewardship in the Disciples of Christ," *Encounter* 47 (Winter 1986): 63.

[3]Clark Williamson has defined these two aspects of God's character as the essence of the gospel. See Clark Williamson, "Theological Reflection and Disciples Renewal," in Michael Kinnamon, ed., *Disciples of Christ in the 21st Century* (St. Louis: CBP Press, 1988), p. 90.

[4]Winfred Ernest Garrison, *An American Religious Movement* (St. Louis: The Bethany Press, 1945).

[5]Garrison, *Religion Follows the Frontier* (New York: Harper & Brothers, 1931), p. xi.

[6]In this way, Whitley was also heavily dependent upon H. Richard Niebuhr's work, especially *Social Sources of Denominationalism* (New York: New American Library, A Meridian Book, Reprint Edition, 1975), originally published in 1929.

[7]Whitley, *Trumpet Call of Reformation* (St. Louis: The Bethany Press, 1959), p. 34.

[8]See, for example, the two classic textbook treatments of Disciples history: W. E. Garrison and A. T. DeGroot, *The Disciples of Christ: A History* (St. Louis: The Bethany Press, 1948); and William E. Tucker and Lester G. McAllister, *Journey in Faith* (St. Louis: The Bethany Press, 1975).

[9]Those who understand history as progressive, getting better and better, are similar in perspective to the nineteenth-century belief in progress shared by postmillennialists; those who understand history as automatically getting worse are similar in perspective to those who defended premillennialism in the same period. See chapter five for a discussion of these two perspectives as they existed among early Disciples of Christ.

[10]In a "Prologue" to his book, *Medieval History: The Life and Death of a Civilization* (New York: Macmillan Publishing Co., second edition, 1975), Cantor goes into much greater detail related to the uses and abuses of history than is afforded me here. His clear presentation of the topic, first read by me early in my graduate school life, influenced my approach to history in general. See especially pages xix-xxiii. I have taken the liberty to edit, by the use of brackets and elipses, Cantor's words. His original quotation included the word *myth* as a negative factor in conditioning social action. Such a negative use of the word has a long history, especially in Western culture, to denote something that is either "precritical" or "irrational." Yet, in more recent days, religious scholars in the West have grown in their appreciation for much more positive meanings of the word *myth*. For a good exposition of the word *myth* as it is understood as a container for "the sacred stories of oral cultures or in the scriptures of historical religions," see William E. Paden, *Religious Worlds: The Comparative Study of Religion* (Boston: Beacon Press, 1988), especially pp. 69-92.

[11]See Toulouse, "Church History as a Dialogue Partner in the Quest for a Christian Identity," *Union Seminary Quarterly Review* 42 (No. 3, 1988): 42.

[12]The first of these, thanks to a book written by Ronald Osborn and an essay written by Larry Bouchard, has more recently joined restoration and unity in most Disciples historiography to form a threefold picture of the most important commitments of early Disciples life. See Ronald E. Osborn, *Experiment in Liberty* (St. Louis: The Bethany Press, 1978); and Larry D. Bouchard, "The Interpretation Principle: A Foundational Theme of Disciples Theology," in Bouchard and L. Dale Richeson, ed., *Interpreting Disciples: Practical Theology in the Disciples of Christ* (Fort Worth: Texas Christian University Press, 1987), pp. 1-26.

[13]Anthony L. Dunnavant has summarized some of this work in his "Evangelization and Eschatology: Lost Link in the Disciples Tradition," *Lexington Theological Quarterly* (Spring 1993), particularly pp. 47-51. Among the Disciples, Dunnavant has been one of the primary historians emphasizing the importance of the eschatological context for early Disciples. See Dunnavant, *Restructure* (New York: Peter Lang, 1993), p. 5; and Dunnavant, "Core Values and Disciples Culture: A View from the Inside," unpublished paper delivered at the Annual Meeting of the Religious Research Association, Nashville, TN, on 9 November 1996, p. 3. In this latter paper, Dunnavant presents what he describes as four core values for early Disciples life: freedom, apostolicity, unity, and evangelization. These values, he argues, are held within a context which "might be termed providential and eschatological." Stephen V. Sprinkle's 1988 *Discipliana* article also lifted up the importance of Campbell's eschatological beliefs as he discussed his doctrine of the church: see Sprinkle, "Alexander Campbell and the Doctrine of the Church," *Discipliana* (Summer 1988): 24-25. A recent essay by a Disciples minister has also examined the subject: see Tim Crowley, "A Chronological Delineation of Alexander Campbell's Eschatological Theory From 1823-1851," *Discipliana* (Winter 1994): 99-107. The importance of this theme for the Stone-Campbell movement has only recently received full (and somewhat controversial) treatment in the new history of the Churches of Christ written by American religious historian Richard T. Hughes, himself a member of the Churches of Christ. See *Reviving the Ancient Faith: The Story of Churches of Christ in America* (Grand Rapids, MI: William B. Eerdmans Publishing Company, 1996); see also Richard T. Hughes and C. Leonard Allen, *Illusions of Innocence: Protestant Primitivism in America, 1630-1875* (Chicago: The University of Chicago Press, 1988), especially pp. 108-112, 121-33, 171-187. David E. Harrell, another historian in the Churches of Christ, gave some attention to early millennialism in his book *Quest for a Christian America: The Disciples of Christ and American Society to 1866* (Nashville: Disciples of Christ Historical Society, 1966), see especially pages 39-61. See also the interesting essay by William D. Howden, "The Kingdom of God in Alexander Campbell's Hermeneutics," *Restoration Quarterly* 32 (1990): 87-104. An interesting non-Stone-Campbell perspective on Campbell's millennialism is found in the Appendix to Ernest Tuveson, *Redeemer Nation: The Idea of America's Millennial Role* (Chicago: The University of Chicago Press, 1968), pp. 215-231.

[14]Hughes, *Reviving The Ancient Faith,* p. 45. Actually, in this sentence, and in his book generally, Hughes is failing to distinguish between Campbell's understanding of the millennium and his understanding of the kingdom of God. For Campbell, as the fifth chapter will make clear, these two realities were very different.

[15]"Reply to Mr. Waterman," *Millennial Harbinger* (April 1934): 156.

# 1

# BORN IN AMERICA
## DISCIPLES OF CHRIST IN CONTEXT

---

*Dearly beloved brethren, why should* we *deem it a thing incredible that the church of Christ, in this highly favored country, should resume that original unity, peace, and purity which belong to its constitution, and constitute its glory?*

Thomas Campbell,
*Declaration and Address,* 1809[1]

---

## Introduction

From the time they set foot on America's shores, the first colonists sensed a new freedom in the air. They did whatever they could to protect it. Over the years, the price of their freedom, and the freedom of their descendants, had been high. Many died early on when the first winter simply outlasted them. Others died before medical centers could be established and disease could be treated under sanitary conditions. Still others died when Native Americans tried in vain to protect their own understanding of freedom. As early battles with these misunderstood people demonstrated all too well, colonists often defined freedom in ways that excluded the freedom of others. When, in 1619, a ship named *Jesus* delivered twenty black indentured servants to Virginia, this story of exclusion gathered momentum in yet another direction. By 1800, one person in five in America was black; most of them were slaves. The human cost of freedom for them was high as well.

17

Where did the American all-consuming quest for freedom come from? Did the Puritans in Massachusetts, the Catholics in Maryland, the Dutch Reformed in New Amsterdam, the Baptists in Rhode Island, the Quakers in Pennsylvania, the Anglicans in Virginia, the various religious and nonreligious renegades in Georgia (an early dumping ground for English criminals), and the great majority of colonists outside the membership of any congregation all have some inherent understanding of the principles of the Declaration of Independence some one-hundred-plus years before it was written? How did such a diverse group of people ever come to form a nation in the first place? How did they come to think of themselves as "free" Americans above any other identification they might have had? The latter question has perplexed scholars for generations.

One thing is certain: American identity did not just suddenly appear out of nowhere. It took more than a century to develop. No doubt the so-called Great Awakening, a religious revival that swept America during the second quarter of the eighteenth century, had something to do with it. The revival left many colonists with the feeling that God had reserved a special place in divine providence for this land and issued a special purpose for its people. Yet many other religious, political, and social elements combined with this one to forge the American sense of self. The covenant theology of the Puritans mixed with the rationalist bent of John Locke. Colonists threw into the concoction a smattering of English common law, the best elements of the Enlightenment, and a rather romantic vision of the old Roman republic.[2] When this compound of ingredients had simmered long enough, a uniquely American flavor began to emerge.

By 1750, at least in the view of its inhabitants, the land known as America became synonymous with liberty. When that happened, the Revolution became inevitable. Every move taken by the English king or by Parliament, no matter how innocent the intent, was interpreted by the developing American mind as an intrusive obstacle to liberty. Any objective study of the various British acts, and American responses to them, confirms that leaders in England and America had lost the ability to communicate reasonably with one another. Americans had come to share a world view that British rulers could not understand. Americans did not really understand it themselves. In spite of what large numbers of confused American ministers preached from their pulpits during the days leading up to and during the revolution, King George III and his minions were not the forces of the antichrist. But the sentiment helped win the victory anyway. The cost of freedom remained high.

Only in the four or five decades after the revolution (1780-1830) did the full impact of this freedom truly permeate the everyday life of the average citizen in the newly formed republic. Coinciding in time with this phenomenon, and breathing in deeply the air of its influence, the story of Disciples really begins. The Christian Church (Disciples of Christ) is the largest mainstream Protestant denomination to be born in America. Like all religious movements, its beginnings were greatly affected by the nature of its surrounding culture. A brief examination of the social context in which Disciples were born provides insight into some aspects of the uniquely Disciples approach to Christian faith.

A study of the period after the Revolution has described it as the time when "the democratization of American Christianity" took place. Ordinary people took matters of faith into their own hands and began to reject the power and authority of the elite religious establishment. Movements like those of the Disciples, the Baptists, the black churches, and the Methodists "did more to Christianize American society than anything before or since."[3]

Methodists, a new group just prior to the revolution, grew to 500,000 strong by 1830. Baptist congregations multiplied from 500 to 2500. Black congregations appeared all over the landscape. Disciples, a group that did not even exist at the time of the revolution, became one of the six largest Protestant groups in America by 1850. What social conditions helped to make such phenomenal growth possible? Several factors in American life after the revolution tended to favor these groups. The most important one, perhaps, might be defined as the development of a crisis in the area of authority in American life.[4]

In attacking so strenuously the authority of British tradition and its elitist institutions during the war, Americans also, by implication, eschewed the establishment of their own powerful institutions. Traditional respect for authority based upon class or education or particular social position in society rapidly diminished. At the time of the war, America possessed very few institutions capable of holding the loyalty of vast numbers of citizens anyway. So where was authority in the culture to rest? If one listened to the rhetoric of the revolution, and most Americans did, the answer was simple: it was to rest in the people.

One thing the majority of Americans seemed confident about was their common distrust of institutional authority. The post-revolution period was the era of the common people. The decades after the war were those of the "real American Revolution," the time of a major "shift away from the Enlightenment and classical republicanism toward vulgar democracy and materialistic individualism."[5] Shortly after the war, Thomas Jefferson and his growing republican movement plugged into this sentiment of the masses and encouraged the common people to believe in themselves, and in the importance of their own freedom and individual sovereignty. Jeffersonian republicanism helped to sever the cords between the present and the past. The past no longer held the key that would unlock the hidden wisdom of the ages. Wisdom could be found in the present. Wisdom resided in the common folk.

The years surrounding the turn of the century witnessed the rise of American individuality. Society began to place supreme importance in the will of the people or, perhaps more accurately, in the will of individual persons. The notion of authority, as a result, was transformed. Authority became something individuals, of their own free will, chose to vest in someone or something. It was no longer automatically the province of institutions or offices held by individuals in those institutions. Authority rested in the will of the people. Such a change also affected the ultimate understanding of where truth could be found. Truth no longer emanated from the top down; rather it arose from the will and understanding of the common people. Such an atmosphere created an increased premium on the skills of persuasion. Leadership fell more to those who could persuade, who could speak the language of the people, than to those who had been groomed by class or education to assume it.

Jeffersonians responded to this development, and encouraged it, by creating a new style of newspaper and print media. In the two decades after 1790, the number of newspapers alone grew from 90 to 370. Bolstered by new print technology, this new press appealed to the ordinary citizen like no print media ever had before. Exploiting the general distrust of elitist power, this new medium of communication spoke directly to the concerns of the common person on the street. And those people responded with votes for Jefferson and others like him.[6]

Other social currents fed this prevailing tide of the times. First, Americans experienced incredible growth in both territory and population. In 1800, with a territory of just under one million square miles, the population in America rested at around five million. By 1850, America covered over one and a half million square miles and encompassed a population of over twenty million. Expansion toward the West, combined with high birth rates, contributed to this phenomenal growth. The ready availability of free land helped Americans moving west establish a strong sense of individual self-worth.

Second, this expansion contributed to the demise of the power of the East Coast establishment. Americans, especially on the frontier, were an independent lot. These pioneers were not the most likely group to sit quietly on the sidelines while someone else told them what they had to do. Individuals on the frontier demanded a much more active role for themselves. The frontier attitude discouraged those in the educated Eastern centers of power from attempting to establish themselves on the frontier. This left the territory even more vulnerable to the power and attraction of new political and religious movements more attuned to the mood of the masses.

Obviously, these developments were not lost on a new breed of religious leaders. In fact, the social conditions themselves brought forth a new style of religious leader.[7] These new religious leaders tapped into the interest and concerns of the common people. They stood as outsiders over against the claims of the powerful institutions and their educated leaders. They possessed a seemingly boundless energy and optimism. Their sermons, preached in the frontier vernacular of the people, exhibited a good deal of hostility toward traditional orthodoxy and offered the people the hope of a religious reformation. They encouraged the people to think for themselves and to establish churches they could control.[8]

The established churches, such as the Congregationalists, Episcopalians, and even the Presbyterians, had difficulty achieving any success in this kind of environment. Many of the ministers in the East had associated openly with the Federalist Party, opposing the republican movement of Jefferson. This fact was not easily forgotten on the frontier. Further, the church polity of these established churches was too rigid. They could not educate, and then ordain, ministers fast enough to meet the expanding needs of the frontier. The Methodists, Baptists, and Disciples, on the other hand, quickly ordained people, educated or not, directly on the scene. These new ministers were of the people and preached the kind of down-home messages the people were eager to hear.[9]

This was the context for the development of numerous religious groups and social experiments; the Mormons, Brook Farm, New Harmony, Fruitlands, Shakers, and the Oneida Community all emerged during these years. Such an environment was also tailor-made for the emergence of a new religious group like the Disciples. All the cultural trends fit neatly into the religious package they offered. For this reason, many American religious historians have recognized Disciples as the quintessential American denomination. A brief survey of early Disciples leaders and their methods indicates some of the reasons this assessment is more than likely accurate.

## *The Birth of the Disciples*

The history of the Disciples is distinguished by the names of many people, women and men, who over the years have contributed to events later defined by historians as important moments in the life of the tradition. Some of these names are not as well known as they should be; this fact leaves Disciples historians rich material for many more years of investigation, especially as they seek over this next decade to uncover and write about the many areas where women and minorities have played such important, but as yet largely unrecognized, roles. However, when one examines the early life of the history, the period of its beginnings, the names of four major personalities generally appear at the top of the list: Barton Stone, Thomas Campbell, Alexander Campbell, and Walter Scott.[10] Each of these personalities, in his own way, illustrated the strengths and weaknesses of the environment around him. These were men who fit the times, and, as a result, they were men who greatly contributed to the growth of a new religious movement.

## Barton Stone

Barton Stone was born in Maryland in 1772. As a fifth-generation American, Stone is the only one of these four "founders" of the Disciples tradition to be born in America. Like so many other Americans from the East Coast during this period, Barton Stone could claim his share of distinguished relatives. He was second cousin to a signer of the Declaration of Independence and in the direct line of the first Protestant governor of Maryland.[11] Shortly after the death of his father, Stone and his family moved to an area near the border between North Carolina and Virginia. The move had more significance for Barton Stone's future than anyone could have known at the time.

Hoping to pursue a law career, Stone entered a Presbyterian log college on the North Carolina border, about thirty miles from his home. A Presbyterian minister by the name of David Caldwell had established the college in 1765. Though the Stone family belonged to the Anglican Church, Barton Stone found himself caught up in the religious excitement circulating among the Presbyterians in this area. Within a year or so of his arrival at the college, Stone was converted by the preaching of a revivalistic Presbyterian minister, William Hodge. He promptly gave up his hopes for a career in law and decided to be a Presbyterian minister. The Presbyterians accepted him as a candidate for ministry and he was promised a license to preach.

While waiting for his license to be granted, Stone traveled to Georgia where he accepted a teaching position at Succoth Academy, a Methodist school in Washington, Georgia. While there he met some prominent ministers, who became his close friends and influenced his approach to Christian ministry. Hope Hull, principal of the school and a Methodist minister, and John Springer, a Presbyterian minister and a strong believer in religious toleration, both acted as models for the young Stone as he began his route to ministry.

Both men reflected the prevailing American mind-set. They were liberal in their attitudes toward the doctrines of others, respecting the individual's right to search for and define his or her own understanding of religious truth. Though they were deeply concerned to communicate the gospel in clear and unmistakable ways, they were not much interested in defending creedal orthodoxy. As was true of many of the new style of ministers, they believed certain strands of orthodoxy had become oppressive and had a tendency to interfere with the individual's right to seek religious truth. Hope Hull also expressed personal sympathy for the republican movement (yet another religious expression of the prevailing political emphasis on freedom) among Methodists, which stressed local congregational autonomy. All these characteristics became prominent in Stone's own ministry.

Within a year, Stone returned home and received his license to preach. Six months later, in the fall of 1796, he had moved on to Kentucky, where he became the supply minister to two Presbyterian congregations, one located at Cane Ridge and the other at Concord. About two years later, after he accepted the calling of both congregations to become their minister, he received his ordination at the hands of the Transylvania Presbytery. As an ordained minister in these two churches, Stone ministered in a particular social context, which in itself exercised considerable effect upon the direction of his life's work.

Stone's ministry came to life in the midst of the American frontier in the decade after the successful completion of the American Revolution. Due to increasing awareness of the implications associated with religious liberty, congregations across America began to forge new ways to reach outsiders with the message of the church. Religious liberty freed all American citizens from a civil authority poised to enforce religious ends. The revolution drove that message home even more. Churches, like other established societal institutions, could no longer count on an automatic membership composed of people ready to bow to the authority of their messages. Ministers, especially those on the frontier, had to learn to rely on other methods to gain support for the messages and endeavors of their congregations.

Ministers who hoped to reach the independent people of the national period had to begin to rely on persuasion to fill their congregations.[12] Pastors could no longer count on state subsidies. Therefore, they had to persuade people that the message they preached was worthy of financial and personal support. Encouraged by the successes experienced by those who had begun to utilize the mass media effectively, frontier ministers learned to reach larger audiences with their messages. They developed the technique of mass revivals.

As a method to fill churches and gain support for religious enterprises, revivalistic practices flourished on the American frontier. Revivalism tended to avoid the expression of ambiguous and divisive theological points. Instead, it emphasized the simple points of the gospel. True to the pragmatism that characterized so much of the American mind, both then and now, most ministers on the frontier concentrated on trying to make their churches grow. Too much stress on theology seemed only to get in the way of congregational growth. Instead, responding to the culture around them, the most successful ministers spoke directly to the hearts of their hearers and touched their spirits with words laden with emotion and passion.

In the early nineteenth century, around 1800, people all over America began to think in terms of either being religious or intelligent. It was not easy to be both. The most important thing in many religious circles was to feel your religion. Religious leaders who failed to take the spiritual feelings of the people seriously also failed to develop strong churches. The revivalist-oriented denominations knew better. Given their natural distrust of the powers of orthodoxy and tradition, they were more able to accept the spiritual expressions of people as legitimate in whatever form they emerged. They did not feel any compulsion to evaluate them according to some orthodox measuring stick.[13]

Barton Stone had encountered revivalistic preaching during his college days. In fact, he had been converted under its power. But it was on the frontier that Stone saw how revivalistic preaching could empower apathetic churches. A great wave of revivalistic preaching broke out around 1800 in gatherings known as "camp meetings." Many years later, historians would use these events to describe the impact of the Second Great Awakening as it swept through its western phase. Stone traveled nearly two hundred miles from home to witness a camp meeting in Logan County, Kentucky, in the early spring of 1801. Even though he saw some strange emotional fanaticism associated with the revival at Logan County, he also witnessed the conversions of hundreds of people. Believing these conversions to be the work of God, Stone decided to work for revival closer to home.

When Stone returned to his own congregations, he set about the task of planning a "sacramental meeting" at the location of the Cane Ridge meeting house. As the revival movement headed toward Cane Ridge, it gathered momentum. By the time the Cane Ridge Camp Meeting was held, August 7–12, 1801, attendance at such meetings had reached its highest numbers. Somewhere between ten and thirty thousand people gathered at Cane Ridge during this five-day period. Methodist, Baptist, and Presbyterian ministers preached on rough, hastily built platforms. There were no indications of sectarian differences among them. All of them, in the language of the frontier people who were gathered before them, preached with persuasion toward a common goal: the conversion of sinners. The crowds, worn out and overexcited, soon witnessed a tremendous outbreak of emotion. Stone described fits of falling, jerking, dancing, barking, laughing, running, and singing.[14]

The camp meeting at Cane Ridge had a significant impact on Stone. Though he did not endorse all the emotionalism associated with the revivals, he could not help but be impressed by the way ministers of different denominations cooperated with one another to increase spiritual vitality among churched and unchurched alike.

Not everyone shared Stone's enthusiasm. Many Presbyterian ministers in the area of the revivals were distressed that so many of the preachers at Cane Ridge and other camp meetings did not have ordination credentials. Many of the preachers were uneducated and were preaching salvation for everyone, instead of those whom God had especially elected. These Presbyterian ministers, with good reason, were deeply concerned that much of the Presbyterian belief system was being challenged by these revivalistic meetings.

The cultural trend toward individual liberty in all matters did not much encourage belief in Presbyterian orthodoxy. The Jeffersonian emphasis on the sovereignty of the will of the individual tended to dilute the appeal of strict Calvinism.[15] Presbyterian doctrine emphasized the fact that God saved human beings through a process of election, a process that operated independently of individual human will. Human beings could not "choose" to be saved; they were either elected by God or they were not. Salvation came only for those whom God had elected. For those who stood outside of election, no amount of special pleading or action of personal will could change their ultimate status before God. For this reason, one can easily see how the camp meetings threatened Presbyterian doctrine.

Over the next two years following the Cane Ridge meeting, two of the Presbyterian revival preachers, Richard McNemar and John Thompson, faced charges levied by the presbytery. Both men were charged with preaching doctrine contrary to the Westminster Creed (they preached that Christ died for all human beings and not just the elect). Before the two years had passed, Barton Stone and two other revival-oriented ministers, Robert Marshall and John Dunlavy, had chosen to side with the accused ministers. In September of 1803, the five Presbyterian ministers declared their independence from the jurisdiction of the Presbyterian Synod of Kentucky. At the time of their withdrawal from the synod, these five ministers formed the independent Springfield Presbytery. They intended, at this point, to remain identified as Presbyterian ministers.

Within ten months following this action, these ministers, now six in number, met at Cane Ridge and decided that the Springfield Presbytery ought to be dissolved. Together, they issued a document entitled "The Last Will and Testament of the Springfield Presbytery." With this statement, these ministers and their congregations left the Presbyterian fold and began a loose association of congregations to be known simply as "Christian" churches. Therefore, this short statement marks the birth of a group of Christian congregations in southern Ohio and northern Kentucky to which present-day Disciples trace their history. The "Last Will and Testament" stressed the Bible as the only authority for Christians and expressed the desire to "sink into union with the Body of Christ at large."

Their "Last Will" expressed their desire to develop congregations with the ability to choose their own ministers, thus denying the power and authority of the established churches. They expressed their hope to ordain candidates to ministry who would "preach the simple gospel...without any mixture of philosophy, vain deceit, traditions of men, or the rudiments of the world."[16] In these and other ways, their brief document echoed the most important tenet of their time: freedom from the coercion of either established authorities or tradition. Even though four of these six signers would abandon the new independent movement early in its history, Barton Stone provided enough leadership to see the movement grow to some degree of maturity and prominence. By the time of the 1832 merger between the congregations related to Stone and the congregations related to the Campbells, Stone's "Christians" numbered well above ten thousand members.

## Thomas and Alexander Campbell

A few years after the publication of "The Last Will and Testament," Thomas Campbell, a forty-five-year-old Scotch–Irish Presbyterian minister who had never heard of Barton Stone, arrived in Philadelphia. The calendar read May 13, 1807. Campbell's family remained behind in Ireland, where he had only recently resigned his ministry at the Old Light Anti-burgher Seceder Presbyterian Church in Ahorey. As the name of his church indicated, Thomas Campbell had seen the effects various divisions had wreaked upon the life of his own denomination. Unsuccessful in his own efforts to heal the latest of the divisions in Ireland, Campbell hoped to find new opportunities for his family and for his own ministry in America. Before much time had passed, the Presbyterian synod assigned Thomas Campbell to preaching duties in southwest Pennsylvania. Within six months, however, another minister had charged that Campbell, among other things, had refused to use Presbyterian creeds as terms of communion. In ministering to isolated citizens on the frontier who were without ministers, Campbell included "other branches of the Presbyterian family" (and perhaps others) in his invitation to the Lord's supper. [17]

Though the ruling body of the Presbyterian Church in Pennsylvania "rebuked" Campbell, it sent him back to his home presbytery in good standing. The members of the presbytery did not welcome him back with open arms. Instead they refused to appoint him to any ministerial position. In September of 1808, Campbell withdrew from the presbytery and began preaching in private homes in the area of Washington, Pennsylvania. Nearly a year later, Campbell and a few others organized the "Christian Association of Washington." Association members adopted as their motto the words "Where the Scriptures speak, we speak; where the Scriptures are silent, we are silent." In September of 1809, the Christian Association published Campbell's *Declaration and Address* in order to express the principles and objectives of their organization.

In this important early document in the history of Disciples, Thomas Campbell declared his movement's own independence from the establishment. In the first sentence, he declared that "we are persuaded that it is high time for us not only to think, but also to act, for ourselves." "Every man," he wrote, "must be allowed to judge for himself, as every man must bear his own judgment—must give account of himself to God." Thomas Campbell, like Barton Stone, believed that the only hope for the renewal of Christianity in America rested in a return to "simple evangelical Christianity, free from all mixture of human opinions and inventions of men."[18] Such a return demanded that individuals read the Bible and judge for themselves what it had to say. As the quote at the beginning of this chapter indicates, Campbell possessed an optimistic hope that America provided the context where such a glorious reformation of the church could succeed.

While these events were taking place in America, Thomas Campbell's family was trying to reach America. Their first effort resulted in a shipwreck. During that experience, Thomas' eldest son, Alexander, made a final commitment to pursuing a ministerial vocation. Following the shipwreck, the family lived for a year in Glasgow, Scotland, where Alexander took advantage of the educational opportunities afforded by the University of Glasgow. He also met ministers associated with the Haldane movement. Named after James Alexander Haldane and his brother Robert, the Haldane movement promoted the establishment of primitive Christianity among all Christians, regardless of denominational affiliation. One particular minister, Greville Ewing, presided over a training school for Haldane ministers and had himself recently become acquainted with the religious writings of John Glas and Robert Sandeman. These two men had also formed a movement of Christians that emphasized the restoration of the primitive church.

Alexander Campbell and the rest of the family finally arrived in America in the fall of 1809. In mid-October, they were reunited with Thomas Campbell on the road about three days' journey from Washington, Pennsylvania. Alexander, now twenty-one, carefully read his father's *Declaration and Address*. As he read, he discovered that his father shared many of the ideas he had encountered while at Glasgow. Together, in a frontier setting well suited to religious reconstruction, they set out to reform American Christianity, hoping to lead it in a return to the ways of the primitive church.

As one of the first steps in this reformation, the Christian Association took steps to establish itself as a congregation. Known as the Brush Run Church, members of the congregation assumed a congregational form of government, and, following the practice of the Haldanes and the testimony of scripture, decided to observe the Lord's supper on a weekly basis. Members chose Thomas Campbell as their elder, and licensed Alexander to preach. Nearly eight months later, on January 1, 1812, the congregation ordained the younger Campbell to Christian ministry.

Campbell recalled one of the very first meetings (June 1811) of this new congregation from the perspective of many years later (1842). The "sixty or seventy disciples, gathered out of various denominations," assembled "under an oak," near a "table...spread in the woods." Using a portion of the "discourse" still extant, Campbell offered readers of *The Millennial Harbinger* a glimpse of the message he preached that day. The text, he said, was Job 8:6–7, "If thou art pure and upright, though thy beginning [be] small, yet thy latter end shall greatly increase." Portions of the sermon clearly illustrate the anti-institutionalism of the day, as well as the theme of individual freedom that so cogently filled the post-revolutionary air. The message also demonstrated Campbell's great confidence that this new reformation in religion would succeed.

> Ignorance and superstition, enthusiasm and fanaticism are the fruits of these human institutions which have displaced the Bible or re-fused to admit it as its own interpreter....We commence our career as a church under the banner of "*The Bible, the whole Bible, and nothing but the Bible,*" as the standard of our religious faith and practice....Our inferences and opinions are our own....Christians are the sons of liberty—the Lord's freed men. The right to choose and to refuse the opinions of men is the essence of liberty....We are a weak band, an humble beginning; but so much the better. So were they of Galilee—such were they of Saxony—and such were the founders of this great nation.[19]

Later, when Alexander Campbell's leadership brought the member-ship of the congregation to decide that the Bible required the adoption of believer's baptism by immersion, Brush Run Church began a relation-ship with a nearby Baptist Association. For a number of years after 1815, the Campbell reforming movement carried on its work from within the shelter of one of the accepted American denominations. The relation-ship between the Reformers and their host denomination, the Baptists, however, grew stormy as time passed.

Though the two groups shared a common baptism, they argued over its connection to formal "remission of sins." The Baptists were also dis-turbed by Alexander Campbell's distinctions between the relevance of the Old Testament and New Testament messages for Christian living (based upon his understanding of three different dispensations repre-sented in scripture, the most relevant for Christians being the "Christian dispensation," from Pentecost forward). There were also some differ-ences in the way both groups approached the question of ministry and its relationship to the administration of the Lord's supper. Even more friction resulted from the fact that Baptist congregations, at this time, were required to subscribe to the Philadelphia Confession of Faith. Though the Baptists granted Brush Run an exception to this policy, they resisted making additional exceptions for other Reformer congregations who hoped to enter Baptist life. The conduct of those Reformers associated with Brush Run Church had obviously caused many Baptist leaders to question the relationship between the two groups.

One of the main sources of the problem stemmed from Alexander Campbell's brilliant use of the new tactics made available by the proliferation of popular newspapers. Like the Jeffersonians before him, he exploited the popularity of the press by using it to attack his enemies and to set forth his own agenda. Beginning in 1823, he founded a periodical, entitled *The Christian Baptist*, through which he spoke frankly, often without tact, about all the important religious issues facing American congregations. The more he elaborated in clear language his own understanding of Christianity, the less comfortable the Baptist leadership felt about his presence in their midst. There is little doubt, however, that Campbell's career as a popular religious journalist, both in his earlier days at the helm of *The Christian Baptist* and his later days after 1830 as the founding editor of *The Millennial Harbinger*, had much to do with the overwhelming growth of the Disciples movement.

During the decade preceding 1830, both Baptists and Reformers grew increasingly distant from one another. Local congregations containing both elements began to split apart, and Baptist associations began the process of separating from any congregations refusing to subscribe to the Philadelphia Confession. Finally, in 1830, members of the Mahoning Baptist Association in eastern Ohio, the only association among the Baptists controlled by the Reformers, decided to dissolve the association and cut all their Baptist ties. From that point on, these Reformers, now separated from any recognized denominational identity, increasingly became known as "Disciples." As Disciples, they were able to set forth, in clear tones, their own message.

The prevailing intellectual currents of the day were an active influence behind the work of Alexander Campbell and other early Disciples. Disciples were indeed indebted to the work of Francis Bacon, John Locke, and other Enlightenment Christians of the seventeenth and eighteenth centuries. The familiarity of both Campbells with the strong European intellectual tradition, shared by a few other of the early leaders among Disciples, indicates most clearly that it would be a mistake to view Alexander Campbell and the early Disciples tradition as simply a product of the American frontier.

Alexander Campbell, as the most rigorous of the early Disciples, reflected most clearly the ideas of this European background. Samuel Pearson described it as follows:

[Campbell] accepts without question the demand of the age that religion, like science, be based on empirical evidence and that theologians be guided, in the words of Charles Hodge, "by the same rules in the collection of facts, as govern the man of science." This notion creates no difficulties for Campbell because he has accepted the notion, common in his day, that the Bible is a book of facts which can be used to defend the claims of Christianity....[Clearly dependent upon Locke] Campbell was not troubled by a conflict between faith and reason or between the facts of revelation and the facts of science. Revelation provided facts which were not otherwise available to reason, but these facts were in no sense contrary to reason.

Campbell's reasonable formulation of faith, with its origins in Francis Bacon and John Locke as much as in the Bible, stood Disciples in good stead as they branched out to become a group of their own. As Pearson argued so well, it enabled Disciples to present a gospel that stood between the two great temptations of the time period: the pure emotionalism of many revivalist preachers and the pure rationalism prevalent among many of the eastern seaboard preachers.[20]

Between 1830 and 1860, Disciples became respectable members of mainstream Protestantism. Their ministry moved toward education and settled pastorates, their congregations toward attracting a middle-class membership, and their leaders toward responsible reputations in the eyes of the "established" ministry. Alexander Campbell brought notoriety to the cause of his movement through his building reputation as a talented debater. His celebrated 1829 debate with Robert Owen, the famous social reformer, brought Campbell a new measure of respect from his Protestant peers in ministry and served as a testimony to the orthodoxy of his own beliefs.[21] When increased immigration after 1830 began to feed an already vibrant anti-Catholicism in America, Alexander Campbell emerged as one of Protestantism's most articulate representatives of a moderate anti-Catholic sentiment. In 1837, he engaged Roman Catholic John B. Purcell, archbishop of Cincinnati, in a widely publicized eight-day debate on the tradition and beliefs of the Catholic Church.[22] Campbell's developing reputation as a highly respected defender of Protestant orthodoxy, aided by these two public debates, helped him to lead his movement from obscurity on the frontier to its later location as a central force in the life of the Protestant mainstream in America.

### Walter Scott

The strength of this new independent movement of Disciples owed much to the previous efforts of Walter Scott. Walter Scott hailed from Moffatt, Scotland, where he had been born on All Saints Eve, 1796. He traveled to America in 1818 and, within the next year, made his way to Pittsburgh. When he arrived in Pittsburgh, he became a teacher in a school founded by a minister named George Forrester, who also happened to be the pastor of a small Haldane congregation nearby. Forrester's unexpected death a few months after Scott arrived on the scene left both the church and the school under Scott's care. As he read the books in Forrester's library, he came across the writings of James A. Haldane, John Glas, Robert Sandeman, John Locke, and others.

By the time Scott met Alexander Campbell in the winter of 1821– 1822, he had already decided that the only creed necessary to Christian faith was the great Christian confession "Jesus is the Christ." When Campbell and Scott met, they discovered very similar concerns. Their mutual interest in John Locke led them to affirm that the gospel was eminently reasonable. They believed that preachers should simply present the biblical evidence supporting the fact of Jesus' messiahship. Any rational person would be persuaded of the gospel's truth and led to acknowledge the fact that "Jesus is the Christ," thereby becoming a Christian. Though this approach to evangelism shared the persuasive character of religion on the American frontier, it rejected the emotionalism of the revivalism so often associated with persuasive techniques on the frontier.

In order to counter revivalistic emotionalism, as well as to develop an effective evangelistic technique, Walter Scott developed a five-finger exercise to describe the logical process by which one could become a Christian, a quick way to explain what he defined as the "true gospel." The first three steps involved human action: (1) confess faith; (2) repent sins; (3) undergo baptism. The last two steps belonged to God and were associated with the third step: as baptism is completed, (4) God forgives; and (5) the Holy Spirit is granted (as is eternal life). Scott's method provided what had been lacking among Campbell's Reformers. Prior to Scott, the Reformers merely constituted a movement for reform within the Baptist churches. Under Scott's leadership, the Disciples developed into a separate religious body. His role in Disciples life enhanced the growth of congregations, contributed to the development of an early sense of Disciples identity, and helped Disciples avoid some of the excesses associated with other revivalistic efforts on the American frontier.

Though the preaching of the Disciples emphasized the priesthood of the individual and stressed the individual's right to read and interpret the Bible without outside interference, Walter Scott and other early Disciples reacted against the way revivalists asserted that people had to look inside themselves for some proof of the presence of the Spirit. Scott's reasoned approach to evangelism took for granted the belief that the role of the Holy Spirit commenced only after a believer had been baptized into the church.

Early Disciples leaders rested the great knowledge and experience of the love of God, not upon merely personal faith, but rather upon the more corporate acts in the life of the church, such as baptism, the Lord's supper, and prayer and confession in the midst of a congregation. For the Campbells and other early Disciples leaders, the power of the Holy Spirit manifested itself in the midst of the gathered church, not in sectarian or private religious claims. Disciples have stressed that the united church, founded upon the testimony of apostolic claims, constituted the only place where Christians could discover and experience the true spiritual power of Christian life. This approach contradicted the emphasis on the personal or individual experience of the Holy Spirit that was so much a part of American revivalism.[23]

## Conclusion

Obviously, Disciples were shaped in some ways by the context provided by American revivalism. There has been a long-standing tendency in Disciples history to avoid elaborate theological statements. In common with most nineteenth-century revivalists, early Disciples believed that theological opinions too often led to division. They were best left to the realm of personal opinion. Disciples also emphasized the participation of lay people in a way thoroughly consistent with the cultural and religious context of revivalism on the nineteenth-century frontier. The freedom of religion in America, combined with the emphasis on personal liberty pervasive in the culture, had increased substantially the participation of lay people in congregational life. But this lay emphasis among Disciples did not completely give way to the individualism that was rampant on the frontier. It did, however, as a later chapter explores, share some of the same frontier suspicions of clergy who were educated and professionally trained in schools located on the East Coast.

Disciples were born in the context of a resurgence of freedom among the common people. In religious life, this freedom had been curtailed for centuries by a hierarchical church life that required unthinking assent to creeds and clerical authority. The Disciples movement translated the cultural obsession with freedom into a religious declaration of the right of all common people to think through the claims of religion for themselves. From the culturally accepted intellectual ideas of his time, Campbell fashioned a rational, scholarly, and critical approach to the Bible that encouraged individual access to scripture while, at the same time, it discouraged individual misuse of scripture. Early Disciples so succeeded in speaking to, and from, their times that the Disciples expression of faith has been described as "an American apologetic."[24]

The effect of the American context on Disciples life has been obvious to most historians of American religion. When Sidney Mead, for example, offered his scholarly assessment of the development of American denominational life, he concluded that there were basically three religious ideas "prevailing during the Revolutionary epoch in which the denominations began to take shape." These three ideas are defined as follows: "the idea of pure and normative beginnings to which return was possible; the idea that the intervening history was largely that of aberrations and corruptions which was better ignored; and the idea of building anew in the American wilderness on the true and ancient foundations." The Disciples of Christ were "typically American" as they embodied all three of these ideas.[25]

These three ideas all have to do with the early Disciples commitment to the principle of "restorationism," the topic of a later chapter. Yet it may just be possible that Mead missed a more important and, in fact, more basic Disciples principle that was perhaps more indicative of the American cultural context than was any of the three religious ideas he mentioned. I am referring to the Disciples commitment to the priority and right of all individuals to read and interpret scripture for themselves. Indeed, no aspect of early Disciples identity fit the times better than this one.

Did the social and cultural context of Disciples dictate to them what particular emphases they would raise and make their own? That is not an easy question. Certainly, we live in the world as finite beings who are greatly affected by the ideas that circulate around us. Early Disciples were indeed products of their culture. As is true in the history of all Christian groups, in certain instances of Disciples history it is sometimes hard to tell whether the gospel or the culture had the upper hand.

It is fair to say that the congruence between the trends of the culture and the interests of early Disciples greatly contributed to Disciples strength. That congruence no doubt also affected the development of their method and their message. Many years ago, H. Richard Niebuhr argued that the "definition of religious truth" cannot avoid the effect of the "exigencies of church discipline, the demands of national psychology, the effect of social tradition, the influence of cultural heritage, and the weight of economic interest."[26] All these factors certainly contributed to the formation of the Disciples theological mind.

Yet Christians must also say more. Social and cultural influences do not explain the whole of our faith. Belief in a God who acts in the world means we affirm that God transcends culture. Our experience of God in Christ enables us to face the world with a different understanding than the various cultural understandings that surround us. Early Disciples, in their commitment to be a biblical people, in their effort to seek apostolic norms for the church, and in their hope to unite the church, often exemplified for the world the reality of this transcendent resource standing behind their life and work. In many ways, the reformation they started in

the nineteenth century, from its very beginnings, offered a serious con-
demnation of the present state of affairs in American religion.

## Questions for Reflection and Discussion

1. What cultural themes would you identify as evident in some of the ideas and activities of the early founders of the Christian Church (DOC)? For example, how is the high value placed on autonomy of the local church, or emphasis on the individual's right to read the Bible, related to the context of American life just after the revolution?

2. Can you name some ways in which our current Christian under-standing is dominated by American middle-class, democratic, individu-alistic, majority race, or gender considerations, or other such interests? In what ways are these consistent or inconsistent with the gospel?

3. What differences existed between Campbell's movement and the Baptists?

## Notes

[1] Thomas Campbell, *Declaration and Address*, and Barton W. Stone and Others, *Last Will and Testament of the Springfield Presbytery*, with brief introduction by F.D. Kershner (St. Louis: Mission Messenger, 1978), p. 34.

[2] See Bernard Bailyn, *Ideological Origins of the American Revolution* (Cambridge: The Belknap Press, 1967), particularly pp. 22-54.

[3] Nathan O. Hatch, *The Democratization of American Christianity* (New Haven and London: Yale University Press, 1989), p. 3.

[4] See Hatch, chapter two, "The Crisis of Authority in Popular Culture," pp. 17-46.

[5] *Ibid.*, p. 23.

[6] *Ibid.*, p. 24f.

[7] See Sidney E. Mead, *The Lively Experiment: The Shaping of Christianity in America* (New York: Harper & Row, 1963), p. 121.

[8] See Hatch, particularly chapters 1, 3, and 4.

[9] *Ibid.*, p. 59f.

[10] The general biographies of these four individuals are related in greater detail in the two general histories of the Christian Church (Disciples of Christ): Lester G. McAllister and William E. Tucker, *Journey in Faith: A History of the Christian Church (Disciples of Christ)* (Saint Louis: The Bethany Press, 1975); and Winfred Ernest Garrison and Alfred T. DeGroot, *The Disciples of Christ: A History* (St. Louis: The Bethany Press, 1948). More specific texts have also appeared. The dates of most of these studies indicate that the field is wide open for fresh interpretations of these figures. See, for example, Charles C. Ware, *Barton Warren Stone, Pathfinder of Christian Union* (St. Louis: The Bethany Press, 1932); Lester G. McAllister, *Thomas Campbell: Man of the Book* (St. Louis: The Bethany Press, 1954); Robert Richardson, *Memoirs of Alexander Campbell, Embracing a View of the Origin, Progress and Principles of the Religious Reformation Which He Advocated*, 2 vols. (Philadelphia: J. Lippincott, 1868, 1870); Winfred E. Garrison, *Alexander Campbell's Theology, Its Sources and Historical Setting* (St. Louis: Christian Publishing Co., 1900); Harold L. Lunger, *The Political Ethics of Alexander Campbell* (St. Louis: The Bethany Press, 1954); James M. Seale, editor, *Lectures in Honor of the Alexander Campbell Bicentennial, 1788-1988* (Nash-

ville: Disciples of Christ Historical Society, 1988); Dwight E. Stevenson, *Walter Scott: Voice of the Golden Oracle* (St. Louis: Christian Board of Publication, 1946); William Austin Gerrard, "Walter Scott: Frontier Disciples Evangelist" (Ph.D. Dissertation, Emory University, 1982).

[11]Charles Crossfield Ware, *Barton Warren Stone: Pathfinder of Christian Union* (St. Louis: The Bethany Press, 1932), p. 4.

[12]Mead, *The Lively Experiment,* particularly chapter 2, "From Coercion to Persuasion," pp. 16-37.

[13]*Ibid.,* pp. 121-129.

[14]John Rogers, ed., *Biography of Eld. Barton Warren Stone, Written by Himself: With Additions and Reflections* (Cincinnati: Published for the author by J.A. and U.P. James, 1847), pp. 39-42.

[15]See Hatch on this point, p. 179f.

[16]"Last Will and Testament," in McAllister and Tucker, *Journey in Faith,* pp. 77-79.

[17] See Robert Richardson, *Memoirs of Alexander Campbell, Embracing A View of the Origin, Progress and Principles of the Religious Reformation Which He Advocated,* Volume One (Cincinnati: Standard Publishing Company, 1897), p. 224f. Richardson specifies that Thomas offered communion to "other branches of the Presbyterian family...who had not, for a long time, had an opportunity of partaking of the Lord's Supper, and he felt it his duty, in the preparation sermon, to lament the existing divisions, and to suggest that all his pious hearers, who felt so disposed and duly prepared, should, without respect to party differences, enjoy the benefits of the communion season then providentially afforded them." It is not known whether Campbell also invited Christians other than from "other branches" of Presbyterianism. Certainly his arguments supported taking that further step, and, of course the movement did take that step rather early. See Campbell's arguments as set forth in these pages of Richardson.

[18]Campbell, *Declaration and Address,* p. 23f.

[19]Campbell, *The Millennial Harbinger* (January 1842): 10-13. The emphasis is Campbell's.

[20]Samuel C. Pearson, "Faith and Reason in Disciples Theology," in Kenneth Lawrence, ed., *Classic Themes of Disciples Theology: Rethinking the Traditional Affirmations of the Christian Church (Disciples of Christ)* (Fort Worth: Texas Christian University Press, 1986), p. 114f, and p. 122.

[21]See Robert Owen and Alexander Campbell, *Debate on The Evidences of Christianity; Containing an Examination of the "Social System," and of All the Systems of Skepticism of Ancient and Modern Times,* 2 vols. (Bethany, Va.: Alexander Campbell, 1829).

[22]Richard Edward Lessner argued, in his doctoral dissertation, that anti-Catholicism was the strongest nativist strain in Disciples life from 1830-1925. See Lessner, "The Imagined Enemy: American Nativism and the Disciples of Christ, 1830-1925" (Ph.D. Dissertation, Baylor University, 1981). See Alexander Campbell and John B. Purcell, *A Debate on the Roman Catholic Religion* (Cincinnati: J. A. James and Co., 1837).

[23]On understanding the five-finger exercise as a response to the emotionalism of revivalism, Scott usually emphasized the gift of the Holy Spirit as a gift given to believers rather than being bestowed by God prior to conversion (associated with emotionalism in revivalism) in order to convict a sinner; see, for example, Scott, *The Gospel Restored* (Cincinnati: O. H. Donogh, 1836), p. 97, and pp. 244-245. This paragraph also depends upon the insights of W. Clark Gilpin, "The Integrity of the Church: The Communal Theology of Disciples of Christ," in Lawrence, ed., *Classic*

36    *Joined in Discipleship*

*Themes*, pp. 35-37, 46.

[24]Samuel C. Pearson, "An American Apologetic: Disciple Articulation of the Christian Faith," *Encounter* 46 (Summer 1985): 255-273.

[25]Mead, *The Lively Experiment*, p. 111.

[26]Niebuhr, *Social Sources of Denominationalism*, p. 15.

# 2

# THE INTERPRETATION PRINCIPLE
## THE FREEDOM TO EMBRACE DIVERSITY

---

*I have endeavored to read the scriptures as though no one had read them before me, and I am as much on my guard against reading them to-day, through the medium of my own views yesterday, or a week ago, as I am against being influenced by any foreign name, authority, or system whatever.*

Alexander Campbell,
*The Christian Baptist* (April 1826)[1]

---

## Introduction

The recent body of work produced by scholars of the early republic has made it increasingly clear that the idea of religious freedom continued to expand in meaning after the American Revolutionary War. Prior to the war, Christians exercised their right to religious freedom whenever they attended the church of their choice. After the war, in the context of the intensifying clamor for expanding individual rights, the notion of religious freedom itself took an individual turn. It came to mean that individuals possessed the right to ignore traditional and institutional authority in religious matters. This remained true even when that authority rested in the long-respected practices of the church of their choice. Religious freedom came to mean "power should be surrendered to the people."[2]

The newfound power of religious liberty often expressed itself in individual ways. Lucy Mack Smith, the mother of Joseph Smith, founder of the Mormons, attended numerous churches of various denominations and finally concluded that none of them taught the truth. She sought and found a minister who would baptize her as a solitary Christian with no connection to any established church. Lucy's decision to stand as a solitary Christian illustrates well the more radical side to the cultural trend toward individualism. In most Christians, it surfaced in less isolating ways. Christians now demanded the right to interpret God's word for themselves as part of what religious freedom guaranteed to them as American citizens.[3]

Though Stone and the Campbells were far less radical than Lucy Mack Smith, they were profoundly affected by the cultural emphasis on the primacy of the individual conscience. The trend neatly reinforced their own Christian sensibilities. They quickly learned to exploit it by translating it into religious language and forming a community specifically designed to enhance and protect the right of individuals to interpret scripture for themselves. This early message of Disciples provided hope for people who had about given up on ever hearing the voice of God above the conflicting claims of the various denominations surrounding them. These types of individuals were both challenged and attracted by Disciples preachers who told them they could join a congregation that expected them to read and interpret the Bible for themselves.[4] The early Disciples movement, with its phenomenal record of growth, no doubt owed much to precisely this set of circumstances.

Through the years, Disciples have maintained their commitment to the individual's right of access to the gospel. A major portion of Disciples identity is rooted in our fundamental desire to be not only a biblical people but an interpretive people. The Disciples passion for the interpretation principle has been described as an act of "piety." That description emphasizes that the interpretation principle is foundational to how Disciples live. Not only does our expectation of active interpretation of scripture reflect this piety, but our promise to confess Christ does so as well. Disciples have pledged to let their lives interpret what they mean by their confession that "Christ is Lord."[5]

## The Interpretation Principle at Work

Because they lived in the midst of a cultural crisis in authority, nineteenth-century Disciples faced a particularly strong temptation to misuse the Bible. In a culture where all authorities are suspect, and where an individual's rights are primary, it would be easy to use the Bible to assert personal biases and establish personal agendas. Early Disciples leadership was aware of this temptation. And they acted to ward it off. Their antidote consisted of at least three interrelated focuses, which together provide a picture of the interpretation principle at work.

The first of these focuses emphasized the need to be clear about Disciples assumptions regarding the nature of the Bible.

## Disciples Assumptions Regarding the Nature of the Bible

First and foremost, founding Disciples were, like most Christians around them, committed to the divine inspiration of scripture. The Bible represented God's message to humanity. "The Word of God," Alexander Campbell wrote, "is but a specific embodiment of the Holy Spirit." Inspired by the Holy Spirit, the authors of these texts communicated to human beings "the mind and will of God."[6]

Disciples strongly asserted the authoritative nature of the Bible. People could depend upon the Bible to tell them the truth about themselves. In its pages, they could discover the key to understanding not only their past but their present and future as well. The Bible stood as the one place the Christian, and the church, could turn to discover God's will. While all authorities around them might crumble, the Bible remained dependable.

The founding Disciples' consideration of the Bible as canon, as authoritative source, also included an understanding that the Bible contained propositional truths that could be stated in clear and unmistakable terms. They turned to the Bible to discover the precise wording of all doctrine to be believed, and all matters of practice and structure for the church. This had the effect of encouraging people to regard the Bible, especially the New Testament, as a "constitution" for Christian life. In fact, they used this word to describe its function for both the Christian and the church.

This helps to explain the early Disciples belief that individual Christians who were willing to approach the Bible without bias would arrive at a common interpretation of all the necessary aspects of Christian existence. Upon this belief, the Disciples' hopes for unity were based. They believed in what Fred Craddock has described as "the principle of clarity." Any reasonable, right-thinking individual could open the pages of the Bible and, regarding at least the matters pertaining to human salvation and the governance of the church, arrive at a clear undisputed understanding with which other reasonable people would agree. Craddock's image for this principle is a good one. Founding Disciples, he said, regarded scripture as "a loudspeaker announcement for general consumption."[7] All it took to heed the announcement was a bit of common sense, the ability to read, and the will to act.

Disciples did recognize, however, that scriptural "declarations"—those passages usually connected with a "Thus saith the Lord"—often led to "inferences." This second stage of biblical interpretation could be rather cloudy at best. At the very least, every reasonable person needed to recognize, as Thomas Campbell put it, the "manifest distinction between an express Scripture declaration, and the conclusion or inference which may be deduced from it."[8] Early nineteenth-century Disciples claimed that only the former ought to be binding on the Christian and the church. As the Disciples grew and developed, Alexander Campbell utilized a broader concept, that of the "necessary inference," to seek a biblical foundation for the practical demand for greater cooperation between congregations.[9]

Clearly, Disciples depended rather heavily upon the New Testament as a kind of smaller canon within the larger canon of scripture. Eugene Boring has argued convincingly that Alexander Campbell's authoritative center in the Bible, and therefore, "the inner core" of his own particular canon, resided principally in the book of Hebrews. This book perfectly suited Campbell's overriding theological interest in the history of salvation.

Indeed, Disciples consistently asserted during this period that the Bible's subject matter was, above all else, the history of salvation. According to the founders, the Bible's primary testimony is to what Campbell described as the "moral facts" of God's "work of redemption." Boring's brief summary of Campbell's perspective is worth quoting:

> The content of the Bible [for Campbell] is summarized by the "mighty acts of God" in history, framed by creation and eschaton, with the event of Jesus Christ as the definitive center. The nature of the Bible is testimony to these events, not speculative theory....The object and content of Christian faith is thus not a Christological theory about *Jesus*, but an *act of God.* this is what Campbell meant by emphasizing that christian faith is a matter of acts, not theories; a matter of Bible, not creeds and theology. Although later Disciples could see that he drew the line too neatly and too easily between "fact" and "theology," the insight that faith is not directed toward creeds and dogmas but toward the God who has revealed redemptive love through mighty acts in history—supremely in the historical figure of Jesus Christ—has become one of the abiding "classic themes" of Disciples thought.

Campbell divided the Bible into three "dispensations," only the last of which should be viewed as ultimately normative for matters pertaining to church life. The first dispensation, a fancy word for time period, covered the period from Adam to Moses and was given the name "Patriarchal" (Genesis 1 to Exodus 19 in the Bible). The giving of the law on Sinai started the second dispensation, the "Jewish," which lasted until Peter delivered his sermon on Pentecost (Exodus 20 to Acts 1). The third dispensation, "the Christian," began with the granting of the Holy

Spirit at Pentecost and continues to the *eschaton* (Acts 2 to Revelation 22). Note, therefore, that the most authoritative books for the church naturally rested primarily in the Acts and the epistles, and excluded both the Old Testament and the Gospels.

Campbell used his dispensational theology to reach decisions regarding which passages in the Bible should be considered most relevant to Christians. It provided him with a discriminatory sense that he applied to scripture. Because he believed that revelation itself was progressive, he was able to claim that passages depicting God as a vicious warrior resulted from an incomplete comprehension of revelation. In his view, Paul's epistles contained a more complete impression of God. Though Campbell's dispensational outlook would be out of fashion today, it did enable him to "affirm the whole Bible without being bound to defend all the Bible says about God."[10]

Their defense of the divine inspiration of scripture did not prevent Disciples from being critical in their approach to the Bible. Indeed, the Disciples definition of the divine inspiration of the Bible also had a flip side. Alexander Campbell regularly asserted his belief that the Bible must also be viewed as a human book. "The language of the Bible," he wrote, "is *human* language." Christians, he warned, should not view everything in the Bible as supernatural for "communications purely supernatural occupy by far the least portion of the sacred books." "There are many things presented to our minds," Campbell wrote in 1828, "which did not originate in heaven, or which did not pertain to heavenly things."[11]

This recognition did not mean that Campbell admitted that the Bible contained errors. Rather, he emphasized only that the authors of the books, especially when dealing with historical facts or circumstances, wrote out of their own memory and experience. Not every word of the Bible, therefore, was inspired in the same way as those words that contained supernatural truths. "It would be a great reproach upon the four evangelists [Matthew, Mark, Luke, and John]," explained Campbell, "to represent them as believing every jot and tittle of the words of the Messiah and of themselves to have been inspired, when not any two of them narrate the same parable, conversation, sermon, or aphorism in the same words."[12] Though the ideas were inspired, the words were not.

The fact that the Bible was a human book as well as a divine book meant that Disciples needed to study the Bible as they would study any other book. God spoke through human words. No other verbal or written vehicle of communication was available. "If, then," Campbell asked, "God speaks in human language, must not His communications be submitted to the same rules of interpretation as all other verbal communications?"[13] Campbell's answer to this question moves the discussion to the second focus of the interpretation principle.

**Interpretation Must Follow General Rules of Interpretation**

The social milieu of denominational life afforded ample opportunity to witness the misapplication of scripture in action. From their very beginning, Disciples felt a sense of urgency about the necessity to call American Protestantism back to the central message of the gospel. Given their context, this is certainly understandable. All around them, denominational leaders argued with one another about issues unrelated to the gospel. Disciples feared these irrelevant arguments threatened the continued existence of the church. In response, they asserted the fundamental integrity of the biblical text.

Even though Disciples believed in the "principle of clarity," they nevertheless recognized that even the clearest messages of the Bible could be misapplied and misunderstood by those who were careless in their approach to scripture. Again, examples surrounded them. The Bible, even though it spoke clearly, did not speak by itself. Interpretation, even in cases of scriptural declarations, had to be applied. Alexander Campbell often addressed the situation. The different sects, he wrote, "make the Bible bow to their own system, received by tradition from their fathers." They refuse to "make their own system bow to the Bible." He believed the same to be true of most individuals. Each person has a tendency to view the Bible "through the medium" of a personal system.

> Just as if A, B and C should each put on different colored glasses; A puts on green spectacles, B yellow, and C blue; each one of them looks through his own glasses at a piece of white paper, and each concludes he is right, not remembering that he has his spectacles on. Thus to A it appears green, to B yellow, and to C blue. They begin to argue on the subject, and it is impossible for any of them to convince another that he is wrong—each one feels a conviction next to absolute certainty that *his* opinion is right. But D, who has no spectacles on, and who is standing looking on, during the contest, very well knows that they are all wrong; he sees the spectacles on each man's nose, and easily accounts for the difference.[14]

So far as Campbell was concerned, the "D" might as well have stood for "Disciples." But even Campbell did not take it for granted that Disciples would read the Bible without spectacles. Disciples, just like anyone else, could be prone to use "false principles of interpretation," or, at least, misapply "the true principles." All Christians, concluded Campbell, needed to approach the Bible with shared and agreed upon scientific principles. Only through this method would common interpretations truly emerge. "Were all students of the Bible taught to apply the same rules of interpretation to its pages," he wrote, "there would be a greater uniformity in opinion and sentiment than ever resulted from a simple adoption of any written creed."[15]

Campbell set forth seven such rules of interpretation. Basically, as numerous Disciples scholars have indicated, his rules paralleled the grammatico-historical method worked out by the humanist scholars during the Renaissance. His rules sought the "plain meaning" of the text. Boring's recent study of Campbell's biblical method points out that these rules were, at one time, part of "the staple hermeneutical diet of every Disciples minister," but they "are little known now."[16] Campbell's use of these rules did not negate his belief that the Bible spoke clearly; rather, they supported that belief. Once individuals applied these principles properly, they could not, in his view, miss the plain meaning of scripture.

Campbell did not utilize what today is known as "higher" or "historical criticism," even though the development of it was proceeding in Germany during his lifetime. The question of whether or not he knew about its development currently remains an open one.[17] Historical criticism considers all aspects of the original context of the biblical text. It addresses the matter of authorship, questions related to the sources, purposes and motives operating behind the text, and the events of the time that might have had an impact upon the author who wrote the text. Today's mainstream biblical scholars, including those among Disciples, make full use of historical criticism.

Whether or not Campbell would have used these principles had he known of them is a question we do not have enough information to answer. We can, however, point out that Campbell was on the cutting edge of critical biblical scholarship well known in this country at the time of his writing. As Boring has pointed out, his rules of interpretation anticipated some of the developments of historical criticism. This is especially true of his first rule.[18] A listing of these rules will demonstrate clearly enough that Campbell assumed a fairly critical approach to his work of interpretation and encouraged ministers and lay people on the American frontier to do the same.

This is not a trivial observation. One must remember that educated ministers and lay people were not the norm on the frontier. At least on this point, Campbell and Disciples might have been taking on a task with little likely prospect of success. Yet they were committed to making the effort. In spite of the difficulties they faced, they exerted their energy to close the gap between scholars, ministers, and laity by attempting to provide all members of the church with the necessary tools to interpret the Bible for themselves.[19]

**Rule I.** On opening any book in the sacred scriptures, consider first the historical circumstances of the book. These are the order, the title, the author, the date, the place, and the occasion of it.

**II.** In examining the contents of any book, as respects precepts, promises, exhortations, etc., observe who it is that speaks, and under what dispensation he officiates. Is he a Patriarch, a Jew, or a Christian? Consider also the persons addressed—their prejudices, characters, and religious relations.

**III.** To understand the meaning of what is commanded, promised, taught, etc., the same philological principles, deduced from the nature of language, or the same laws of interpretation which are applied to the language of other books, are to be applied to the language of the Bible.

**IV.** Common usage…must always decide the meaning of any word which has but one signification; but when words have according to…the Dictionary more meanings than one, whether literal or figurative, the scope, the context, or parallel passages must decide the meaning.

**V.** In all tropical [figurative] language ascertain the point of resemblance, and judge of the nature of the trope, and its kind, from the point of resemblance.

**VI.** In the interpretation of symbols, types, allegories, and parables, this rule is supreme. Ascertain the point to be illustrated; for comparison is never to be extended beyond that point—to all the attributes, qualities, or circumstances of the symbol, type, allegory, or parable.

**VII.** For the salutary and sanctifying intelligence of the oracles of God, the following rule is indispensable: We must come within the understanding distance. There is a distance which is properly called the speaking distance, or the hearing distance, beyond which the voice reaches not, and the ear hears not. To hear another, we must come within that circle which the voice audibly fills. Now we may with propriety say, that as it respects God, there is an understanding distance. All beyond that distance cannot understand God; all within it can easily understand him in all matters of piety and morality.

These seven rules of interpretation offer a picture of the critical mind Campbell assumed whenever he approached scripture. Disciples, throughout the years following Campbell's death, have, for the most part, continued in this critical tradition. These rules are "public, populist," and "personal."[20] Campbell and his followers struggled over time to wrest control of scriptural interpretation from the elite scholars and church leaders who pontificated on the meaning of scripture to the uneducated members of the congregation. Part of Disciples strategy included the effort to make interpretation a public process, subject to common rules of interpretation. Included in this approach was the effort to make scripture more accessible to lay people within the church. Finally, Campbell emphasized that all biblical interpretation also has an intensely personal side to it. Campbell put it this way:

> The man of God reads the Book of God to commune with God, "*to feel after him and find him*," to feel his power and his divinity stirring within him; to have his soul fired, quickened, animated by the spirit of grace and truth...God speaks: he listens. Occasionally, and almost unconsciously, at intervals he forgets that he reads, he speaks to God, and his reading thus often terminates in a devotional conversation with God....The Bible reading of all enlightened Christians generally terminates in a sacred dialogue between the Author and the reader.[21]

Campbell's principles bequeathed to later Disciples a willingness to interact with, rather than ignore, the critical developments of the scientific community. This Campbellian concern for the importance of the interaction between biblical interpretation and scientific principle, like its twin emphasis on the interaction between faith and reason, has greatly affected Disciples development. Disciples scholars have remained committed to the use of scientific method in their search for biblical truth. This commitment has enabled contemporary Disciples, in the tradition of their ancestors on the American frontier, to express a credible faith, one that commands the attention of the reflective unbeliever.

**Private Interpretation: Rights and Limitations**

The interpretation principle at work among Disciples had three focuses that were intended to protect the general integrity of the biblical message and to serve as an antidote to the prevalent misuse of scripture in America. This third and last focus emphasized both the rights and limitations attached to private interpretations of scripture. Though Disciples protected absolutely the individual's right to interpret scripture, they did place limits on how those individuals could utilize their personal interpretations. This precaution was absolutely consistent with their concern that the church be protected from the elitist interpretations of the powerful few.

Thomas Campbell defined this focus as early as his *Declaration and Address* in 1809. As he spelled it out, it had at least three aspects to it. First, the church of Christ will not establish anything, in matters of faith and practice, "for which there cannot be expressly produced a 'Thus saith the Lord,' either in express terms or by approved precedent." He meant by this that the church could only require of its members, in matters of "doctrine, worship, discipline, and government," only those things that appear as direct commands in scripture, or as clear biblical examples that one might reasonably expect the gathered congregation to follow. Regarding the latter, for example, there is no command to celebrate the Lord's Supper weekly anywhere in scripture. Yet scripture seems to indicate that it was celebrated each time the faithful gathered. Therefore, it stands as an "approved precedent."

Second, Campbell placed a further restriction on the church and its leadership. No one in the church was to interfere "directly or indirectly with the private judgment of any individual," so long, that is, as that private judgment did not contradict either an "express declaration" or an "approved precedent" of scripture. This aspect of the Disciples approach to scripture has produced one of the strongest traditions of toleration known to any denominational group in the world. Individuals are not to be denied church membership just because they do not "see with our eyes as to matters of human inference." Disciples recognized that the "inviolable right" to private interpretation was bound to produce divergent opinions on various issues. They did not want these opinions to become excuses to leave the church or to split it. Thomas Campbell hearkened back to the differences of viewpoint present between Jewish Christians and Gentile Christians described in the book of Acts and concluded, with the author of Ephesians, that Christians should be "forbearing one with another in love."

The third and final dimension to this focus placed a restriction on the individual. Since individual interpretation of scripture leads to individual inference, and such inferences are "imperfectly if at all perceived," no inferences ought to be exalted "above the express authority of God." No individual has the right to demand personal inferences be recognized or affirmed by other members of the church. In fact, Campbell recommended that individuals go one step further in their self-restraint. If anyone is offended because of a personal practice some other individual bases upon private judgment, the latter individual should forgo the practice in question to preserve the peace and unity of the congregation.[22]

Disciples used this third focus of the interpretation principle at work to stifle conflict within the congregation. Basically, early Disciples had a "live and let live" attitude regarding what they viewed as matters of personal opinion. This approach has its strengths. It has long established toleration as a hallmark of Disciples identity. Yet it also has its weaknesses. It too easily separates sources for developing "faith" ("express declarations" and "approved precedents") from sources behind human "opinion" (inferences from scripture; matters where scripture has no declarative word).

This separation is tied to the early Disciples understanding of scripture as propositional truth. Even though Disciples no longer hold to that view, the idea of an identifiable separation between matters pertaining to "faith" and those pertaining to "opinion" has remained strong. Since founding Disciples emphasized that the church could not speak with authority in areas of "opinion," many later Disciples have continued to say that only individuals (and not the denomination) should express opinions on matters where there is no declarative statement to be found in scripture. The church, in other words, must not use interpretation to make "inferences," no matter how biblically based, regarding controversial issues. This long-held belief has made our denominational social witness a very controversial topic among Disciples.

Many believe the church is compelled to speak and to act in areas of social concern as part of its mission in the world; others, probably constituting the majority of Disciples, want to restrict controversial opinions and actions to individuals. Personally, I long for the day when Disciples might discover a vital identity as members of a church willing to address, with speech *and* action empowered by the gospel, the unpopular, controversial, and hard issues facing human existence in our time. These days, *that* day seems less rather than more likely to be upon us anytime soon.[23]

## Conclusion

These three focuses of the interpretation principle do contain many obvious strengths. We are a diverse people. But we are also a tolerant people. All of our most influential mainstream leaders from Stone and the Campbells forward have defended this principle of free and rational inquiry. This approach to scripture has saved Disciples from the ever-present temptation to establish any particular biblical interpretation as normative for the denomination, or the whole church. The tolerance of this posture has enabled us to admit that, as a denomination, we do not possess the key to all truth. We can still learn from others.

At times, in our present denominational life, there are signs that we occasionally lose sight of this commitment to toleration and diversity. In General Assembly debates and, occasionally, in journalistic diatribes, one or another special interest group in the church, or individual in the church, gives in to the temptation to launch a personal attack on the views of others within the denomination. Special interest groups are bound to form within the life of a church. There is nothing inherently bad about small groups of people with shared interests organizing to discuss and promote those interests in the general life of the denomination. Yet when any group temporarily loses its commitment to toleration, and begins to accuse others of heresy or unacceptable ideas, it would do us all some good to recall the third focus first set forth by Thomas Campbell. I like the way Larry Bouchard has captured Disciples identity at this point:

> ...because we have valued freedom of interpretation so highly, we can use no single source of doctrinal interpretation to define the center of our community as we make claims on behalf of the whole of Christianity....No reasonable methods of interpretation or conclusions are arbitrarily foreclosed, so long as they seriously confront the scriptural witnesses as a matter of ultimate concern.[24]

To say that we must be tolerant is not the same as saying that the denomination should never make claims on behalf of the whole of Christianity or speak the gospel with *authority*, even in controversial areas pertaining to issues of justice and peace. When the General Assembly or any other "official" entity in our church life publishes some document or pronouncement (hopefully with full theological and biblical rationale), members of our congregations know that they are not bound by it. Yet they also should believe that it deserves their prayerful consideration.

It is a tradition among Disciples to protect the full and free expression of minority dissent within our gathered church life. Minority groups surrounding any given issue deserve to hear the very best theological and biblical rationale the majority can muster in support of its formal statements. Conversely, the majority needs to take seriously the theological and biblical arguments set forth by minority groups within Disciples life. Churches developing their institutional life during the glory days of democracy, and if ever there was such a church it is our own, too often assume that the voice of the majority is the voice of God. It just may be, more often than we would care to admit, that, on some issues, the minority offers better representation of the divine will and intention. In such cases, we can only hope that its voice will be heard clearly above the din.

Mutual respect of one another as members of God's family, even when we cannot respect one another's positions, is essential if the unity of church life is to continue. Any group as diverse as Disciples must recognize that total agreement on particular issues relating to church life will be rare. But members must also recognize that the church must continue to do its work. If total agreement were required before the church could work or speak, the church would have a good deal of silent free time on its hands.

Our commitment to the interpretation principle has made us a "people of the book." We have always taken the Bible seriously. We have always taken lay education seriously. Sometimes, admittedly, we have not dedicated ourselves to studying the Bible as we should. And, further, perhaps we have not always done as complete a job of education as we might have. In both these areas, we have occasionally talked a better game than we have played. But we are, for the most part, a biblically centered people. The Bible is our first resource when we encounter difficulty or conflict. Though we differ widely in our personal understandings of the Bible, most all Disciples view it as the major authoritative resource for Christian life and practice.

Because the Campbells and other early leaders took the Bible seriously, they provided future Disciples with a critical spirit with which to approach scripture. Disciples generally do not approach scripture flippantly or haphazardly, not unless they do injustice to the strong Disciples tradition that preceded them. The advent of historical criticism has moved the critical spirit in directions the founders did not necessarily anticipate. Yet today's Disciples scholars still exemplify the seriousness of effort and dedication to the result that characterized the work of the Campbells. It is no secret that the advent of higher criticism around the turn of the century (1900) caused a serious rift between certain Disciples scholars, most notably between Herbert L. Willett and John W. McGarvey.[25] Yet both men remained Disciples, and, different as they were in their approaches to the Bible, both still represented the Disciples critical spirit in the best sense. And both of them were dedicated to sharing the results of their scholarly work with the people in the pew.

The evangelization carried out by Disciples to spread both the gospel and their own understanding of the interpretation principle successfully reached many people on the periphery of cultural life. Disciples helped to provide for these people a community-oriented haven in the midst of a chaotic social setting. They helped these formerly alienated individuals to understand themselves in light of a biblical world view and affirmed them as individuals who mattered and who had the right, even the responsibility, to search God's word for themselves. They listened to their hopes and their dreams and enabled them to see those individual visions as important components in God's will for their lives. In this area, later Disciples have had a good example to follow.

Finally, the interpretation principle emphasized the public nature of interpretation. Disciples have, from their very beginning, recognized that interpretation should take place in the context of the whole church, not just the public arena composed by the members of any particular denomination. The Campbells, in fact, did not recognize that any particular Disciples denomination existed. Therefore, Disciples have been blessed with a general tendency to do biblical interpretation out in the open, informed by the ideas and understandings of the whole of Christianity. In the intervening years since the Campbells, we have come to realize more than they did just how important the witness of Christian tradition is in this process as well. We probably would not have been able to do so, however, had they not bequeathed to us such an exemplary critical spirit of inquiry.

The interpretation principle as understood by the founders, on the other hand, has produced occasional problems in the life of our church. Most of these problems stem from their situation both in terms of their time and their culture. First, nineteenth-century Disciples shared with others of their time a belief that the Bible contained statements of propositional truth, especially in the realm of what they referred to as "express declarations ['Thus Saith the Lord']." Even though Campbell and others recognized the human dimension to the Bible's language, they failed to see that all language about God is necessarily limited by its human dimensions. No human language can "capture" revelation and deliver it intact, free of the taint of human finitude or sin. It is dangerous to take any language about God literally, or, as theologians would say it, univocally. There simply cannot be an exact one-to-one correspondence between our words and the reality of God's activity and character. Human language can only point in the direction of what we mean when we talk about God or attempt to describe the truth of God's revelation.

The second point is built upon the recognition asserted in the first point. Since God has no other avenue for the mediation of God's word to humanity except through some form of human agency, the Bible itself must be understood as a book affected by the limitations of the human condition. It is a human book, divinely inspired, but nonetheless a fully human book. For all their emphasis on the necessity of interpretation, early Disciples were unable to understand that the Bible itself is a collection of human interpretations of God's revelation, or, alternatively, the "mighty acts of God in history." As later historical criticism has revealed, the four gospels are not literal histories, as Campbell and other early nineteenth-century Protestants assumed, but rather are differing theological formulations of the life of Jesus. The inability of early Disciples to recognize this dimension of biblical interpretation, when combined with their general propositional approach to the Bible, frequently degenerated, especially in the second generation, into an unfortunate form of rigid biblical literalism that tended to produce an intolerant mind-set.

Fred Craddock mentioned in his 1981 Forrest F. Reed Lectures the general tendency of Disciples to practice what he described as the "principle of finality."[26] This principle also resulted from the Disciples belief that the Bible contained propositional statements of truth. It surfaced in the way Disciples attempted to use scripture to "prove" particular "truths." Early Disciples, therefore, had a tendency, when they approached scripture in this manner, to be overly convinced they could arrive at final truth. This method of interpretation, practiced by many nineteenth-century Disciples preachers, made it too easy for them to identify the heretics and too confident that their own position always sided with the angels. Given events near the end of the nineteenth century, and again several decades into the twentieth century, one might reasonably conclude that the principle of finality, when joined to the right of individual judgment, lay at the heart of the two major schisms in the life of the Disciples. What Disciples had believed would lead to simple and effective union, instead led to two very serious divisions.

The passing of time has taught Disciples to take themselves a little less seriously. It has also brought them to a more sophisticated understanding of biblical authority and inspiration, one less prone to biblical literalism and intolerance. Yet they still have problems. Both liberals and conservatives in their midst have been known to abuse the scripture. Some have not taken the Bible seriously enough in setting forth their positions on particular issues. In this way, they have not been true to their Disciples heritage. Others have used private interpretations of the Bible to claim they possess the only truth on a given issue. In this way, they have not been true to their Disciples heritage.

In such cases, perhaps Disciples should return to the antidote established by their founders in response to such behavior. Disciples could focus more intentionally, informed by the whole of Christianity, on the matter of putting their interpretation principle to work. They could be more deliberate about elaborating, in a public manner, their assumptions about the nature of scripture. They could concentrate their educational efforts to help congregations reach a better understanding of the nature of sound rules of biblical interpretation. Finally, they could more carefully protect and reasonably limit (in the spirit of Thomas Campbell) the rights, privileges, and responsibilities of personal biblical interpretation. Such a return to the best aspects of the interpretation methodology from their denominational heritage might just enable Disciples to enter the twenty-first century as a more conscientiously biblical people.

## Questions for Reflection and Discussion

1. The whole subject of interpretation raises the question of the *truth* of our interpretations (based upon the recognition that "a person's interpretation can be more or less true to the text being interpreted"). Can you describe some different types of truth claims? How are things we have believed to be true either verified or falsified?

2. Note Alexander Campbell's concern to let the scriptures speak on their own terms. Describe your understanding of how the Bible speaks to us (does scripture ever speak completely or fully on its own terms?). In other words, is it possible to read scripture without simultaneously interpreting scripture?

3. What constituted the early movement's antidote to the abuse of scripture (what forms the heart of the interpretation principle at work)? What are the strengths and weaknesses of these focuses (for example, how does the third of these principles affect the ability of the church to speak

to social problems not literally or directly addressed in the Bible—in your view, is this effect a strength or a weakness?)?

4. What are the implications for our interpretation of the Bible of the statement that "all language about God is necessarily limited by its human dimensions"?

## *Notes*

[1] Quoted in Howard E. Short, *Doctrine and Thought of the Disciples of Christ* (St. Louis: Christian Board of Publication, 1951); *The Christian Baptist* (April 1826): 229.

[2] Nathan Hatch, *Democratization of American Christianity*, p. 77.

[3] The story of Lucy Mack Smith is told in Hatch, *Ibid.*, p. 43.

[4] *Ibid*, p. 24. Hatch treats the "Christian" and "Disciples" movements specifically in pp. 68-81.

[5] Larry Bouchard, "The Interpretation Principle: A Foundational Theme of Disciples Theology," pp. 20, 22. Bouchard's excellent article defined the Disciples confession as "performative speech"—"not a proposition but an action that...places the person under the religious imperative to interpret the confession throughout his or her life."

[6] *The Millennial Harbinger* (September 1851): 483.

[7] Fred B. Craddock, *The Bible in the Pulpit of the Christian Church: The Forrest F. Reed Lectures for 1981* (Claremont: Disciples Seminary Foundation, 1982), p. 5.

[8] Campbell, *Declaration and Address*, p. 60.

[9] Michael Wilson Casey, "The Development of Necessary Inference in the Hermeneutics of the Disciples of Christ/Churches of Christ" (Ph.D. Dissertation, University of Pittsburgh, 1986).

[10] M. Eugene Boring, "The Formation of a Tradition: Alexander Campbell and the New Testament," *The Disciples Theological Digest* (1987): see especially pp. 8-18.

[11] Quoted in Royal Humbert, ed., *A Compend of Alexander Campbell's Theology* (St. Louis: The Bethany Press, 1961), pp. 40, 42. Boring addressed this question as well; see "The Formation of a Tradition," pp. 6, 34-38; Campbell quotes originally found in *The Millennial Harbinger* (January 1846): 17; and *The Christian Baptist* (December 1828): 499.

[12] Quoted in Humbert, ed. *A Compend*, p. 43; originally in *The Millennial Harbinger*, (September 1837): p. 397.

[13] *The Millennial Harbinger* (August 1832): 339.

[14] *Ibid.*, p. 343.

[15] Humbert, *Compend*, p. 50; originally, *The Millennial Harbinger* (January 1846): 13.

[16] Boring, "The Formation of a Tradition," p. 22.

[17] See Boring, *Ibid.*, and Thomas H. Olbricht, "Alexander Campbell in the Context of American Biblical Studies, 1810-1876," *Restoration Quarterly* 33 (First Quarter, 1991): 13-28.

[18] Boring, *Ibid.*, pp. 24-25.

[19] Campbell's rules of interpretation are quoted in Humbert's *Compend*, pp. 54-56. They are found in their entirety in Campbell, *Christianity Restored: The Principal Extras of the Millennial Harbinger, Revised and Corrected* (Rosemead, California: Old Paths Book Club, 1959), pp. 95-99. This book is a handy collection of Campbell's writings on his "principles of interpretation," with essays by Campbell addressing the different types of biblical language (pp. 15-95).

[20]Boring, "The Formation of a Tradition," p. 23.

[21] *The Millennial Harbinger* (January 1839): 38.

[22]Thomas Campbell, *Declaration and Address*, especially pp. 26, 64, 66-67.

[23]Disciples have been involved in organized and cooperative benevolence work for over 100 years. Yet, social concern (applying Band-Aids) is different from social transformation (the attempt to transform societal structures which cause the wounds). Disciples have done the former well, but, as a church, rarely have worked meaningfully on the latter. The decision of the Division of Homeland Ministries to restructure its departments, accomplished in 1991 and including the dissolution of the Department of Church in Society, has raised the question in some Disciples' minds about whether modern Disciples are doing any better empowering the denomination in this area than previous generations before them. For a brief sample of the history of this Disciples tendency, see Mark G. Toulouse, "Social Transformation: Past," *Midstream* 26 (July 1987): 459-472.

[24]Bouchard, "The Interpretation Principle," p. 15.

[25]See M. Eugene Boring, "The Disciples and Higher Criticism: The Crucial Third Generation"; and Leo G. Perdue, "The Disciples and Higher Criticism: The Formation of an Intellectual Tradition," in D. Newell Williams, ed., *A Case Study of Mainstream Protestantism: The Disciples' Relation to American Culture, 1880-1989* (Grand Rapids: William B. Eerdmans Publishing Co., 1991), pp. 29-70, and 71-106 respectively; see also Anthony Lee Ash, "Attitudes Toward the Higher Criticism of the Old Testament Among Disciples of Christ: 1887-1905" (Ph.D. Dissertation, University of Southern California, 1966).

[26]Craddock, *The Bible in the Pulpit of the Christian Church*, p. 26f.

# 3

# THE RESTORATION PRINCIPLE
## A QUESTION OF AUTHORITY

---

*...simply returning to the original standard of Christianity, the profession and practice of the primitive Church, as expressly exhibited upon the sacred page of New Testament scripture, is the only possible way that we can perceive to get rid of those evils....Let us do as we are there expressly told they did, say as they said; that is, profess and practice as therein expressly enjoined by precept and precedent, in every possible instance, after their approved example; and in so doing we shall realize and exhibit all that unity and uniformity that the primitive Church possessed, or that the law of Christ requires.*

Thomas Campbell,
*Declaration and Address, 1809*[1]

---

## Introduction

With these words, Thomas Campbell wrote passionately about how the church might overcome the tragic divisions so characteristic of its existence in the world. He knew the pain of divisions in the church all too personally. As recently as three years before he wrote these words, just one year before he left Ireland for America, his own church body divided yet again, adding one more adjective to its name. These divisions helped to set his mind on the question of Christian union.

As he studied the question, the solution to division seemed simple to him and to most of those early reformers who gathered with him to form the Christian Association of Washington, Pennsylvania, in 1809. "Don't you see how easy it is?" one can almost hear him say, "All we need do is read the Bible and do what it says the early Christians did. What better example could we have?" The major problem contributing to division, in

55

Campbell's view, had to do with "the imposing of our private opinions upon each other as articles of faith or duty." Where do Christians get the right to judge and reject others by what they form as personal opinions and practices? The answer to the problem of division, the elder Campbell wrote, would present itself when Christians moved away from the practice of trusting too much in their private opinions and moved toward the model of the "profession and practice of the primitive church, as expressly exhibited upon the sacred page of New Testament scripture."[2]

Such is the heart of what is known as the "restoration" of the Christian church. Early Disciples were not the only group to formulate ideas related to restorationism. Various independent church movements such as those of Haldane, Glas, and Sandeman had believed that too many Christian churches had cluttered Christian beliefs with human inventions devoid of any biblical roots. For these believers, and for early leaders in the Disciples tradition as well, the restoration idea represented the path to the purity and simplicity of the original faith, a faith uncontaminated by either time or history. This idea found fertile soil in America where the recent democratic revolution had profoundly diminished the authority of inherited orthodoxies.

The American frontier afforded a particularly suitable place for Disciples to act on their ideas. Two historians writing on the Churches of Christ have listed five reasons why the frontier provided such a rich context. First, the land itself possessed a kind of inherent innocence, a place where purity seemed to be a part of the landscape. Second, the people on the frontier viewed democracy as the type of government God intended for human community. Such an attitude encouraged the belief that the church could also be transformed into what God intended for it to be. Third, optimism resulting from new freedoms acquired in the social sphere, especially in the area of politics and economics, fed Christian hopes for the arrival of the Christian millennium. Advocates made a strong case that restorationism could help to accomplish that reality more quickly. Fourth, restoration ideas supported the aims of younger, more dynamic movements in their quest to break ties with the established churches. Fifth, in the context of a confusing array of people and institutions offering authoritative answers, restorationism told people they could turn to the Bible and discover the answers for themselves. These attributes of the frontier prepared the way for the carefully formulated message of Disciples restorationism.[3]

## *The Restoration Principle: A Commitment to Biblical Faith*

Thomas Campbell, Alexander Campbell, Barton Stone, and Walter Scott were committed to the belief that Christians can best understand human experiences through reference to the Bible. Their restoration mind-set stemmed from this commitment. They assumed that all matters necessary to right doctrine and faith could be found in the scripture. Early Disciples, therefore, were a people of the Bible. They read and studied it carefully, and, foreign as the practice sounds to many Christians today, even memorized large portions of it. Theirs was a movement back to the Bible in an age when many religious groups had seemed to them to place creeds over the truths revealed in scripture. In this way, they carried on the tradition of Martin Luther and other Protestant reformers who sought to place the Bible above the authority of the institutional church. As Alexander Campbell described it, the Bible is "the fountain and source of light and life, spiritual and eternal."[4]

Alexander and Thomas Campbell lifted up the authority of scripture alone because they believed that the authority of scripture testified directly to the lordship of Jesus Christ. They began with the theological affirmation that the authority of Christianity could not rest in any human doctrine, but arose ultimately from the revelation of God in Christ. For the Campbells, this was the central fact of history. Since they discovered that revelation in the Bible, they placed the Bible at the center of the life of their congregations. For in the biblical representations of God, the world, themselves, and their neighbors, they discovered pictures disclosing the meaning of the gospel and the meaning of human existence.

It is true that their passion for the biblical witness could, and did in some cases, degenerate, in the next generation, into an unfortunate biblical literalism that tended to worship the words more than the message. Nevertheless, these women and men were committed to take the Bible seriously as an integral ingredient to any recipe for Christian growth and maturity.

Disciples restorationism also addressed the question of what faithful continuity with the gospel of Jesus Christ might mean. Alexander Campbell and others recognized that the lives of Christians in the first century had been touched by the same gospel that now touched Americans on the frontier. Their expression of restorationism sought to do justice to the oneness of purpose and faith that existed between the earliest Christians and themselves. Restorationism grew out of their early and deep concern to explore the meaning of their responsibilities in this area. To their everlasting credit, early Disciples were concerned to express their own faith in the context of affirming a definite historical and faithful continuity with the whole Christian church in all times and all places, stemming back even to the apostolic faith of the earliest Christian churches.

In their phrase "No Creed but Christ," these early Disciples also hoped to capture the essence of the centrality of Christ as an authority for Christian life and work. In their restoration mind set, they attempted to give life to their conviction that the church of Christ needed to stand separated from the methods and practices so evident in the corrupted social institutions of secular society. Restorationism, in fact, grew out of the theological principle that the church belongs to God, not to its membership, and must do what it can to discern the will of God if it hopes to work and serve meaningfully in the midst of a hurting and broken world.

Before it was anything else, restorationism represented a commitment to the overarching recognition that God reigns in the church. Early Disciples women and men sought a church unaffected by either human self-interest or self-righteousness. They looked around them on the American frontier and came to the accurate conclusion that individuals sought a dependable authority from which they could discover the meaning of life. Churches on the frontier appeared to have lost the ability to meet this need. As Disciples interpreted the scene, they concluded that these churches had substituted human authority for divine authority. Restorationism arose from the Disciples desire to restore divine authority to its rightful place. "Upon the whole, we see one thing is evident," observed Thomas Campbell, "the Lord will bear with the weaknesses, the involuntary ignorances, and mistakes of his people, though not with their presumption."[5] At its best, restorationism aimed to address the problem of human presumption. But, at its worst, it constituted a misreading of history.

## *The Restoration Principle: Interpreted as a Misreading of History*

Knowledge of historical events inevitably leads those who live in the present to an ever greater understanding of themselves. So people who are interested in learning more about themselves usually cast a backward glance through history. As they look back, they occasionally succumb to that great temptation to turn history into nostalgia. They think to themselves: "Weren't those days something? The world was much simpler then. No threat of devastating world war, no widespread dealers of drugs, no pollution, and no diet fads, or, more importantly, no guilt as a result of ignoring diet fads."

Of course, in the old days, religious understandings were so much simpler as well. Religious leaders of a century or two ago were much more confident that they knew the right answers than their descendants are today. Ambiguity did not seem to loom as large for them as it does for religious leaders today. Certainty was much easier to come by. No one seemed to have doubts in those days. Look at the great early leaders of the Disciples tradition, Thomas and Alexander Campbell, Barton Stone, Walter Scott, and later leaders like Caroline Neville Pearre, Jessie Trout, and Mae Yoho Ward. All strong, forceful, full of faith. Ah, yes, those were the "good old days."

These kinds of reminiscences make up the powerful attraction of nostalgia. Nostalgia sees history as a simpler time, a safer time, a more certain time. It leads people to believe they would all be better off if only they could return to "the good old days" of less pollution and more piety, less anxiety and more certainty. It gives the impression that the present's only hope is in recreating the past. In reality, however, nostalgia is really one of the great enemies of history because it distorts the true picture. The good old days were never really as good as nostalgia paints them.

In some ways, the restoration commitment among early Disciples became an exercise in nostalgia. The unity that Campbell and others sought never materialized. Instead, Disciples have been through two painful divisions within their own history. Why is this the case? Most modern Disciples have come to understand that the restoration approach itself was flawed by faulty presuppositions. Increasingly, they interpreted it as a misreading of history. In order to understand how this was the case, it is first necessary to understand the presuppositions supporting the Disciples commitment to restorationism.

Presuppositions are simply those things a person "supposes" are true and upon which everything else that person believes somehow rests. In many cases, presuppositions are held unconsciously, perhaps even taken for granted. That is what can make some of them dangerous. Cultures also have presuppositions. White Anglo-Saxon Protestant (the infamous WASP) culture was built, in large measure, on the foundation of racist and religiously biased presuppositions. As the Civil Rights Movement of the 1950s and 1960s clearly demonstrated, cultural presuppositions, or any other presuppositions for that matter, die hard.

Within a seminary, one of the first tasks professors set for themselves is challenging students to identify their own religious presuppositions. Maturity demands a willingness to confront and challenge one's own presuppositions. When people honestly explore and critique their own presuppositions, both they and their presuppositions usually emerge transformed. They no longer take their presuppositions for granted. Many reformulate their presuppositions to some extent so that they become more properly understood as thoughtful "suppositions," continually available for later reflection, perhaps even reformulation. These thoughtful persons usually become willing, with a great deal of humility, to engage in a genuine give-and-take dialogue with others about the nature of their Christian faith.

At least two presuppositions contributed to the development of the nostalgic understanding of the primitive church held by nineteenth-century Disciples. As Protestantism adopted new biblical, scientific, and historical methods of inquiry, however, these presuppositions were challenged and ultimately transformed. By the midpoint of the twentieth century, Disciples presuppositions about both the nature of the Bible and the nature of the church had undergone serious reconstruction. As a result of this reconstruction, Disciples were forced to abandon their earlier commitment to the restoration of the church.[6]

## The Nature of the Bible

As restorationists, most nineteenth-century Disciples viewed the Bible, particularly the New Testament, as a "constitution" enabling them to reproduce the primitive and unified church in all times and in all places. In the second generation, this view of the Bible led to an increased tendency to read the Bible as a law book. It became more important to talk about what the Bible prescribed than how it revealed God as a God of grace. This approach to the Bible led to serious problems for Disciples. The message of the gospel often got bogged down in rigid scriptural legalism. This basic presupposition affirming the Bible as "constitution" began to be overturned toward the end of the nineteenth century.

A shift in the Disciples approach to scripture occurred as increasing numbers of Disciples ministers became familiar with the higher critical approach to scripture. Higher criticism developed in Germany and slowly made its way to North America where it had a profound effect upon American biblical studies. The method contributed to the ultimate dissolution of a view of the world that had been built by some American Christians upon the twin doctrines of verbal inspiration and biblical inerrancy. Higher criticism, for many, swept away the credibility of both of these doctrines.

This new form of biblical criticism[7] went beyond the textual (lower) criticism practiced by Campbell. Campbell focused on determining the original wording of the text. As indicated in a previous chapter, higher (historical) critics addressed larger questions of background, date, authorship, literary characteristics, sources, and other such considerations. This newer form of criticism began to challenge traditional assumptions related to the Bible. Its conclusions challenged Mosaic authorship of the Pentateuch and, more troubling for many Disciples, the apostolic authorship and historical reliability of the Gospels. Higher criticism also uncovered the degree to which the culture and the needs of biblical time influenced the expressions and content of the biblical text itself.

A majority of contemporary Disciples have come to understand that the Bible, authoritative as it is in representing God's word of salvation to human beings, is also a book that, to some degree, represents the cultural concerns of those who contributed to the writing of its pages. Today's Disciples understand more completely than their predecessors did that all human thinking, even that of those who witnessed to the revelation of God through the pages of the Bible, is enmeshed in history and colored by one's cultural point of view. Earlier Disciples, in their restorationism, tended to contain the gospel in the shell of a first- or second-century world view. For example, some Disciples over the years have banished women to the captivity of a first- or second-century understanding of women. This misreading of the Bible and its relationship to culture also stood behind the defense of slavery offered by many nineteenth-century Disciples.

The pivotal figure in introducing Disciples to the new understanding of religion and culture emanating from higher criticism was Herbert L. Willett.[8] As the Dean of Disciples House at the University of Chicago from 1894, a professor of Old Testament in the Divinity School from 1896, a contributing editor in the newly reconstituted *Christian Century*, and regular contributor to the *Christian-Evangelist*, Willett exercised considerable influence among more educated, liberal-leaning, and urbane Disciples. A prolific writer, Willett led in the effort to educate Disciples laity in the liberal vision afforded by the new spirit of American Protestantism, of which higher criticism was only one component.

Beginning before the Civil War, but really taking root after 1870, a rebirth of spirit swept American Protestantism. A new, fresh daring in the area of intellectual inquiry acted as the central feature of this rebirth. Protestants became interested in the importance of human experience for theology. This caused the practice of theological reflection to take a turn. Many Protestants shifted their search for knowledge of God away from reference to creeds or doctrinal systems and toward thinking about their experience of God in the world around them. Some late-nineteenth-century theologians expressed the hope that this quest could open new understandings of the human condition and bring human beings to fresh encounters with God.

The new spirit of intellectual freedom and creativity circulating among Protestants at this time soon found new avenues of expression. Developments in science led to related developments in theology. Charles Darwin published *The Origin of the Species* and the evolutionary hypothesis began to challenge Christianity's literal dependence upon the biblical creation story. Part of this new theological awareness also addressed the nature of history itself. Religious scholars became concerned with tracing human development within and through history. They combined their new concern for the study of human religious experience with this new sense of historical development.

As a result, theologians began to appreciate the fact that even the Christian witness had changed and developed through time. God, it seemed to them, had adapted the gospel message to the intellectual and emotional and ethical capacities of different times, places, and peoples. This awareness brought these scholars to a greater appreciation for the diversity of Christian faith and expression, both past and present. The history of Christian doctrine became a new area of study for theologians. As the nineteenth century came to a close, theologians the world over warned their Christian communities about the fundamental incompatibility between dynamic Christian faith and literal dependence upon any form of sterile theological orthodoxy, however expressed.

Pastors and theologians also began to pay more attention to the way the religious needs of their congregations were changing in a developing urban culture. As they addressed themselves to these needs and to experiencing a God they found active in the midst of these needs, they simultaneously worked to gain a greater appreciation for the needs and hopes of all members of the human race. They were aided in this effort by the development of several new academic areas of inquiry, including the psychological and sociological study of religion.

The study of comparative religion also emerged as an academic discipline. A new historical science, it concentrated on exploring such questions as the relationship of Israel to Canaanite culture and religion, or the relationship between the theology of New Testament writings and the thought present in Greek and Roman culture. Eventually, this discipline branched out to include comprehensive studies of the histories and beliefs of various world religions, like those of Buddhism and Hinduism. Some Christian theologians began to entertain and explore the possibility that God was also at work in these non-Christian religious expressions.

Disciples did not share all the assumptions of this new context. Many Disciples did not share any of them. Others selectively picked and chose their way through the new avenues of knowledge rapidly becoming available to them. The social context of these changes provided the background for the controversies that flowed through Disciples life well into the twentieth century. Regardless of the possibility of controversy, however, many theologians and ministers did begin to recognize as legitimate the various conclusions reached by way of higher criticism. As they did so, their assumptions about the nature of the Bible began to change.

The Bible, in their view, contained a record of human experiences of God's revelation. It resulted from particular human encounters with the revelation of God in history. For Willett, for example, the Bible's authority and inspiration did not rest in the words of the Bible, but rather in the experiences of the people of Israel and the early Christian community. The Bible was inspired by a people's profound discovery of God in their lives. People of faith experienced God and recorded their stories in such powerful ways that the stories themselves make readers aware of the presence of God in their own lives.

Beginning with Willett, Disciples leadership began to reach the conclusion that the Bible is a book that leads its readers to an experience of the revelation of God for themselves. It is not, in and of itself, the revelation of God. Its value and authority does not rest in its literal containment of revelation. Rather, it rests in its ability to witness to the revelation of God in creation and in history and to direct human attention to the possibility of real, personal, and communal interaction with God. The Bible remains the primary authoritative source for Christian life and faith among these Disciples. Its authority, however, stems more from the spirit of the text than the literal word of the text. This new view of the Bible, settling into Disciples life after the turn of the century and over the next fifty years, led many Disciples to a reevaluation of earlier views related to the nature of the church.

## The Nature of the Church

Disciples of the nineteenth century believed that all local gatherings of Christians in the first and second centuries were perfectly unified in all essential matters of faith and organization. This presupposition was central to the early Disciples commitment to restorationism. It rested on several other presuppositions. Early theologians of our movement were convinced that Christ had successfully communicated to his apostles what God intended for the establishment of the church. They also were convinced that these apostles recorded accurately God's vision of the church in the Bible, just as it had been communicated to the apostles by Christ, including all necessities relating to its "doctrine, worship, discipline, and government" (as Thomas Campbell liked to phrase the matter). Finally, nineteenth-century Disciples believed the "primitive" church had followed these instructions to the letter. They affirmed, therefore, that all Christian congregations in the earliest era of Christianity were united around one common purpose and according to one uniform understanding of the church.

The context provided by higher criticism challenged all these earlier affirmations. Beginning with their renewed theological understanding of the church as an organization which, try as it may, can never escape its historical relativity, Disciples have concluded that the church has never seen a golden age when it was pure and without blemish. Though inspired and driven by a sincere commitment to divine purposes in history, the church can never completely escape either its historical existence (and, therefore, its relative and finite existence in history) or its humanity (and, therefore, its sinfulness).

Historical research over the last century has corroborated what the increased theological sensitivity of Disciples has concluded about the nature of the church. Disciples, and other mainline Protestants, now know that the early church only gradually developed in its self-understanding. Jewish, Greek, and Roman elements all combined to affect its development as an institution, both in its structure and in its thought. History has revealed very clearly the fact of diversity in the early church. There never was one ancient church, but instead, an assortment of early churches. The practices, church government, and, yes, even the faith of these early congregations were quite diverse depending on geographical location and cultural influences. For example, the congregation in Antioch differed considerably from the congregation in Jerusalem. Even as these two fellowships undoubtedly shared a common love for Christ, they defined the nature of the Christian life, for the individual and for the church, quite differently (refer to Acts 15, for example). In other words, there really never existed some singular unified early church Disciples could restore in the modern period.

Early Disciples possessed another idea about the nature of the church that went unchallenged until the developments of the late nineteenth and early twentieth centuries. In their understanding, God's church had to be an unchanging institution: the same yesterday, today, and tomorrow. Therefore, their view of the early or primitive church included their belief that the church could not have changed and remained God's church. Most of today's Disciples have abandoned this notion as well. The increased theological awareness leading modern Disciples to recognize the human character of the church has also led them to recognize the impossibility of affirming an unchanging church. Though the life of the Holy Spirit within the church is permanent and is dependably present, the church as a human institution can only provide flesh for divine purposes in fleeting and necessarily impermanent ways. Even where divine purposes may be unchanging, the church is rooted in its own historical and cultural setting and is, therefore, constantly changing and developing.

Disciples ministers today generally recognize that biblical writings reveal an early church life continually developing according to the needs of various times and circumstances. Changing times brought new and changing ways to express the gospel. While some Disciples developed this understanding near the turn of the century, others continued to depend upon a more static reading of the Bible. Some nineteenth-century Disciples refused to admit organs into the worship life of their congregations on the basis of such readings. Others, however, adapted to the ways of the world altogether too easily. Some spent more money on ornate organs than the mission endeavors of the church itself.

By 1906, a separate movement of churches among Disciples had gathered under a new name and a distinct identity, including their own listing in the federal census of that year. Disciples congregations joining together to form the Churches of Christ (Non-Instrumental) retained many of the nineteenth-century restorationist commitments that many of the mainstream Disciples were beginning to question. Their rigorous understanding of restorationist views caused the leaders of this movement, represented by ministers like Tolbert Fanning and David Lipscomb, to oppose the Disciples adoption of state and national missionary societies throughout the last quarter of the nineteenth century. The split between the two groups of congregations resulted from much more complicated religious and cultural origins than are suggested by their developing differences over the question of organs in worship, or the adoption of societies in missionary endeavors. Most of those divisive origins, however, can be traced to the response of both groups to the basic issue of change in church life.

Mainstream Disciples gradually came to accept the theological understanding that the church, by its very nature, is a changing institution. Once they recognized that change was not all bad, they also realized that the church needs to be more conscious of its changing nature. Congregations ought to assess the quality of change by whether it provides for continued or more effective faithfulness to the gospel. Today's Disciples believe this to be a much more productive enterprise for the church than the nineteenth-century restoration attempt to find ways to live in the first century again, an attempt that denied the reality of change altogether.

## The Restoration Principle: Revisited

Can the restoration principle be reinterpreted in a way that can have meaning for contemporary Disciples? Perhaps a positive answer to that question resides in those aspects of that principle that were most concerned with seeking the essence of biblical faith. Many concerns of the early Disciples appear to coincide with more recent developments within worldwide Christianity. Within the ecumenical movement today, there is a serious effort to recover a meaningful definition of what is meant by the term "apostolic faith." By pinpointing the "permanent" or "essential" aspects of apostolic faith, many ecumenical leaders hope to further the cause of Christian unity and strengthen the witness of the church in the world. At a World Council of Churches consultation in Rome in 1983, a working definition of the term was developed:

> The term "apostolic faith" as used in this study does not refer only to a single fixed formula or a specific moment in Christian history. It points to the dynamic, historical (*geschichtliche*) reality of the central affirmations of the Christian faith which are grounded in the witness of the people of the Old Testament and the normative testimony of those who preached Jesus in the earliest days ("apostles") and of their community, as attested in the New Testament. These central affirmations were further developed in the church of the first centuries. This apostolic faith is expressed in various ways, i.e., in individual and common confessions of Christians, in preaching and sacraments, in formalized and received creedal statements, in decisions of councils and in confessional texts. Ongoing theological explication aims at clarifying this faith as a service to the confessing community. Having its centre in the confession of Jesus as Christ and of the triune God, this apostolic faith is to be ever confessed anew and interpreted in the context of changing times and places in continuity with the original witness of the apostolic

community and with the faithful explication of that witness throughout the centuries.[9]

This search for apostolic faith seeks to find the unity beneath the
diversity of even the early period. Biblical criticism has revealed more
completely the multifaceted dimensions of theological reflection at the
time of the early church. Yet around what commitments did these diverse
understandings revolve? Are there normative biblical Christian beliefs
to be shared by all Christians? What does it mean to be faithful to the
apostolic witness of the Christian church? The problem is the same one
the Campbells were concerned with on the American frontier. Many of
the important questions are the same. These concerns, in fact, have a
long history. In the early centuries of the church's life, Irenaeus,
Tertullian, and Augustine all addressed these questions using whatever
tools they had available to them. John Calvin, and the Reformed tradition
in general, sought to guide the sixteenth-century reformation by
reference to the New Testament precepts and precedent. Campbell's
restorationism, no doubt influenced at least in part by the work of the
Protestant reformers, spoke to these concerns for his time. Our time is
increasingly attempting to speak to them under the rubric of
"apostolicity."

Today's "central affirmations" of apostolic faith, like those of the
Campbells, are gleaned from the biblical witness, and generally, however
expressed, grouped around four major categories. Recently, an
ecumenical leader set forth these central affirmations "descriptively" as
"dimensions of the apostolic faith."[10] The first dimension is the confession
that Christ is "God and Savior." The emphasis within this aspect of the
apostolic faith is to affirm the "incarnational claim" that God is in Christ,
that Christ represents God faithfully for humanity, and that Christ is
the one through whom Christians understand the meaning of their
redemption. This confession finds varying expression among different
traditions, but all members of the Christian tradition affirm the biblical
witness about Jesus as standing at the center of God's activity in history.

Second, apostolic faith also affirms the "guidance and inspiration of
the Holy Spirit." Usually, this affirmation finds its life in the Lord's supper, baptism, and preaching, though some traditions emphasize particular gifts of the Holy Spirit. The biblical witness, however, makes clear the
presence and power of the Holy Spirit for the work of the church and the
edification of Christians.

Third, the apostolic faith emphasizes "the authoritative witness of
the Scriptures." Two characteristics seem to define the present Christian
approach to the Bible. Critical biblical methods are increasingly accepted
within the life of the church today. Accompanying this growing acceptance of all aspects of developing biblical criticism as an interpretive

method contributing to the clear meaning of scripture for our day is a general ecumenical emphasis on the primary authority of the biblical witness. Of course, there remain significant numbers of Christian groups today who emphasize the "self-interpretive" nature of the Bible based upon their view that the Bible contains the literal and directly inspired words of God.

The fourth dimension of apostolic faith speaks to the nature of the church. Apostolic faith affirms "the Church as the Community of Faithful Worship, Witness, and Service in the World."[11] The shape of this "worship, witness, and service" has varied throughout history. Yet the history of the church is replete with examples of how the faithful community has attempted to fulfill its promise as a community set apart to serve God in the world. Contemporary traditions share the present task of "faithful worship, witness, and service" with the one church through history and is informed by the testimony of its life.

Every group is different in the fine and detailed shades attributed to these four aspects of apostolic faith. The Disciples commitment to restorationism brought all four of these emphases to special light from the very beginning of the Disciples movement. Disciples have always been christocentric as a people. Their historic focus upon Christ, expressed in their "No Creed but Christ" phraseology, clearly delineated their belief in the absolute centrality of God's act in Christ for the redemption of humanity and the foundation of the church.

The primacy of the Holy Spirit has generally been interpreted within Disciples tradition through an emphasis upon the role of the Spirit in the life of the church. Alexander Campbell's emphasis on the corporate dimensions of Christian existence highlighted the early Disciples understanding of the importance of the Holy Spirit for the church's ongoing life and witness. The acts of Christian worship, particularly baptism, the Lord's supper, reading of scriptures, preaching, and prayer, all served as ordinances where the work of the Holy Spirit revealed both the presence of Christ and the real power of God's redeeming grace.

Restorationism grew out of the early Disciples affirmation of the centrality of scripture. Over the years, Disciples have maintained their identity as a biblical people. The shape of that identity has changed some through their growing acceptance of historical criticism as a biblical interpretive tool. But the fundamental identity of Disciples as a people of the Bible has remained the same. For a time in Disciples life, after the time of Willett, Disciples appeared to be heading toward a fragmentation of their biblical witness, where one method operated in the Disciples congregations and another in the Disciples academic community, and neither had much to do with the other. Today, there is a growing awareness of the need for congregation and academy to work together in the interpretation of the Bible. Yet much work is yet to be done.

Biblical interpretation performed in the context of academic life among Disciples should maintain an ultimate intention and ability to serve the life of the church. The Disciples adoption of biblical criticism, despite what some Disciples conservatives have charged, has never illustrated the choice of some to believe the biblical critics rather than to believe the Bible. Contemporary Disciples are learning more and more how the modern methods of biblical interpretation do not threaten the authority of scripture properly conceived, but rather serve to enable scripture to speak with greater clarity and integrity, and therefore greater authority, in matters affecting Christian life and apostolic faith. The biblical message defines the gospel, relates the experience of the redeemed community of faith, and witnesses to the unity of the body of Christ. Alexander Campbell, even though he held basic presuppositions regarding the nature of the Bible that are different from those held by most Disciples today, knew at least as well as contemporary Disciples that the community's apostolic faith is formed in these "essentials" only through its faithful approach to scripture.

The fourth dimension of apostolic faith was also present in the restoration emphasis of early Disciples. The early leaders asserted the essential unity of the church's life from the very beginning of the Disciples movement. Their concern for the vitality of the church's "worship, witness, and service" is evident throughout the ecclesiastical, literary, and social landscapes they left behind, the first littered by their steeples and mission stations, the second by volumes of their pages, and the third by their benevolent institutions. Restorationism served as their method by which these Disciples hoped to bring this dimension of their commitment to the apostolic faith to life. However flawed their restoration understanding might have been about the nature of the primitive church life, they never wavered from their more important insight that the essence of the church is one, a singular body whose head is Christ.

I believe that the restoration principle, at its central point, served Disciples as an attempt to find and express continuity with the apostolic faith. They affirmed the simplicity of faith, but also asserted that true faith had defined characteristics. When present-day Disciples revisit the restoration principle, they should discover an early Disciples search for the integrity of faith. There is something we can learn from that search. Accompanying our contemporary recognition that the Bible cannot serve as a "constitution" in our midst should be the equally important recognition that the Christian faith does possess certain identifiable characteristics. Individuals and congregations cannot practice and believe whatever they choose to practice and believe, contradicting or ignoring these dimensions of apostolic faith.

All of us, individuals and congregations alike, must measure our activities by these strands of apostolic faith. Does what we do serve the gospel,[12] the truth of which is authoritatively displayed in the biblical witness to it? Is what we plan consistent with the ministry and witness of Christ as reconciling, redeeming, and liberating incarnation of God? Is it one with the witness of the Holy Spirit, made manifest to us through our worship? Do our lives and our activities serve the real unity of this great body of Christians known as the church, of which Disciples constitute only a small portion?

Individuals and congregations in the church do not have to reach total agreement as to the precise method of God's forgiveness and redemption of human beings, or the accurate means of Christ's incarnation, or some singular definition of Christ's humanity and divinity, or the proper lines of just how the Bible is inspired, or the definitive understanding of how the Holy Spirit works, or the final determination of how the church is one in all times and all places. In these matters, the Campbell approach seems best: leave them to the realm of personal opinion. In asserting the truth of these general claims (rather than a dogmatism about *how* each of these claims is true) the church provides a witness to the central affirmations of apostolic faith and discovers a guide to the appropriate expression of its own life and work. This is, in essence, what the early Disciples tried to accomplish through restorationism.

## Conclusion

Disciples, with their doctrine of the restoration of the church, sought "the mountain of the LORD's house" (Isaiah 2:1). Though they ended up on another human hill, they were on to something. The early Disciples commitment to restorationism became sloppy, was prone to nostalgia, and later expressed itself as a misleading biblical literalism. Nevertheless, these people struggled to give expression to a great truth. Through their restoration principle, they sought a way to sweep out the weak and empty loyalties that had cluttered the human soul of the church. They sought a way to free Protestantism from worship at human altars. They wanted to find an anchor of divine authority that would offer stability to Christians who found themselves floating from one buoy of human authority to another.

Though Disciples eventually rejected as illusory a restorationism resting upon a singularly unified early church, their early restorationist vision arose from their desire to be true to Christ as Lord. Though their early expressions of it tended too easily to dismiss some seventeen centuries of history and Christian tradition in order to return to a primitive first-century version of church life, early Disciples earnestly sought the voice of God as the guide to contemporary understandings of the worship, witness, and service of the church. Restorationism rested upon the theological recognition that no human authority can ever provide an adequate basis for Christian life and work and hope; these rest in God alone. This theological affirmation provided Disciples of Christ with a great sense of identity and a single-minded focus in terms of mission. The value of the Disciples vision of a church dependent upon God's authority alone rested in its ability to act as a critique of the ways of the world, and how those ways had crept into the ways of the church. In spite of the problems occasioned by early restorationism, this vision could, and sometimes did, lead to self-analysis and concern for a biblical way of working in the world. The restoration principle revisited as concern for the dimensions of apostolic faith could do the same for the church today. Further, acknowledgment and acceptance of the diverse ways of affirming these dimensions of apostolic faith could lead Disciples to an even greater appreciation of the way different nuances of faith actually strengthen, rather than weaken, the Christian witness in the world.

## Questions for Reflection and Discussion

1. Restorationism, at its heart, is concerned with the integrity of the church. What areas of concern might you define as constituting the integrity of the church?

2. In what ways did the early Disciples' commitment to restorationism represent a "misreading of history"? In other words, what are the presuppositions of restorationism which have been challenged both by historical inquiry and by increased theological awareness?

3. Can you list presuppositions (inherited or developed, conscious or unconscious) of your own, related to your faith (for example, in relation to your understanding of the mission of the church, or the nature of the Bible), that you have reconsidered in the past, have had challenged recently, or believe you ought to be willing to reconsider in the future?

4. If the church develops, affected by time and circumstances, how can the church best meet the difficult issues facing it today (sexuality issues, abortion, medical ethics)?—would you describe the church as ahead of or behind the culture (and why)? In any given controversial issue, how does the church's present position represent an accommodation to cultural norms of a passing era (as was the case with slavery or, later, segregation)?—how does the present position represent a gospel challenge to developing cultural norms?—how does the proposed new position represent accommodation to developing cultural norms ?—how does it act as a challenge, based upon the gospel, to prevailing cultural norms?—is it possible that the proposed position is both a new accommodation and a gospel challenge? How should the church proceed since there are rarely ever clear answers to any of these questions?

5. In what ways do the four "central affirmations" found in modern understandings of "apostolic faith" represent concerns historically important to Disciples?

6. Disciples restorationism expressed a concern for the theological recognition that "no human authority can ever provide an adequate basis for Christian life and work and hope; these rest in God alone." Of what use is this theological principle when human beings also should recognize that they can never be absolutely certain they have accurately discerned the mind of God? How would you assess your ability to see God's will and intention in views different from your own?

## Notes

[1]Campbell, *Declaration and Address*, p. 77.

[2]*Ibid.*

[3]Richard Hughes and Leonard Allen, *Discovering Our Roots: The Ancestry of Churches of Christ* (Abilene: Abilene Christian University, 1988), pp. 90-93.

[4]Alexander Campbell, *The Christian System* (Cincinnati: H.S. Bosworth, fourth edition, 1866), p. 15.

[5]Thomas Campbell, *Declaration and Address*, p. 65.

[6]See, for example, Ralph G. Wilburn, "A Critique of the Restoration Principle: Its Place in Contemporary Life and Thought," in Ronald E. Osborn, ed. *The Reformation of Tradition*, Vol. 1, *The Renewal of Church: The Panel of Scholars Reports* (St. Louis: The Bethany Press, 1963), pp. 215-264.

[7]The word *criticism* is utilized in the context of the phrase "biblical criticism" to mean "scholarly, discerning, and careful."

[8]M. Eugene Boring, "The Disciples and Higher Criticism: The Crucial Third Generation," and Leo Perdue, "The Disciples and Higher Criticism: The Formation of an Intellectual Tradition," in D. Newell Williams, ed., *A Case Study of Mainstream Protestantism: The Disciples' Relation to American Culture, 1880-1989* (Grand Rapids: Eerdmans Publishing Co., 1991), pp. 29-70 and 71-106 respectively.

[9]Quoted in George Vandervelde, "The Meaning of 'Apostolic Faith' in World Council of Churches' Documents," in Thaddeus D. Horgan, ed., *Apostolic Faith in America* (Grand Rapids: Eerdmans Publishing Co., 1988), p. 24.

[10]See Horgan, "Dimensions of the Apostolic Faith," in *Ibid.* The following four dimensions are discussed briefly in pp. 59-63.

[11]*Ibid.*, p. 62.

[12]Clark Williamson defines the gospel as "the gracious promise of the love of God offered freely to each and all, and, therefore, the command of God that justice be done to each and all of those whom God loves." Williamson, "Theological Reflection and Disciples Renewal," in Michael Kinnamon, ed., *Disciples of Christ in the 21st Century* (St. Louis: CBP Press, 1988), p. 90.

# 4

# THE ECUMENICAL PRINCIPLE
## SEEKING THE UNITY OF GOD'S CHURCH

*We envision full communion as a dynamic and growing relationship that is more than just accepting one another as we now are. It is a mutual commitment to grow together toward a vision of the church that enriches our theological traditions, enhances service and mission, and deepens worship. We will find diverse expressions of what it means to live in full communion in Christ as we experience life together.*

"Resolution on Ecumenical Partnership"
General Assembly of the Christian Church
(Disciples of Christ)
Indianapolis, Indiana, 1989[1]

## Introduction

Of the literally hundreds of books and essays written to analyze and interpret the Disciples understanding of church unity, all authors are agreed on at least one item: Disciples of Christ, from their very beginning, have been deeply committed to the principle of Christian unity. Kenneth Teegarden, general minister and president emeritus of the Christian Church (Disciples of Christ) has an interesting way of phrasing this commitment: "The ideal of Christian unity is to Disciples of Christ what basketball is to Indiana, hospitality is to the South, and nonviolence is to Quakers." His point, of course, is simply to say that Christian unity "is part of our identity."[2]

In some ways, the early commitment to Christian unity naturally fit the context. As Disciples were being born, the various states were making a commitment to political unity. If union could be accomplished in politics, it certainly should be within reach for the church. Perhaps

73

the context of political union provided Disciples with an extra incentive as they sought Christian union.[3] On the other hand, their nineteenth-century commitment to unity was unique among American Protestants. Since most Protestants possessed institutional and denominational identifications they appreciated, they no doubt affirmed vested interests in those areas that early Disciples did not share. Unity, in some instances, could threaten those interests. And though the concern to restore primitive Christianity was common to many different groups during this time period, only the early Disciples situated it alongside the accompanying belief that the apostolic witness demanded unity among all Christians. To some degree, therefore, Disciples were swimming against the cultural stream on this question. As they did so, they repeatedly attacked denominationalism as a "sin" of major proportions.

Pride in denominationalism, rather than disdain for it, characterized the general religious context on the American frontier in the early 1800s. After all, these years were but a few removed from the glorious victory for religious liberty secured through the new American constitution. Most Christians viewed denominationalism as a part of the positive outcome of the process that secured religious liberty. The American constitution ensured the success of the denominational system. Christians were guaranteed their freedom to place their membership with any denominational group and to worship with that group in whatever manner, within reasonable limits, seemed appropriate to them. It is understandable, therefore, why many Americans sharing the individual orientation of the frontier were more interested in defending the denominational system than they were in attacking it.

Early Disciples, however, saw denominationalism as an affront to Christian unity. This caused them to denounce it in no uncertain terms. On June 28, 1804, Barton Stone's actions indicated as much when he joined with several other ministers in dissolving the Springfield Presbytery. At that time, Stone and these other ministers wrote that it was their desire for the presbytery to "sink into union with the Body of Christ at large."[4] In 1809, in another state and among a different group of reformers, Thomas Campbell issued his *Declaration and Address*. Among its many prominent expressions stressing church unity, one finds Campbell's wholehearted belief that "division among Christians is a horrid evil." The "bitter jarrings and janglings of a party spirit" so clearly evidenced among the denominations, said Thomas Campbell, had to be overcome.[5] Is it any wonder why the Christians of Kentucky and the Reformers or Disciples of Pennsylvania gravitated toward one another?

By 1830, these groups had both established congregations in some of the same areas, particularly in Kentucky, Ohio, Tennessee, and Indiana. As these congregations came into contact with one another, they could not help but notice similar patterns of belief, including a commitment to both restorationism and believer's baptism. Particularly striking to them, however, was their equal dedication to the cause of church unity and its accompanying disavowal of all party names. In 1827, for example, Barton Stone wrote an open letter in *The Christian Messenger* to Alexander Campbell. The letter, written for the purpose of offering a rebuttal to some of Alexander Campbell's views of Jesus Christ, indicates that even early leaders of what would become the Disciples movement could not agree about how they would speak of Christ's relationship to God. More to the point, however, the letter praised Campbell for maintaining the "courage of a David, tearing away the long established foundations of partyism, human authoritative creeds and confessions." "Your religious views," Stone told Campbell, "in many points, accord with our own."[6] These two groups, it seemed to many of their members, were destined to unite with one another. Yet, their road to union did have its potholes.

## Unity Between Christians and Disciples in 1832

As most who have researched the event have indicated, union between Stone's "Christians" and Campbell's "Disciples" would probably have never happened if it had required the total agreement of both leaders.[7] As editors of their own religious journals, both Stone and Campbell avidly read each other's editorial work. Occasionally, they commented on each other in their own papers. In August of 1831, Stone addressed directly the question of union between the two groups. He told his readers that the "Christians" were ready and willing to unite even though there were some differences of opinion between the two groups. On the other hand, however, he pointed out that the "Disciples" saw these differences as serious obstacles to union. Stone listed two major differences as the reasons why Campbell's group of "Disciples" congregations were hesitant to unite with the "Christian" congregations.[8]

The first of these had to do with the fact that the "Christians" practiced open communion and open membership. Stone preached immersion for the remission of sins, but he admitted the unimmersed to church membership. Regarding the Lord's supper, Stone told Campbell that he found nothing in the Bible "to forbid me to commune with unbaptized persons at the Lord's Table." Campbell, in 1830, instructed Stone that "it is not enough to say there is no command against it. If it is not commanded by the Lord, it is human, and all human institutions are will-worship, and, as such, obnoxious to the curse."[9] In Campbell's opinion, such an argument applied to both open communion and open membership. Later, both Campbell and Stone would reach consensus agreement on these two issues, each of them giving a little and getting a little, but at the time of the union of the two movements, they definitely expressed serious disagreements about both matters.

Stone listed a second reason why Campbell's "Disciples" seemed opposed to the union. He claimed they opposed the name "Christian" because no one could really deserve to wear the name. Further, in what almost sounds like one child arguing with another about who crossed the finish line first, Stone informed Campbell that the doctrines taught by "Disciples" were "taught by us many years ago." For his part, Campbell denied that Stone's movement preceded his own on any of the truly important questions. Though he admitted that Stone was an early proponent of "anti-creed, anti-council, and anti-sectarian" religion, he argued that the Disciples were the first to give real meaning to the "ancient gospel and ancient order of things" as the basis for church unity. Campbell eagerly engaged Stone in the child-like argument over who could claim "first place" in the origin of ideas.

Regarding the question of names, of "Christians" or "Disciples," Campbell answered that "the controversy about the name...is, and must necessarily be, one of subordinate importance." Having said that, however, he then spent two full pages describing why the name "Christian" was less appropriate than the name "Disciples." "Disciples" had more biblical basis than "Christian," claimed Campbell. Besides, some Unitarians were known to go by the name of "Christian" only. Though Stone had some leanings in this direction himself, Campbell did not want to be closely associated with Unitarians, even if it only meant sharing a common name. Obviously, the way Barton Stone and Alexander Campbell felt about this name issue helps to explain why present-day churches in the denomination are often called "Christian churches" while most members of those churches are known as "Disciples." It also helps to explain why we are known as The Christian Church (Disciples of Christ). Kenneth Teegarden has an interesting insight on the name itself: "The generic first part, *Christian Church*, points to our objective of unity; the distinguishing second part, *Disciples of Christ*, reminds us that we have not arrived."[10]

One definitely gets the feeling from reading Stone and Campbell that, had it been left up to them alone, any formal unity between their two movements would never have occurred. Barton Stone received help from ministers in both movements in bringing about a successful merger between them. Two Disciples ministers, "Raccoon" John Smith and John T. Johnson, brother to Richard M. Johnson, the Vice President of the United States, established close connections with congregations from the "Christian" movement located in Kentucky. John Rogers, a "Christian" minister, also worked in Kentucky and became friendly with Johnson, Smith, and other "Disciples" ministers in that region. These three men met together with Barton Stone in the late fall of 1831 and planned several mass meetings to be held in Georgetown and Lexington in late December and early January.

The Georgetown meetings fostered optimism that the union between "Christians" and "Disciples" could really take place. The next week, in Lexington, the two groups made it official. John Smith and Barton Stone, each representing their groups, stood up to speak to the issue. Stone invited Smith to make the first remarks. "God has but one people on the earth," Smith told his listeners.

> Let us, then, my brethren, be no longer Campbellites or Stoneites, New Lights or Old Lights, or any other kind of lights, but let us all come to the Bible, and to the Bible alone, as the only book in the world that can give us all the Light we need.

Stone, in response, turned to Smith and said, "I am willing to give him, now and here, my hand." All those assembled sang a song together and, on Sunday, January 1, 1832, ratified the union by celebrating the Lord's supper together.[11] Stone urged the congregations to "let the unity of Christians be our polar star."[12]

The resulting union between these two independent religious movements was not insignificant given the frontier context. The nineteenth century is better known for church splits, particularly from its beginning through the time of the Civil War, than it is for church mergers. Outside of limited cooperative endeavors between Presbyterians and Congregationalists that resulted in some joint congregations, and the two groups (Millerites and Sabbatarians) forming the Seventh-Day Adventists, this event marks the only other union of two distinct religious groups in nineteenth-century America. The numbers of people involved were not large, somewhere between twenty to thirty thousand combined members. Virtually no social or economic differences separated the members of the two movements. All the congregations involved were located within the same general region of the country. All these things greatly contributed to making unity possible. Yet, the accomplishment of full union still remains impressive.

The union was not without its difficulties, however. Even at Lexington, the two groups of congregations were unable to unite successfully until 1835. There remained serious methodological and doctrinal differences between the two groups. Leadership questions arose as well. Campbell tended to overpower Stone, and the two continued to snipe at one another in the pages of their journals. Yet, the process uniting the various congregations of the two movements gradually continued. In spite of all their differences, the leaders of the "Christians" and "Disciples" shared a deeply rooted theological conviction: they affirmed that the unity of the church did not arise out of human origins, but rather must be experienced as the gift of God. Unity, in other words, must be regarded as an essential characteristic of God's true church. These early Disciples simply could not escape their belief that a fragmented church is really no church at all. This conviction, no doubt, served them well during the tense early days of their union.

Another interesting aspect of this union results from the role local congregations played in making it successful. Even though lay people were present at Lexington, the actual decision to unite came from the leaders. Yet, neither movement had any effective institutional structure to implement such a decision. The ultimate uniting of these movements depended entirely on the will and action of local congregations coming together in various cities and towns across the region where both groups lived. Though "Raccoon" Smith and John Rogers served as traveling evangelists to encourage the unification of congregations, the people in the pews and their local ministers had to take the action. Undoubtedly, Walter Scott's activities as an evangelist on behalf of the united church greatly aided the union effort as well. Yet, the point remains that local congregations made the effort successful.

In our day and time, when union talks take place at leadership levels and rarely reach the congregational ear, local ministers need to give special attention to the nature of union discussions and attempt to relay information to the people in the pews of their congregations. No matter how successful talks between church leaders are these days, real unity of the church will only materialize when local congregations are able to worship together, listening to the preached word together and passing the elements of the Lord's supper to one another. Unity, in all cases, must be local and tangible or it is something less than true unity. Early "Christians" and "Disciples" knew this fact and they possessed a congregational passion for Christian unity often lacking in Disciples congregational life today.

Agreement reached between impersonal church structures is, perhaps, a first step. Yet, unity is not complete until it is practiced at the local levels of congregational life. Working to achieve church unity is not simply the task of the general minister and president of the Christian Church (Disciples of Christ), or even simply a major responsibility of the Disciples General Board. Christian unity, as our ancestors seemed to know better than we, must be the task of the whole church and all its members.

Both Campbell's "Disciples" and Stone's "Christians" were also aided in their movement toward unity by the assumptions they shared about its nature. Members of the two groups had long been nurtured in the belief that unity between churches would be automatic as members of those churches returned to the practice of the simple gospel. Human opinions, they were told, had caused the deep divisions in the life of the church. Once individuals and Christians stopped the practice of making human opinion the basis of church membership, the separation between various Christians and churches could be resolved. Simple and reasonable preaching about how God acted in Christ to save human beings, backed by the testimony of the Bible, would lead lost people to make rational decisions to become Christians. It would also lead churches to reclaim the purity of biblical faith. True church unity would automatically follow, and, in the case of the "Christians" and the "Disciples," it actually did.

Yet, as the previous chapter has shown, this commitment to a church unity that rested upon restorationism soon faced troubled days. Occasionally, it led the emerging Disciples movement, after 1832, to a form of self-righteousness that tended to isolate it from the work of Christian unity. From 1832 until the turn of the century, Disciples did not take any significant strides in this area. More serious work on behalf of church unity would have to wait until Disciples came to a new and different understanding of the nature of Christian unity. Where early Disciples defined it in terms of imitating early church patterns, later Disciples defined it in terms that recognized the developing and growing witness of a diverse church in the modern world. This change in perspective began to take place near the end of the nineteenth century and the beginning of the twentieth century.

## A Change in Theological Perspective

By about the time the nineteenth century gave way to the twentieth century, a few Disciples leaders had come to share many of the theological assumptions defined in the last chapter, those occasioned by higher criticism and the arrival of Darwinian theory. These changes in theological perspective definitely aided in the formation of a transformed understanding of Christian unity among Disciples. In the midst of these changes, however, at least one major aspect of the Disciples understanding remained the same. Early-twentieth-century Disciples still regarded Christian unity as having its basis in an individual's relationship to Christ. Therefore, Disciples continued to understand unity as the gift of God. Christian union is an essential attribute of the body of Christ. It simply *is*; it is not something that human beings create.

These more modern Disciples also felt the same way their earlier ancestors had felt about denominationalism, with one exception. Similar to those who had preceded them in time, Disciples around 1900 still viewed denominationalism as a "sin." Yet, more of the Disciples leadership, especially those in seminaries or Divinity schools, were reaching the understanding that Disciples themselves participated in this "sin." They began to assert that, no matter how much Disciples may have denied it or may continue to deny it, Disciples of Christ must also see themselves as a denomination.

This recognition brought with it the more important affirmation that, therefore, Disciples should fall under the same judgment so willingly laid upon all other denominations. No longer could Disciples view themselves and their theology as being free of human opinions. Instead, they gradually accepted the fact that even their own movement had not ever been free of the influences of historical and cultural development. These leaders began to assert that "Each denomination, including the Disciples of Christ, was a partial and relative expression of a faith which would be fully known only in unity."[13] Hence, modern Disciples discovered, in coming to terms with the shortcomings of their own identity, yet another justification for seeking the unity of the church.

There was, however, a point at which these later Disciples departed rather seriously from earlier understandings of Christian unity. Alexander Campbell, Barton Stone, and other early Disciples had viewed unity as something the church had to return to or "restore." Restorationism claimed that the early church had been united. This unity was lost due to the increasing divisive influence of human opinions. The key to restoring that unity, early Disciples leaders believed, involved a return to the simple gospel, stripped of human opinion. As we have seen, however, later Disciples abandoned this commitment to restorationism. Instead, as a result of a slow migration to a new theological context, they arrived at a greater appreciation of historical development and its effect upon Christianity.

With a new appreciation for the diversity of the gospel message in different times and circumstances, these later Disciples expressed a more open appraisal of the work of other denominations. Their increasing awareness of human inability to capture the divine message in its entirety led them to the recognition that Disciples of Christ were not all that different from other Protestant denominations struggling to find the most appropriate forms of Christian expression and witness. They became more humble about their own understandings and a good bit more tolerant of the expressions of others. This insight enabled later Disciples to work more creatively toward the Christian unity sought by their ancestors.

### An Ecumenical Church in the Twentieth Century

In Disciples church life the word ecumenical surfaces with frequent regularity. However, I have found that many people in Disciples congregations are still not quite certain about what the word itself means. The word is derived from the Greek word *oikoumene*, which means "the inhabited earth." In its current usage, the word defines the modern Christian effort to establish meaningful unity in both proclamation and mission between all the Christian communities of "the inhabited earth." The modern ecumenical movement emerged as a by-product of Protestantism's changing sense of itself at the end of the nineteenth century. Its first major international manifestation occurred in 1910 with the convening of the Edinburgh World Missionary Conference. Two years earlier, however, the ecumenical spirit blossomed among American churches with the formation of the Federal Council of the Churches of Christ in America (FCC).

Disciples of Christ were charter members of this new American ecumenical organization. In becoming members, Disciples were also making a statement to themselves and to others concerning their movement's status as a denomination. In order to be a member of a "federation" of churches, a group first needed to recognize itself as a "church" rather than a "movement." Disciples leaders definitely wrestled with this issue; whether members of congregations realized it at the time is another matter altogether. The question did not, however, prevent Disciples from a distinguished participation in this form of the ecumenical movement from its very beginning, continuing, of course, with our current participation in the National Council of Churches of Christ in the USA (NCC), the successor organization to the FCC. Several Disciples have fulfilled influential leadership roles in these circles, especially people like Mossie Wyker (president of United Church Women—now known as Church Women United), Edgar DeWitt Jones (president of the FCC), Roy G. Ross (general secretary of the NCC), and J. Irwin Miller (president of the NCC). Late in 1990, Joan Brown Campbell, a Disciples woman, was named the new general secretary (chief executive) of the NCC.

Disciples also had a hand in the formation of the World Council of Churches in 1948. Ever since that date, Disciples have taken their responsibility in this organization very seriously, sending full delegations to every meeting and responding in writing to most of its deliberations (both those addressing "Life and Work" and "Faith and Order"). Of course, Disciples missionary leaders, as is indicated in later chapters, also attended the many worldwide ecumenical meetings relating to the modern missionary movement. This participation has had a profound effect upon the Disciples in the twentieth century and has led their leadership to a more responsible expression of Disciples understandings of the Christian faith.

As mentioned above, 1910 is counted as the pivotal year in worldwide ecumenism. It might also be counted as the pivotal year for Disciples in their own structured participation in the quest for Christian unity. Peter Ainslie, pastor of Christian Temple in Baltimore, led Disciples of Christ in the formation of a new organization committed to ecumenical concerns. This commission became known as the Council on Christian Union and, since 1954, has been called the Council on Christian Unity. This organization, as Ainslie originally had envisioned it, has served as the Disciples lifeline to larger ecumenical developments outside the denomination's life. Its current president, Paul A. Crow, Jr., stands in a long line of distinguished Disciples leaders who have viewed furthering the unity of God's church as a major feature of their ministerial calling. Under the leadership of such dedicated and gifted servants in the cause of unity, Disciples have once again renewed their deep commitment to church unity and, since 1910, have worked hard to find a way to bring it to fuller expression.

## General Disciples Ecumenical Efforts Since 1910

For a brief period around 1918 to 1920, Disciples participated in conversations with Presbyterians and about seventeen other churches in a plan to unite churches under the new name "The United Churches of Christ in America." The discussion came to be known as the "Philadel-phia Plan." This plan really only suggested an initial federation of the churches, much like that previously accomplished in the Federal Council of Churches, but it did state that the ultimate goal included actual or-ganic union of these churches. In order to accomplish that goal, it hoped to establish progressive steps whereby denominations could begin to submit to the oversight of the central body. Before it really got off the ground, however, the plan simply died for lack of strong support. Many of the groups feared that the new organization might be viewed as com-petition to the FCC. Even the northern Presbyterians who had initially suggested the idea dropped the initiative after only two years.

Disciples of Christ possess, however, a rather long history of negotia-tions with the Baptists on the topic of church unity. This history dates all the way back to the 1815 formal admission of the Brush Run Church to membership in the Redstone Baptist Association. One should also re-member, of course, that Alexander Campbell's first religious journal was named *The Christian Baptist.* The emphasis by both groups over the years on baptism by immersion for believing adults has most certainly aided the overtures each has made to the other. Initial overtures in 1841 (by the Disciples) and 1866 and 1871 (by the Baptists) did not yield much fruit. The turn of the century brought more promising possibilities. In 1904, the Disciples and the Freewill Baptists had a very productive meeting. Yet, these Baptists also were engaged in a reuniting effort with the American Baptists which began to attract their attention. This re-union they completed in 1909. Brief efforts in 1929 with the American (formerly Northern) Baptist Convention failed when many Baptists feared that the differences between baptismal views were greater than they actually were.

More serious discussions between the two groups emerged in the 1940s. The Disciples and Baptists were able to join together in the comple-tion of several joint ventures in ministry during this period. They pub-lished a hymnal, joined one another in cooperative ministry on several college campuses, and even had a few congregations join one another in local ministries. The two groups even held their conventions in the same city in 1952, but shortly thereafter, the discussions between the groups dissolved into thin air. Though the two churches had some theological differences related to their understandings of baptism, and practical differences related to the Lord's supper and the role of creeds in the church, their conversations most likely broke up over pragmatic anxieties related to the ongoing nature of their denominational institutions.[14]

In 1946, the Disciples also participated briefly in what came to be known as the Greenwich Plan of church union. This plan originated when the Congregational Christian Church requested the FCC to sponsor a plenary session on the union of those churches that had already recognized one another's ministries and sacraments. Only eight or nine religious bodies expressed interest in the proposition. Since the FCC declined to host the meetings, these churches formed a conference to organize the interested churches. Disciples leader C. C. Morrison, the editor of *The Christian Century*, presented the initial form of the plan. Under this plan, each denomination would retain its own identity in the beginning, though each was expected to find a way to merge rather quickly into a united church. The plan was pursued for about ten or twelve years, but it never developed into a form the participants felt was ready for presentation to the church bodies each of them represented. The Greenwich plan slowly passed away. Most of the churches involved soon poured their energies into a new effort at union between several church bodies that appeared on the scene in 1960.

Before Paul Crow became president of the Council on Christian Unity in 1974, he was busy representing Disciples in this new ecumenical development. He served as the first general secretary of the Consultation on Church Union (also referred to as COCU) from 1968 to 1974. COCU has its origins in a sermon originally preached on December 4, 1960, at Grace Cathedral (Episcopal) in San Francisco by Eugene Carson Blake, the stated clerk of the United Presbyterian Church. Blake proposed that the United Presbyterian Church and the Protestant Episcopal Church jointly discuss the possibility of forming a united church ("truly catholic, truly evangelical, and truly reformed") with the Methodist Church and the United Church of Christ. Since the Disciples were already involved in union conversations with the United Church of Christ by this time, the group quickly expanded to include Disciples. Members of the Evangelical United Brethren were involved in discussions with the Methodists so they were also included. Soon the movement was joined by the African Methodist Episcopal Church, the African Methodist Episcopal Zion Church, the Christian Methodist Episcopal Churches, and the Presbyterian Church in the United States. Since COCU was founded in the early 1960s, the Methodists and the Evangelical Brethren have united, and the two Presbyterian groups have united. The International Council of Community Churches has joined the effort. These changes bring the total number of churches involved to nine.

84    *Joined in Discipleship*

As is indicated by the leadership provided by Paul Crow and other Disciples, Disciples participation in COCU has been extremely important to the denomination's participation in unity endeavors over the last three decades. During the 1980s, COCU produced a very important theological "consensus" statement. The document, entitled *The COCU Consensus: In Quest of a Church of Christ Uniting*, was completed in 1984 and then recommended to the assemblies of all the member churches for reception.[15] After over three years of careful study and deliberation by various local congregations, study that was encouraged and fostered by the Disciples Council on Christian Unity, the 1989 Disciples General Assembly, meeting in Indianapolis, affirmed the consensus as consisting of "a sufficient theological basis to proceed with the covenanting acts and the uniting process to be proposed by the COCU churches in the mid-1990s."[16]

At the 1987 General Assembly in Louisville, it became clear that some congregations were concerned about whether or not the Disciples of Christ would be giving up some areas of denominational control if they affirmed the consensus. Some congregations found language related to a COCU "Council of Oversight" particularly troubling. In 1988, COCU acted in such a way as to alleviate these types of concerns expressed by some of the member churches. The consensus, according to the COCU meeting of that year in New Orleans, was to be affirmed in the context of a new document entitled *Churches in Covenant Communion: The Church of Christ Uniting*. This newer statement explored the meaning of churches "covenanting" together. It offered a shift in approach, away from any commitment or hope to merge these denominations and toward a recognition of a new form of church unity, described as "covenant communion." Covenanting does not require any "uniformity in structure" whatsoever. In fact, "the churches may maintain, for as long as each may determine, their own structure and traditions, including present forms of worship, systems of ministerial selection, training and placement, their international, confessional and communion relationships, and their mission programs."[17] Thus assured, the 1989 General Assembly in Indianapolis received *The COCU Consensus* with "gratitude and hope."[18]

The 1995 General Assembly, meeting in Pittsburgh, experienced similar controversy surrounding business item 9519. That business item contained the formal response of the Disciples to the proposals growing out of the 1988 meeting of COCU in New Orleans. Since 1988, the nine individual member churches of COCU have been studying the proposal that they find new ways to share their common life together under the rubric of "The Church of Christ Uniting," a "new ecclesial reality." Since 1988, the proposal facing the COCU churches has not been built upon the hope of forming a new denomination. Rather the "richly varied cultures, traditions and institutional forms of the several churches will continue to be distinguishable." But through the "Church of Christ Uniting" these nine churches have been asked to recognize their unity in those things deemed "essential to the church's life, namely: faith, sacraments, ministry, and mission."[19] If these churches accept the new covenant communion, the "Church of Christ Uniting" will become the successor to the Consultation on Church Union. COCU will have new words standing for its letters.

The controversy surrounding the business item stemmed largely from the activities of Disciple Renewal (DR). A resolution (9521) submitted to the assembly by several Texas Panhandle congregations associated with DR expressed the concern that congregations choosing not to participate in the COCU proposal might be treated differently from those who do participate. The resolution was defeated because the General Assembly concluded that the *Design* already assured congregations and ministers certain freedoms that spoke to these concerns. In a document entitled "The Pittsburgh Proclamation," circulated by the group after the vote at the General Assembly, DR leaders claimed that acceptance of the "Church of Christ Uniting" proposal had caused Disciples to abandon their "plea for unity based on mutual acceptance of the essentials of the biblical faith," and accept instead such things as the role of bishops, apostolic succession, and homosexual ordination. In addition to this conservative opposition, some more liberal Disciples also feared the COCU proposal depended too much on "such tired ideas as 'apostolic succession,' the Apostles' and Nicene creeds, and inherently hierarchical and patriarchal episcopal structures."[20] These fears were usually relieved once the COCU shift toward covenant communion was more carefully explained. The fears of Renewal leadership were not so easily addressed. In response to what Disciple Renewal described as the abandonment of the Disciples tradition, the Pittsburgh Proclamation called congregations to join together in a new "fellowship of Disciple heritage churches." Disciple Renewal, by way of this proclamation, gave way to the Disciple Heritage Fellowship. This fellowship of Disciples congregations emphasizes, among other things, salvation in Christ alone and the infallibility of the Bible.

In spite of this organized opposition to 9519, the business item passed easily with a large majority of delegate support on the floor of the General Assembly. In early 1996, the Administrative Committee of the General Board, led by General Minister and President Richard Hamm, passed a business item (1471) intended as a "pastoral response" to the concerns raised by Disciple Renewal and others at the General Assembly. This Administrative Committee action reaffirmed the Disciples commitment to "freedom of individuals and congregations to be directed by their own consciences, free of coercion from others."[21] It assured congregations and pastors who might choose not to participate in the COCU covenant communion of their full acceptance within Disciples life. With their vote

86    *Joined in Discipleship*

to approve covenant communion, Disciples of Christ became the fifth church to pass the proposal out of the nine churches considering it. As of this writing, there are now eight denominations who have approved the proposal: the Christian Methodist Episcopal Church, the International Council of Community Churches, the Presbyterian Church (USA), the United Church of Christ, the United Methodist Church, the African Methodist Episcopal Church, and the African Methodist Episcopal Zion Church (these latter three denominations have approved the proposal since the Disciples General Assembly). The Presbyterian Church (USA) approval is contingent upon their ability to work out the necessary constitutional amendments related to the process. The remaining denomination, the Episcopal Church, continues to work on the proposal. COCU hopes to celebrate the inaugural liturgy marking the birth of the "Church of Christ Uniting" in the year 2001. Michael Kinnamon describes the hopes captured by "covenant communion" in the following way:

> Covenant communion is not a perfect plan—whatever that might mean! But, *if taken seriously*, it would be a way of saying that "Disciples" and "Methodist" and "Presbyterian" are fine adjectives but lousy nouns. The noun that defines us together is *Christian*. We are Christ's and Christ is not divided. In a world of individualism and fragmentation and fear of those who are different, this is a witness God calls us to make. [22]

The original *COCU Consensus* document (1984) depended in great measure upon another theological consensus document produced by the World Council of Churches. In 1982, after many decades of work, the Faith and Order Commission of that organization produced a document entitled *Baptism, Eucharist, and Ministry* (BEM).[23] This BEM document demonstrated impressive theological agreement on these three aspects of Christian life and expression. A very diverse group of approximately 120 theologians approved the document. These theologians represented Baptists, Methodists, Disciples, Presbyterians, Pentecostals, Roman Catholics, Anglicans, Eastern Orthodox, Seventh-Day Adventists, and other such groups. Though BEM noted continuing differences among Christian groups on these topics, it attempted to set forth the lines of convergence that appear possible as these churches seek some unity of expression. It is a document that has helped each of these groups to learn from the other groups, and has invited them to grow toward more mutual understanding and acceptance of one another.

The Disciples Council on Christian Unity wrote a report on the BEM document that was received by the 1985 Disciples General Assembly meeting in Des Moines, Iowa. The General Assembly voted to forward this report "to the World Council of Churches as a preliminary Response of the Christian Church (Disciples of Christ)" to the document itself.[24]

The BEM document and the COCU consensus document, which relies heavily upon it, have caused Disciples to take their own need for theological reflection in critical areas of their faith more seriously. Disciples have been pleased to find within these documents affirmation of some of the essential and classical concerns of the Disciples of Christ tradition. They have also been challenged by these statements to push themselves toward theological maturity in these and other areas of their Christian life. In recent years, Disciples, in their General Assemblies, have received theological statements submitted by the Disciples Commission on Theology (associated with the Council on Christian Unity) addressing baptism, the ministry, and the Lord's supper, prepared in response to these types of ecumenical conversations.

Perhaps the most pragmatic contribution to Disciples made by these two major ecumenical statements stems from the inspiration they have offered for the union conversations between the Christian Church (Disciples of Christ) and the United Church of Christ. One of the most often asked questions in local congregations on the topic of union conversations is "Why, among all the denominations in the world, have Disciples hooked up with the United Church of Christ?" The answer to this particular question has at least two facets to it. First, as previous paragraphs have indicated, the United Church of Christ is not the only denomination with whom Disciples have seriously discussed the possibility of organic church union. Second, there is, in the case of the United Church of Christ, a common heritage that makes serious union negotiations a natural occurrence. This latter factor deserves some attention.

**The History of an Ecumenical Partnership**

The Disciples and the United Church of Christ (UCC) share common roots that extend all the way back to the late eighteenth and early nineteenth centuries. Barton W. Stone's close connection with three particular ministers and the churches that followed their leadership set the stage nearly two hundred years ago for these more recent unity talks. One of these ministers, James O'Kelly immigrated to America from Ireland in 1778 at the age of 21. In his early years as a Methodist itinerant minister, he found that the Revolutionary War themes of the day, particularly those emphasizing equality and liberty, captivated his mind, heart, and spirit. Acting from this newfound perspective, O'Kelly launched an offensive against the authority of Bishop Francis Asbury. In 1792, at the first General Conference of the Methodist Episcopal Church, O'Kelly set forth a resolution calling for a more democratic appointment process for Methodist ministers. When the conference voted against the resolution, O'Kelly withdrew from the organized Methodist church.

Over the next six years, some eight thousand ministers and church members joined O'Kelly to form their own more democratic church. For a brief period between 1793 and 1794, the movement took "Republican Methodists" for a name. Then, in August of 1794, declaring that they had decided to take the Bible as their only authority, these Republican Methodists settled on the "Christian Church" as their new name. Another former Methodist minister, Rice Haggard, had suggested the new title to O'Kelly. Ten years later, just after Barton Stone and his friends dissolved the Springfield Presbytery, Rice Haggard joined their small group. He showed up just as the group appeared to be struggling over the issue of a name. For the second time in ten years, Haggard suggested the name "Christian." Stone, like O'Kelly before him, announced the search for a name was over.

As part of their interest in seeking a return to primitive Christianity, O'Kelly's churches sought equality between all ministers (no bishops or superintendents need apply), congregational autonomy (including the right of congregations to call their own ministers), and complete freedom for all ministers and church members to interpret the Bible for themselves. This similarity in emphases between O'Kelly and Stone led to increasing contacts between their movements. Many of Stone's earliest ministers had some previous association or continuing relationship with this earlier group of Christians.

Meanwhile, in rural New England, a couple of Baptist ministers were finding themselves increasingly discontent with Baptist ways. One of them, Abner Jones, started a new congregation in Lyndon, Vermont, in 1801. When the church hung up its name, it read simply "Christian Church." Jones was soon joined by a second Baptist minister named Elias Smith. A radical Jeffersonian, Smith hoped to rebuild congregational life according to republican principles.[25] Together, Jones and Smith began to establish a network of Christian congregations. These congregations, like those of O'Kelly, shared a strong restorationist mind-set. Sometime before 1826, the congregations working with Jones, Smith, and O'Kelly cooperated closely enough with one another to be known as the "Christian Connection." A good many of Stone's congregations and ministers were also loosely associated with the group. Campbell's congregations, on the other hand, kept their distance because Campbell opposed the way Christian Connection leaders in New England openly espoused unitarianism. Though he never made an issue of it, Stone himself preferred unitarianism to trinitarianism. When the Stone/Campbell merger began to spread after 1832, the Christian Connection, still claiming the allegiance of at least some of Stone's churches, went off on its own.

The Christian Connection, otherwise known as the General Convention of the Christian Church, eventually established headquarters in Dayton, Ohio. In 1890, and again in 1923, unity talks were held briefly between the Christian Connection and the National Council of Congregational Churches. By 1931, these churches united with one another and formed the General Council of Congregational and Christian Churches. Within a few years of their union, the Congregational and Christian Churches began conversations with another recently united denomination, the Evangelical and Reformed Church. A little more than twenty years later, in 1957, these churches successfully merged to form the United Church of Christ (UCC).

As this brief history indicates, Disciples and UCC congregations, given their common history, are hardly strangers to one another. For some congregations associated with the UCC, union with Disciples would constitute a kind of homecoming. Besides sharing the space, and occasionally even the buildings, of the American frontier, these two movements, through time, have also shared similar aims and purposes. Both groups have sought to further the cause of Christian unity. Each denomination's leadership has grown to theological maturity under the tutelage of the ecumenical conversations fostered by the Consultation on Church Union (COCU). Even in practical matters, the churches resemble one another. Each group's polity protects the right of local congregations to select ministers and own property. Both groups ordain women and believe the theological foundations of ministry dictate support and advocacy for women in ministry. Over the years, many pastors from each tradition have held dual standing in both denominations, and members of the two churches have moved freely from one to the other.

Obviously, there are some differences between the two churches, most notably in the area of the sacraments. Yet, these differences have not kept the two groups from seeking to become one. Conversations between them go all the way back to at least 1912. Serious conversations began shortly after the 1957 formation of the United Church of Christ. Between 1961 and 1966, several meetings were held. When COCU began its own strong deliberations, the Disciples and the UCC decided to suspend their own talks and devote their energies to the wider ecumenical conversation. When it became clear that COCU talks would take considerable time, the two denominations began their own conversations again. In 1977, both the General Synod of the UCC and the General Assembly of the Disciples authorized a two-year study examining the question of total organic union between them.

This two-year study yielded the proposal that the two churches needed to covenant with one another to work for six more years, between 1979 and 1985. A Steering Committee was elected to guide the process. Membership was composed of ten representatives from each church. The two church presidents, Dr. Avery D. Post and Dr. Kenneth L. Teegarden, served as co-chairs of the committee. During the next six years, hundreds of churches from both traditions participated in study of the possibilities of accomplishing organic union. Though the Steering Committee found pockets of meaningful support for unity when it compiled the results of the study, it also found a considerable degree of opposition and a great deal of apathy about the prospect of real union. Congregations and individuals feared a general loss of denominational identity, stated that the technical requirements of union might detract from mission purposes, and displayed a general distrust of national leadership.

The Steering Committee began to back off the prospect of organic unity, a merging of the two churches at every level, and began to talk more in terms of a pragmatic unity of "witness, service, fellowship, worship, and proclamation of our common faith." With this shift as the backdrop, the committee recommended that the churches enter into an "ecumenical partnership." The partnership recommended to both churches in 1985 had three primary marks: "(1) commitment to respond together to the mission God has entrusted to the church; (2) theological work to equip our churches as they grow toward full communion; and (3) common worship with frequent and intentional sharing in the Lord's Supper/Holy Communion."[26] As part of the second of these primary marks, the Steering Committee asked that an Ecumenical Partnership Committee be asked to develop recommendations by 1989 that would lead to "full communion" (not to be understood as "full unity") between the two churches. The 1985 general meetings of both churches received and affirmed the recommendations of the Steering Committee. Four years later, the General Assembly of the Disciples and the General Synod of the United Church of Christ both passed a resolution declaring that "a relationship of full communion now exists between our churches." This relationship rests on five pillars of acceptance and cooperation. Each of these is rooted in scripture and based upon the theological understandings reached and explored by both the "COCU Consensus" and the BEM document.

### Five Pillars of Full Communion

These five points are set forth by a 1989 resolution affirmed by the General Synod of the United Churches of Christ and the General Assembly of the Christian Church (Disciples of Christ). For both groups, "full communion" does not constitute satisfaction with the status quo, but rather looks forward to "a dynamic and growing relationship." Though theological rationale is not always clearly provided within the resolution itself, it is assumed in most cases. I have taken the liberty to address that rationale in my own way in the brief description that follows. A closer look at each of these five pillars affords us the opportunity of exploring some of the major theological assumptions supporting ecumenical progress in today's Christian church.[27]

(1) *"Common Confession of Christ."* This pillar is built upon the common theological presupposition shared by both churches, as set forth in their resolution, that "God...was in Christ reconciling the world to God's

self, the One in whom 'we live and move and have our being'" (2 Cor. 5:19; Acts 17:28). Standing behind this common confession is the whole notion of *covenant*. In one of the early study documents produced by the Steering Committee, leaders in the two churches affirmed that the Bible uses the word *covenant* to describe a "dynamic reality: God's binding embrace, God's gracious initiative in laying claim to human life." Members of the committee recognized that God always takes "the initiative in the formation of covenantal relationships." They also recognized that the meaning of the covenant cannot be reduced "to one understanding or dimension."

Two different traditions of covenant exist in the Old Testament.[28] On the one hand, God's covenant with Israel, sealed on Mount Sinai with Moses, is seen to be conditional, depending upon whether Israel obeys the challenge God has laid down for the people of God (Ex. 24). Will Israel obey God's laws or not? (Ex. 19:5; 1 Kings 6:12; 9:1–9). In this understanding of covenant, the covenant itself requires those who are a part of it to be concerned with justice and to walk humbly with God (Micah 6:8).

On the other hand, the Old Testament also describes a covenant like the one made with Noah, Abraham, or David (Gen. 9:9–17; Gen. 17; 2 Sam. 17:14–15). In this covenantal relationship, God promised to fulfill God's promises regardless of human obedience. For these three biblical characters, God's grace came in the form of an unconditional and unmerited gift. Out of the depths of their hearts, each of them came to understand that such grace could only be fulfilled as each of them truly learned the meaning of stewardship. All that they had and were came from God. This recognition led them to be responsible stewards of themselves, the resources they found at their disposal, and the whole of the created order.

These two notions of covenant have long stood in tension with one another. The tension has continued even in the Christian community as it came to see itself as standing under the "new covenant" relationship with God as the "new Israel" (Lk. 22:20; Heb. 7–10; Gal. 6:14–16). Both sides of this tension, however, point to the fact that the covenant rests in God's grace. Without God's gracious activity, there would be no covenant and, therefore, no human response. For Christians, the offer of God's grace calls those who receive that grace to the fulfillment of responsibilities, not because they are threatened, or because they hope to gain God's favor, but because God's grace has enabled a faithful human response born of love and gratitude. God's divine initiative empowers Christians to be "response-able," and thus gives them the ability to address the demands of God pertaining to the establishment of justice and the embodying of mercy in a broken and divided world. In this way, the concept of covenant speaks as much to human relationships as it does to the divine-human relationship. It is through this covenantal relationship with God that Christians who confess Christ know themselves to be in covenant with each other working on the behalf of all the peoples of the world, the entire family of God. In this, their common confession of Christ, the members of the Disciples and the UCC churches announced that their status of "full communion" rests securely on a foundation established by God's redemptive activity in Christ. To this point in their history as ecumenical partners, their greatest opportunity to join one another in common confession of Christ came through their common worship experiences in the summer of 1993 when the General Assembly of the Disciples met in a "common gathering" with the General Synod of the United Church of Christ under the theme "Partners for the Glory of God." This common meeting between the General Assembly and the General Synod, held in St. Louis, was considered successful by both churches and a repeat of the event is planned for the year 2001.

(2) *"Mutual Recognition of Members."* This second pillar affirmed what might be referred to as the concept of "mutuality." At the time of their beginning, Disciples directed their message to other denominations. They treated other Christians as aliens until those persons came to the full truth as defined by Disciples. In the intervening years, Disciples have recognized their own limitations and have learned not to take themselves so seriously that they are unable to see the fullness of God's faithful community. Ecumenical conversation has taught them that they have much to learn from the expressions of faith found in other Christian communities.

In this second affirmation of full communion, both the Disciples and the UCC churches recognized that "the baptism administered by the partner church is a valid sacramental act." In this way, both churches asserted that "Baptism involves the gift of God's grace and the response of faith. Through baptism, all Christians are united by the Holy Spirit in the one universal church." Based upon this theological affirmation, the Disciples and UCC churches agreed to the "transfer of membership" between their local congregations "by letter." Neither church, by virtue of this theological principle, gave up its own normative approach to the practice of baptism. Instead, as stated by the 1989 document, their commitment to one another in this way merely represented "an affirmation that differences of practice need no longer divide the churches." As the BEM document stated it, the images of baptism as practiced by various churches are "many but the reality is one."[29]

This action between these two limited representatives of God's church points to the wider affirmation that God wills all Christians to live as one together, regardless of their differences. Paul, when confronted with bickering between Christians, warned that the house of Christ cannot be divided (1 Cor. 1:12–13). The message the Disciples and the UCC churches have attempted to send to one another and to other Christians is one of full acceptance in spite of some profound differences existing between them. In this effort, they have worked to "Welcome one another...for the glory of God" (Rom. 15:7). In welcoming one another, the early Christian community could come to affirm the fact that diversity is a gift of God, given for the "common good" of the community (I Cor. 12:4–11). Mutuality is a current expression of this biblical insight.

(3) *"Common Celebration of the Lord's Supper/Holy Communion."* Since these churches confess Christ in common, and since they recognize one another's baptism and accept one another's members in each other's congregations, it naturally follows that they should share in the Lord's table together. This section of the 1989 resolution asserted that the Lord's supper constitutes "the most powerful sign of Christian unity (I Cor. 10:17)." It followed this affirmation with the theological rationale that supports it: "Through the life, death, and resurrection of Jesus Christ, God has reconciled us to God's self, and offered us a new relationship of love and unity with one another. Celebrating the sacrament together, we are responding as one family with thanksgiving to what Christ has done for us, praying as one people that the Holy Spirit will lead us into deeper truth and unity, and remembering as one pilgrim people the promises of hope and salvation." With this statement, the general bodies of the two denominations requested that "congregations...geographically near each other...find ways to share the sacred meal together at least once or twice a year, and to consider more frequent eucharistic services."

(4) *"Mutual Recognition and Reconciliation of Ordained Ministries."* In this section of their resolution, Disciples and UCC churches affirmed one another's "ordained ministries" as belonging to the "one ministry of Jesus Christ." Of course, the ministry of Jesus Christ is not limited merely to the ordained clergy. It includes all those who claim the name of Christ's followers. Christ lived as one who served the people of God, and as one who proclaimed God's reign among them. In the same way, Christ sends all Christians into this form of ministry in the world. Yet, there is a more specialized way to talk about ministry. The ordained ministry of the church, the work of women and men who dedicate themselves to become ministers of Word and sacraments, has a long history. The ordained ministry does what it can to facilitate and enable the wider ministry into which all Christians are called.

In ecumenical conversations between groups like the Disciples and UCC churches, current ordained ministries are seen as an extension of the ministry performed by Christ in his life, death, and resurrection. Christ performed a ministry that represented God to all humanity. Empowered by the presence of the Holy Spirit, the ordained ministry of today's church continues the ministry of Jesus Christ. If it is to be true either to its heritage in Christ or to its calling by the Holy Spirit, the ordained ministry in any time and every location must serve on behalf of the church universal, not simply act in the name of a particular denomi- nation. In the context of their full communion, Disciples and UCC churches state their mutual recognition of each church's ministries as belonging to the ministry of Jesus Christ. Ministers in one church will be recognized as ministers in the other church. Each may serve, when invited, as minister to the other. Though ministerial credentials are immediately recognized, each minister will need to go through the standard processes established by each denomination to gain official "standing" within the denomina- tion. If a minister in either church is called to serve as a congregational minister in the other denomination, the minister will need eventually to demonstrate some familiarity with the history and identity of the de- nomination before complete ministerial standing within the denomina- tion will be granted. Changes to the Disciples "Policies and Criteria for the Order of Ministry" were made by the General Assembly in 1995 as a part of declaring as complete the reconciliation of ministries between the two churches. These changes define the meaning of, and indicate the processes associated with, such terms as "ordained ministerial partner" (all ordained ministers in either church) and "ordained ministerial part- ner standing" (those individuals ordained within one church who have completed the process of approval for individual ministerial standing in the other church).[30]

(5) *"Common Commitment to Mission."* This fifth pillar of full com- munion between these two churches recognized that "unity and mission are inseparable." As John 17:21 states it, unity is essential to success in mission: "that they may all be one…so that the world may believe that you have sent me." The modern ecumenical movement has affirmed with Emil Brunner that "the church exists by mission, just as a fire exists by burning."[31]Therefore, mission is not an option for the church; rather it, like unity, is part of the church's very essence. When the church is not engaged in mission, it ceases to exist as church. As the church is one, so must also the mission of the church be one. As these two denominations entered into full communion, they recognized the diversity of this one mission of the church.

> The mission of the church takes many forms. The church engages in mission through worship, through proclamation of the gospel, and through action. In worship, the church recalls and celebrates the mighty acts of God in creation, redemption, and providence. Thus graciously renewed in faith, hope, and love, its people are sent out in the power of the Holy Spirit to be ambassadors, witnesses, and servants of Christ in the world. In proclamation, the church tells the story by which its own life is defined. As it confesses unam- biguously the Christ in whom it lives, the church invites all who will

to enter its fellowship of life in Christ. In action, the church embodies God's justice, peace, and love. As the church reaches out to others, both individually and systemically, it manifests God's reconciling purpose and saving reign in all the earth.[32]

Based upon this definition, the Disciples and UCC churches made a "deliberate commitment to engage in mission together, wherever and whenever possible." This 1989 commitment bore fruit nearly six years later as the two churches committed to one another to work as one church in the conduct of all their mission work. In 1995, meeting in General Assembly at Pittsburgh, Disciples affirmed the Common Global Ministries Board of the Christian Church (Disciples of Christ) and the United Church of Christ. The United Church of Christ General Synod meeting in 1995 also approved the joint board. The mission enterprise of both denominations is now guided by this common board, and all work in overseas ministry is now an integral part of the ecumenical partnership. [33]

## Conclusion

Unity is far from a simple topic to consider. Throughout their history, Disciples have been deeply committed to it, but only marginally successful in achieving any approximation of it in their own life and work. Disciples, in the early nineteenth century, stood on the cutting edge of ecumenical understanding. By the twentieth century, ecumenical theological development had passed them by. The union between Stone's Christians and Campbell's Disciples in 1832 stands as the lone absolute success story in the tradition's history. Some of its success may no doubt be attributed to the fact that it occurred in a day before institutional structures and congregational apathy could stand in the way of uniting. Where structures have evolved in modern denominational life, among congregations that seem no longer to care about unity as a goal, they have made it enormously difficult for two different groups to approach the question of actual organizational unity.

There are, of course, different types of unity. Some Christians emphasize the spiritual unity of the church without acknowledging any need to bring that spiritual reality into physical representation. There is, they claim, an absolute distinction to be made between the "invisible church" (the spiritual reality) and the "visible church" (the earthly reality). For these Christians, the visible church is not, and never can be, the physical incarnation of the invisible church. What is important for them is the spiritual reality. Some Disciples, over the years, have remained satisfied with spiritual unity without desiring to press on to other more tangible forms of union.

Others, while recognizing the impossibility of making the invisible and visible church synonymous, emphasized the need for practical unity.

This enabled Christians to work together in the cause of mission without untidy preoccupations with doctrinal differences or structural incompatibilities. As Disciples became increasingly involved in world mission, they discovered that practical unity could aid them in taking the message of Christ to a lost world. Through comity agreements with other denominations, they divided the territory and trusted other denominations to aid them in the task of global evangelization. Practical unity, sometimes without any strong theological base, has been a part of Disciples existence throughout most of this century.

Still other Christians emphasize that organic unity is the only kind of unity that really matters. Organic unity is concerned with visible structural manifestation of the oneness that constitutes the church. These Christians refuse to make a distinction between the invisible church and the visible church. All Christians are called to be members of God's one church. There is only one church, and that church should be fully and completely united. Denominations represent the fragmentation of that one church. As long as the church is divided, and as long as denominations take their own status too seriously, the church is less than it can and should be. It is sacrificing some of itself. As comfortable as denominational identity is, those who rest within it must understand that the very essence of the church is perverted when denominations continue to live at ease with the human divisions their members have created. The Disciples and UCC churches, though they have been unable to accomplish complete organic unity with one another, have at least demonstrated their dissatisfaction with the status quo. They have forged a relationship of full communion with one another that will encourage future dialogue and stimulate steps toward more mature expressions of their commitment to a unified church.

The modern ecumenical movement pursues expressions of more visible unity between different Christian traditions. Currently, as illustrated by the "Church of Christ Uniting" proposal, the ecumenical movement has moved away from seeking structural mergers and has begun to emphasize the need for establishing a covenantal relationship between churches. This earnest and continuing quest for more visible representations of unity does not translate into the attempt to find some lowest common denominator type of theology that all church traditions can affirm. Rather, as maturity in ecumenical life has developed, it has been defined by more acceptance of the fullness and diversity of theology. Perhaps Disciples have made their greatest contribution to modern ecumenical understandings at precisely this point.

Throughout this last century, Disciples have insisted that nothing human beings have constructed (theology, structures, creeds, etc.) should keep the church from realizing a more fundamental and visible unity. Differences of opinion must not be interpreted as ultimate obstacles to true Christian unity. The early Disciples aversion to creeds as a test of fellowship has often expressed itself as a defense of freedom in matters of biblical interpretation and theological expression. Disciples, as modern ecumenists, have argued that diversity is one of the great gifts God has given the church. They have been both willing and able to grow in their own theological insights through their encounter with the theological reflections of others. As they have done so, they have also encouraged the same growth in others.

## Questions for Reflection and Discussion

1. What differences existed between the movements of Stone and Campbell?

2. What does it mean to say that unity must be experienced as the gift of God, that it is an essential characteristic of God's church? How can the church understand the various types of understandings of the unity of the church (spiritual, pragmatic, organic) in light of this theological affirmation?

3. The role of the congregations was essential in bringing about the unity between Disciples and Christians in 1832. How might congregations become more active in ecumenical endeavors today? How does your congregation live out the vision of the Disciples commitment to church unity?

4. How did theological changes and the dawn of the twentieth century affect Disciples in their approach to the topic of church unity?

5. Which of the five pillars of full communion between Disciples and the UCC, and the theological points accompanying them, are most helpful for you in underscoring the importance of working toward church unity (and why is this the case)? How has a study of past ecumenical efforts (either the history since 1910, or the history of an ecumenical partnership) among Disciples helped you in your understanding of Disciples' work in this area today?

## Notes

[1]See item 8915, "Resolution on Ecumenical Partnership," *Business Docket and Program: General Assembly of the Christian Church (Disciples of Christ) in Indianapolis, Indiana, July 28-August 2, 1989*, pp. 308-310. Also printed in *Year Book & Directory of the Christian Church (Disciples of Christ)*, 1990, pp. 259-261.

[2]Kenneth L. Teegarden, *We Call Ourselves Disciples* (St. Louis: The Bethany Press, 1959), p. 36.

[3]C. J. Dull made this very interesting point in an e-mail message to me dated 14 April 1996. It is likely the context of political union helped feed the Disciples emphasis on union within the church.

[4]"The Last Will and Testament of the Springfield Presbytery," quoted in McAllister and Tucker, *Journey in Faith*, p. 78.

98    *Joined in Discipleship*

⁵Campbell, *Declaration and Address*, p. 47, p. 24.
⁶*Christian Messenger*, (July 1827): 204.
⁷An excellent history of this 1832 union is found in Paul A. Crow, "The Anatomy of a Nineteenth-Century United Church: The Mingling of the Christians and the Disciples," The 1982 Russell Disciples Heritage Lecture at Brite Divinity School, *Impact* 9 (Fall 1982): 19-37; also Crow, "The Anatomy of a 19th Century United Church," Sesquicentennial Lectures, Lexington Theological Seminary, *Lexington Theological Quarterly* 18 (October 1983): 1-53; see also William J. Richardson, "Lexington in 1832: Unity 'in Each Place,'" *Lexington Theological Quarterly* 17 (April 1982): 71-76; and Henry E. Webb, "The Union of Christians and Disciples: Lexington, Ky., January 1, 1832," *Lexington Theological Quarterly* 17 (July 1982): 31-36.
⁸*Christian Messenger* (August 1831): 180.
⁹*The Millennial Harbinger* (October 1830): 474.
¹⁰Teegarden, *We Call Ourselves Disciples*, p. 49.
¹¹John Augustus Williams, *Life of Elder John Smith* (Cincinnati: R.W. Carroll and Co., 1870), pp. 452-455.
¹²*Christian Messenger* (September 1832): 266.
¹³The ideas discussed in this paragraph and the one before it are dependent on the insights of W. Clark Gilpin in his article, "Issues Relevant to Union in the History of the Christian Church (Disciples of Christ)," *Encounter* 41 (Winter 1980): 15-23.
¹⁴See Paul A. Crow, "The Christian Church (Disciples of Christ) in the Ecumenical Movement," in George G. Beazley, ed., *The Christian Church (Disciples of Christ): An Interpretive Examination in the Cultural Context* (St. Louis: The Bethany Press, 1973), pp. 276-278. Crow points out that the most "thorough analysis of these conversations" is found in Franklin E. Rector, "Baptist-Disciple Conversations Toward Unity," in Nils Ehrenstrom and Walter G. Muelder, ed., *Institutionalism and Church Unity* (New York: Association Press, 1963), pp. 253-274. Much in these pages is dependent upon Crow's excellent discussion of ecumenical activities in his article. One should also see Michael K. Kinnamon, "A Special Calling: Christian Unity and the Disciples of Christ," in Larry Bouchard and L. Dale Richeson, ed., *Interpreting Disciples: Practical Theology in the Disciples of Christ* (Fort Worth: Texas Christian University Press, 1987), pp. 248-273.
¹⁵See Gerald F. Moede, ed., *The COCU Consensus: In Quest of a Church of Christ Uniting* (Consultation on Church Union, 1985).
¹⁶See Resolution 8927, "Resolution on the COCU Consensus: In Quest of the Church of Christ Uniting," in *Business Docket and Program: General Assembly of the Christian Church (Disciples of Christ) in Indianapolis, Indiana, July 28-August 2, 1989*, pp. 343-344.
¹⁷See *Churches in Covenant Communion: The Church of Christ Uniting* (Consultation on Church Union, 1989), p. 9.
¹⁸Resolution 8927, "Resolution on the COCU Consensus: In Quest of the Church of Christ Uniting," p. 344.
¹⁹See *Churches in Covenant Communion*, pp. 1-2; see also business item "No. 9519: Formal Action of the Christian Church (Disciples of Christ) In Response to *Churches in Covenant Communion: The Church of Christ Uniting*," in *Business Docket and Program, "Becoming A Dwelling Place For God": General Assembly of the Christian Church (Disciples of Christ) in Pittsburgh*, Oct. 20-24, 1995, pp. 307-313.
²⁰Quoted in Michael Kinnamon, "What's all the Fuss about COCU? *The Disciple* (March 1996): 24. The "Pittsburgh Proclamation," as far as I know, has not been published. Copies of it can be ordered from the Disciple Heritage Fellowship. Resolution 9521, entitled "Policy Statement Regarding Disciples Pastors in Congregations Who Choose Not To Participate in the COCU Covenanting Process," is found in *Business Docket and Program, "Becoming A Dwelling Place For God": General Assem-*

*bly of the Christian Church (Disciples of Christ) in Pittsburgh,* Oct. 20-24, 1995, pp. 315-316.

[21]This is quoted from Business Item 1471 of the Administrative Committee of the General Board. My copy of it was attached to a letter widely distributed by Richard L. Hamm on 1 February 1996 to inform Disciples of this action. The published minutes of the Administrative Committee contain a record of this resolution. The Administrative Committee met January 28-30, 1996, and acted on this resolution on January 30, 1996.

[22]Michael Kinnamon, "What's all the Fuss about COCU?" p. 24.

[23]See *Baptism, Eucharist, and Ministry: Faith and Order Paper, No. 111* (Geneva: World Council of Churches, 1982). See also William H. Lazareth, et al., *Growing Together in Baptism, Eucharist, and Ministry: A Study Guide* (Geneva: World Council of Churches, 1982).

[24]See 8537, "Report on Baptism, Eucharist, and Ministry," in *Business Docket and Program: General Assembly of the Christian Church (Disciples of Christ) in Des Moines, August 2-7, 1985,* pp. 280-285.

[25] Hatch and others have pointed out that Smith began, in 1808, the first religious newspaper in America. Its title indicated the context of radical cultural freedom: *The Herald of Gospel Liberty.* See Hatch, *Democratization of American Christianity,* p. 70.

[26]See "Report and Recommendation of the Steering Committee on the Covenant Between the United Church of Christ and the Christian Church (Disciples of Christ)," item no. 8513 in the *Business Docket and Program,* 1985, pp. 237-246.

[27]Quotations below, unless otherwise indicated, come from Resolution 8915, "Resolution on Ecumenical Partnership," in *Business Docket and Program: General Assembly of the Christian Church (Disciples of Christ) in Indianapolis, Indiana, July 28-August 2, 1989,* pp. 308-310; also printed in *Year Book & Directory of the Christian Church (Disciples of Christ),* 1990, pp. 259-261.

[28]These two notions of covenant are discussed in the "Study Series on *The Covenant* between the Christian Church (Disciples of Christ) and the United Church of Christ." See especially the first section of the study series entitled "Living in Covenant." The Christian Board of Publication published the study series pamphlets in June of 1981.

[29]*Baptism, Eucharist, & Ministry,* p. 8.

[30]See Resolution 9518, "Changes And Or Additions to the 'Policies and Criteria For the Order Of Ministry of the Christian Church (Disciples of Christ)' Which Will Facilitate the Implementation of the Mutual Recognition and Reconciliation of Ordained Ministers in the Ecumenical Partnership Between The Christian Church (Disciples of Christ) and the United Church of Christ," in *Business Docket and Program, "Becoming A Dwelling Place For God": General Assembly of the Christian Church (Disciples of Christ) in Pittsburgh,* Oct. 20-24, 1995, pp. 305-307.

[31]Brunner, *The Word and the Church* (London: SCM Press, 1931), p. 108.

[32]This quotation is from resolution 8915, "Resolution on Ecumenical Partnership," in *Business Docket and Program: General Assembly of the Christian Church (Disciples of Christ) in Indianapolis, Indiana, July 28-August 2, 1989,* p. 310. Quotations in this section not otherwise attributed are also from this source.

[33]See Resolution 9529, "Resolution on Affirmation of the Common Global Ministries Board and of Overseas Partner Churches by the Christian Church (Disciples of Christ) in the United States and Canada and the United Church of Christ, USA," in *Business Docket and Program, "Becoming A Dwelling Place For God": General Assembly of the Christian Church (Disciples of Christ) in Pittsburgh,* Oct. 20-24, 1995, p. 327.

# 5

# THE ESCHATOLOGICAL PRINCIPLE
## GOD WITH US

---

*This work shall be devoted to the destruction of sectarianism, infidelity, and antichristian doctrine and practice. It shall have for its object the development and introduction of that political and religious order of society called THE MILLENNIUM, which will be the consummation of that ultimate amelioration of society proposed in the Christian scriptures.*

Alexander Campbell
"Prospectus" for *The Millennial Harbinger*[1]

---

## Introduction

Alexander Campbell inaugurated the pages of his new journal, *The Millennial Harbinger*, with the words that head this chapter; his translation of Revelation 14:6–7 accompanied them: "I saw another messenger flying through the midst of heaven, having everlasting good news to proclaim to the inhabitants of the earth, even to every nation, and tribe, and tongue, and people—saying with a loud voice, Fear God and give glory to him, for the hour of his judgments is come: and worship him who made heaven, and earth, and sea, and the fountains of water." These verses from the Bible graced many of the title pages of the journal through the next thirty-five years. As the title to his journal itself indicates, these words had special significance for Campbell. In short, Campbell, and early Disciples with him, possessed an eschatological hope. And that hope exercised a formative influence on their Christian identity.

What is the "eschatological principle"? As the church has used the word "eschatological," it has traditionally meant the "doctrine of last

101

things." Campbell wrote at length about "last things," including such themes as prophecy, the millennium, and the "everlasting kingdom of God." But a better overarching definition for this eschatological principle as it operated for Campbell might more truly be "God with us," for this is how Campbell understood the Christian hope he described. His vision of the last things was proleptic (the kingdom of God is both "already and not yet"—the church lives in the present "as if" the kingdom has come in all its fullness, even though the fullness of the kingdom is beyond time). It arose from an understanding of God's activity in history. The early Disciples' interest in eschatology helped to provide the movement with both its "evangelistic zeal and its grounding in Christian hope."[2] The unfolding of "last things" was merely the result (and goal) of what God had been doing in history since creation. To speak of "last things" one also has to tell the story of "first things." Campbell approached eschatology from this perspective

The eschatological principle among early Disciples is certainly deserving of consideration as one of the most important marks of their early identity, equally significant to, if not in some ways more formative than their commitment to biblical interpretation, restorationism, and church unity. Eschatology forms and affects the movement's early theology, in its first generation, perhaps more profoundly than its commitment to any of the other three "founding principles." This principle emphasized the saving work of Christ, and, as a result, nourished the Disciples' decidedly christocentric character. Its focus was on the past, present, and future of God's salvation in Jesus Christ. Disciples' commitment to it shaped their understanding of what it meant to be Christian and to believe in a God who intervened in history on their behalf. Before defining in detail the various elements of Campbell's postmillennialist eschatological perspective, we should take a brief look at the millennial influences operating on his social context.

## Contextual Considerations

### Millennialism in its Varied Forms

In nineteenth-century America, millennialism came in many flavors. Unlike today, most Christians had a deep and abiding interest in millennialism. They often discussed their likes and dislikes, especially when someone showed up with a flavor they did not like. The major arguments stemmed from just how to interpret the book of Revelation, especially what to do with Revelation 20:4–6:

> Then I saw thrones, and those seated on them were given authority to judge. I also saw the souls of those who had been beheaded for their testimony to Jesus and for the word of God. They had not worshiped the beast or its image and had not received its mark on

their foreheads or their hands. They came to life and reigned with Christ a thousand years. (The rest of the dead did not come to life until the thousand years were ended.) This is the first resurrection. Blessed and holy are those who share in the first resurrection. Over these the second death has no power, but they will be priests of God and of Christ, and they will reign with him a thousand years.

The church described this "thousand year" reign as the millennium (from the Latin *mille*, meaning thousand, and *annus*, meaning year). The problem various interpreters had, however, was reaching agreement about its nature, its location, the time it was to take place, and the relation of Christ's return to it. Would Christ reign literally or spiritually? Would the millennium be in heaven or on earth? Would Christ return before or after the millennium? Did Christ's resurrection inaugurate the millennium or is it yet to come? Is the first resurrection actually a physical resurrection or a spiritual one that indicates the revival of the martyrs' spirit within the church itself? These questions divided the nineteenth-century church. Americans entered the fray with great enthusiasm.

The term "premillennialist" has usually been reserved for those who take the view that Christ will inaugurate the millennium with his literal second coming. Though there are different versions of premillennialism, most adherents in nineteenth-century America believed the saints would be physically resurrected and reign with Christ. Some described the millennium as a thousand years on earth, while others emphasized the millennium as just another way to talk about Christ's eternal reign. Still other premillennialists argued that the millennium would last 365,000 years, believing that every day in prophetic terms meant a year in history. But all premillennialists held in common the belief that Christ's return would precede the millennium.

Throughout history, especially during times of crisis, Christian voices have found premillennial beliefs especially attractive. During the second and third centuries, a time when Christians faced occasionally intense periods of persecution, most early interpreters of the book of Revelation believed that Christ would soon return and establish a period of millennial blessedness, though they disagreed about the particulars related to the millennium itself. Church history knows these Christians by the name of "Chiliasts" (from the Greek word *chilioi*, meaning "thousand").[3] This chiliastic perspective gave Christians in the second and third centuries hope in the midst of suffering, much like the book originally did for its initial audience. Most of today's scholars date Revelation from the 90s, during the persecution under the Roman emperor Domitian, or the early 100s, during the reign of Trajan. Others, usually more conservative in orientation, date the book from Nero's persecution during the mid-to-late 60s.

In general, premillennialists have been very pessimistic about the future. They describe the unfolding of history as if it were a downward spiral. In the view of the premillennialist, things went bad with the fall of Adam and Eve and have only gotten worse since. There will come a time when God will simply get fed up with all the evil and sin and say "that's enough." At that point, Christ will return and put an end to human foolishness. This view had many defenders in the nineteenth century. A good number of Disciples, including Barton Stone and Walter Scott, were attracted to it. A new version of premillennialism, dispensational premillennialism, appeared near the end of the nineteenth century and was popular among the Plymouth Brethren, but few Disciples were affected by it. Many twentieth-century fundamentalist and neo-evangelical Christians have been introduced to it through either the Scofield Bible or Hal Lindsey's book *The Late Great Planet Earth.*[4]

Once Christianity became the religion of the empire, Chiliasm ceased to be fashionable. In fact, the church was slow to accept the book of Revelation as scripture. By the year 400, the western church had accepted it, but the Greek Church waited nearly a century longer. The Syrian and Armenian churches were much slower to accept its canonical status. In general, "amillennialists" surfaced and carried the day in millennial interpretation. The amillennialists rejected a literal thousand years. Some spiritualized the millennium and believed themselves to be living in it. As a present reality, it began either with the birth of Christ or, perhaps, with his resurrection. Christ's reign is in heaven and represented on earth by the church. Augustine understood the millennium in this way. Others described by the name of amillennialism understood the millennium as a past event or as merely a purely symbolic allusion to the perfection or completion of God's action, either in the final events or even in the present.[5] Nineteenth-century America had few representatives of amillennialism. To my knowledge, no early Disciples defended amillennialism as the proper view.

By far the most popular view of the millennium among evangelical Christians in nineteenth-century America was the one known as "postmillennialism." The name originates from the belief that Christ would return at the end of the millennium rather than at its beginning. A few early American puritans, notably John Cotton and Jonathan Edwards, defended a postmillennialist view. Its most influential advocates arose in the eighteenth century outside America. These included Daniel Whitby (1638-1726), of Salisbury Cathedral, and Dutch scholar Campegius Vitringa (1659-1722). Alexander Campbell mentioned both men favorably in his writings. Many premillennialist Christians accused Campbell of representing the "Spiritualist school" of Whitby. Campbell defended Whitby as an orthodox Christian but claimed never to have read firsthand any of his work on the subject. Campbell's opponents were not far wrong, however. Campbell's views on the millennium were very similar to the theories espoused by Whitby.[6] Both emphasized a figurative, rather than a literal, first resurrection, and connected it with a renewed and invigorated church.

Unlike premillennialism, postmillennialism usually exhibits a profound optimism about the spread of the gospel and the success of the evangelistic mission of Christianity. Defenders of the view have asserted that the success of the church would usher in the millennium without need of any supernatural event. In their understanding, the millennium is a historical period characterized by religious peace and spiritual fulfillment. Most nineteenth-century scholarly postmillennialists emphasized that the millennium resulted from the grace of God rather than the action of human beings. But the view has always had a high regard for the potential success of human efforts on behalf of the evangelistic spread of the gospel and, in some circles, for the effects the gospel could have on the social sphere. In the American setting, popular postmillennialism often placed great emphasis on the ability of human efforts to bring in the millennium. In some corners, including among the Disciples, it became attached to America's efforts to civilize and democratize the rest of the world.

The context of the early nineteenth century in America was especially suited to millennial enthusiasm. For many of the citizens of the new nation, innocent and free, the kingdom of God seemed very near. In addition, revivalism "tended to dwell upon the ancient millennial expectation of a golden age to come, whether inaugurated by the personal return of Christ or established by the preaching of the gospel."[7] The Second Great Awakening reaped a mighty harvest of new religious movements, among them the Shakers, the Mormons, and the Millerites. The first two of these movements attracted some early Disciples and, given their early stability, kept them. The Shakers made serious inroads among Barton Stone's Christian movement, whereas the Mormons snatched the more radical among early Disciples leadership. These defections might have had a moderating effect on early Disciples millennialism.[8] The Millerites are another story. In the beginning, they were a movement existing within a number of different denominations. Their consolidation into the Seventh-Day Adventists came later. Most of the Disciples attracted by the Millerites remained with the Disciples. The Millerite movement provided a backdrop for many of the eschatological conversations among early Disciples, especially during the 1830s and 1840s.

### The Millerite Movement and Disciples

A farmer in Low Hampton, New York, named William Miller was converted in 1816, at the height of revivalistic excitement. He joined the Baptist church and immediately began to take account of the book of

Revelation. After a number of years, he began to publish his calculations concerning the return of Christ. Using prophecies in Daniel and the book of Revelation, Miller became confident that Christ would return in the early 1840s, eventually settling on sometime between March 21, 1843, and March 21, 1844. When the latter date came and went, Miller, with the help of biblical exegesis among his followers, made an adjustment to a final date of October 22, 1844.

On the morning of October 23, tired believers experienced what has often been described as the "great disappointment." Some followers became Shakers. Others made adjustments in their theologies and remained hopefully expectant of a second advent of Christ sometime in the near future. Miller found himself excommunicated by his Baptist church in New York. He died in obscurity in 1849. Ellen Gould White expressed her belief that the temple was cleansed in heaven, rather than on earth, on that date. She blamed Christianity's failure to observe the Sabbath for Christ's decision not to return and established among Miller's "disappointed" the core of what would become the Seventh-Day Adventist Church.

American religious historians hypothesize that three events enabled Miller to achieve a widespread reputation. First, his musings were published in book form in 1836. Campbell, who wrote often of Miller, could not help but chuckle about Miller's concern for "copy-right" covering his written material:

> I know it is difficult for those who believe the theory to act in a manner consistent with it. Even Mr. Miller himself...has secured the copy-right of his book for some ten years after the end of the world, as if such a right could secure it against the general conflagration![9]

Second, a serious economic depression occurred a year later, known in American history as the Panic of 1837. This crisis may have caused many Americans to find hope in an immediate appearing of Christ. Third, Joshua V. Himes, a minister in a Boston church associated with the New England Christians, discovered Miller in 1839 and began to act as his public relations manager. He set up tours, hired new evangelists to promote the message, founded and edited two journals (the *Midnight Cry* in New York and the *Signs of the Times* in Boston), and even published a hymnbook called *The Millennial Harp*. At its most successful point, there were some "50,000 convinced believers and there may have been as many as a million others who were skeptically expectant."[10] Some Disciples were found in both camps, those "convinced" and those "skeptically expectant."

Premillennial enthusiasm among some Disciples ran high well before the popularity of the Millerite predictions. Most Christians shared

~~the belief that the~~ age of the world was nearing 6000 years. Pre-millennialists attached to this the belief that the second coming was most likely near because of that fact. Regardless of how Christians viewed the relationship between the second coming and the millennium, many agreed that the millennium itself represented the Sabbath (the seventh and final thousand year period of human history). Campbell did not dispute, except in some minor details, the mathematical calculations (dates, etc.) used by the premillennialists. But he did not believe their "certainty" about them was justified. Nor did he share their "literal" understanding of the events that were to transpire. Campbell preferred "figurative" or "spiritual" interpretations.[11]

Nevertheless, as early as the August edition of the first year of the *Harbinger's* existence, Alexander Campbell provided significant space for expositions of premillennialism, even while he wrote his own series of articles on the millennium.[12] Its author, writing under the pseudonym of "Daniel," believed Campbell fair enough to give "both sides." Daniel's series of articles ran for nearly a year, argued the premillennial interpretations strongly, and questioned the "sober senses" of those who held to postmillennial understandings.[13] In addition, Campbell published a series of extracts from a popular-selling premillennialist book written by James A. Begg. Originally published in England in 1831, it went through five editions in less than a year. A brother of the book's author published it in America and sent Alexander Campbell a copy of the volume. Though he thoroughly disagreed with Begg's interpretations, Campbell published excerpts in two issues during 1832, along with content from a pamphlet generally supporting the views in a third issue that year.[14]

Samuel M. McCorkle, who called himself "layman," and served as a preacher for the movement in the area around Rockville, Indiana, provided the most comprehensive treatment of premillennialism to appear in the *Millennial Harbinger*. Calling McCorkle a "bold adventurer," Campbell introduced the series of essays with his promise to "give this brother a fair hearing...because the subject deserves more profound attention than any other, except it be the personal remission of sins." [15] McCorkle took full advantage of the opportunity. He published a series of fifteen articles, between February 1833 and May 1834, containing mostly the content of a small book he had published with a Nashville press in 1830.[16]

During the fall of 1834, Campbell began writing a series of articles on "The Millennium" over the name of "the Reformed Clergyman." Given the controversial nature of the premillennial/postmillennial debate among Disciples, Campbell evidently decided his most pointed comments about the matter would best be presented while writing with a pseudonym.[17] McCorkle and the "clergyman" sparred in the pages of the *Harbinger* from 1834-1838 as Campbell followed his millennial series with a long series of fourteen essays entitled "Prophecies." The heart of their disagreements, of course, centered on the relationship between the advent of Christ and the millennium. In 1835, McCorkle attacked at Campbell's most vulnerable spot:

> Nothing superior to the present dispensation can rise out of it. Can more be expected in the future than has been done in the past?...How visionary it is to expect the sword to be turned into a ploughshare under man's management; under the present order of things. Millennial perfection cannot rise out of the present dispensation; and if it were universally established on earth, it could not be preserved half a thousand years under human administration.[18]

The spirited exchanges between the men continued. After Campbell began his longest series of articles in 1841, this time writing under his own name, McCorkle attacked him directly about halfway through the series by exclaiming: "The idea of evangelizing the world—of getting up a Millennium by human effort, is perfectly visionary, or preposterous; and I wonder that a man of your research and discrimination to remain so long in gestation with a chimera having so little foundation in God's word...Good God! what is man?" Campbell, tiring of the "indefatigable Layman," promised to lay before the reader any "new idea" set forth by McCorkle, "provided only, it be not preceded with the interjection 'good God!'—a form of speech that comports not, in my humble opinion, with the expectation of the *immediate* return of the Messiah." Campbell also indicated casually that McCorkle had plagiarized the writings of Elias Smith (from 1808) in large chunks.[19] By 1844, McCorkle found himself much more comfortable publishing in Barton Stone's *Christian Messenger.*[20]

Campbell hated the pessimism associated with premillennialism, especially respecting its "paralysing influence" upon Christian motivation for evangelizing the world.[21]

> To be convinced of it we have only to observe the conduct of those who are now looking for the immediate personal return of the Lord before the extension of his kingdom, and compare it with that of those who expect it after the Millennium. The former have almost, and they ought to have altogether, abandoned all effort and prayer for the conversion of the Jew and the Greek....In 1843 the day of judgment commences, and conversion ceases; and why should they who believe this engage in sending the gospel to foreign lands, or in translating the scriptures into foreign languages, or in any great enterprize [*sic*] that looks beyond a period so nigh—just at the

door....The expectants of the immediate personal return are, indeed, laboring to awaken their families and friends and neighbors to a preparation for that awfully grand and glorious event....But farther than this their theory will not suffer them to go.[22]

This is a theme Campbell sounded throughout the Millerite movement's influence among Disciples. "Penitence superinduced by affliction, and repentance originating on a death-bed, have long since been of doubtful reputation," he wrote. "Panic fears and impulses are not the eloquence of Christ's gospel." Converts won in this way, he argued, would only relapse once the "disappointment" occurs.[23]

The most profound support among early Disciples for premillennialism of the Miller variety came from Walter Scott and the pages of *The Evangelist*. Some background may be relevant here, but only to provide context and not to be understood as the cause for Scott's support of William Miller. By 1840, Walter Scott and Alexander Campbell were feuding fairly openly and regularly in the pages of their journals. They had long, sometimes hot, disagreements about whether the movement ought to take the name "Christian" or "Disciple." Scott argued for the former, Campbell for the latter.[24] But the rift was more serious than this between them. Scott understood an article published in the *Harbinger* to accuse Scott and the *Evangelist* of heresy; whether Campbell intended this reading or not is impossible to judge from the context of the article. Further, Scott took exception to Campbell's judgment that the *Evangelist* rose up "to assist us in this grandest and noblest of enterprizes [sic]."[25]

It is clear from Scott's writing about Campbell during these years that he felt the editor of the *Harbinger* treated him with less respect than he deserved for his efforts on behalf of the restoration movement; Scott felt Campbell had too much pride in his own efforts and too little ability to appreciate the efforts of others. In other words, Scott believed Campbell treated him like a second-class citizen. Campbell's claim that the *Christian Baptist* "led the way in the present effort at reformation" did not settle well with Scott, who responded,

> Would the person who led the way in the present effort to re-establish the true gospel [Scott meant himself here] be permitted to use such language, and to speak of all who are now engaged in this effort as coming up to his assistance? I think not.[26]

In Scott's understanding, he had been responsible for the "introduction of the true gospel" since "there was no party in existence in which any one could enjoy primitive christianity in peace" until he preached the "ancient gospel." Campbell, to Scott's liking at least, had never acknowledged that fact. Instead, Campbell gave primary credit to his writing in the *Christian Baptist.* But Campbell and Scott simply could not reach a common agreement on who was most responsible for how "'This Reformation' in its infantile but distinct and separate form" originally emerged. According to Scott, however, "it never once occurred to me to think of myself apart from the Harbinger. For whether he wrote or I spoke, we co-operated for the glory of God and the good of souls." But Scott remained convinced that it regularly occurred to Campbell to think of himself apart from Scott.[27]

After a peace meeting between the two in Cincinnati toward the end of 1839, an anonymous attack on Scott's paper was published in the *Harbinger.* Campbell immediately claimed it happened by accident while he was out of town. Scott asked for the name of the author so that he might go directly to him to "settle it with him according to the laws of Christ." Campbell refused to divulge the name, claiming that Scott's letter "was not sufficiently respectful." Tired of the condescension and paternalism that accompanied most of Campbell's references to him, Scott wrote:

> Thrice do we find in his late piece the words *"beloved brother"* italicized and quoted as taken from the Evangelist. This is a bold push to put a man at fault. Now the Harbinger has designated us beloved brother often enough as all know: and it would be a very easy matter for us to quote, italicise, and comment on the expression as being found in his own writings, but alas! this is a poor way to heal wounds....We most sincerely wish to the brethren that peace which it appears we ourselves are not destined to enjoy. Yes, may grace, mercy, and peace be with the brethren through our Lord Jesus Christ.[28]

As these conflicts illustrate, Scott had no difficulty taking stands contrary to those of Campbell on any particular issue. With respect to millennialism during these years, he defended a position Campbell regularly repudiated in his own journal. The *Evangelist* had been decidedly premillennial since at least the mid-1830s. In a series of articles entitled "The Second Coming of Christ: The Cloud," Scott laid out his understanding of the literal second coming at the beginning of the millennium.[29] By 1840 Scott began to lay hold of Millerite ideas concerning the immediate return of Christ.[30] Over the next few years, he came to understand Miller's perspective as "the hope of the gospel" which "neither you nor I nor any other christian can reject."[31] Campbell expressed shock "that any one should, under the plea of preaching the *one* hope of the Christian, plead for the proclamation of '*the second advent near,*' as that one hope."[32] By the end of 1842, Scott chided the Disciples for their "ignorance of the prophetic word, of which this great and flourishing reformation has just caused [*sic*] to be ashamed."[33]

Scott's premillennialism had more support than such statements might indicate. At least four other Disciples journal editors were thorough premillennialists, and three of those were rather enthusiastic supporters of Miller's immediate expectations. Arthur Crihfield (*The Orthodox Preacher)*, Nathaniel Field (*the Israelite)*, and John R. Howard (*The Bible Advocate)* all expected Christ to return soon, and 1843 seemed as good a year as any. Barton Stone (*Christian Messenger)* had supported premillennialism from the early 1830s, and expressed interest in Miller's speculations without offering the kind of fervent support evidenced in Scott and some of the other editors. Of the four founders of the movement, Stone expressed the least confidence in human ability to accomplish anything meaningful. He retained the basically low view of human nature he had inherited from Presbyterianism and had zero interest in Christian participation in politics or in working for the general improvement of the civil sphere. Though supportive of church unity, to be accomplished by a return to the ancient church, Stone possessed a rather "sectarian, antimodern bias" on all other matters.[34] Some of the later confusion about the level of proper Disciples participation in social and political affairs no doubt had some of its origin in these different approaches the founders took to the millennium.

Alexander Campbell began taking notice of Miller, whom he described as "more imaginative than learned in prophecy," as early as 1840. On several occasions, he published extracts from Miller's writings.[35] Though he had high regard for Miller as a "good and exemplary Christian," he had "no sympathy for [the] theory." He believed it to be "an incalculable mischief to the cause of a suffering and degraded Christianity."[36] Believing the theory to lack scriptural warrant, Campbell concluded, "I have never met with so much confidence, supported by so little reason and evidence, on a subject of so much importance, of such mighty magnitude, as I have witnessed in Mr. Miller and his party on the whole subject of the coming of the Lord and the things that are to follow."[37] The fact that a number of Disciples, "some of our more intelligent and influential brethren,"[38] were favorably disposed to the Millerite theory bothered Campbell considerably. In February 1843, just one month before Miller's twelve-month period marking the end of the world, Campbell expressed his concern about what might happen to Disciples if they continued in their Millerite enthusiasm:

> I advise all of our brethren to be always ready to die any day, and every day; but I caution them against suffering themselves to be greatly excited about the end of the world in 1843. I do this with a great respect to those who differ from me; but I do it because of the injury which might accrue to a cause dear to us by every tie of sympathy and humanity, whose influence and success cannot but

be injured by suffering themselves to become enthusiasts in a cause plead [*sic*] by a class of individuals no way distinguished for learning, Christian intelligence, or good sense in the Christian or current acceptation of these words.[39]

Ultimately, the believing Disciples suffered the "great disappointment" of October 1844 along with everybody else. Most of them remained Disciples. For the most part, they remained chastened premillennialists who became wary of setting dates. Stone died in 1844, but his successors at the *Christian Messenger* announced a moratorium on millennial speculation. After Walter Scott's experience with Miller, he became an enthusiastic postmillennialist, pushing belief in human progress much further than Campbell ever did.

Premillennialism remained a factor in Disciples of Christ life well after the "great disappointment" of the Millerites. Those congregations aligned with the Churches of Christ after 1906 were destined to spend many years of the twentieth century fighting a battle over premillennialism, eventually defeating it.[40] For Disciples, at least through the beginning of the twentieth century, before historical criticism taught their scholars to read the visions of Revelation more in terms of its author's day than their own (and before events like the Holocaust and Hiroshima challenged the optimism of even the most enthusiastic among postmillennialists), Alexander Campbell's postmillennialism served as the norm for most of those who landed in the mainstream of the Disciples of Christ after the Civil War, but it became more specific and less nuanced.[41] By the end of the second generation, about the time Disciples and Churches of Christ split, eschatological themes, as a central part of Disciples identity, had receded to the point of almost disappearing altogether. No Disciple took great scholarly interest in Revelation or published a well-circulated commentary on it between the one written by Barton W. Johnson around 1880 and the one published by M. Eugene Boring in 1989.[42]

Between 1830 and 1860, Campbell wrote enough material in the *Millennial Harbinger* related to prophecy, providence, the future life, the second coming, and the millennium to fill two very large books. Of the four founders, he was the only one to espouse a consistent view through the entire spectrum of these years. He believed strongly in the importance of these topics for Christian faith. As a result, he proved an able defender of postmillennialism. His version of it had a decidedly Disciples twist to it, especially as he defined his understanding of the "kingdom of heaven." If today's Disciples are to understand the importance of this eschatological principle for early Disciples identity, both in terms of its benefits and deficiencies, they have to start with an analysis of Campbell's postmillennialism.

## Campbell's Postmillennialism
### The Millennium

Campbell approached the topic of the millennium boldly in terms of interpretation, but with some caution in terms of dogmatism. Above all, he acknowledged that the book of Revelation, with all its allusions and symbols, posed a great difficulty for any who would be interpreter of its pages. "The finite never can comprehend the infinite," he wrote.[43] But he never doubted that the millennium would come, and most likely that it would come soon. He did his best to figure out the dates historically, trying to build his own chronology for when Christians might expect the millennium to begin. As he did so, he talked of the "*probable* evidence, and probable evidence not of the superlative degree." In his debate with Robert Owen, he fixed the date for the "cleansing of the sanctuary" for sometime around 1847 (just four years different from the date chosen years later by William Miller).[44] This phrase came from Daniel 8:14, a passage of scripture used by most interpreters as a key to unlocking the future date of the Christian millennium. The difference between Campbell and Miller in their dating methods was only minimal; but they had considerable difference between them in how they understood the phrase "cleansing of the sanctuary."

Miller connected it with the second coming of Christ, at which time the earth was to be purified by fire or some other way. He therefore understood "the sanctuary" to represent the earth. Campbell believed it to be symbolic for the church.[45] In his debate with Owen, and throughout his writings about the subject in the *Harbinger*, he expressed his belief that the purification of the church would begin soon, if it had not already begun with the restoration of the ancient gospel. The sects were "all too narrow and too weak" for the founding of the "Millennial Church." "There is now…the *Ancient Gospel*, which is long enough, broad enough, strong enough for the whole superstructure called the Millennial Church— and that it will alone be the *instrument of converting* the whole human race, and of *uniting* all christians upon one and the same foundation."[46]

> When we put to sea under this banner [*Millennial Harbinger*] we had the port of Primitive Christianity, in letter and spirit, in profession and practice, in our eye; reasoning that all the Millennium we could scripturally expect was not merely the restoration of the Jerusalem church in all its moral and religious characters, but the extension of it through all nations and languages for one thousand years. To prepare the way for such a development of Christianity several things are essential—1st. The annihilation of partyism. 2d. The restoration of a pure speech. 3d. The preaching of the original gospel. 4th. The restoration of the Christian ordinances. 5th. Larger measures of the Holy Spirit, as promised to those who seek

for it in the appointed way. To these five points, as means of the triumph of the gospel over idolatry, infidelity, impiety, immorality, and corrupt religion, we have for years been directing the inquiries of our readers.[47]

In these passages, Campbell clearly connected the successful restoration of the church to his hope that the millennium might begin soon. This connection between looking back and looking forward is consistent throughout his writings on the subject.[48]

Campbell's "purification of the church from all the defilements of the grand apostacy," besides being intimately connected with the ancient gospel, contained a strong note of anti-Catholicism.[49] He believed the "little horn" of Daniel 7:20 referred to the papacy and was bound for destruction. He interpreted passages from Revelation 13:12–18 to refer to the papacy and directly connected it "and all clerical dynasties, Protestant and Papistical" with the antichrist.[50] This anti-Catholic note accompanied most Protestant interpretation of the book of Revelation, regardless of the views of how the millennium would begin. American Protestants believed the church's triumph was to exclude Catholics because of the hierarchical and national connections associated with the Catholic Church. American Protestants viewed Catholic presence in America as a real "threat to American liberties."[51] The millennial purification of the church would destroy all human governments along with four great evils: "Mahometanism, Papalism, Paganism, and Atheism." [52] These were the rivals to Christian dedication. One of Campbell's problems with premillennialism stemmed from his dedication to the idea that these rivals had to be defeated within history (before Christ came again), rather than beyond it. Otherwise, they, rather than Christ, would win the battle of the kingdoms in history. Campbell also looked for the complete conversion of the Jews within history, based upon his reading of Paul.[53]

He approached the scriptures surrounding the millennium with an odd mixture of literal and figurative interpretations (these are the terms used by the writers of the time). The first resurrection spoken of in Revelation 20 was figurative rather than literal, and signified the revival of the martyrs' spirit within the church. But the thousand years was literal, rather than a figurative period symbolic of the triumph of God's justice. He believed it to be a literal period to conclude history and that it would be preceded by the literal triumph of the church (aided by the Holy Spirit) over its enemies.

Campbell's understanding of the millennium provided him nearly an unmitigated optimistic view of history. He expected God's ultimate purposes for history to be fulfilled historically. The millennium would be a time of unparalleled human happiness accompanied by the reign of absolute divine justice. Accompanying these views, Campbell shared with other Protestants in America a "faith in progress" and an overarching confidence in American institutions as the instruments of civilization and culture for the rest of the world. Even on the eve of the Civil War, Campbell could wax eloquent about "the great fact that this world is but as it were awaking from sleep—emerging from superstitions and barbarisms of all sorts."

> Why, it was but yesterday that the mariner's compass was discovered, that printing was shown to be practicable, that steam power was laughed at as an absurdity, and the electric telegraph ridiculed as the hobby of a vagarian's brain. A new world has been found and settled almost within the span of sire and son—and that world is yet but experimenting in its government. Still more than all, far off in the East...there are races, nations and tribes, upon whom the light of truth, science, or even semi-barbarism, has never yet dawned.[54]

Both the early Campbell and the more mature Campbell could speak confidently and uncritically once in a while about the role of America in leading these "nations and tribes" to truth. Occasionally, Campbell folded his cultural parochialism in with his millennialism and produced a rather strong dose of ethnocentrism. He was not above mixing in a tad of racism as well:

> In our country's destiny is involved the destiny of Protestantism, and in its destiny the destiny of all the nations of the world. God has given, in awful charge, to Protestant England and Protestant America—the Anglo-Saxon race—the fortunes, not of Christendom only, but of all the world.[55]

This Anglo-Saxon racism and nationalism is far more prominent in the later Walter Scott than in any of Campbell's writings. After Scott left premillennialism behind and became an ardent defender of postmillennialism, his version of it differed from Campbell's in quite a number of respects. Chief among these differences, he attached a political interpretation to the "cleansing of the temple." This caused Scott to emphasize the political role of the United States and Great Britain in bringing in the millennium. In his latest book (1859), he declared the governments of these two nations were proof that "the Messiah who was to come is come."

> Let us look to America as the first of the Messianic nations....After all these revelations, may we not with every reasonable prospect of being gratified, cherish the pleasing assurance that society will at no distant period be essentially changed in Europe as it has been in the United States....May God hasten on the deliverance of all nations....Seeing God was pleased to foretell that he would create a new government and a new people, and seeing it was exceedingly

proper to choose a *new world* to do it in, it may be that in the government and people of the United States we have an historical illustration of the grand prophecy....We are all Anglo-Saxons—the offspring of the grandest nation on earth—the British nation....Most of all to be dreaded in this matter is the infusion into our country of foreign mind, foreign spirit—either from within or from without....Already two disturbing forces grievously agitate the republic, namely: 1. The Negro. 2. The Papist. The first seizing the soil, the last the balance of power....it remains for the reader to decide whether the United States is not one of the new Messianic governments predicted by the prophets; and whether there is not far more of reason than romance in our views of the matter?[56]

Since Campbell understood the millennium to be associated with the renewal of the church, not of existing governments, Campbell consistently stated his belief that none of the world's nations "can become a kingdom of Jesus Christ until all kingdoms become his."[57] The millennium would transform all existing governments; therefore, he tended to place no ultimate value upon existing governing institutions, nor did he express much interest in undertaking their reform. Writing in his *Christian System*, Campbell expressed the sentiment that, since Pentecost, "the governments of this world have either been directly opposed to [the kingdom], or, at best, pretended friends; and therefore their influence has always been opposed to the true spirit and genius of the Christian institution."[58] Though Campbell naively believed in human progress, and occasionally stated his optimism that America would contribute meaningfully to that process, his theological view of the kingdom of God did not allow him easily to combine nationalism, racism, and the millennium as a consistent expression of his eschatological views.

Few Disciples today would affirm Campbell's belief in a literal millennium, and fewer still would share his anti-Catholic and other culture-bound views of the end times. Campbell's experience instructs us that faith is never immune to the influences of the culture that surrounds it. Christians of all times need critically to discover ways to develop tension between faith and culture. Campbell's eschatological principle did lead to important theological insights that enabled a measure of self-transcendence for early Disciples in their relation to culture. It is at these points that his eschatological views are especially important for today's Disciples.

### Prophecy and Eschatology as the Fulfillment of the History of God's Salvation

Alexander Campbell approached his interpretation of the millennium with a broader angle of vision than many other interpreters did.

The key to understanding prophecy for Campbell rested in placing all prophecy and eschatology first in the context of God's saving acts in history. He concerned himself with unwrapping this salvation history in a way that would reveal the true character of both the millennium and the eternity to follow it.

> Instead of beginning and ending with the Apocalypse, we begin at the beginning of the book of creation, providence, and moral government [by which Campbell meant the events recorded within the Old Testament]. We proceed to that of redemption [the New Testament] and treat the subject *historically....*[59]

Campbell shared with the Reformed tradition this theological confidence that a sovereign God guided all of history toward some particular end, from the very beginning of creation to the dawning of the eschaton. This God stands above history (the transcendence of God), but is not unconcerned with it. God acts within and through history (the immanence of God) to bring salvation to humanity and to mold human history in the direction of the kingdom of God.

Throughout his lifetime of writing on these themes, Campbell remained consistently *historical* in perspective. He valued history and the church's record of God's activity within it. This historical consciousness formed the very heart of his eschatological understanding, and it gave him, and the mainstream of Disciples life after him, a commitment to the dynamic, rather than static, construction of human existence.[60] Human history is going somewhere. It is not standing still. God has an ultimate purpose yet to be worked out. The kingdom of God has broken in; the world is being changed. Neither the saved individual nor the church itself can afford to stand still. Salvation is linked with the kingdom of heaven, and the kingdom of heaven is leading the saints to the end of time when God's kingdom will be fully known. Creation, history, Israel, salvation, the kingdom, the saints, the church: all these terms had eschatological significance for Campbell, and they all led to one conclusion: God is working unceasingly to bring human history to the divine conclusion planned for it since before creation. As Campbell put it: "Before he had laid the corner stone of the material universe, or pronounced the first fiat, the end—the development and the consummation of it, were stereotyped in his Omniscient mind."[61] God has willed it and it will be done.

Campbell's understanding of the different dispensations of history arose from his eschatological perspective. He broke history into different dispensational segments (Patriarchal, Jewish, Christian), and these segments indicated just how God "dispensed" salvation during those times. These dispensations revealed the "sacred history" of God's salvation.[62] He began with Genesis and, in series after series of articles, carefully moved through Revelation, covering, according to him, "the route which sacred history takes; and this, so far, is the best hint we can give to those who have patience to search devoutly and intensely for the coming glories of Messiah's reign." [63] All these stories, in his view, pointed forward to the ultimate instrument of God's salvation, Christ. In order to understand more thoroughly how this eschatological principle helped to keep the early Disciples on a christological center, and to understand how this christocentrism ultimately pointed back to God, we need to review briefly Campbell's understanding of the kingdoms (note the plural) of God.

## The Kingdoms of God

Perhaps there is no element of Alexander Campbell's theology that is more misunderstood than his beliefs related to the kingdom of God. On the one hand, it is true to say that "Campbell viewed the kingdom of God as a constitutional monarchy in the here and now and, for all practical purposes, equated the kingdom and the church."[64] But one has to say more because Campbell said a great deal more. Which kingdom are we talking about here? For, on the other hand, and more important as an element within Campbell's theology, there was another kingdom, a transcendent eschatological kingdom of God that would replace this temporal "constitutional monarchy." This latter kingdom, in Campbell's theology, was one without beginning and without end, where God reigned forever and ever. This reign of God stood before creation, and God plans for it to extend beyond creation. But before that purpose could be accomplished, God had to make contingency plans. The sins of humanity made those plans necessary.

Campbell generally talked of three kingdoms. But when his eschatological theology is considered as a whole, he referred to a fourth kingdom as well. Three of these four kingdoms are present within and subservient to the fourth kingdom, the overarching and transcendent kingdom of God, though citizens of one are not necessarily citizens of any other. These three temporal kingdoms (the kingdom of nature, the Jewish kingdom of God, and the kingdom of heaven) more accurately represent "reigns:"

> frequently the original word *basileia* [mostly translated "kingdom"] ought in preference to be rendered *reign*, inasmuch as this term better suits all those passages where *coming* or *approaching* is spoken of: for, while reigns or administrations approach and recede, kingdoms have attributes and boundaries which are stationary. Reign and Kingdom of God, though sometimes applicable to the same subject, never contemplate it in the same light. They are, indeed, as intimately connected as the reign of King William and the kingdom of Great Britain. The former represents the administration of the

kingdom, and the latter the state over which this administration extends.[65]

The overarching kingdom is always God's kingdom, no matter which of the kingdoms Campbell talked about, whether those kingdoms refer to the reign of God or Christ over creation, Christ's reign over Christians, or God's reign over Israel.

*The Kingdom of Nature.* Campbell occasionally wrote about a kingdom of nature. By this term, he meant God's reign over creation into which all creatures are naturally born. God is the "benevolent Creator." In Eden, human beings sinned. This sin against the Creator left the human race without hope. But God had a remedy. God warned the serpent that the last word belonged to God. "I will put enmity between you and the woman," said God, "and between your offspring and hers; he will strike your head, and you will strike his heel [Genesis 3:15]." Campbell read this passage as a promise of redemption. This promise, claimed Campbell, opened "a large but yet undefined area of hope." It guaranteed a final triumph. Even during the times before God's covenant with Abraham, and before the giving of the law at Sinai, God expressed the divine purpose to redeem creation and to address what sin had done in the world.

The kingdom of nature was a divine kingdom, not simply a natural one. God reigned over the kingdom of nature through God's Word. God created nature originally through God's Word (John 1). Campbell, like other Christian theologians of his time, stressed Christ's connection to the pre-existent Word of God. The Word, associated with Christ, existed with God in creation—"all things have been created through him and for him." Christ is the "firstborn of all creation" and "in him all the fullness of God was pleased to dwell" (Campbell often quoted this passage from Colossians 1:15–20). God reigned over nature, but, through human sin, the kingdom was usurped by Satan. God reclaimed it through Christ. Even before the birth of Christ, God handed over the kingdom of this earth to the Word because Christ was the key to its redemption.[66] For Campbell, the kingdom of nature existed, therefore, from creation. Into this kingdom all human beings are born and, because of their sin, this kingdom will exist as a separate kingdom until the end of history. This kingdom of nature illustrates the sovereignty of God and of Christ over all creation, past—present—future, even where human beings within creation do not recognize their relationship to the benevolent Creator.

*The Kingdom of God (also known as the First Kingdom, or the Kingdom of Law).* During the Patriarchal dispensation (Genesis 1– Exodus 19), the kingdom of nature existed by itself. With the beginning of the Jewish dispensation (Exodus 20–Acts 1), God offered the Jewish people a new kingdom, "the kingdom of God," because "God was in a peculiar sense their King." This kingdom is often referred to as the "first kingdom" because it was the first kingdom of salvation history, occasioned by the sin of humanity after creation. In his book *Christian System*, one can find Campbell's references to both the Jewish "kingdom of God" and the "kingdom of nature" as kingdoms of flesh, kingdoms into which one is naturally born. From the time of the Exodus and the giving of the law at Sinai, all Jews were born into "the kingdom of God" or the "kingdom of law." Everyone else was born into the "kingdom of nature," including those Jews born before this "first" kingdom of God was established over Israel. But because God chose the Jews, he became their king in a special way, establishing the kingdom of God over them.

> For certain purposes he selected them, distinguished them, and took them under his own immediate protection. He gave them laws, ordinances, and customs, which had both a specific and general influence, and were preparatory to a new and better order of society.[67]

God condescended "to appear in the character of *King of the Jews*, and to make them a *kingdom of God*, as preparatory to the appearance of his Son, who is predestined to be the king of the whole earth, and to have a kingdom which shall ultimately embrace all the nations of the world."[68]

This kingdom of God for Jews temporarily took the place of the kingdom of nature for them. Until Pentecost, Jews were born into this temporary kingdom of God, while other races and peoples of other nations continued to be born into the kingdom of nature. After Pentecost, Jews were naturally born once again into the kingdom of nature because this "first kingdom" was terminated at Pentecost. The "lawful subjects" of this "first kingdom" were "all the descendants of Jacob, without regard to regeneration."[69] This kingdom must not, however, be confused with the transcendent and everlasting kingdom of God. Instead, it represented the kingdom of law, the temporal reign of God over the people of Israel. This kingdom served as a "type" for the "second kingdom," prefiguring and pointing ahead to the coming "reign of heaven," or "kingdom of Christ."

This kingdom of God over Israel represented the "kingdom of God of this world." The "second kingdom" would be the "kingdom of God not of this world." This first kingdom had its seed in the promise of God to Abraham that he would be blessed, his name made great, and from him would come a great nation. The second kingdom had its seed in the promise to Abraham that he would be a blessing to all the families of the earth (Genesis 12:1-3). God's covenant with Israel at Mount Sinai with Moses fulfilled the first promise; the ascension of Christ and the sending of the Holy Spirit at Pentecost fulfilled the second promise. With Moses, Israel became "a holy nation, a peculiar people." But this kingdom was "temporal, and its blessings temporal and earthly." Whatever "*spiritual* privilege" the Jews enjoyed were enjoyed on the same basis as the Jewish Patriarchs (Abraham, Isaac, Jacob) had experienced—"by faith in the second promise." Not all Jews looked forward in faith. Jews without faith in the second promise were the "natural children" of Israel, while those with faith became "the spiritual children of Israel."

> The whole nation were his literal and natural children; and such of them as believed the second promise and understood it were not only his natural children, but his [spiritual] children in the same sense in which all *believing Gentiles* are by virtue of the second promise constituted the children of Abraham.

This kingdom of God testified to God's activity in history. It represented God's future in Israel's present. The history of the kingdom is filled with "remarkable providences." It is a record of a "sacred history, or the remarkable instances of God's providence to the Jews and Patriarchs." As such, it represented "the foundation of the sacred dialect of the new institution....All the leading words and phrases of the New Testament are to be explained and understood by the history of the Jewish nation and God's government of them." This is why Campbell approached eschatology, the future hope, by taking a look backward first. God acted in relation to Israel and bestowed divine favor upon the Jews.

> They were the *called* and *chosen*, or the *elect* of God as a nation. As such, they were *delivered, saved, bought*, or *purchased*, and *redeemed.* God is said to have *created, made, formed*, and *begotten* them. As such, he is called their *Father*, their *God*, their *Redeemer*, their *King*, their *Saviour*, their *Salvation*; and they are called his *children, sons*, and *daughters*; *born to him*, his *house, people, inheritance, family, servants.*[70]

These words are all italicized within Campbell's passage. In other words, for Campbell, the entire grammar of Christian faith is found in the story of God's activity with and reign over the Jews.

**The Kingdom of Heaven (also known as the Second Kingdom, the Kingdom of Christ and God, the Kingdom of Favor—or Grace).** The kingdom of God among the Jews, as Campbell interpreted it, continued some 1500 years, from the time of Sinai to the time of Pentecost (Exodus 20—Acts 1). And then it ended. The Jewish dispensation ended as suddenly as it began, in a day. The Disciples emphasis on Pentecost has been one of the hallmarks of Disciples tradition and heritage. For Campbell, it was at Pentecost that Christ was made "Lord of all for the sake of that community of ransomed humanity called his church, or kingdom."[71] Not only did the church historically enter the world at Pentecost, the reign of the kingdom of heaven began at that time as well.

"For our part," wrote Campbell, "we must believe that the Kingdom of Heaven began, or the Reign of Heaven literally and truly commenced, in one day." At Pentecost, Christians were "saved from their sins," and "received a kingdom which cannot be shaken or removed."[72]

Pentecost, then, launched two great happenings: the birth of the church and the arrival of the kingdom of heaven (Campbell's preferred name for this kingdom). This is why some historians have confused the two in Campbell's thought. The relationship between the two was essential. The emergence of the church depended upon the arrival of the kingdom of heaven. Without it, the church would not have been born. Now that the kingdom has arrived, the members of the church have become its subjects. Every proper kingdom, according to Campbell, has subjects (members of the church), a constitution (God's will—the plan of salvation since before time began), a king (Christ), a territory (the whole earth), and laws (those found in the apostolic writings in the New Testament, though he emphasized the "supreme law" to be love of Christ and love for one another). The church, composed of the kingdom's subjects, was simply one of five aspects to the fullness of the kingdom of heaven.[73]

All of history looked forward to Pentecost and the establishment of this kingdom. The "spiritual children" of Israel had faith in this kingdom. And now they were fulfilled by its arrival. The "unbelieving Jews were rejected and repudiated as the visible and formal people of God" when this kingdom arrived. The kingdom was taken from them and given to those who would show its fruits (Matthew 21:43). Though they continue to exist as "a *monumental* people," they no longer represent the people of God as a nation.[74] Campbell followed Paul (Romans 11), however, in his belief that all Jews would become believers at some point in the millennium.

This theological belief in the arrival of the kingdom of heaven at Pentecost had interesting implications for the practice of the church in at least five areas: its authority, its worship and prayer life, its ordinances, its ethics, and its mission. The church's whole identity, in fact, evolved from the call of the gospel that spoke to the meaning of history and its culmination. Each of these areas of the church's life in early Disciples history reflected this understanding of the kingdom of heaven. Authority, for Disciples, could not rest in any human place (opinions, creeds) since Christ was king. Disciples needed a "thus saith the Lord" or an approved precedent (a practice of the early church approved by the authority of the apostles, given by Christ) before they could speak with authority.[75]

Disciples worship was thoroughly centered in Christ, but its practice was completely governed, not by the gospels, but by the epistles, for those books addressed the period following Pentecost. This event marked when the kingdom of heaven commenced. This belief was so strong among early Disciples that they refused to speak the Lord's Prayer, even if they were in the company of a group of worshipers from another tradition who were reciting it. Campbell claimed that the prayer, as indicated by the part of it that prays "thy kingdom come," was "literally answered some three years after it was presented." The apostles never taught it to anyone. They preached that the "kingdom or reign of Christ" had already come. "We may, indeed," wrote Campbell, "both pray and labor to enlarge his kingdom, but no intelligent Christian can now pray, thy kingdom or they reign come."[76] Disciples today usually pray this prayer as a part of their worship life since, sometime after the turn of the century, as Campbell's influence waned, their ministers shifted their understanding of the "kingdom" in the prayer to refer to the kingdom of God rather than the reign of Christ.

This theology of the kingdom of heaven also profoundly affected the mission of early Disciples. The kingdom arrived in full power at Pentecost. The Holy Spirit filled the church at its beginning and made it "fully adequate to the conversion of the whole world."[77] The church looked to the final establishment of Christ's kingdom in the millennium and understood itself to be the instrument of God for evangelizing the world. This eschatological hope compelled the church to attend to the matter of evangelism. Members of the church did not do so because they feared a shrinking church, or because they equated the kingdom of heaven with church growth, or because they needed to raise a larger budget to underwrite the church building or pay the church staff. Nor did they evangelize because they visualized a quick end to the world. They did so because they had become partakers in God's history of salvation. Their glimpse of the kingdom of God called them to the task at hand, spreading the good news of God's salvation in Jesus Christ to the world. Early Disciples stood firmly in the broader Christian tradition as they practiced an evangelism so thoroughly grounded in the gospel and in Christian hope.[78]

As previous chapters have indicated, Disciples of Campbell's generation also recognized that the church's mission included both restoration and church unity. The "apostasy" of the church since the days of Pentecost made both tasks necessary. As the church, through time, had fallen away from the gospel, it had become fragmented and now largely rested on human opinions and human authorities. For Campbell, and most of the early Disciples, their commitments to restoration and unity arose from their vision of the eschatological kingdom. The Christian hope pictured one church, pure and undivided. As Campbell put it, in light of the kingdom of God, "We...should hang our Sectarian trumpets in the hall and study ecclesiastic wars no more." The millennial church is one church. There will be no petty squabbles in God's kingdom. Disciples were empowered by this hope. Their millennial vision pulled them toward the future, even while they looked to the past to gain a greater understanding of the plan of salvation so evident within human history.

Finally, Campbell considered the Christian ordinances, or sacraments, to be the "means of all spiritual enjoyment" in this present kingdom of heaven. His list of ordinances included not only baptism and the Lord's supper, but also preaching and fasting and prayer. Through them, argued Campbell, Christians experience the grace of God. Baptism by immersion, "being born of water and Spirit (John 3:5)," actually constituted admission into the kingdom of heaven. As citizens of this kingdom, "sin cannot lord it over them; for they are not under law, but under favor [by this term, Campbell meant 'grace']."[79] Campbell's understanding of these different kingdoms allowed him greater latitude than others had when considering just who might enter the "everlasting kingdom of God." This openness gained rather famous expression in the Lunenberg letter of 1837, when Campbell affirmed that infant-baptized people might be saved. Lesser known is the fact that as early as June of 1829, Campbell used an essay defining the three kingdoms to explain that, though infant-baptized people do not enter the kingdom of heaven, the temporal kingdom of Christ, they could "enter into the third kingdom, the kingdom of glory."

> I am prepared to say that my opinion is, and it is but an opinion, that infants, idiots, and some Jews and Pagans, may, without either faith or baptism, be brought into the third kingdom, merely in consequence of the sacrifice of Christ; and I doubt not but many Paidobaptists of all sects will be admitted into the kingdom of glory.— Indeed all they who obey Jesus Christ, through faith in his blood, according to their knowledge, I am of opinion will be introduced into that kingdom. But when we talk of the forgiveness of sins which comes to christians through immersion, we have no regard to any other than the second kingdom, or the kingdom of favor. I repeat it again—there are three kingdoms: the Kingdom of Law, the Kingdom of Favor, and the Kingdom of Glory; each has a different constitution, different subjects, privileges, and terms of admission.

The most interesting implication, and Campbell clearly spelled it out later in this essay, as well as in his *Christian System*, was that there are those in the kingdom of heaven ("Favor") who might not enter the kingdom of "glory." Full participation in the kingdom of heaven demanded an ethical and obedient life. Otherwise, one could not be assured of being born into the next kingdom, the kingdom that really counted. Human beings "cannot enter into the third and ultimate kingdom through faith, immersion, or regeneration." How then does one enter the eternal kingdom? One cannot get there by faith alone, "but by being counted worthy of the resurrection of the just." It requires also "the obedience of faith." Christ says one enters the kingdom "because I know your good works, your piety, and humanity. I was hungry and you fed me, etc." [80]

> Because forgiven, they should forgive; because justified, they should live righteously; because sanctified, they should live holy and unblamably; because reconciled to God, they should cultivate peace with all men, and act benevolently towards all; because adopted, they should walk in the dignity and purity of sons of God; because saved, they should abound in thanksgivings, praises, and rejoicings, living soberly, righteously, and godly, looking forward to the blessed hope.[81]

This perspective led to a great emphasis in Campbell, and among early Disciples, on obedience in Christ, on the ethics of being Christian. If one were not obedient, did not live ethically and cultivate peace, one would not see the eternal kingdom. This comes close to "works righteousness."[82] The grace of God brings one into the kingdom of favor, but to be admitted into the kingdom of glory, one had to do more. But Campbell always emphasized the role of God's Holy Spirit in transmitting, diffusing, and sustaining an obedient and spiritual life after baptism. Christians are granted a new "state or condition," from which they should be able to act in obedient ways. In other words, God's grace enables obedience: "God never commanded a being to do any thing, but the power and motive were derived from something God had done for him."[83] Campbell's presumption was that a person with no inclination toward obedience could not truly have received God's grace and therefore could not be born into the kingdom of glory, even though he or she might have been baptized into the kingdom of favor.

Criticism from scholars alleging that Campbell equated the kingdom with the church, or that he did not possess a vision of a transcendent kingdom that could empower a countercultural or ethical vision, is not exactly accurate. Campbell's ethical posture was clearly rooted in his eschatological vision of this everlasting kingdom of God.[84] A disobedient Christian who died without bearing the fruits of baptism simply did not stand much of a chance of being born, after death, into the kingdom of glory.

*The Everlasting Kingdom of God (also known as the Third Kingdom, or the Kingdom of Glory).* Three kingdoms pertaining to the history of salvation are now in view: the kingdom of law, the kingdom of favor, and this "third kingdom," the kingdom of glory. This last kingdom is the transcendent one, the final one, the ultimate eternal kingdom of God. It is different in character from any of the previous kingdoms. This kingdom has no beginning and no end. It is not a temporal kingdom like the kingdom of nature or the other two kingdoms which commenced, after the occasion of human sin in the garden, with an aim to set in motion the history of salvation. This kingdom preceded creation and will continue after the story of history is done. From the King (God) reigning over this eternal kingdom, the other "reigns" received their authority and their purpose for existence.

The careful reader of Campbell recognizes, then, that Jesus himself, in Campbell's view, lived under the "old Kingdom of Law." He did not live in the kingdom of heaven, the Christian dispensation, as that time did not begin until Pentecost. The kingdom of heaven, therefore, is the reign of the triumphant and ascended Christ, anointed and empowered by God, not the reign of the earthly Jesus. At Pentecost, God anointed Christ the "Monarch of the universe." The "great God and Father of the universe…invested" Christ with "regal authority." Christ is the king, but his kingdom is temporary. It is a "remedial reign." It possesses the purpose "to put down sin." When that has been done, when Christ returns and establishes his authority over all history by his complete and utter triumph over sin and all the enemies of God, the kingdom of heaven will end and give way to the everlasting kingdom of God.

The temporary nature of Christ's kingdom is an important theological point for Campbell. And those who confuse Campbell's belief in this "everlasting kingdom of God" with what Campbell writes about the kingdom of heaven will miss the point entirely.[85] The whole history of salvation, of God's activity in history, has pointed toward Christ, and the conflict of history itself is resolved in Christ. But, in the end, when history concludes, Christ will return all authority to the One to whom it ultimately and always belonged. (See Paul's statement of this in 1 Corinthians 15:24–28.) The "sceptre" is handed back to God. Christ "gives up the kingdom," and "the government of the universe will assume its ancient order." The eternal kingdom of God remains and "God [will] be supreme monarch again."[86] Put simply, the christocentric focus of early Disciples always brought the Christian back to God. The narrative of the history of salvation in Jesus Christ ultimately belongs to, and always points us to, God.

## Conclusion

Alexander Campbell's eschatological views certainly appear somewhat strange to the modern Disciple. His approach to the book of Revelation is dated when viewed from our perspective today. It is conditioned by nineteenth-century American culture in troublesome ways, especially in its anti-Catholic bias and its overconfidence in human progress. Today's Disciples are schooled in a different understanding of Revelation, one pegged to the author's context as a message of hope for Christians of his time who were persecuted (the "contemporary-historical" view, sometimes called the "preterist" or simply "historical" view), rather than as a book which lays out a blueprint for precisely how the long-range future is to unfold, of which we are living near the end (sometimes called the "church-historical" or "continuous-historical" view, the view held by Campbell).[87] Though his possessed some distinctive Disciples features, Campbell's interpretation represented the most popular reading of his day, as our mainstream biblical scholarship does in its own way today. When exposed to the "contemporary-historical" reading of Revelation, which was gaining a foothold in German biblical scholarship in the early 1840s, Campbell rejected that reading, and expressed his disappointment that his favorite American biblical scholar, Moses Stuart, had adopted it. "What a singular aberration from common sense for so distinguished a man!"[88]

Today's Disciples biblical scholars accept a reading closer to Stuart's than to Campbell's. In spite of differences between his approach and our approach, Campbell's careful biblical scholarship in this area produced insights we should reflect as Disciples today. His concern for reading the prophetic material in the context of the whole content of scripture helped him to develop and set forth a fundamental understanding of a God who seeks our redemption and calls us into the future with hope. The early Disciples' vision of that future demanded of Christians an integrity that matched their calling. Interestingly enough, Disciples Professor M. Eugene Boring's commentary on Revelation, though using a different type of interpretation in reading the book ("contemporary-historical" rather than "church-historical"), reaches very similar conclusions to those of Campbell when he interprets theologically what the book tells us about who God is, who Christ is, what they do, and what it means for the present to be given a future resting in the certainty of the faithfulness of God.[89]

Though Campbell's theological reflections on prophecy, the millennium, and the various kingdoms are complex and potentially confusing, they can be summed up easily enough. In all his writings about eschatology, Campbell expressed a supreme confidence that God had a stake in human history. He firmly believed that God is with us (after all, this is the meaning of Emmanuel—see Matthew 1:23). God has entered human time and changed it, made it into something it would not and could not be otherwise. The salvation of God has made our own time significant and important. History is meaningful; these days we are living —each and every one of them—have genuine meaning. The eternal God has transformed human time by acting within it. God as a living actor in history is one who can be and is encountered by human beings. These encounters are the stuff of eschatology.

Campbell interpreted history as the interval between eternities. Before history, there was God. After history, there is God. And God is in history. History is this in-between time and serves as the container for the story of human life, the "incomparable fortunes, good and bad." The

Bible tells this story and reveals God, "the source of universal being—the father of eternity—the spring of all life, and the fountain of all bliss," in a way that is adapted to "the capacity, conditions, and circumstances of fallen humanity." And just as history has been changed, eternity has itself been changed. Because of history, the eternity following history will be different from the one before it. Because of God's grace, because of God's activities in history, "the Christian, that native of heaven, and pilgrim of time" possesses "the radiant hopes of a bright and boundless future": an eternity with God.[90]

Campbell's eschatological principle had its center in Christ. In and through Christ, God has been working out divine purposes in history. Christians stand in the midst of a time that is being redeemed. And when time ends, the anointed Christ presents a redeemed creation to our God who reigns eternally. In their eschatological faith, Campbell and other early Disciples saw beyond themselves to the edge of God's time, that time beyond time, and they learned the meaning of Christian hope. They also learned the meaning of Christian discipleship and the responsibilities accompanying it. The eschatological perspective requires of Christians a special orientation toward the mercy and justice found at the center of the kingdom of God.

No wonder Campbell and other Disciples spent so much time thinking and writing about baptism and the Lord's supper. These two central sacraments of the church collapse God's time into our time and bring Christians to a firsthand encounter with God's grace in the here and now. Among the many other ways it shaped early Disciples identity, the eschatological principle provided early Disciples a firm foundation for their sacramental theology.

## Questions for Reflection and Discussion

1. How did ideas floating around in the American context divide early Disciples leadership in their approaches to the book of Revelation and to the idea of the millennium in general? To what extent can you identify cultural influences on our own approach to the questions of who God is, how God acts today and will act in the future, what history is, the role of our nation in history, and who should be counted in or out of God's kingdom?

2. In what ways did Campbell approach the topics of "prophecy" and "eschatology" historically?

3. Describe what it meant to Campbell to be "christocentric." In what ways did Campbell's theological understanding of who Christ was, and what Christ has done and is doing, ultimately point to God?

4. How did Campbell understand the concept of the kingdom(s) of God? In what ways did he describe these different kingdoms and how do they relate to the overarching purposes God has in mind for history?

5. How did Campbell's understanding of the "kingdom of heaven" affect his understanding of the work of the church, especially in such areas as authority, worship and prayer life, ordinances, ethics, and mission?

## Notes

[1]"Prospectus," *Millennial Harbinger* (January 1830): 1.

[2]Anthony L. Dunnavant, "Evangelization and Eschatology: Lost Link in the Disciples Tradition," *Lexington Theological Quarterly* (Spring 1993), p. 50.

[3]See Arthur W. Wainwright, *Mysterious Apocalypse: Interpreting the Book of Revelation* (Nashville: Abingdon Press, 1993), especially pp. 21-31, for a discussion of millennialism in the early church. Wainwright points out that not all these Christians were chiliasts; some doubted whether Revelation actually was an inspired book that belonged in the church's canon. This book is an excellent accounting of the history of millennialism in all its complex forms. These initial paragraphs are dependent on Wainwright's analysis.

[4]See Hal Lindsey, *The Late Great Planet Earth* (New York: Bantam Books, 1973).

[5]Wainwright, *Mysterious Apocalypse*, pp. 33-34, and p. 12.

[6]For a discussion of postmillennialism in general, see *Ibid.*, pp. 77-81; for Campbell's comments about Whitby and Vitringa, see "Historic Prophecy, no. 1," *Millennial Harbinger* (March 1832): 133; for comments about Whitby particularly see "Coming of the Lord, no. 25," *Ibid.* (July 1843): 294; and "Coming of the Lord, no. 26," *Ibid.* (October 1843): 441. Campbell did state that he had read of Whitby's views in Scott's *Evangelist.* Walter Scott quoted from Whitby in "Modern Opinions Respecting the Apocalyptic Millennium," *The Evangelist* (July 1835): 155-162. For Whitby's view, see "A Treatise of the True Millennium," in *Paraphrase and Notes on the New Testament,* 2 Vols. (London: Awnsham & John Churchill, 1703), 2:247-278. Campbell actually credited Englishman Joseph Towers with the most formative influence in shaping his views on the millennium. See "The Millennium, no. 3," *Ibid.* (April 1856): 184. Towers' book, title unknown, appeared first in London in 1796 and later in America in 1808. It is interesting that Campbell, in retrospect, in 1856, credited Towers with a heavy influence on his views of the millennium, because in 1835 an anonymous letter to Walter Scott's *Evangelist* charged Campbell with plagiarizing "Towers on the Prophecies." See Eusebius, "The Letter Men and Allegorists," *Evangelist* (July 1835): 153-155.

[7]See Winthrop S. Hudson and John Corrigan, *Religion in America: An Historical Account of the Development of American Religious Life* (New York: Macmillan Publishing Company, fifth edition, 1992), especially pp. 180-195.

[8]This is David E. Harrell's point; see Harrell, *Quest for a Christian America: The Disciples of Christ and American Society to 1866* (Nashville: Disciples of Christ Historical Society, 1966), pp. 36-38.

[9]"Coming of the Lord, no. 1," *Millennial Harbinger* (January 1841): 11.

[10]For this story of Miller, and the connection with these three events, I am dependent on the brief treatment given Miller in Hudson and Corrigan, *Religion in America,* pp. 192-194.

[11]See Campbell, "Coming of the Lord, no. 17," *Millennial Harbinger* (July 1842): 303-308.

¹²See "Millennium, no. 1," *Ibid.* (February 1830): 53-58, through "The Millennium," *Ibid.* (April 1831): 165-168.

¹³See "Prophecies, no. 1" through "Prophecies, no. 8," in *Millennial Harbinger* (August 1830): 373-375, through the *Millennial Harbinger* (June 1831): 261-266.

¹⁴See "The Coming of the Lord," *Millennial Harbinger* (June 1832): 255-262; "Literal Fulfillment of Prophecy," *Ibid.* (July 1832): 322f; and "Twelve Short and General Reasons," *Ibid.* (September 1832): 438-444.

¹⁵"The Prophecies," *Ibid.* (February 1833): 49.

¹⁶Campbell first reviewed McCorkle's views in "The Millennium," *Ibid.* (April 1831): 165-168.

¹⁷"Conceal my name till the end of the seventh volume of the Harbinger, that I may be heard without favor or affection—prejudice or partiality." "The Millennium, no. 1," *Ibid.* (September 1834): 459.

¹⁸McCorkle, "Reply to a Reformed Clergyman, no. 3," *Ibid.* (August 1835): 368.

¹⁹Campbell quotes McCorkle in "The Coming of the Lord, no. 10," *Ibid.* (December 1841): 576-578, and makes his comment on pp. 578-579. On the charge of plagiarism, see Reformed Clergyman, "The Millennium, no. 5," *Ibid.* (January 1835): 6; see also Eusebius, "The Letter Men and Allegorists," *Evangelist* (July 1835): 153-155, who agrees that McCorkle plagiarized Smith, but attacks Campbell on a similar point.

²⁰On this point, see Richard T. Hughes, *Reviving the Ancient Faith: The Story of Churches of Christ in America* (Grand Rapids, MI: William B. Eerdmans Publishing Company, 1996), pp. 106-107.

²¹"The Millennium, no. 5," *Ibid.* (January 1835): 11.

²²"Coming of the Lord, no. 1," *Ibid.* (January 1841): 11.

²³"Coming of the Lord, no. 16," *Ibid.* (June 1842): 262.

²⁴For example, see Scott, "Divine Authority for Our Name," *Evangelist* (March 1840): 51-56; and "Arguments for 'Disciple' Examined," *Ibid.*, 60-62; and "Cleansing of the Sanctuary, no. 4, Christian Name," *Ibid.* (June 1840): 122-128.

²⁵See particularly Walter Scott, "Unity of Spirit," *Ibid.* (April 1840): 79-82.

²⁶Scott, "The Harbinger," *Ibid.* (July 1840): 157-161.

²⁷See Scott, "The Harbinger," *Ibid.* (September 1840): 201-203; see also "Our Course," *Ibid.* (November 1840): 241-242.

²⁸See Scott, "The Harbinger," *Ibid.* (July 1840): 161.

²⁹The series entitled "Second Coming of Christ: The Cloud," began in the pages of the *Evangelist* (August 1934): 174, and ran through 1836. Scott may have entertained postmillennial views earlier in his ministry: see particularly, Philip (the pseudonym used by Scott), "On the Millennium, no. 1," *The Christian Baptist* (July 6, 1826): 80-81. This series has a postmillennial feel to it, though he is not explicit on the relationship between the coming of Christ and the millennium.

³⁰See the series of articles entitled "Cleansing of the Sanctuary" that ran through 1840 in *Evangelist*; see particularly the first of these essays in the May 1840 issue, p. 9. This point is also made by David E. Harrell in the lecture he presented at Brite Divinity School for the Walter Scott Bicentennial Celebration. See Harrell, "Walter Scott and the Nineteenth Century Evangelical Spirit," unpublished manuscript, p. 9f.

³¹Scott, "Reply to Bro. Church," *Evangelist* (September 1842): pp. 199-205.

³²"Coming of the Lord, no. 23," *Millennial Harbinger* (May 1843): 219.

³³Quoted in Harrell, "Walter Scott and the Nineteenth Century Evangelical Spirit," p. 10. The reference is from Scott, "To The Brethren," *Evangelist* (October 1842): 236-237.

³⁴See Richard Hughes who has developed this side of Stone in *Reviving the Ancient Faith*, pp. 106-113, though I think he makes too much of it when he claims it as the root of the later split between the Churches of Christ and the Disciples. For an

early expression of Stone's premillennialism, see the exchange of letters between Stone and Elder William Caldwell; see *The Christian Messenger* (October 1833): 312-314; *Ibid.* (December 1833): 365-367; *Ibid.* (May 1834): 140-148. For his more excited essays on the immanence of the second coming, see Stone, "The Coming of the Son of God," *Ibid.* (April 1842): 166-170; and Stone, "The Signs of the Last Days," *Ibid.* (August 1842): 301-306; and *Ibid.* (October 1842): 363-367.

[35]For the quote, see Campbell, "Coming of the Lord, no. 2," *Millennial Harbinger* (February 1941): 54; for the first reference to Miller, see "The End of the Present Dispensation in 1840," *Ibid.* (June 1840): 269-270.

[36]For the first quote, see "Coming of the Lord, no. 13," *Ibid.* (March 1842): 97; for the second, see "Coming of the Lord, no. 20," *Ibid.* (February 1843): 55.

[37]"Coming of the Lord, no. 18," *Ibid.* (August 1842): 334.

[38]"Coming of the Lord, no. 20," *Ibid.* (January 1843): 49.

[39]"The Orthodox Preacher," *Ibid.* (February 1843): 93-94.

[40]See Hughes, *Reviving the Ancient Faith*, pp. 137-167.

[41]Beginning with Robert Milligan, this brand of postmillennialism became much more specific with reference to dates and attempted to tie specific historical events to the immanent end. Milligan wrote a series of twenty articles on prophecy, the size of a good book, for the *Millennial Harbinger* beginning in January 1856 and continuing through August 1857. For a couple of examples on the specificity of events and dates, see "Prophecy, no. 9," *Ibid.* (August 1856): 428-435, where he discusses the roles of contemporary Russia and Turkey, the latter of which he predicts will fall by 1892; and "Prophecy, no. 11," (November 1856): 607, where he dates the expected conversion of the Jews at around 1922; and "Prophecy, no. 20," *Ibid.* (August 1857): 430, where he predicts that the Jews will return to Palestine in around 1892, be converted around 1922, and by 1957, "they will with the blessing of God and the co-operation of Gentile believers, carry the victories of the cross to the remotest parts of the Earth, and introduce the golden period of the Messiah's reign." M. Eugene Boring's soon-to-be-published book on Disciples biblical interpretation (*Disciples and the Bible*. St. Louis: Chalice Press, 1997) cites passages from the last forty-two pages of Milligan's *Scheme of Redemption* that carry dates close to these. Boring points out that Milligan's work takes a "scholastic turn" compared to the work of Campbell.

[42]Boring's book on biblical interpretation reveals that Barton W. Johnson continues the postmillennial posture defined by Campbell. Johnson's commentary is entitled *Vision of the Ages, or Lectures on the Apocalypse* (Delight, Arkansas: Gospel Light Publishing Company, fourth edition, 1881). Boring's commentary is *Revelation* (Louisville: Westminster/John Knox, 1989). By the time of Herbert Willett and Edward Scribner Ames, the eschatological principle changed considerably in its details. Willett's view of the second coming of Christ remained postmillennial in a more modern sense of the word, but was entirely "spiritual" rather than physical. See Willett, *Basic Truths of the Christian Faith* (Chicago: The Christian Century Foundation, 1903), p. 78. With Ames, the visible kingdom of God on earth became "an inner kingdom of life and righteousness." See Ames, *The New Orthodoxy* (Chicago: The University of Chicago Press, 1918), p. 83. For a description of how liberal versions of "building the kingdom of God" took precedence, especially in terms of mission, in the early twentieth century, see chapter 8.

[43]"The Millennium, no. 3," *Millennial Harbinger* (April 1856): 184. Campbell expressed this sentiment often in his writings: see, for example, "The Conversion of the World," *Christian Baptist* (January 5, 1824): 42; "A Restoration of the Ancient Order of Things, No. 1," (February 7, 1825): 48; "The Millennium," *The Millennial Harbinger* (April 1831): 167; "Coming of the Lord, no. 1," *Ibid.* (January 1841): 6; and "Prophecy, no. 3," *Ibid.* (December 1860): 669.

⁴⁴Campbell deals with the differences in dates between himself and Miller in "Coming of the Lord, no. 13," *Ibid.* (March 1842): 97-99.

⁴⁵See "Coming of the Lord," numbers 13, 17, 18, 22, and 26, published in *Ibid.* (March 1842): 98; (July 1842): 305; (August 1842): 333; (April 1843): 187; and (October 1843): 445.

⁴⁶Campbell, "Millennium, no. 1," *Ibid.* (February 1830): 58.

⁴⁷Campbell, "Millennial Character of the Harbinger," *Ibid.* (December 1840): 562.

⁴⁸Hughes argues Campbell gave up his connection between restoration and millennium and instead placed his hope for the millennium in American civil religion. See Hughes and Allen, *Illusions of Innocence*, pp. 170-187. The substance of that chapter originally appeared in Hughes, "From Primitive Church to Civil Religion: The Millennial Odyssey of Alexander Campbell," *Journal of the American Academy of Religion* (March 1976): 87-103. I say more below about my disagreement with Hughes on this point. See footnote number 55.

⁴⁹For the quote, see "Coming of the Lord, no. 22," *Ibid.* (April 1843): 187.

⁵⁰Campbell, "Historic Prophecy, no. 2," *Ibid.* (May 1832): 218-219.

⁵¹See Hughes on this point, *Reviving the Ancient Faith*, pp. 32-37. Hughes points out Campbell's developing interest in defending the interests of Protestantism in general, which gave him a broader and more liberal vision than many within the early Disciples movement.

⁵²Campbell, "Coming of the Church, no. 1," *Ibid.* (January 1841): 6. Numerous other references could be cited here.

⁵³Campbell, "Coming of the Church, no. 3," *Ibid.* (March 1841): 97; see also "Coming of the Lord, no. 25," *Ibid.* (July 1843): 295.

⁵⁴Campbell, "The Millennium," *Ibid.* (June 1858): 336. A passage similar to this one, in its confidence in progress, is found early in Campbell's writings, in 1834, in "The Millennium, no. 3," *Ibid.* (November 1834): 549. By 1862, however, Campbell wrote with great despair: "Of all the monstrosities on which our sun has ever shone, that of professedly *Christian* nations glutting their wrath and vengeance on one another with all the instruments of murder and slaughter, caps the climax of human folly and gratuitous wickedness." See Campbell, "Moses, the Oldest of Prophets," *Ibid.* (April 1862): 169.

⁵⁵Quoted in Harrell, *Quest for a Christian America*, p. 53. The quote is from the *Millennial Harbinger* (August 1852): 462. Harrell details the combination of national destiny, racism, and millennialism in this chapter; see especially pp. 44-53. Hughes, *Illusions of Innocence*, chapter 8, pp. 170-187, argues that there was a shift in Campbell toward a consistent national form of millennialism in his later years. I do not see it any more evident there than it is in his earlier years, and it is never the dominant characteristic of his millennialism, but rather resides as an occasional and limited, but nonetheless real, part of it throughout his life. For Campbell's references to Anglo-Saxon triumph, see Harrell, p. 47. It is interesting to note that Campbell's references in this regard are usually in the context of public addresses commemorating a public holiday like July 4, or orations delivered in a secular or political context. Through the countless pages of texts dealing with prophecy and millennium in thirty years of the *Millennial Harbinger*, I found no explicit references either to Anglo-Saxons or to America's role in bringing in the millennium. Though I was influenced by Hughes' arguments before reading the material in the *Millennial Harbinger* for myself, I have since concluded that Campbell did not offer any consistent or direct associations between the millennium and the "religion of the republic" in his later years. In general I found consistent emphases connecting the hopes of restoration and the hopes of millennialism throughout Campbell's writings on the topic; his writings on the millennium and the second coming contain vastly more regular men-

tion of the "ancient gospel" than mention of the "progress of civilization." Besides the reference I have already mentioned, see "Millennium" (December 1956): 699 for another later reference. In this essay, Campbell also affirms the Apostles' Creed, and adds to it, as setting forth the "facts" of the ancient gospel that need to be believed (see pp. 701-702). I do believe Hughes has contributed greatly to our historical understanding of Campbell by demonstrating that Campbell came to a greater appreciation of his association with Protestantism as he became older.

[56]Walter Scott, *The Messiahship or Great Demonstration, Written For the Union of Christians on Christian Principles, as Plead for in the Current Reformation* (Cincinnati: H.S. Bosworth, 1859), pp. 298, 313, 321-322, 332-333, 335.

[57]Campbell, "Everlasting Gospel, no. 2," *Ibid.* (March 1833): 119. This theme appeared in his *Christian System* and throughout his writings on the millennium during these thirty years.

[58]Campbell, *Christian System,* p. 159.

[59]Campbell, "The Millennium, no. 3," *Ibid.* (April 1856): 187. The emphasis is his own.

[60]This remained true even though later generations lost any connection between this dynamism and eschatological views.

[61]*Ibid.* See also Campbell, "Millennium, no. 4" *Ibid.* (May 1856): 270: "There is one oracle of our Apostle Paul that commands much thought, and which furnishes a very safe sign-post…in our pathway along the lines of the prophetic chart.… It reads thus: 'The gifts and callings of God are without change of purpose' or 'repentance,' on his part [Romans 11:29]. He has a scheme, a purpose, a plan in creation, providence, moral government, and in redemption, from which he never departs.…Now such being the fact through the entire domain of animated nature, ought we not to realize the Divine power and wisdom as acting wholly under the promptings of Divine goodness, and as directed and controlled by it?…In tracing all the meanderings of the stream of prophecy, from the first prophetic promise or covenant vouchsafed to fallen man, however it may appear to us to change its course, we shall find that it is moving forward in the most direct and consistent line, and in perfect good keeping with every Divine attribute, developing the moral and spiritual grandeur of the absolute monarch of universal being.…The history of this symbolic nation is but the history of a *special providence,* documented with the most interesting details and evidences."

[62]As he put it in his *Christian System:* "That sacred history, or the remarkable instances of God's providence to the Jews and Patriarchs, are the foundations of the sacred dialect of the new institution." See *Christian System,* p. 142.

[63]See the series on prophecy written under the pseudonym of the "Reformed Clergyman" that appeared in the *Millennial Harbinger* from January 1837–November 1838. The quotation is from "Prophecies, no. 6, *Ibid.* (August 1837): 377. The term "sacred history" was used often by Campbell. Campbell's "Coming of the Lord" series, his longest running series, ran from January 1841–October 1843, and covered the same territory, as did his series on "The Millennium," running sporadically from February 1856–June 1858, and his series entitled "Prophecy" running from March 1860–March 1862.

[64]Hughes, *Reviving the Ancient Faith,* p. 93. Hughes compares Campbell and Stone on this point and argues that Stone places a hope in a transcendent kingdom of God, "envisioned the kingdom as God's final, triumphant rule, which will be made complete only in the last age," and Campbell did not. This is not exactly accurate. Campbell, as this section of the chapter makes clear, talked about several kingdoms, each having their purpose in the scheme of things, but the most important of the kingdoms was represented in the final and transcendent reign of God in the "everlasting kingdom."

## 134    Joined in Discipleship

[65] *Christian System,* p. 149.

[66] For Campbell's emphasis on creation, and on Christ as the "firstborn of creation," see "Coming of the Lord, no. 2," *Millennial Harbinger* (February 1841), particularly pp. 49-51; and "The Millennium, no. 2," *Ibid.* (March 1856): 132-135. The biblical passages quoted here were used by Campbell in the KJV but are here presented in the NRSV. When quoting Campbell's use of scripture within larger quotes of Campbell, the KJV is used in this chapter. For statements on this kingdom of nature, see *Christian System,* p. 160; see also Campbell, "Query," *Millennial Harbinger* (January 1833): 12.

[67] Campbell, "The Three Kingdoms," *The Christian Baptist* (June 1, 1829): 557.

[68] *Christian System,* p. 139.

[69] "The Three Kingdoms," p. 557.

[70] For a detailed explanation of the Kingdom of God among the Jews, see *Christian System,* pp. 134-145; see also "The Three Kingdoms," p. 557-558.

[71] "Millennium, no. 5" (May 1856): 275.

[72] *Christian System,* pp. 164 and 171. Walter Scott shared this view of the kingdom of heaven being temporal and separate from the transcendent kingdom of God: see *The Gospel Restored: A Discourse* (Cincinnati: Printed by O.H. Donogh, 1836): pp. 197-199.

[73] See William D. Howden, "The Kingdom of God in Alexander Campbell's Hermeneutics, *Restoration Quarterly* 32 (1990), pp. 90-91, on this point. See also W. Clark Gilpin, "The Integrity of the Church," pp. 29-48. Campbell's discussion on these five elements of the kingdom of God is found in *Christian System,* pp. 148-160.

[74] "Millennium, no. 5," p. 275. See also, *Christian System,* p. 166.

[75] See, for example, "Response," *Millennial Harbinger* (1834): 608-611. Stephen V. Sprinkle emphasized that, for Disciples, early ecclesiology grew out of this eschatological view; see Sprinkle's, "Alexander Campbell and the Doctrine of the Church," (Summer 1988): 19-25.

[76] Campbell, "Prophecy, no. 8," *Ibid.* (July 1861): 398-399. Isaac Errett shares this view of the Lord's Prayer as late as 1889: see, Errett, *Evenings With the Bible: New Testament Studies,* Volume III (Cincinnati: Standard Publishing Company, 1893), p. 206.

[77] *Christian System,* p. 177.

[78] The connection between evangelism and mission is especially linked in Dunnavant's "Evangelization and Eschatology," pp. 43-54.

[79] For Campbell's quote on church unity, in the previous paragraph, see Campbell, "Millennium and Prophecy, No. 1," *Millennial Harbinger* (January 1857): 26. For the quote immediately preceding this footnote, see "The Three Kingdoms," p. 557. See also "Query," p. 12.

[80] "The Three Kingdoms," 557-558. The Lunenberg letter is found in *The Millennial Harbinger* (September 1837): 411f. See also *Christian System,* p. 233, which is a rewriting of this 1829 essay in the *Christian Baptist.* In this section of *Christian System,* Campbell talks about the "three kingdoms" and "three salvations." Obedience is emphasized throughout *Christian System.* See, for another example, p. 241. In the book, Campbell rewrote the indented quote above to be a little less explicit about the "infants, idiots, deaf and dumb persons, innocent Pagans wherever they can be found, with all the pious Pedobaptists" who he said "we commend to the mercy of God." See p. 233.

[81] *Christian System,* p. 187.

[82] See "The Three Kingdoms," p. 558. Elsewhere on this page: "But if the justified draw back, or the washed return to the mire, or if faith die and bring forth no fruits—into the kingdom of glory he cannot enter. Hence good works through faith, or springing from faith in Jesus, give a right to enter into the holy city—and this is a

right springing from grace or favor....And while men are saved by grace, or brought into the second kingdom, (for all in it are said to be saved in the New Testament style) by favor, they cannot enter the heavenly kingdom, but by patient continuance in well doing."

[83]See also *Christian System,* p. 176, where the quote immediately preceding this reference and the following quote are found: "But the remission of our sins, our adoption into the family of God, our being made heirs and inheritors of the kingdom of glory, are consequent upon faith and the obedience of faith.... the creature may throw away that life by refusing to sustain it by the means essential to its preservation and comfort."

[84]This, contrary to Hughes, *Reviving the Ancient Faith,* p. 94.

[85]For Campbell's use of this term, "everlasting kingdom of God," see, for example, *Christian System,* p. 161; and "Query," p. 12.

[86]*Christian System,* p. 147. See also p. 154.

[87]See Boring, *Revelation,* pp. 47-51, for a brief definition of these various "types of interpretation."

[88]See "Coming of the Lord, no. 25," *Millennial Harbinger* (July 1843): 293. Campbell greatly appreciated the scholarship of Moses Stuart. When Stuart adopted the "German Professors' interpretation of prophetic times," Campbell stated: "I never was more disappointed in reading any treatise on prophecy, than in perusing that of Professor Stuart."

[89]See Boring, *Revelation.*

[90]See Campbell, "Coming of the Lord, no. 2," *Millennial Harbinger* (January 1841): 5-6.

# 6

# THE SACRAMENTS
## "ENJOYMENT OF THE PRESENT SALVATION OF GOD"

---

*Any sceptic, of little ingenuity, may attempt to turn faith, or testi-
mony, or baptism, or the Lord's supper, into ridicule, because of
the ignorance that is in him. All Christian ordinances are but
means of grace, and each and every one of a special grace peculiar to itself; so that no one can be substituted for another, or
neglected, without the lack, or loss, of the blessing in the Divine
will and grace connected with it.*

Alexander Campbell,
*The Millennial Harbinger* (December 1855)[1]

---

## Introduction

Alexander Campbell is the single most important figure in the development of early Disciples sacramental theology. One should, however,
recognize from the beginning that Alexander Campbell refused to use
either the word *sacrament* or the word *eucharist* when talking about either baptism or the Lord's supper. He claimed that both these names
were of "human origin." Proclaiming that one should speak of "Bible
things by Bible words," Campbell preferred to use the word *ordinance* to
describe these two events.[2] Though the word *ordinance* does appear in
the Bible, it never appears there in reference to either baptism or the
Lord's supper. Campbell, however, believed that Jesus Christ "ordained"
or "instituted" both baptism and the supper. For that reason, he utilized
ordinances, and, occasionally, institutions to refer to them.

Campbell's concern with finding God's design for the church led to
his attempts to define those things Christ ordained for the church. He

137

regarded Christ's ordinances as essential for the proper ordering of the church's life. Without proper attention to them, Christians would be unable to restore the ancient pattern. And, in Campbell's view, there were more than merely two ordinances. Christ ordained preaching, fasting, prayer, and the confession of sins as much as he ordained baptism and the Lord's supper. All of these activities served, in Campbell's words, as "means of our individual enjoyment of the present salvation of God."[3]

Campbell's substitution of ordinance language for sacramental language was really more a semantic change than a substantive one. Though he talked of more than two ordinances, he defined the word *ordinance* in much the same way other Protestants defined the word *sacrament.* For later Disciples, however, avoidance of sacramental language assumed more substantive content than Campbell ever intended by it. Late-nineteenth- and early-twentieth-century Disciples generally emptied Disciples theology of its earlier understanding of the ordinances as a means of grace. For them, sacramental language indicated a fascination with magical formulas and the priestly authority associated with the church's power to dispense or withhold God's grace at its own will.

In their overreaction to such language, later Disciples began to lose Campbell's own understanding of the importance of the ordinances as the modes through which "the grace of God acts upon human nature."[4] Disciples scholars have demonstrated rather convincingly that Alexander Campbell's theological concerns regarding the ordinances stood squarely in the Reformed tradition.[5] Alexander Campbell, after all, was a Presbyterian before he was a founder of the Disciples, and the Presbyterians, as indicated in the Westminster Confession, used the word *ordinance* interchangeably with the word *sacrament.*

Campbell never intended, in his refusal to use the word *sacrament,* to deny that God acts through the ordinances to communicate the divine grace of God's forgiveness. "We teach, and have always taught," wrote Campbell in 1855, "that the Holy Spirit works upon the understanding and affections of saints and sinners, by and through his word and ordinances."[6] This thoroughly Reformed view of the ordinances as a means of grace received through faith is not a view lay Disciples hear much today. But it was a theme sounded clearly by most of the early Disciples leaders. Further, it was consistent with their emphasis on the communal nature of the church and upon the work of the Holy Spirit in the life of the church.

It is within the context of this general discussion of Campbell's emphasis on the ordinances as means of grace that one may arrive at an understanding of the theological meaning of baptism and the Lord's supper in early Disciples tradition. Early leaders, however, experienced difficulty communicating the richness of this meaning even to their own congregations. At one point, as early as 1832, Barton Stone lamented

the way people approached the Lord's supper: "I fear the common remark is too true, that very little solemnity and devotion is manifest in the
celebration of this ordinance among our brethren."[7] Does this remark
hold true for Disciples today, not only for the supper, but for baptism as
well? Are these two sacraments taken for granted today? Have Disciples
lost the rich meaning once associated with these sacraments? Some Disciples think so. If they are right, uncovering the traditional theological
heritage in these areas might lead Disciples to a revitalized appreciation
for what these acts accomplish and represent in the life of the church.

## *Baptism*

### The Beliefs and Practices of the Founders

When his daughter Jane was born on March 13, 1812, Alexander
Campbell made a decision that altered the course of Disciples history
dramatically. As he thought about her impending baptism, he started
more seriously to question the biblical foundations of infant baptism.
Prior to this point, both of the Campbells had expressed some awareness
that infant baptism had no real scriptural precedent, but neither of them
had chosen to make it an issue.

When Thomas Campbell spoke to a group of Christians in the home
of Abram Altars a few summers earlier (1809), he had ended his remarks with the words "Where the Scriptures speak, we speak; where the
Scriptures are silent, we are silent." One of those gathered, Mr. Andrew
Munro, believed such a motto meant the end of infant baptism. At that
time, the elder Campbell did not believe that to be the case, but he was
willing to stand by the motto even if it were to have those kinds of
consequences. Later (1811), when three members of the newly established Brush Run Church refused to participate in the Lord's supper
because they had not been baptized, Thomas Campbell agreed to immerse them. He performed their baptism by immersion even though he
had not been baptized in this manner himself. By his remarks, it is clear
that he opposed any form of rebaptism, but, at the same time, he believed baptism by immersion probably constituted the most biblical form
of baptism.

Alexander Campbell felt much the same way his father did about
baptism. Infant baptism might not be the best baptism, but it was baptism
nonetheless. In June 1811, the younger Campbell put it this way: "As I
am sure it is unscriptural to make this matter a term of communion, I
let it slip. I wish to think and let think on these matters."[8] Yet after Jane
was born, Campbell's restudy of the baptism question led him to
conclude that infant baptism could not really count as true baptism.
Therefore, he decided not to baptize Jane. He also concluded that all
those who had been sprinkled as infants needed to experience biblical

baptism. Since infant baptism was no baptism, Campbell reasoned, the immersion of adults who had been sprinkled as infants was not really rebaptism. Instead, it constituted their first true baptism.

This momentous conclusion changed the course of Disciples history. On June 12, 1812, a Baptist preacher baptized both Campbells, their spouses, and three other members of the Brush Run Church. With this act, the Campbells and their followers proclaimed that the restored church depended upon a particular form of baptism. All other baptism was no baptism at all. Their earlier potential for large-scale unity with other Christian movements now evaporated. Where the form of baptism had been a matter of opinion, it now became a matter of law. Since only the Baptists practiced the proper baptism, their group offered the only immediate hope for Disciples who sought progress in their search for Christian unity. When Campbell's Reformers entered Baptist life, they had no way of predicting how stormy their new relationship would become.

By the time the storm finally erupted, Campbell and other leaders among the Disciples had become acquainted with Barton Stone and the numerous congregations of Christians associated with one another under his leadership. Though there were differences between them, especially in areas related to baptism, the Lord's supper, and authority in ministry, compromises were reached quickly. The two groups gravitated toward one another. On the baptism question, Campbell's views carried the day. Prior to merging with Campbell, Stone preached immersion for the remission of sins, but both he and his congregations advocated the admission of the unimmersed into church membership. Campbell's approach to baptism ultimately led Stone to question his own inconsistency between preaching one thing and allowing a different practice to prevail in the congregational setting. On the other hand, Stone's tolerance for the unimmersed remained important throughout his life. He refused to say that immersion was necessary to salvation, and, as time would show, Campbell eventually joined him in that opinion. Stone, however, certainly held it with more conviction than did Campbell.

Alexander Campbell's initial concern for the nature of baptism turned on the questions of its proper "action" and its proper "subject." Both these questions have to do with the form of the sacrament. How and upon what subject was baptism to be performed? At first, he was most interested in finding the proper way to perform baptism. His commitment to restorationism naturally led him to this concern. If the church hoped to be restored, it must do things like the primitive church did them. Campbell's commitment to unity also led him to this concern. If congregations and denominations were to be united, they must have a unified witness in their performance of baptism.

Campbell concluded that immersion was the proper "action" and that only a believer could be the proper "subject." It is, in fact, a misnomer to refer to the Disciples understanding of baptism as "adult immersion." It is, rather, "believers' immersion." Only those individuals, wrote Campbell, who express "repentance towards God, and faith in Christ— are the proper subjects of this ordinance." When congregations prepared to immerse "proper subjects," they were fulfilling the New Testament form of baptism.[9]

This overriding desire to deal with "form" questions has a long history in Disciples life. Occasionally, in fact, it seems as if Disciples are much more concerned with "form" than they are with "meaning." This is particularly true for the history of the sacraments in Disciples life, especially where congregational life is concerned. Most congregations throughout Disciples history have been deeply concerned with maintaining the proper form of the sacraments, but few congregations have spent equal energy engaging questions related to their proper meaning.

Though Alexander Campbell began with the question of form (both in terms of "action" and "subject"), he quickly moved on to the question of meaning, what he referred to as the "design" of baptism. In fact, when he considered which of these was the most important, the form or the meaning, he said quite clearly that the "*design* of this institution has long been thrown into the shade because of the wordy and impassioned controversy about what the *action* is, and who may be the proper *subject* of it." And in his view, the design constituted "the only value of it." In his 1853 book on the topic of baptism, he stressed the importance of the meaning of the institution in these words:

> Now, it must be confessed that, whatever importance there may be in settling these questions, that importance is wholly to be appreciated by the *design* of the institution. This is the only value of it. The question concerning the value of any action is incomparably superior to the question, What is the act itself? or to the questions, Who may perform it? or, Upon whom may it be performed? We are, therefore, induced to believe that the question now before us is the all-interesting important question—indeed, the transcendent question in this discussion.[10]

Campbell summed up the meaning of baptism by offering the phrase "baptism for the remission of sins."[11] Because of this summary, Campbell's detractors often accused him of holding to a magical understanding of baptism, as well as to a kind of "works righteousness" with regard to salvation. When Campbell addressed baptism and salvation, he often sounded as if salvation depended on a mechanistic process rather than a divine act. Nevertheless, he saw the process as God's process, dependent upon God's grace, not human action, for its power and effect. Ultimately, this is why Campbell had to admit that even people baptized as infants could be saved.[12]

Campbell must have worn out several pens trying to help his readers understand that "baptism for the remission of sins" meant, not a baptism unto salvation, but rather, as *The Christian System* expressed it, "a formal, distinct and specific absolution, or release from guilt." He stated emphatically that baptism "has no abstract efficacy." On this point, he offered his strongest argument against infant baptism.

> Without previous faith in the blood of Christ, and deep and unfeigned repentance before God, neither immersion in water, nor any other action, can secure to us the blessings of peace and pardon. It can merit nothing.[13]

In putting the matter this way, Campbell did not intend to say that God did not act meaningfully in baptism. Nor was he willing for baptism to be regarded as "a mere ceremonial introduction into the church—a way of making a profession of the Christian religion." If that view of baptism had been intended by God, wrote Campbell, the precept associated with baptism would have been "repent and be baptized, every one of you, for admission into the church."[14]

Campbell, like Luther and Calvin before him, instead insisted that baptism was one of the "indispensable provisions of remedial mercy." "Baptism," Campbell explained, "is a sort of embodiment of the gospel; and a solemn expression of it all in a single act." In other words, penitent believers are the recipients of a divine action in baptism. In the act of baptism, God makes "a solemn pledge" and offers "a formal assurance" that sins are forgiven. Christians "are thus publicly declared forgiven, and formally obtain the assurance of our acceptance and pardon, with the promised aid of the Holy Spirit to strengthen and furnish us for every good thought, and word, and work."[15] For Campbell, as Clark Williamson has stated it, baptism "is a sign of God's grace toward us and a way of our saying 'yes!' to that grace."[16]

There were social or communal dimensions to Campbell's understanding of baptism as well. He did not presume it to be purely an individual act affecting only the penitent believer who underwent baptism. It was, first and foremost, a public act. Baptism occasioned the remission of all past sins, through faith in Christ, and Christians are "publicly declared forgiven."[17] Part of baptism's inherent meaning has to do with its *public* declaration of God's forgiveness and grace offered in Christ. Baptism, through its identification with the burial and resurrection of Christ, focuses the hearts and minds of those present on Christ alone, the source of human salvation.

Second, in baptism the participant is adopted by God, "born into the Divine family."[18] In contrast to the Baptists and some others around him, Campbell ultimately did not link baptism with the accomplishment of membership in a local congregation. Instead, he asserted that baptism completes one's adoption into the family of God, the church in all times and all places. Baptism seals the penitent believer to the body of Christ; it operates as a sign of the participant's permanent separation from all other tribes or peoples. In common with all other Christians present, the believer's baptism accomplishes a "separation to God," which in turn unites that believer with all other Christians, both in past and present time.[19] As the "Preamble" to the Disciples *Design* puts it, "Through baptism into Christ, we enter into newness of life and are made one with the whole people of God."

These two aspects of the corporate dimension of baptism, the public declaration of God's forgiveness and the welcoming of the subject into the family of God, have often been neglected by contemporary Disciples. Occasionally, one might even hear of a Disciples minister who has consented to the performance of a private baptism, set in a context outside the worship life of the congregation and restricted in attendance to only the immediate members of the family. Such private baptisms nullify completely this very important communal aspect of the meaning of baptism, and for that reason are, under normal circumstances, best avoided.

Campbell's emphasis on baptism as a "separation to God" also spoke to the ethical implications of baptism. One of the "consequents" of baptism, wrote Campbell, is "sanctification," defined as "the act of separating a person or thing from a common to a special and spiritual use." For Campbell, there was "a natural and necessary connection" between baptism and sanctification. While sanctification depends entirely upon faith, "repentance and baptism are severally essential to the exhibition, development, and perfection of the Christian."[20]

The major force in accomplishing sanctification is the work of the Holy Spirit. "Of this separation or sanctification to God," as Campbell put it, "the Holy Spirit…is the personal agent and author, his word the instrument, and the blood of Christ, apprehended and received by faith, the real, cleansing, and purifying means."[21] Though the talk of "agent" and "instrument" and "means" can become confusing, the ethical result of baptism was clear to Campbell: the Christian who emerges from baptism should demonstrate a changed character. Separated to God and enrolled in the family of God, the baptized Christian is empowered by the Holy Spirit to turn full attention to the service of God in all areas of personal and social life.

For some Disciples theologians, Campbell's emphasis on the meaning of baptism, in all its individual, communal, and ethical aspects, has had considerable importance. For others in the life of the tradition, Campbell's emphasis on proper form has seemingly outweighed his emphasis on proper meaning. Even for Campbell himself, form questions took on such an importance that he found it difficult, if not impossible, to relate his deeper theological insights concerning baptism to any tangible expressions of the unity of the church during the remainder of his life. Throughout the first half of the twentieth century, several Disciples scholars (like W. E. Garrison, Frederick D. Kershner, Charles Clayton Morrison, and William Robinson, to name a few) have delved into the question of meaning in baptism and written about it.[22] None of their efforts, however, ever resulted in a denominational reexamination of the issue. Today's renewal of baptismal theology among Disciples really resulted from other factors.

**Baptism Among Disciples Today**

Recent ecumenical conversations have produced two important documents that occasioned renewed Disciples activity in the area of baptismal theology. First, in 1982, the World Council of Churches' Faith and Order Commission published its remarkable text, *Baptism, Eucharist, and Ministry* (BEM), for reception by churches the world over. Second, two years later, the Consultation on Church Union (COCU) published *The COCU Consensus: In Quest of a Church of Christ Uniting*. Disciples scholar James O. Duke participated directly in the preparation of this latter document. These two publications, as noted in chapter four, have been received and studied by Disciples.

These ecumenical discussions have led Disciples to a renewed appreciation for the meaning of baptism as set forth in Alexander Campbell's early writings. Further, the historical and critical scholarship developed after Campbell have led today's Disciples to recognize more honestly the shortcomings in traditional Disciples understandings of baptism. The Disciples Commission on Theology (related to the Disciples Council on Christian Unity), after studying the historical and theological baptismal tradition among Disciples in light of the recent ecumenical convergence, published a document entitled "A Word to the Church on Baptism." This 1987 report is described as "an emerging theology of baptism among Disciples." Affirmed by the delegates to the 1987 General Assembly in Louisville, Kentucky, the report has been recommended to Disciples congregations across the country for study. The Commission's report revisits some of the old Disciples' baptismal territory, while, at the same time, it breaks new ground. It has resulted in at least four important principles that help to define modern Disciples baptismal theology.[23]

1. *The baptismal theology represented within "A Word to the Church on Baptism" marks a thoughtful return to the tradition of Alexander Campbell.*

In order to facilitate discussion among Commission members, Clark Williamson prepared a lengthy study of the Disciples baptismal tradition. His study offered a critical appraisal of the thought of the founders, especially that of Alexander Campbell. The Commission's report affirmed Campbell's theological approach to the meaning of baptism.[24] It stressed that Campbell's approach to baptism was firmly rooted in both the New

Testament witness and the Reformed theological tradition. With these two sources operating as resources, Campbell defined baptism as dependent upon God's grace. Along with his recognition of the priority of God's action in baptism, Campbell equally emphasized the need for a meaningful and "faith"-ful human response to God's grace.

In his critical appraisal of Disciples tradition, Williamson assessed the relative appropriateness of Campbell's entire baptismal theology. After first emphasizing the strengths of Campbell's understanding, he treated the apparent weaknesses of Campbell's position. Williamson pointed to five specific weaknesses in Campbell's thoughts about baptism: (1) Campbell failed to deal with the entire biblical witness, largely excluding the experiences and models of the Jewish people. (2) Campbell made immersion, the "action" of baptism, too prominent in his overall understanding. Though he emphasized "meaning" as the "only value," his legalistic mind-set concerning immersion often overshadowed the deeper theological insights he had to share. (3) Campbell's preoccupation with immersion, when combined with his belief that all other churches were "sects," sharply inhibited his ability to pursue unity. (4) Campbell's restoration emphasis, and his view of the biblical witness, caused him to overlook the diversity of the early Christian communities, even with regard to baptism (see 1 Cor. 1:10–17). And (5) Campbell expressed too much confidence that immersion, almost by itself, would lead to the development of a church distinct and separated from the world.[25]

The Commission, in its report, also noted other problems developed in later years. Shortly after the death of Alexander Campbell in 1866, Disciples leaders moved into a phase marked by both a misunderstanding of Campbell's theological positions and a tendency to become more concerned with dogma than grace. Building on Campbell's own emphasis on immersion, Disciples in this later period, sometimes known as the period of "Disciples' scholasticism," made immersion the only issue in baptism. Immersion assumed the status of law. Many Disciples came to assert that there was no salvation without immersion, turning baptism into a "good work" upon which salvation depended. The report acknowledged that remnants from this more legalistic posture remain in some portions of Disciples life today.

In order to speak to this issue, the members of the Commission point out that the New Testament witness with regard to immersion is more diverse than previously supposed. A critical reading of the New Testament sources also reveals a greater concern for "meaning" than for either "action" or "subject." The discovery of the *Didache* just seven years after the death of Campbell illustrates even more the difficulty of claiming that immersion was the only early form of baptism. This early-second-century document testifies to the acceptability of a threefold baptismal affusion (pouring water over the head three times) in the name of the

Father, Son, and Holy Spirit. Probably written even before a few books of the New Testament, the document indicates that immersion, though normally preferred and performed in running water, was not the only baptismal practice acceptable to Christian churches.

2. *An increased understanding of baptism as "sacrament," "an expression of God's grace in a visible sign," led the Commission on Theology to "recognize that both infant and believers' baptism can be authentic practices in the one church of Jesus Christ."*

Following the understanding reached in both the BEM and COCU documents, members of the Commission recognized that baptism is characterized by "two essential elements—divine grace and human response." The report emphasized that both infant baptism and believers' baptism reflect some of each of these elements, "but each practice also risks the loss of part of that full meaning." Infant baptism, while bearing powerful witness to the sole authority of God's grace in constituting human salvation, tends to downplay the importance of human response. Believers' baptism, while stressing the need for an individual commitment to God, tends to "minimize the priority of God's grace." While both practices fall short of providing the fullness of meaning embodied within the act itself, both also provide a witness, as the BEM document puts it, to "God's own initiative in Christ and express a response of faith made within the believing community."[26] Therefore, though this report acknowledged that, among Disciples, believers' baptism is the "normative (standard) practice," it also called for the recognition of infant baptism as an acceptable and meaningful alternative form of baptism.

Today, most Disciples congregations practice open membership. All Christians, upon a profession of their faith and some form of baptism, are accepted to congregational membership. Disciples membership policies are now more in line with Alexander Campbell's definition of what makes one a Christian: "But who is a Christian? I answer, everyone that [sic] believes in his heart that Jesus of Nazareth is the Messiah, the Son of God; repents of his sins, and obeys him in all things according to his measure of knowledge of his will."[27]

Yet the report leaves unaddressed one of the important implications of its recommendation to accept infant baptism as a legitimate alternative to believers' baptism. These days, as a result of their changing perspective toward open membership, Disciples face a new challenge. It is not too unusual to find members in Disciples congregations who have children baptized as infants in other denominations. While infant baptism stresses the initiative of God's grace in salvation, the "full fruit of baptism" (as described in the BEM document), requires a personal response from the recipient of baptism, usually expressed in churches practicing infant baptism at the point of confirmation. Ecumenical dialogue has emphasized the church's responsibility to nurture the development of baptized infants until such time as they are able to express their personal commitment to Christian faith.

The public nature of the act of confirmation marks an important stage of faith for the person baptized as an infant. It symbolizes both a self-conscious identification with the church and a personal affirmation of God's gracious act in baptism. Disciples congregations need to be able to provide a meaningful ceremony equivalent to that of confirmation for those who were baptized as infants. As members of the one church, Disciples are responsible for the nurture and confirmation of those baptized infants who come to them from other traditions. Disciples should remain aware of this responsibility, or they will be faltering in the fulfillment of their role as members of the church. As Disciples fulfill this responsibility, they will also enjoy a rediscovery of the truth that all forms of baptism require a responsible program of Christian nurture.

3. *Following Campbell's understanding that baptism is "God's gift of grace," and recognizing that infant baptism is a legitimate form of baptism, the members of the Commission also endorsed the ecumenical realization that "baptism is to be administered only once."*

Both the BEM and COCU documents discussed the question of rebaptism and reached the conclusion that rebaptism is an inappropriate activity. The Report of the Commission indicated four reasons why the prohibition of rebaptism is necessary: "(1) since baptism depends on God's grace and not simply on the 'readiness' or 'worthiness' of the person, rebaptism calls into question what God has done in that moment (whether or not we 'remember' it); (2) rebaptism questions the sacramental integrity of other churches; (3) baptism marks incorporation into the one church and not simply into any one denomination; and, (4) baptism is not a momentary experience, but marks the beginning of a lifelong growth in Christ."

The biggest difficulty with this ecumenical understanding occurs at the point of a genuine pastoral concern. Occasionally, ministers meet with individuals who are anxious about their personal experience of having had a conversion experience after baptism. Some of these persons request rebaptism. Ministers can spend time counseling these individuals regarding the meaning of their baptism. In spite of the fact that these individuals cannot remember it, infant baptism demonstrated the reality of God's grace working in their lives, even leading them to the point of their later conversion experience. The Commission recommends that ministers become familiar with liturgical ways to reaffirm the baptismal faith for these individuals, without repeating the baptismal sacrament itself. Such services are valuable not only for those who have been baptized as infants, but for those who were baptized as believing adults as well. The Council on Christian Unity for the Christian Church (Disciples of Christ) maintains copies of renewal services developed in recent years.

4. *Following ecumenical understanding, and reaffirming the pattern established by Alexander Campbell, the "Word to the Church on Baptism" stresses that baptism "should be administered, whenever possible, during public worship."*

Baptism offers an important teaching opportunity to the congregation as it performs the act. Today, many Disciples congregations baptize only once a year, at Easter time. Often, that service is held on a Sunday afternoon rather than during the regular worship hour. Such a pattern is unfortunate since many committed members of the church, under these conditions, rarely witness baptism. As the report states, "baptism is…an important teaching opportunity during which the whole community may be encouraged to deepen its understanding of what it means to be Christian." Part of this understanding lies in the relationship between sacrament and service. Baptism in the midst of the worshiping community offers the opportunity to remind those gathered that there is an intimate connection "between baptism and participation in God's mission in and for the world."

An important aspect of the meaning of baptism emphasizes the separation of the newly baptized individual to God and to the family of God, represented by those present at worship. If few members of the congregation witness the baptism, the richness of this aspect of its meaning is quickly diluted. The need for continuing Christian nurture of those the church baptizes, and the accompanying pledge among those present to participate in that nurture, also makes it desirable that baptism take place within the context of the worshiping community. Finally, baptism itself may serve as an opportunity for those present to reaffirm their own baptismal vows. If baptism is conducted outside the confines of regular worship, many members will be denied the opportunity to reaffirm the rich meaning of their own baptisms.

## The Lord's Supper

### The Theological Context

On Pentecost Sunday in 1943, just under twenty-two months before the Germans put him to death in Flossenbürg for his resistance to Hitler, Dietrich Bonhoeffer, the well-known German theologian, sat in his prison cell and composed a letter to family and friends. He told them he had been thinking about the joyfulness of God's Spirit, and how the reality of silent prisoners "pacing up and down in their cells" served as such a contrast to that joyfulness. "If I were a prison chaplain here," he wrote, "I should spend the whole time from morning till night on days like this, going through the cells; a good deal would happen." The next morning, before he had finished his letter to them, he received the Pentecost gift they had sent to him. He searched for a way to describe what its arrival meant to him. The only expression he could find was sacramental:

I really cannot tell you what happiness such things give one. However certain I am of the spiritual bond between all of you and myself, the spirit always seems to want some visible token of this union of love and remembrance, and then material things become the vehicles of spiritual realities. I think this is analogous to the need felt in all religions for the visible appearance of the Spirit in the sacrament.[28]

In Bonhoeffer's words, one quickly discovers a depth of meaning that transcends the simple act of remembering. Something else is going on here. Using the sacramental analogy, he is trying to say he experiences something *real* in this Pentecost gift. The material gift somehow actually conveys the spiritual reality. The sacramental quality Bonhoeffer describes means more than mere memory or thoughtful recollection; it conveys an actual experience of present grace.

Throughout the history of Christianity, Christian theologians have struggled over the theology of the sacramental experience associated with the Lord's supper. That long struggle has produced several distinct views about what actually happens at the Lord's supper. Is Christ physically present in the elements (the bread and wine) themselves, or simply spiritually present in the act of communing with one another? Is Christ really present at all? Not only have Catholics and Protestants had difficulty finding agreement on any of these points, but even Luther, Calvin, and Zwingli, all leaders of the Protestant Reformation, failed to reach complete agreement among themselves on these points.

Among Protestants, the debate has always been one centered on whether or not the supper is to be celebrated primarily as "memorial" or, alternatively, as an act in which the bread and cup actually become means of grace, communicating the present action of God by conveying the present spiritual grace of Jesus Christ to the participants in some real way. There have been some differences between Protestant traditions holding to the second view, but they have generally agreed on a central emphasis on the "real presence" of Christ in the sacrament. Until more recent years, efforts to move these two groupings of Protestants, those who emphasized "memorial" and those who emphasized "real presence," toward consensus have proven unsuccessful. The success of the reception of *Baptism, Eucharist, and Ministry* (BEM), however, revealed that a new day has dawned. Ecumenical dialogue has now achieved considerable consensus regarding this aspect of the Lord's supper.

In some ways, the new ground results from articulating a fuller appreciation for the early understanding of the Greek word *anamnesis*, the word used for "memorial" in the Bible. Its meaning in the Bible,

Christians within the ecumenical movement argue, carries more depth than simply to suggest "memory." Early Christians understood the word *anamnesis*, when connected to the sacrament, to carry with it an understanding of living communion with the resurrected Christ, and an active recalling of that Christ to the present mind and heart. The past collapsed into the present. Therefore, BEM emphasized that the "biblical idea of memorial as applied to the eucharist refers to this present efficacy of God's work when it is celebrated by God's people in a liturgy....Christ himself with all that he has accomplished for us and for all creation...is present in this anamnesis, granting us communion with himself."[29] Such an understanding of "memorial" has narrowed considerably the gap that once existed between the "remembrance" Protestants and other Protestants who defend "real presence."

In the second generation of Disciples, the emphasis on memorial became the predominant one. Disciples of this generation, however, did not emphasize this understanding of the term *anamnesis*. Instead, in the tradition of Zwingli, they emphasized mostly the "remembrance" aspect of the supper, nearly to the complete exclusion of any recognition of the present action of God in the table. The emphasis for them was upon the emblems of the table as reminders of the *past* action of God in Christ. This tended to rob the Lord's supper of its ability to act in the present as a specific embodiment of the gospel offered in our time, not some past time. The approach of late-nineteenth-century Disciples to the table also tended to emphasize human action over divine action. The person who remembered the past sacrifice of Christ could also renew her or his strength to follow Christ.

In contrast to Zwingli, and to the practices of many nineteenth- and twentieth-century Disciples congregations, Luther and Calvin stressed the immediacy of God's activity of grace in the Lord's supper. For them, the supper did not evoke merely a call for devotional human action, but rather represented an active demonstration of the love of God in Christ. Campbell's own view of the supper emphasized this activity of God in the supper. Today, Disciples are recovering this deeper meaning of the action of God and the presence of Christ in the Lord's supper. Ecumenical dialogue has occasioned a greater appreciation for the earliest Disciples tradition on this question.

### The Recovery of the Early Tradition

For Campbell, as pointed out early in this chapter, the ordinances of the church were not limited to just baptism and the Lord's supper. His list of the ordinances included the Lord's Day, preaching, the reading and teaching of the scriptures, prayer, fasting, ordination, and even marriage. All these things were ordinances because they served as the modes through which the grace of God acts upon human nature. "All the ordinances of Christianity," he wrote, "are means of grace."[30] They constitute "the indispensable moral means of spiritual life and health."[31] The action of God in the Lord's supper, wrote Campbell in *The Christian Baptist* in 1825, "inscribes the image of God" upon every Christian's heart.[32]

As is evident here, when Campbell talked about the meaning of the Lord's supper, he began with an emphasis on divine action, not human action. He emphasized somewhat more clearly than contemporary Disciples that it is God who acts and it is we who receive. The Lord's supper, for Campbell, was more than mere remembrance, more than just a symbol that Christ is present in worship. It dramatically demonstrated that God was acting in the very midst of the gathered community. In the supper, God, through the Holy Spirit, acts to convey the reality of divine forgiveness and acceptance to all human beings. For Campbell, the Lord's supper participated in the church's proclamation that God forgives sinners.

Campbell did not believe that the elements of bread and wine ever underwent any magical transformation. Neither did he have a mechanistic understanding of the role of either the bread or the wine, as if grace were poured through them into the human body. They were nothing but bread and wine. But he did believe in the importance of the role of the Holy Spirit in acting through the symbols of bread and wine for the good of the development of Christian character.

The Holy Spirit works in the Lord's supper to provide assurance for Christians that the grace of God has saved them. The Lord's supper acts out the story of God's love in such a way that Christians discover the root of their identity. They learn who God is (the one who loves). They learn who Christ is (the one through whom we understand ourselves as loved by God). They learn who they are (the ones loved by God).[33]

The role of the Holy Spirit in the Lord's supper brings up another aspect of the traditional theological debate surrounding this sacrament. The debate among "real presence" Protestants, the Roman Catholic community, and the Eastern Orthodox community has centered on how the presence of Christ becomes effective and real. This discussion has turned on the "invocation of the Spirit." The Greek word in question is *epklesis* (to call upon). Is there some special moment in the Lord's supper when Christ's promised presence arrives, and is it due to the repetition of certain words or formulas expressed in the form of prayers? In its commentary, the BEM document expressed the differences in this way:

> Some are content merely to affirm the presence without seeking to explain it. Others consider it necessary to assert a change wrought by the Holy Spirit and Christ's words, in consequence of which there is no longer just ordinary bread and wine but the body and blood of Christ. Others again have developed an explanation of the

real presence which, though not claiming to exhaust the significance of the mystery, seeks to protect it from damaging interpretations.

Without attempting to define the specifics of the role of the Spirit,
BEM affirmed "the indissoluble union between the Son and the Spirit."
Making it clear that the sacrament should not be regarded as either
"magical" or "mechanical," the ecumenical convergence represented in
BEM asserted:

> The bond between the eucharistic celebration and the mystery of
> the Triune God reveals the role of the Holy Spirit as that of the One
> who makes the historical words of Jesus present and alive. Being
> assured by Jesus' promise in the words of institution that it will be
> answered, the church prays to the Father for the gift of the Holy
> Spirit in order that the eucharistic event may be a reality: the real
> presence of the crucified and risen Christ giving his life for all hu-
> manity.

BEM has demonstrated that most Christian groups are coming to
understand the importance of prayer in the observance of the Lord's
supper. At least one element of the church's prayer needs to speak to the
role of the Holy Spirit. As BEM stated it, "The church, as the community
of the covenant, confidently invokes the Spirit, in order that it may be
sanctified and renewed, led into all justice, truth and unity, and empowered to fulfill its mission in the world."[34] The "Word to the Church on the
Lord's supper," presented to the 1991 Tulsa General Assembly by the
Disciples Commission on Theology, stressed the importance of this aspect of prayer at the table. It urged elders and others who pray at the
Lord's supper to include a petition for the presence of the Holy Spirit.
The document also suggested that it is "appropriate in communion prayers
to focus on our remembrance of the sacrifice of Jesus Christ, our antici-
pation of God's ultimate victory, our awareness of the presence of Jesus
Christ among us, and our appreciation for the richness of meaning con-
veyed by the Lord's supper."[35]

With Luther and Calvin, Campbell believed the grace mediated by
the ordinance is received only by faith. God announces God's love at the
table. Will Christians understand themselves in relation to it? Will it
make a difference in their lives? Reformed Protestantism, and Campbell
along with it, has always asserted that faith is necessary for the announcement of God's love to make a difference in the life of the individual.
Modern Disciples scholars are stressing this aspect of the supper once
again as well. As James Duke has phrased the matter, "apart from faith
ordinances have no efficacy; a promise that is not believed conveys no
assurance."[36]

For modern Disciples, therefore, the divine action present in the supper is accompanied by the call to human response and action. Some Christians in history have turned this scenario upside down by demanding that certain human actions were necessary prior to approaching the table. Anxious Christians often wondered whether they were worthy of participation in the Lord's supper. Through the history of Christianity, various norms of ethical conduct were attached to Paul's comment about examining oneself in order to avoid unworthy participation at the table. Campbell, for his part, viewed the issue of worthiness more in a Calvinist sense than a Catholic one.

John Calvin claimed that those Christians personally convicted by a sense of their own misery and unworthiness were the ones who were truly ready to hear the good news of the supper, for they represented those who realized most clearly that their salvation came from outside themselves. They longed to be fed and found "their proper nourishment in the Lord's supper." "In fact," Calvin wrote, "what mockery would it be to go in search of food when we have no appetite?"[37] These words were enormously freeing for all those Christians during Calvin's time who knew that they were unrighteous and would never be able to stand before God if they had to do so on their own accord. Campbell sounded these Calvinist themes himself when he wrote:

> Is not this ordinance a cordial for restoring the languishing, strengthening the week [weak], recovering the sick, and reviving the dying believer? How reasonable, then, is it to argue that languishing, weak, sick, and dying believers must not have it often administered to them, just because they are not in perfect health?[38]

Consistent with their emphasis on the divine action present in the supper, and with their belief that all who are hungry should be fed, Campbell and other early Disciples came to emphasize that it was the Lord's table, not ours. This theological affirmation stands behind the historic Disciples tradition of the "open" table. The tradition of the open table does not have its roots in Campbell, but rather in Stone. Stone, after his break with Presbyterianism, opened participation at the table to all those who confessed Christ. For a time, Campbell barred from the table those who had not been immersed as believers.

Because he approached the Lord's supper through his understanding of its place in the life of the church, Campbell had a difficult time supporting the concept of an "open" table. Around 1830, he chastised Barton Stone for requiring immersion for membership but not for participation at the table. "If this be not to build up with one hand and pull down with the other," he wrote of him, "I have yet to learn how a person can be guilty of such an inconsistency."[39] Campbell's concern for the restored church and its purpose in history made it difficult for him to open the table to those who had not been baptized by immersion as believers. As time passed, however, Campbell's position changed. The logic of his own understanding of salvation demanded the affirmation that God's grace operated independently of the mode of one's baptism. Campbell's increasing awareness that there were Christians among the "pious unimmersed" led him to the practice of the open table. How could the church bar from the table those the Lord had accepted into the kingdom?

In earlier Disciples history, the open table communicated the message that Disciples of Christ did not bar participants from the table because they were baptized by other baptisms. Today, the open table communicates the theological commitment to see ourselves as part of the one church. The table in most Disciples congregations, however, is not totally open. The history of Christianity, as well as Disciples history, has traditionally restricted from the table all those who are not baptized. The church has regarded baptism as a sacrament of incorporation into the life of the church and the Lord's supper as a sacrament of nurture. Therefore, the ecumenical church has understood baptism as a necessary prerequisite for the Lord's supper.

In some Disciples congregations today, children who were baptized as infants sit in worship next to children who are not yet baptized. The baptized children are welcome to participate in communion. Those who have not formally joined the church by making a profession of faith and undergoing baptism, an event that usually transpires around the sixth grade for most Disciples children, are not invited to participate. Some children begin to view baptism as the act that makes one "worthy" to participate in the supper.

One of the problems with this dilemma is the way it is resolved in the congregation. Many congregations simply let the parents decide what they will do with their children. This is in keeping with the Disciples tradition of freedom, but these parental decisions are rarely made with reference to conscious theological reflection. The resulting inconsistencies do not make sense to the children affected most by them. And children, like adults, like for faith to be reasonable. Other congregations, guided by the ecumenical position on this point, simply tell parents and children that baptism must precede participation in the supper. Theological reflection often does not play a part in this decision either.

*On the one hand,* if we honestly believe, as I do, that our children are members of the family of God, even though they are not yet baptized, then on what theological foundation do we bar them from the very celebration of the church that addresses unity for that family? The very act of God at the center of our worship life, which announces God's love and acceptance to all, at the same time, from the perspective of our children, is an act that excludes them. *On the other hand,* if we allow our children to partake of communion without baptism, we create a rather sticky ecumenical problem. History and tradition dictate against it. Our theology of baptism is one of "incorporation," and our theology of the supper is one of "nurture." Incorporation, says the history of Christian tradition, precedes nurture.

The problem remains. Most congregations among us are solving it pragmatically. Whatever seems to work best to avoid undue tension usually wins out. This is not a new dilemma. It has been with those congregations practicing believers' immersion from the very beginning. For some Disciples congregations, however, it has become more acute as both unbaptized and baptized children comingle in the worship life of our congregations. For children, this separation process at the table is at once both clear (based on baptism) and confusing (does God accept the baptized child more than me?).[40]

The 1991 Disciples "Word to the Church on the Lord's Supper" supports the traditional and ecumenical view. Whatever congregations ultimately do with this issue, they need to do it by considering thoughtfully and carefully the theological arguments supporting both sides. The decision in every location, no matter what the decision, should be one that seeks a consistent and theological understanding of the gospel through serious dialogue with scripture, the ecumenical church, and the whole of Christian tradition. Serious theological dialogue on the question can only serve to enrich the worship life of the congregation.

The importance, in Disciples tradition, of mature faith cannot be ignored either. Campbell believed the most important element of human action related to the Lord's table had nothing to do with demonstrating righteousness or any other prerequisite for participation at the table. Rather, he emphasized both a personal and a social response to the supper, both arising from faith. On the personal side, Campbell asserted that Christians, in receiving the elements, were saying to God: "Lord, I believe it. My life sprung from thy suffering; my joy from thy sorrows; and my hope of glory everlasting from thy humiliation and abasement even to death." In other words, at the Lord's supper, by faith, the Christian receives the love of God as expressed through the life of Christ. Here the Christian responds to the message carried in the words of institution (Mt. 26:26–29; Mk. 14:22–25; Lk. 22:14–19, or 1 Cor. 11:23–26), that are read at every celebration of the Lord's supper. These biblical words provide a vivid picture of the meaning of the sacrament.

In this personal encounter with God in Christ in the supper, Campbell asserted that Christians confront their own participation in sin. As Campbell expressed it, "Every time the disciples assemble around the Lord's table, they are furnished with a new argument also against sin, as well as with a new proof of the love of God. It is as well intended to crucify the world in our hearts, as to quicken us to God, and to diffuse his love within us." At the very point when our own identification with sin in the world is made so crystal clear to us, at that moment God extends the grace of the bread and the loaf to us and conveys a message of forgiveness and acceptance. All this in spite of our complicity in the sin that placed Christ on the cross. As Campbell put it: "This institution commemorates the love which reconciled us to God, and always furnishes us with a new argument to live for him who died for us."[41]

The question of how Christians "live for" Christ turns toward the social side of the meaning of the supper. Participation in the supper required identification with the whole community of faith and brought to mind the corporate hope of God's final victory over all the contingencies of history. At the same time, it reminded the church that the healing of creation was not yet complete; Christians, suffering together with Christ, must face their responsibility to stand with those affected by continuing injustice in the world. This identification, hope, and call to responsibility was symbolized through each Christian's offering of the bread and the wine to the neighbor. In Campbell's words:

> Each disciple, in handing the symbols to his fellow-disciple, says, in effect, "You, my brother, once an alien, are now a citizen of heaven; once a stranger, are now brought home to the family of God. You have owned my Lord as your Lord, my people as your people. Under Jesus the Messiah we are one. Mutually embraced in the Everlasting arms, I embrace you in mine: thy sorrows shall be my sorrows, and thy joys my joys. Joint debtors to the favor of God and the love of Jesus, we shall jointly suffer with him, that we may jointly reign with him. Let us, then, renew our strength, remember our King, and hold fast our boasted hope unshaken to the end."[42]

This emphasis on the "family of God" also reinforced the early Disciples emphasis on Christian unity. The supper not only reconciles us with our neighbors, it brings us into relationship with all Christians in all times and in all places.

This belief helps to explain why Campbell and Stone were so dogmatic about the use of just one loaf during the Lord's supper. Campbell argued that 1 Corinthians 10:17 ("Because there is one loaf, we, the many, are one body; for we are all partakers of that one loaf") emphasized the unity of the loaf as a picture of the unity of the church.[43] Barton Stone agreed when he pointed out that the broken bread represented the broken body of Christ, and "Christians united in one body are joint partakers of it." "In the Lord's supper," wrote Stone, "there should be but one loaf, to represent the Lord's body that suffered on the Cross—two or more loaves destroy the very idea of the ordinance, as not representing the one body of Christ suffering and dying."[44]

Not only did they insist that only one loaf be used, but Campbell and Stone agreed that the loaf must be visibly broken during the Lord's supper. Campbell's preferred name for the Lord's supper was, in fact, "the breaking of the bread." As Campbell put it,

> If a loaf is put upon the table, cut or broken, as is the custom in most of the religious sects, the primary idea in the supper is not represented by the partakers. There is no representation of *the breaking of the body* of Jesus. There may be a representation of communion on the broken body; but no symbol of the sacrifice of Christ — no commemoration of the breaking of his body....There can be no exhibition of the breaking of the body of Jesus, if the loaf is broken before the disciples assemble around the Lord's table.[45]

Drawing upon this tradition, the recent Disciples "Word to the Church on the Lord's supper," received by the General Assembly in Tulsa, emphasized that "how we conduct the Lord's supper may have the effect of heightening or diminishing our experience of its meaning." The document asked Disciples congregations to consider setting "aside the sterile practice of using tiny, individual, and pre-cut pieces of bread and little cups of juice or wine in favor of loaves of bread that can be broken in the sight of all the congregation and cups that can be filled and then shared either by dipping or sipping." This practice would better enable a congregation to see the supper as

> a visible and tangible reminder that God's self-revelation occurs in and through earthly media. God condescends to meet us where we are, on earth, and as we are, creatures who are taught and powerfully moved by our sensory experiences. When at the Lord's supper the breaking of bread, the pouring of wine, and the sharing together of food which sustains us are joined with God's Word of Good News and the power of the Spirit, we are nourished by the love of God in Jesus Christ and through that love are made one with another and with the church universal.[46]

Ever since that first celebration of the Lord's supper at Brush Run Church in 1811, the Lord's supper has been central to Disciples church life. This strong history of centrality has enabled Disciples, through their theologians, to assume a prominent place in ecumenical discussions concerned with the liturgical renewal of Protestantism. But among Disciples, there has been no real agreement on what the centrality of the supper really meant theologically. Everyone agreed on its central role in worship, but through Disciples history, not many congregations have contemplated the supper's theological centrality and what that centrality might suggest in terms of their order of worship.

The sample orders of worship found in the writings of Alexander Campbell, Walter Scott, and Robert Richardson all seem to indicate that the early pattern mostly placed the Lord's supper after the "teaching," and the offering after the Lord's supper. Yet most of these early Disciples said plainly that nothing "prescribed" any particular order.[47] Near the end of the nineteenth century, many American churches began to emphasize preaching over sacrament and made the sermon the culmination of the worship service. Many Disciples congregations changed their order of worship to fit the emerging emphasis on preaching. In the twentieth century, the trend is to return to the earlier tradition. Only this time, Disciples are doing so with a greater sense of the theological significance of the supper as the central focus of their worship service.

As the 1991 "Word to the Church" explained, this return to an order where the supper's centrality is pictured by its role as the culmination in worship more accurately follows the general Christian tradition since apostolic times. Theologians throughout history have been fairly explicit about the theological foundations for their placement of the Lord's supper in worship. Calvin and Luther both stressed the link between the Word and the Lord's supper. The Word prepared the heart to be receptive to the meaning of the sacrament. The "Word to the Church" summarized the reason why this order has been the traditional one in the life of the church:

> The reading and preaching of the Word of God calls forth among those who worship a decision for or rededication to the life of faith. Thereafter the faithful approach the Table to make and receive a sign and seal of the Gospel, to commune with the Savior Christ Jesus and all of his disciples, and to receive from this spiritual food new strength and vitality for undertaking our calling of Christian service in the world. Thus the supper is the fitting climax to our public worship.[48]

No one can pretend to prescribe to Disciples congregations the proper ordering of their worship services. All congregations should, however, approach the order of their worship services in a theological frame of mind. What does the way we order our service say about the way we see the Spirit of God acting in our midst? What does it say about how the human being responds to that action of God's spirit? Whatever a Disciples congregation decides about questions related to its order of worship, it should work hard never to lose the great joy of the Lord's supper that, for Campbell, was so much of the reason he regarded it as central to the life of the church. Read these words of Campbell from 1825—they seem especially fitting for a Lord's supper meditation on some Disciples heritage Sunday morning:

With sacred joy and blissful hope [one] hears the Savior say, "This is my body broken—this is my blood shed for you"....While [the breaking of the bread] represents...all the salvation of the Lord, it is the strength of...faith, the joy of...hope, and the life of...love. It cherishes the peace of God, and inscribes the image of God upon [the] heart, and leaves not out of view the revival of [the body] from the dust of death, and its glorious transformation to the like-ness of the Son of God. It is an institution full of wisdom and good-ness, every way adapted to the Christian mind. As bread and wine to the body, so it strengthens...faith and cheers [the] heart with the love of God. It is a religious feast; a feast of joy and gladness; the happiest occasion, and the sweetest antepast on earth...that mor-tals meet with on their way to the true Canaan.[49]

## Conclusion

When Alexander Campbell approached either baptism or the Lord's supper, he saw himself dealing with much more than a question of how or in what way they should be performed by the church. He consistently displayed a deep theological interest in the connection between this act in worship and the identity of the church itself. One of the recurrent themes of Disciples history is the belief that the *true* church of Christ really appears only during those moments when it points beyond itself to the sovereign God of redemption and creation.[50] For Campbell, the visible church had its whole identity wrapped around the redemptive activity of God in history. Baptism and the Lord's supper, in the thought of Campbell, were both testimonies to that reality.

When Campbell sought to define his understanding of these sacra-ments, he went first to apostolic tradition as he found it in scripture. He also sought the witness of the church through time. The early Disciples practice of the sacraments reflected a strange mixture of "Catholic," "Re-formed," and "Free Church" elements in combination with one another.[51] As the recent "Word to the Church" put it, "early Disciples drew upon the resources of scripture and tradition alike in order to direct the churches to worship practices and teachings which would do justice to the funda-mental theological significance of the Lord's Supper."[52]

When modern Disciples of Christ seek to renew sacramental life within their congregations, they are *not* seeking to "restore the true Campbellian practice." Rather, they recognize the need for the theology behind, or meaning transmitted by, the form and practice of their sacra-ments to maintain continuity with the witness of the apostolic period. In the spirit of Campbell, they want their practices to reflect a proper conti-nuity with the apostolic understanding of the action of God in and through human history. This early commitment among Disciples remains with them still. In the present, in fact, it is being revived.

## Questions for Reflection and Discussion

### Baptism

1. As you think through the history of reflection and action pertaining to baptism among Disciples, what would you pick as two major turning points and why? In other words, what two events or developments within Disciples life changed the course of Disciples life in some significant way? What has changed? What are the continuities that remained in spite of the immensity of the changes?

2. If not addressed specifically in the answer to question #1, how have the theological understandings of baptism changed among Disciples from the days of the founders to the present? What is different about the four principles that help to define modern Disciples theology?

3. If it is true that "all forms of baptism require a responsible program of Christian nurture," how does your congregation address Christian nurture in relationship to the topic of baptism (baptism classes, Sunday school sessions focusing on the meaning of baptism in relationship to the Christian life, other events)? In what specific ways does your congregation address the nurture and confirmation of those children in your midst who were baptized as infants?

### The Lord's Supper

1. It might be helpful to place this discussion in the context of the Reformers' views (Luther, Calvin, Zwingli) because, in some ways, Alexander Campbell was indebted to them.

2. What words are used to describe the table in your congregation (Lord's table, Lord's supper, sacrament, ordinance, eucharist, communion)? What particular theological understandings are lifted up or emphasized by the name you use to describe this particular aspect of your worship? If you were asked to describe the "sacramental theology" operating in your congregation, what major points would you mention? What avenues within the congregation are regularly utilized to talk about the meaning of the supper to the life of the church? Do worship committees regularly address these questions? Sunday school classes?

3. After reading this chapter, how would you outline the major features of a Disciples theology of the Lord's supper?

4. What is the relationship between form and meaning in your practice of the supper? For example, what symbols or symbolic actions (crackers, cut or uncut bread, a chalice, individual cups, actual breaking of bread, passing of bread, intinction, etc.) are used, and how are they understood as helping to emphasize the meaning of what we do when we partake in the supper?

5. What does your congregation's treatment of unbaptized children in relationship to the table say theologically? (For example, is it purely a

parental decision? Is it conscientiously treated as a theology of incorporation and a theology of nurture approach? Is it conscientiously understood as a theology of inclusion of all members of the family of God?)

6. The conclusion of this chapter quotes Clark Gilpin's observation that "the true church appears only during those moments when it points beyond itself to the sovereign God of redemption and creation." How does the design of your congregation's worship service enable this kind of happening? What does the way you order your service say about the way you see the Spirit of God acting in your midst? What does it say about how the human being responds to that action of God's spirit?

## *Notes*

[1] *The Millennial Harbinger* (December 1855): 678.

[2] Alexander Campbell, *The Christian System* (Cincinnati: H.S. Bosworth, second edition, 1866), p. 125.

[3] *Ibid.*, p. 174f.

[4] *The Millennial Harbinger* (January 1843): 9.

[5] Clark M. Williamson, "The Lord's Supper: A Systematic Theological View," *Encounter* 50 (Winter 1989): 47-67; Clark M. Williamson, *Baptism: Embodiment of the Gospel*, "The Nature of the Church: Study Series 4 (St. Louis: Christian Board of Publication, published for the Council on Christian Unity, 1989); James O. Duke, "The Disciples and the Lord's Supper: A Historical Perspective," *Encounter* 50 (Winter 1989): 1-28; and Richard L. Harrison, Jr., "Early Disciples Sacramental Theology: Catholic, Reformed, and Free," in Kenneth Lawrence, ed., *Classic Themes of Disciples Theology: Rethinking the Traditional Affirmations of the Christian Church (Disciples of Christ)*, pp. 49-100.

[6] *The Millennial Harbinger* (May 1855): 258.

[7] *Christian Messenger* (September 1832): 280.

[8] Quoted in Garrison and DeGroot, *The Disciples of Christ: A History*, p. 160. For other aspects of this story, see pp. 140 and 158-161.

[9] Campbell, *The Christian System*, p. 57.

[10] Campbell, *Christian Baptism: With Its Antecedents and Consequents* (Bethany, Virginia: printed and published by Alexander Campbell, 1853), p. 248.

[11] *Ibid.*, p. 249f.

[12] See, for example, what has become known as the "Lunenburg Letter," in *The Millennial Harbinger* (September 1837): 411f.

[13] *The Christian System*, p. 58.

[14] *Christian Baptism*, p. 256.

[15] *Ibid.*, pp. 246-247, 257, and 256.

[16] Williamson, *Baptism: Embodiment of the Gospel*, p. 37.

[17] See *Christian Baptism*, p. 256.

[18] *Christian Baptism*, p. 276.

[19] *Ibid.*, see pp. 274-277.

[20] For the importance of sanctification, see *Ibid.*, p. 285f. These other quotes are found on pp. 274 and 275.

[21] *Ibid.*, p. 286.

[22] See, for example, William Robinson, "The View of Disciples or Churches of Christ," in Roderic Dunkerly, ed., *The Ministry and the Sacraments* (London: SCM Press, 1937).

[23]The Commission's "Word to the Church on Baptism" report is published in Williamson, *Baptism: Embodiment of the Gospel,* pp. 46-60.

[24]Williamson's research was ultimately published under the title *Baptism: Embodiment of the Gospel.*

[25]See Williamson, *Baptism: Embodiment of the Gospel,* p. 38f. For a fuller treatment of these weaknesses, see Clark M. Williamson, "Disciples Baptismal Theology," *Midstream* 25 (1986): 200-223.

[26]*Baptism, Eucharist, and Ministry,* p. 12.

[27]*The Millennial Harbinger* (September 1837): 411.

[28]Dietrich Bonhoeffer, *Letters and Papers From Prison* (New York: Macmillan Company, Fourth Printing, 1971), p. 36.

[29]*Baptism, Eucharist, and Ministry,* p. 19.

[30]Alexander Campbell, *Christian Baptism: With Its Antecedents and Consequents* (Bethany, Va.: Printed and Published by Alexander Campbell, 1853), p. 259.

[31]*The Millennial Harbinger* 7 (January 1843): 9.

[32]*The Christian Baptist* (August 1, 1825): 175.

[33]I am indebted to Clark Williamson for this description of the Lord's Supper; see Clark M. Williamson, "The Lord's Supper: A Systematic Theological View," p. 55f.

[34]*Baptism, Eucharist, and Ministry,* p. 22.

[35]See Report 9113, "A Word to the Church on the Lord's Supper," *Business Docket and Program: General Assembly of the Christian Church (Disciples of Christ) in Tulsa, Oklahoma, October 25-30, 1991,* pp. 296-303. This quotation is from p. 302.

[36]James O. Duke, "The Disciples and the Lord's Supper: A Historical Perspective," p. 4.

[37]John Calvin, *The Institutes,* in *John Calvin: Selections from His Writings,* ed. and with an introduction by John Dillenberger (Missoula, Montana: Distributed by Scholars Press for the American Academy of Religion, 1975), p. 518f.

[38]*The Christian System,* p. 318.

[39]*The Millennial Harbinger* (October 1830): 474.

[40]See Colbert S. Cartwright's discussion of this subject in *Candles of Grace: Disciples Worship in Perspective* (St. Louis: Chalice Press, 1992), chapter six.

[41]*The Christian System,* p. 310f.

[42]*Ibid.*

[43]*Ibid.,* p. 305. The translation is Alexander Campbell's (*Living Oracles*). See also Richard Harrison's excellent article, "Early Disciples Sacramental Theology," which discusses these points on p. 73f.

[44]*Christian Messenger* (September 1828): 261-262.

[45]*The Millennial Harbinger* (April 1834): 96.

[46]"A Word to the Church on the Lord's Supper," p. 302-f.

[47]Colbert S. Cartwright deals with this question in his unpublished essay, "Disciples Worship on the American Frontier," pp. 22-30. See also *Candles of Grace,* especially chapter three.

[48]"A Word to the Church on the Lord's Supper," p. 301.

[49]Campbell, *The Christian Baptist,* 3 (August 1825), p. 175. I have, as may be deduced by the ellipses and the brackets, made these changes in the text in order to give attention to a more inclusive style of language for those who might like to use this quotation in a worship setting.

[50]This is a point made by W. Clark Gilpin in "The Integrity of the Church: The Communal Theology of Disciples of Christ," p. 36f.

[51]See Harrison, "Early Disciples Sacramental Theology: Catholic, Reformed, and Free."

[52]See "A Word to the Church on the Lord's Supper," p. 297.

# 7

# FROM MANY ELDERS TO ONE MINISTRY

*Within the church the fundamental ministry is that of Jesus Christ whose servanthood, offered to God in behalf of humanity, defines and gives character to all ministry exercised in his name....By baptism all Christians are inducted into the corporate ministry of God's people and by sharing in it fulfill their own callings as servants of Christ.*

"Policies and Criteria
for the Order of Ministry in the
Christian Church (Disciples of Christ)"[1]

## Introduction

Notions of ministry among Disciples, like all other aspects of their life and thought, were not immune to change. Disciples, as one generation has passed to another, have demonstrated a rather remarkable ability to adapt and adjust to meet the needs of changing times. But this characteristic has also been present within generations; and it also must be understood as an asset of the first generation. The story of the Disciples understanding of ministry indicates, perhaps more clearly than any other topic, just how adaptable the earliest leaders could be.

Previous chapters have explored several smaller examples of that adaptability. Disciples demonstrated from the outset their ability to speak in the language of the time and location in which they lived. The rising individualism of the American western migration helped to shape the Disciples commitment to individual biblical interpretation and believers' immersion. The confusing reality of American denominationalism helped

163

Disciples develop a sense of urgency from which they forged commitments to restorationism, ecumenism, and an open celebration of the Lord's table. This interaction with their culture and the prevailing moods of their time led to their rapid growth and development as a distinct group of Christians in America.

That rapid growth, however, brought with it new and unforeseen problems. Still other problems resulted from the changing cultural setting in which Disciples found themselves after the 1830s. To relieve the pressure these circumstances occasioned in their congregational life, Disciples made adjustments in their understanding of ministry. Though the adjustments were subtle at first, and largely determined by "expedient" circumstances, they did set Disciples feet on a path of significant change. Disciples had no way of knowing it at the time, but these adjustments were but the first step toward joining the Protestant mainstream.

To gain a clear picture of the development of the current Disciples understanding of ministry, it is helpful to divide the history into four periods. Each period possessed its own special characteristics and provided some aspect of the necessary foundation for the wider perspective of ministry developed in subsequent periods. As readers will no doubt recognize, the residue of emphases from past periods still remains among us.

## *1801–1835: Congregational Elders*

If there is one thing that the first generation bequeathed to the remainder of Disciples history, it is the importance of the laity and its role in ministry. This emphasis grew from the natural soil of the frontier. The ethos of those days, as previous chapters have indicated, naturally encouraged the development of leaders from among the people. These leaders tended to be optimistic and, in a sense, blind to their own limitations as leaders. Their optimism, connected with incredible energy, found expression in their tireless efforts to reform—or, perhaps better, transform—every aspect of the religious institutions of their day. They offered new hope to tired souls. Their message carried the promise of newly discovered self-worth for those who came within earshot of it.

Their field of ministry seemed endless. It is hard for us to imagine today but, around 1800, only about 40 percent of the population (using optimistic figures) had even a nominal relationship to the church. The majority of citizens were unchurched. Restoration preachers knew this situation offered them the golden opportunity to establish a new majority of church members by creating new Christians with the message of the primitive gospel, or, as Walter Scott preferred to call it, the "true gospel." By 1835, nearly 75 percent (again, using optimistic figures) had become related to the church.[2] This growth in the American attachment to church life demonstrates a significant enhancement of the importance of church among the citizens of the nation. Success belonged to those who could reach the common people, and who better to do that than converts from among the common people? Disciples, from their very beginning, attracted that kind of preacher.

This general elevation of the importance of the common individual on the frontier resulted in an accompanying large-scale revolt against the power of professional people in society. Truth rested not in the educated and philosophical ruminations of those who practiced the professions, but rather in the results of the arguments waged in the arena where public opinion held sway. People viewed "official" authority with great suspicion.

The cultural trend toward disestablishment also contributed to this anti-professional attitude, especially as it related to the clergy. The "official" separation of church from state was still in its infancy in most places. In fact, Connecticut, New Hampshire, and Massachusetts still had vestiges of legal establishment until 1818, 1819, and 1833 respectively. Old style religious leaders had depended upon the state for support of their ministries. New style religious leaders had to depend upon their powers of persuasion.

Disciples formulated their approach to ministry in this new environment. Born in the midst of this very important historical transition between establishment and disestablishment, Disciples realized the importance of defining a new understanding of ministry for a new age in history. Barton Stone and Alexander Campbell both shared in the more general cultural distrust of the old-line authority in the more established denominations. But their distrust took different forms.

Barton Stone concentrated his complaints in the area of Presbyterian judicial power. Newell Williams has pointed out that Stone "charged Presbyterians with violating their own standards." Presbyterian practice denied the right of any church judicatory to make new laws. They could only enforce the rule of scripture. Stone, and the other signers of the "Last Will and Testament," with good evidence backing them up, charged that the Presbyterian judicatory under which they served had made new laws and used them to bolster its own authority. In the years that followed the dissolution of the Springfield Presbytery, Stone often wrote of his belief that no conference of ministers ought ever "to make laws for the rule and government of the churches."

Yet in most other ways, Stone's view of the ordained ministry differed very little from official Presbyterianism. The office of bishop (synonymous, for Stone, with "pastor" or "elder" as was the case in the Presbyterian tradition) served the local congregation as the preacher. The bishop also administered baptism and the Lord's supper, and exercised church discipline. The "ruling elder" constituted the second office of ministry and served as an assistant to the bishop, but was not allowed to

preach or officiate at the table. Stone never clearly defined his understanding of the office of deacon. Presumably he accepted the Presbyterian view that the deacon should care for the needs of the local congregation and tend to those who were in material need.[3]

Stone and his Christian congregations had a higher view of ministerial authority than the one to be found among the Disciples. Each congregation ideally had a settled minister who alone had the power to
preach and officiate at the Lord's table. Further, the power of ordination
did not rest in the congregation, but rather rested in the ministry itself.
Stone's journal addressed this question in 1827 when the church at Flat
Run recommended one of its members for ordination. The congregation
raised the question, "by whom shall this brother be ordained?" Stone
printed the congregation's report in the *Christian Messenger:*

> After mature deliberation on the subject, it was agreed that as we
> have no account in the New Testament of ordination to the ministry
> being done by the church alone, or by the church in conjunction
> with the eldership, but that as we have particular accounts of it
> being done by the eldership or presbytery, therefore, the eldership
> alone with the recommendation of the church, had the authority to
> ordain, when they concurred with the church in regard to the quali-
> fications of the person to be ordained.[4]

The Christians, therefore, established a conference of bishops (ministers)
charged with the authority to ordain new ministers. The conference of
bishops, however, had no authority to place ministers. That authority
rested solidly in the congregation.

After the union between Christians and Disciples took hold, the views
of Barton Stone on ministry receded into the background and were replaced by those of Alexander Campbell. Campbell, the more overpower-
ing personality of the two, had definite opinions about what the ministry
of the church ought to be. He shared in the general anticlericalism he
found around him. Some of this anticlericalism could have arisen from
his concern for the struggling congregations all around him. Many of
them were without ordained ministry and were therefore unable to celebrate the Lord's supper. In fact, due to their higher view of ordained
ministry, many of the Christian congregations associated with Stone did
not have a weekly Lord's supper for precisely this reason. In cases like
these, where congregations suffered due to what Campbell perceived as
unhealthy deference toward clerical status, Campbell railed against the
clergy and advocated lay administration of the ordinances "when circumstances demand it."[5]

The fact that he led a new religious movement also probably contributed both to his advocacy of the cause of the laity and his
anticlericalism. His congregations had no educational institutions with

which to train clergy. The only real pool of ministers available to the movement rested in the uneducated, untrained laity. More than likely, these and other aspects of the cultural milieu served to reinforce views he had held for some time. He and his father came out of the Secession Presbyterian tradition of Scotland, well known for its opposition to the Catholic and Anglican episcopacy. This sentiment probably took root in both Campbells. Later, due to rough treatment at the hands of various Presbyterian and Baptist authorities, both men developed an accompanying antipathy toward the notion of clerical authority in general.

Campbell's early comments on the clerical profession, coming from his days as editor of *The Christian Baptist*, were caustic, and, according to his biographer and friend, Robert Richardson, those comments somewhat "alarmed" his father.[6] Though his attacks concerning the "arrogance of the clergy" and "the haughtiness of their pretensions"[7] attracted large numbers of readers for his journal and new members for his congregations, he planted an anticlerical seed that took root and grew to be a contributing factor in the division of the movement in the next generation. On the positive side of the ledger, his attack on the "hireling clergy" served to enrich the Disciples commitment to the empowerment of the laity.

The preachers opposed by Campbell were, by and large, the settled and salaried preachers of the various denominations. They were those preachers who had been trained for ministry, authorized by some hierarchical authority, and then sent forth to find a suitable location to exercise their ministry. They were a class of ministers who stood apart from the needs of the frontier. Their education did not prepare them for the context of ministry on the frontier, and they were usually unwilling to offer support for the popular religious movements common among the people in that area. Instead, they tended to support a stable society where clear lines of authority, usually their own, operated. They were most comfortable in locations of order and decorum. They also emphasized their "special calling" to ministry. Campbell did not believe such a calling, even if true, justified claims to special authority. In short, in Campbell's view, "clergy" stood on ceremony rather than Christian commitment. To emphasize his point, he created and published a rather lengthy satirical essay in the style of scripture, which he titled "The Third Epistle of Peter." Excerpts demonstrate both his views on clergy and his sense of humor:

> And let your dwelling places be houses of splendor and edifices of cost; and let your doors be decked with plates of brass....Let your fare be sumptuous, not plain and frugal as the fare of the husband-man who tills the ground; but live you on the fat of the land...."In all your gettings," get money! Now, therefore, when you go forth on

your ministerial journey, go where there are silver and gold...for
verily I say you must get your reward....And when you shall hear
of a church that is vacant and has no one to preach therein, then be
that a call to you, and be you mindful of the call, and take you
charge of the flock thereof and of the fleece thereof, even of the
*golden* fleece. And when you shall have fleeced your flock, and
shall know of another *call* and if the flock be greater, or rather if the
fleece be greater, then greater be also to you the call.[8]

Campbell's view of the ministry set forth three offices: the bishop (or
elder), the deacon, and the evangelist. The first two of these offices were
absolutely restricted to the congregational realm. The third traveled and
preached with the support of a particular local congregation. None of the
three offices was considered to be portable. In other words, an ordained
minister from one congregation could not serve another congregation
without that congregation performing its own ordination ceremony.

Campbell's elders, preferably a plurality of elders in each location,
had total control of the congregation's governance and ministry. One of
them would be appointed the "president," and would assume the primary role of ministry for the congregation. The other elders would assist
in ministry, including such functions as administration of the table and
taking care of matters of discipline as they arose. In most cases, only the
president assumed full-time ministry and received compensation, while
the other elders assumed their roles as part-time volunteers.

Campbell's theology of baptism emphasized that every Christian,
once baptized, became a minister. For this reason, he held that ministry
for the congregation arose from among the laity. Elders did not cease to
be laity once they were ordained; they merely represented the laity in
their function as ministers for the congregation. Campbell's view of the
ministry as one that resided in the gathered community of the laity has
acted as a buffer against ministerial claims to self-sufficiency in Disciples
life. Disciples tradition has consistently realized, thanks to Campbell, that
ministry is dependent upon the gathered congregation of the faithful and
has no independent existence of its own. Disciples have also emphasized
that the life of the community itself is grounded in the life and work of
Christ. And the life and work of Christ is grounded in God. Ministry has
no meaning apart from these realizations. This pyramid of dependencies
has helped to maintain among Disciples a recognition that all ministry,
lay and ordained, has its ultimate foundation in God's gracious act of
redemption.

Campbell's understanding of ministry, as emphasized by his definition of the role of the evangelist, recognized the peculiar nature of the
social setting in which he found himself. The context of the disestablished
church in America forever changed the way the Christian churches could
think about ministry. Formerly, all citizens in a given community were

members of the church automatically, from the time of their birth forward. But, in America, no officially sanctioned parish system existed after disestablishment.

Campbell recognized that this development created two publics the church had to address through ministry.[9] On the frontier, the largest public stood outside any conscientious identification with the family of Christ. The smaller public identified with various congregations. Campbell divided his order of ministry so as to take seriously both of these two publics. The church continues to exist in the midst of these two publics, not only in its proclamation of the gospel, but in its application of that gospel to address the activities and institutions of a public largely apathetic about issues related to justice.

Evangelists, as Campbell defined their role, preached the gospel to the unconverted and established new congregations. They also assumed oversight of congregational spiritual needs until such time as leaders from within the life of the congregation could be trained. In many cases, evangelists maintained pastoral oversight for a time even after congregational elders were ordained.

Though Campbell had the highest regard for the laity as ministers, he still emphasized the need to set some members of the laity apart to perform the special functions of ministry. These laity were ordained by the congregation for that purpose. Those who were thus set apart, dependent upon their gifts, were entrusted with the care of preaching (ministry of word) and the administration over matters pertaining to both baptism and the table (ministry of sacrament). According to Campbell, other lay persons were to perform these functions *only* when ordained elders were unavailable to perform them.

Campbell's conception of the elder differed from our current understanding of the term. For Campbell, the elders (occasionally referred to as bishops) *were* the ordained ministers of the church. They were the people empowered by the congregation to perform the general function of ministry and to fulfill its accompanying role of oversight over the religious community. It was only during the second period that expediency dictated a different formulation of the role of elders in the congregation.[10]

## 1835–1870: Elders Associated with the State or Region

During these years, the frontier areas where Disciples had originated changed considerably. Settlements grew closer together. What had once been largely agricultural territory took on urban characteristics. A middle class of merchants and shopkeepers began to emerge. Wealth began to accumulate. The ratio of farmers to city dwellers in America decreased steadily from 1800 to 1850. The cultural lag between the frontier areas moving out toward the Middle West and industrialized eastern locations began to disappear. Communication improved. All these changes affected the religious development taking place in the territory.

Disciples grew numerically during these years. The geographic area they covered began to increase considerably, especially in the years immediately following the 1832 union of the Christian and Disciples movements. Many Disciples families followed the expanding western lines of the frontier, taking their faith with them. In the next three decades, Disciples grew from approximately 22,000 members to over 190,000 members. This growth was at a rate about four times greater than the growth of the nation's general population.[11] As these frontier areas settled down, so did Disciples. They began to come to a sense of their own identity as a community of people. Their leaders concentrated on developing the relationship between the Disciples mission and the new reality of their situation.

Taking advantage of the improved communication possibilities, congregations began to keep in better touch with one another. Campbell's *Millennial Harbinger*, beginning in 1830, rapidly increased circulation over the old *Christian Baptist*, his previous journal. Disciples leaders became anxious that, as the movement spread, aberrations might appear in the movement that would discredit its fundamental purposes and goals. They longed to keep lines of communication open in order to instruct new churches and ministers in the meaning of the restored gospel. To be a Disciple meant something. Disciples stood for particular principles (interpretive, restoration, ecumenical, eschatological), and those who cared for the integrity of the movement wanted to do what they could to maintain those principles. Leaders felt a sense of urgency to hold things together.

As a by-product of this concern, the importance of education intensified during this period. Leaders believed a proper education would produce a new generation of leaders who could help ensure the Disciples future. Both Walter Scott and Alexander Campbell were involved in this concern for education. Walter Scott served briefly in 1836 as president of the first Disciples college, Bacon College (later Transylvania University). In 1840, Alexander Campbell, who had always advocated education for ministers (though not the pretense that often accompanied it), secured a charter for Bethany College to be "a seminary in learning." For the remainder of his life, he dedicated a major portion of his days and nights to the educational enterprise he set in motion at Bethany. Over 209 known colleges and 205 institutes or academies have been founded over the years by Disciples of Christ.[12] From the 1840s on, education became a feature of central importance in the formation of Disciples character.

Part of this Disciples concern for education grew out of the recognition that a second generation of Disciples needed to be trained in the ways of faith. Many in the first generation had been converted in the heat of revivals or mass meetings. Due to changes on the frontier, such meetings were rarer and less likely to attract crowds. As Disciples congregations found themselves in a more stable environment, they took on more stable characteristics. Emotional revivals fell into the background in favor of protracted meetings where the reasonable aspects of faith (following the example set forth by Campbell and Scott) could be discussed at great length. Over time, education became a subtle substitute for jolting conversions. Children grew up in the congregation, never really knowing anything but church life.

Methodists and Baptists were experiencing the same kinds of developments as Disciples during these years.[13] Because of their stronger institutions, however, they were a few decades faster in their evolution than the Disciples were. Each of these three groups possessed a strong work ethic and a moral sense of obligation to be responsible. As a result, many of their poorer early followers eventually accumulated wealth and used it to build bigger and fancier churches.

All three groups moved toward the development of a more regularized clergy during this period. Candidates for ministry were encouraged to seek a theological education and then were hired as settled pastors for congregations they had never held membership in before. By the end of this period, these educated ministers attracted more professional types of people upon whose wealth the congregation came to depend. Over time, the presence of impoverished people in the urban congregations became rather rare, not because there weren't any in the community, but because the message preached in the churches seemed to address different concerns than they had. Further, not too many people invited them to feel much at home among the middle class when they did attend church.

Many of these developments, especially as they intensified after the Civil War, were at the heart of the later division between Disciples and the Churches of Christ.[14] As Disciples in the more urbanized areas moved toward a regularized ministry and congregational life, dissent began to surface, especially in the rural areas of Disciples life, where comfortable assets were still the exception rather than the rule. McAllister and Tucker comment in their general history that those who could not afford settled clergy hired from outside the congregation were gratified to realize there were none mentioned in the Bible.[15] To be fair, however, one needs also to recognize that these dissenters had the early writings of Alexander Campbell to fall back on as well. After Campbell's death, many second-generation ministers hardened his earlier views into dogma. Therefore, the controversy was more widespread than can be entirely laid at the doorstep of economic, social or class differences. Some who were able to afford settled pastors and fancy organs still opposed them based upon both their understanding of the movement's history and their reading of the Bible. The leadership among Disciples was changing.

A fundamental shift occurred in the practice of Disciples ministry during these years. In the first period, congregations largely generated a ministry from within their own confines of church life. Their elders had no rights of ordination beyond their own congregations.Toward the end of the second period, presiding elders, or preachers, presented themselves to the congregation as educated and qualified to serve. They were largely called to congregations from the outside. Some congregations had difficulty finding elders from among their own gathered communities who were willing to serve full-time. They could, however, afford to bring one in from the outside. This important shift likely originated in the great need for ministers during this period, but no doubt the developing educational enterprise among Disciples also contributed to it, as did both the success of this kind of ministry in other American Protestant churches and the increased complexity of culture itself.

This shift necessarily included the willingness to recognize the legitimacy of elders prepared for ministry in other locations. It became a matter of trust between congregations who shared a common heritage. Increasingly realizing the importance of such trust, Campbell began to assert as early as 1836, in his *Christian System*, an understanding of Christian ministry not all that different from conceptions of many of the denominations he had spent earlier days attacking.[16] In the 1840s, he began to emphasize that the mission of the wider church needed greater attention than could be provided by individual congregations acting on their own. He knew Bethany College needed a fairly wide base of support if it were to survive. He had no doubt, either, that his college helped to fulfill the general mission of the church. The foreign missionary enterprise also demanded a pooled effort if any significant progress was to be made. Such a shift in Campbell's thinking, driven by practical considerations, helped to move Disciples toward what might be described as a rudimentary understanding of the needs of the wider ministry of the church.

Alexander Campbell's developing understanding of ministry had to deal with at least four tensions.[17] First, Campbell recognized the "tension between the need to establish new churches and the needs of ongoing congregations." Second, Campbell understood the tension that existed between "the need of the church to be free from oppressive self-centered and self-serving leadership, and the need of the church for order." Third, as years passed, he struggled with the "tension between the needs of local congregations and the needs of the church as part of the wider church and society." Finally, Campbell came to recognize the "tension between each local community of faith developing its own leadership, and the reality that the churches need educated, paid, full-time leaders."

The first two of these tensions, it seems to me, arose for Campbell in the years prior to 1835, as the movement he led struggled to find congregational expression. The last two of these tensions reached center stage only after 1835, as social conditions and rapid growth drove the congregations associated with the movement closer together, both in terms of geography and mission.

Disciples gradually organized various area, regional, state, and even national bodies to further cooperation among and between their congregations. In the mid-to-late 1840s, Disciples organized several voluntary societies to accomplish specific purposes in mission. Alexander Campbell even became president of the missionary society formed in 1849. In more localized endeavors, congregations began to cooperate with one another to employ evangelists who worked to establish new centers of Disciples work. Often, even these local endeavors issued requests for more general support through the pages of *The Millennial Harbinger.* Soon, before the end of this period, a number of regional "corresponding secretaries" appeared whose task was to assist in the development of churches and in the ordination and placement of ministers.

North Carolina's State Convention, operating rather successfully by 1860, kept a "ministerial roll" of acceptable ministers who had standing in the state. It appointed an "Examining Committee" composed of five ministers in 1872 and charged it to keep an eye on doctrinal matters in the state. By the next year, the state took steps to begin to transfer ordination from purely congregational hands to the oversight of a standing committee of the State Convention.[18] Black Disciples in eastern North Carolina, and in Texas, followed suit within the next decade, well ahead of most other areas of the country.[19] Such structured organization, carrying with it some authority for ordination, no matter how limited, was the exception rather than the rule in the 1860s and the 1870s. The trend, however, was definitely set in the direction of greater cooperation in regional endeavors.

The shift to regional and state identifications did not come easily, however. Many congregations were uncomfortable with such developments. Even some of those who actively supported the regional work were somewhat apprehensive about implications associated with it. Titles given to regional workers, like those of "secretary," and "president," reflect the fact that most viewed the regional work as largely administrative to aid in expansion and development in areas where ministry really mattered. The true work of ministry, they believed, belonged in the congregations. Regional cooperation increased, but there were continuing questions regarding its actual definition as "ministry."

This increasing identification with the work of regions did have its downside however. As events leading up to the Civil War intensified, Disciples tended to break down along regional lines. Though Alexander

Campbell, like Barton Stone, freed his own slaves, he could not quite bring himself to condemn the institution of slavery. If anything, the biblical witness seemed to allow for it. Hoping to hold his movement together, Campbell relegated the matter to the realm of private opinion. As the war neared, many Disciples, North and South, lashed out at each other. Though Disciples did not split at the time, the bitterness lasted well after the war was over. Southern culture found itself under severe attack by the north during the years surrounding the war, enough so that secession and war seemed the only viable option. When political union fell on hard times, union among Disciples became hard to maintain as well. Though the result of the war held the political union together by force, the church did not have to follow suit. When the Churches of Christ formally departed from Disciples in 1906, the split largely followed the sectional lines of the Civil War period.[20] From a membership of approximately 160,000 at the time of the division, the Churches of Christ have grown to somewhere in the neighborhood of 1.3 million active members in the United States alone, the majority of them still located in the southern regions of the country.

After the conclusion of the war, several Disciples leaders struggled to recover a sense of the whole among the leaders of the various factions. Isaac Errett, premier leader of the second generation, established the *Christian Standard* in 1865 and edited it until his death in 1885. His irenic nature and tactful approach to all matters enabled him to gain a hearing among all sides of almost any conflict. When James H. Garrison finally settled in St. Louis and, in 1882, merged two papers into *The Christian-Evangelist*, Errett had some editorial help in furthering this constructive enterprise of building a sense of "brotherhood." Theirs was an uphill battle. The creation of national missionary organizations in 1874 and 1875 aided the efforts to reinforce the self-identity of the group as a whole, but also further alienated those who were fiercely congregational. The conflict had to do with the issue of local congregational authority. About this time, a smaller-scale version of the conflict surfaced within the life of the congregation itself.

## 1870–1960: Ministers of the "Brotherhood"

Newell Williams' study of Disciples ministry revealed how the move toward a settled ministry set up a new and very serious tension in Disciples life.[21] When a young college or seminary graduate came into a new setting as "pastor," what was to be the relationship established between the newcomer and the part-time uncompensated elders of the congregation? These elders owned a strong tradition as part of the ordained ministry of the congregation, even though they were part-time and unpaid. They also possessed a history of practical power in the area of church governance. Was this young neophyte to come in as an equal elder and assume general leadership in every area of the congregation's life?

The tension these questions raised continued throughout this period. John W. McGarvey argued the view that elders should be dominant, and these ministers from the outside should be considered evangelists, necessary only until full-time leadership within the congregation could be developed. He even contended that the minimum age of elders should be set at forty (Campbell set it at thirty), in order to preclude young college graduates from being able to attain to the office of elder. Isaac Errett, on the other hand, argued that age should never be a factor. If these young ministers were trained, held the gifts of ministry, and were called to full-time work in the congregation, they should be immediately ordained as elders. Oversight of the congregation's ministry, said Errett, should reside in the leadership of the full-time elder.[22]

For many years, well into the twentieth century, elders and these outside "evangelists" struggled over territorial questions. Elders in many congregations held onto their right to officiate over the Lord's table, to the point that the full-time minister had nothing whatsoever to do with it. Some of these congregations also had elders strong enough to maintain absolute control over governance matters pertaining to congregational life. During the first half of this period, McGarvey's view, in fact, was the dominant one.

The situation began to change in the decades after the Churches of Christ split from the Disciples. The 1920s saw the development of the so-called "functional plan." The goal of the plan was to "replace 'official' church leaders, a small group of elders,…with a large group of 'functional' church leaders, representative of the congregation, who would work under the guidance of the minister to enlist the whole church in fulfilling the church's ministry."[23] Slowly but surely general boards began to appear in Disciples congregations. These boards were composed of the chairs of various committees charged with particular tasks in the congregation's life. These chairs often were the elders and deacons in the church.

O. L. Shelton's book *The Church Functioning Effectively*, published in 1946, represented the culminating definition of this movement. It had considerable influence among Disciples congregations.[24] As elders began to assume a self-conscious identity as "lay elders," they also began to recognize "ministers" as a new office in Disciples ministry, one distinct from that of "elder." In the intervening time, Disciples have, in most locations, welcomed the minister to assume a position beside the elders behind the table. In the majority of Disciples congregations, the minister presides while elders present the prayers for the loaf and the cup. Such a practice symbolizes well the fact that lay and ordained ministry both originate in the act of God's redemption in Christ.

There are still locations among Disciples where elders preside at the table alone. These remnants of the elder's solitary role at the table are the last tangible reminders of the day when elders were not "lay elders" but were the "ordained" ministers of the congregation. The practice, however, tends to separate the ministry of "word" from the ministry of "sacrament," historically connected in Christian tradition and, in early Disciples history, in the office of ordained ministry. Does affirmation of the "priesthood of the believer," a treasured concept for Disciples and the whole Protestant reformed tradition, guarantee all Christians the right, at all times, to serve as ministers of word and sacrament in the life of the church?

Campbell did not think so. He did, however, assert the right of the congregation to assign these responsibilities to lay people "when circumstances demand it."[25] The minister's presence at the table, as the congregation's appointed representative teacher of the faith, helps to preserve the historic centrality of the Lord's supper as a primary means of teaching the good news of the Christian faith. As the minister is a representative of the church beyond the congregation, the minister's presence at the table also symbolizes the congregation's connection with the entire church of Christ. If, however, for any reason, ordained ministers are unable to officiate, Disciples tradition has always affirmed the right of the congregation to appoint a lay Christian to administer the Lord's supper. Disciples have long asserted that the validity of the Lord's supper as a sacrament of the church is not at all dependent upon whether or not the person who officiates is ordained. But early Disciples equally asserted that, under normal conditions, the one who officiates ought to be one of the elders [ministers] selected by the church for that purpose.

The tradition of using lay elders to offer the prayers at the table is a strong witness to the importance of the ministry of the laity in the life of our denomination. It also symbolizes the central truth that all ministry arises from the laity. Other denominations might benefit from following our practice on this point. Most denominations, Disciples included, would benefit from a serious renewal of lay ministry within the life of the church. In many congregations, beyond their role at the table, elders do not have much to do. Deacons are often limited to the collection of the offering or the passing of the communion trays. In general, Disciples congregations would benefit from a fresh consideration of how they might empower elders and deacons to assume more meaningful roles in the total ministry of the church.

In addition to the tension worked through between elders and ministers during these years, the period beginning around 1870 also witnessed increased awareness of the meaning of Disciples ministry in the context of congregational association at a national level. The organization in 1874 of the Christian Woman's Board of Missions, quickly followed by the establishment of the Foreign Christian Missionary Society, the National Benevolent Association, and other such societies, helped to mold the self-identity of the "brotherhood" as a group of congregations engaged in joint ministry. State and regional organizations, increasingly developing in their own right as centers of ministry, began to work more closely with these national organizations.

Regional oversight of the work of ministry became more prominent during this period. Most regions employed evangelists whose work was financed by the cooperative efforts of congregations in the region. Regional secretaries oversaw the work. All in all, a general matrix of regional oversight, rooted in Campbell's notion of the work of the evangelist, began to appear. By 1939, the annual Disciples convention even recommended that each area develop ordination councils to meet whenever congregations requested ordination of ministers. This council "was to consist of the minister and one or more elders [ministers] from each of three or more Disciples churches."[26] Ordination followed the willingness of at least three of the ministers to sign the ordination certificate. Even though a majority of congregations initially ignored the 1939 recommendation, Disciples slowly shifted authority for ordination from the congregational to the regional level, in recognition that ministry has responsibilities beyond those associated with any one congregation.

Disciples expectations of ministerial education greatly intensified during this period. A recent study of the ministers of larger congregations among Disciples has uncovered some interesting data for three different time periods. In 1909, 95 percent of these ministers had an earned college degree from a Disciples institution, but only 5 percent of them had a seminary degree. By 1942, 84 percent had college degrees from Disciples institutions, and 33 percent had seminary degrees. By 1985, 81 percent had degrees from Disciples institutions, and 97 percent had seminary degrees.[27] These figures are interesting for a couple of reasons. First, by 1942, it is obvious that Disciples ministers were beginning to attend other than Disciples colleges in larger numbers. This trend has continued to the present. Second, the increase in percentage of seminary degrees during this relatively short period of time is dramatic indeed.

This increase provides clear evidence of the way Disciples leadership consistently expressed its commitment to an educated, theologically literate ministry during this period. A study of the Disciples relationship with Yale Divinity School also provides some interesting evidence of this development. By 1920, 105 Disciples ministers had received the seminary degree from the divinity school at Yale University, and 48 more had received the degree from the University of Chicago Divinity School. By 1940, these numbers increased by 183 more at Yale, and by 25 more at Chicago. These figures do not count either the 12 Yale Ph.D.

degrees in divinity granted to Disciples by 1940, or the 36 Ph.D. degrees granted by Chicago during the same time period.[28]

These ministers, educated in ecumenical environments, came to have a strong influence in moving Disciples notions of ministry in ever more inclusive directions. During these ninety or so years, Disciples ministers and congregations became ever more aware of their interconnectedness in ministry beyond the level of congregations, or even states and regions. Ministers encouraged their congregations to recognize these broader responsibilities of ministry. Throughout these ninety years, the leadership of the United Christian Missionary Society, and that of its predecessor societies, modeled the importance of maintaining a vital ministry generated outside the traditional confines of the congregation or region.

The more inclusive understanding of ministry generating from this period did not become so fully inclusive that it was able to overcome its gender bias in church life. After 1870, it became clear to larger numbers of Disciples that women intended to carry out a long and arduous struggle to gain their own rightful place in Disciples ministry. Women ministers appeared during this period, and in ever increasing numbers as the years passed. Prior to 1888, so far as historians are able to determine, there were no "ordained" women ministers among Disciples. The early Christian Connection movement associated with the independent Elias Smith had fairly large numbers of women preachers, some of whom developed considerable reputations by the end of the 1820s.[29] But Disciples leadership frowned on such developments, largely due to its early understanding of scripture as propositional truth, and based upon its interpretation of the Bible's first- and second-century understanding of the role of women.

Clara Celeste Hale Babcock, evidently the first woman minister to be ordained among Disciples, began her enormously successful ministry in 1888. "Sadie" McCoy Crank's ordination dates to March 17, 1892. The ministries of these two women, in spite of obvious success, were hardly readily accepted or supported by Disciples at large.[30] An enlightened Illinois state evangelist in the 1880s by the name of Nathaniel Haynes is one of the few glorious exceptions among leaders of the time. Isaac Errett, and other late-nineteenth-century leaders, fully supported women's work in ministry on the mission field but failed to offer widespread support for pulpit ministry in this country.

This hesitancy to support women in ministry lasted well into the twentieth century; it still exists in significant pockets of Disciples life today. Janet Riley, a Disciples woman, reveals the interesting autobiographical detail that the Dean of the Disciples House at the University of Chicago, when she applied in 1958, informed her that educational financial assistance there was reserved only for men.[31] Most Disciples congregations did not include women in the eldership until well into the

1960s. Ironically, women were ordained long before they found general acceptance as lay elders in the congregation.

Today, women have complete equality in the area of seminary education, but are a long way from being able to claim the same equality in the practice of ministry. Though the Disciples General Assemblies have regularly affirmed, through resolutions, the equality of women in ministry since the 1960s, the general situation in terms of opportunities at the congregational level is only slightly better than it was some twenty years ago.

Women, when they can find work in the congregational ministry, generally fill assistant or associate positions. Some are able to assume pastoral ministry in congregations desperate for leadership and unable to pay adequate salaries because men, who have other opportunities, are unwilling to serve in those locations. Regional and general ministry possibilities for women have improved dramatically over the last decade, but there are only small numbers of these positions available. The increasing, and tragically underutilized, reservoir of seminary-educated women constitutes the greatest untapped cumulative resource available to the congregational ministry of Disciples. A church that affirms its commitment to gender equality in ministry must find ways to practice what it affirms. The integrity of Disciples ministry rests on our learning how to use this reservoir appropriately.

## After 1960: The Church's Ministry

As Disciples, after 1960, worked to develop a fuller understanding of their theology of church, they also discovered their need to take yet another significant step in shaping their theology of ministry. If any one event marks the beginning of this journey, the sermon preached by Presbyterian minister Eugene Carson Blake at the Grace Cathedral (Episcopal) in San Francisco on December 4, 1960, arguably fits the bill as well as any other. This event, as already detailed in chapter four, kicked off Disciples involvement in the Consultation on Church Union (COCU). Ongoing ecumenical conversations as a participant in COCU and, in particular, conversations with the United Church of Christ, have led Disciples to a new appreciation for ministry's need to express both the continuity and universality of the church's nature.

The ecumenical convergence in the theology of ministry, represented in such ecumenical documents as *The COCU Consensus* and *Baptism, Eucharist, and Ministry*, has stressed that the unity of the church does not require uniformity. Yet it has challenged all Christian communities to think of ministry as "the one ministry of Christ that is shared by the whole people of God."[32] When ordained ministers and lay people fulfill ministerial roles in the world, they do not represent merely congregations, regions, or denominations. Rather, they serve as representatives and re-presenters of the one ministry of Jesus Christ in the world. Their ministry should be performed with a view to preserve, not just a particular congregation or denomination, but the unity and health of all Christian churches. Ministry is, as Ronald Osborn so eloquently put it, "identification with God's will."[33] As such, ministry must serve the whole of God's creation by addressing the needs of both church and world.

Ministry celebrates, as Alexander Campbell might have said it, the "facts," or the mighty acts, of God in history. Recent ecumenical discussion concerning ministry has centered upon the basic theological affirmation that "the life, death, and resurrection of Jesus Christ was a ministry of God to all humankind."[34] This ministry is now shared, through the power of the Holy Spirit, with the whole Christian community. The authority and ability to perform ministry comes from God. It is not a creation of the individual, the congregation, the denomination, or even the whole church. Ministry resides in the power of God, through grace, to transform and empower humanity. "The ministry of the one People of God, with all its diversity," proclaimed the *COCU Consensus*, "is the continuation of the saving ministry of Christ."[35]

To the joy of all Disciples, the ecumenical convergence has affirmed that lay ministry is "the primary form of ministry apart from which no other Christian ministry can be described."[36] This lay ministry, into which every Christian is "ordained" at the time of baptism, is a ministry committed to full participation in the ministry of the church. Among other things, lay people witness to the acts of God, participate in worship, seek justice in society, provide pastoral care, intercede for others, and share in the governance of their particular congregations and denominations. All these ministerial tasks should be understood as falling under the general category of the single ministry of God's church.

The COCU document also acknowledged that, within this one ministry of the *laos* (the people of God), some individuals are called by the church to perform particular ministries. These persons are ordained, "consecrated to service," by the church "through the power of the Holy Spirit." These ordained persons "share in the ministry of Christ by representing in and for the church its dependence on, and its identity in, the Word of God." This ordination or consecration does not make one a "professional." Professional status is generally understood as something an individual achieves. Rather, "ordination represents the call of God through the voice of the *one church*" to perform particular ministries belonging to the *one ministry* of the church.[37]

The development represented in emerging ecumenical agreement has motivated contemporary Disciples to contemplate their own theology of ministry more carefully. This more reflective approach resulted as well from the Disciples experience of undergoing years of change in the actual practice of Disciples ministry. Since the 1960s, and proceeding to our present day, Disciples have conscientiously sought a fuller understanding of the one ministry of the whole church.

From within these contexts, Disciples have realized the need to represent more responsibly this wider understanding of ministry within the structures of our own denominational life. Soon after the restructure of our church, the General Board of the Disciples created a Task Force on the Ministry. This task force studied the question of Disciples ministry for two years and finally recommended to the 1971 General Assembly in Louisville that Disciples adopt a document addressing the "policies and criteria for the order of the ministry." In addition to making seminary education a prerequisite to ordination, this document officially recognized for the first time among Disciples that there existed an "order of ministry" through which Christian tradition has been transmitted from one generation to another through time. The task force asked Disciples to affirm that our own forms of ministry belonged to this general "order of ministry."[38]

By linking Disciples ministry to the ministry of the church through all time, in all places, Disciples have returned, in a sense, to their roots. When the Disciples movement began, its leaders struggled to form their ministry according to the design of it they found in the Bible. Alexander Campbell's conception of ministry, whatever else it might have been, remained firmly located in his understanding of the apostolic testimony. Today's ecumenical concern with ministry strives for the same goal. The ministry of the church in contemporary times seeks continuity with the ministry of the apostolic faith.

To seek continuity with the apostolic faith does not mean that the ministry must correspond precisely to the biblical testimony in terms of form. First, there really is no single New Testament form that takes precedence over all other forms. Second, the biblical witness itself provides testimony that the Holy Spirit led the church to adapt its ministry to the ever-developing contexts of its times. Apostolic continuity does mean, however, the serious endeavor of the church to preserve the "apostolic content" of ministry. Ministry must strive to represent the full range of meaning attached to the liberating and reconciling ministry modeled by Jesus Christ. Ministry, therefore, is not limited merely to the church, but must engage the world. "Christ's authority," proclaims the COCU document, "was displayed in his healing the sick, forgiving sins, comforting the afflicted, challenging the arrogant, transforming traditions, and bringing into being a new covenant People in the midst of the old. Christ's authority was also made manifest in his announcement of the end of oppression and of the overturning of unjust power structures through the assertion of God's rule."[39]

The 1971 Disciples document, besides recognizing the existence of the one "order of ministry" through time, also placed Disciples responsibility for the authorization of ordination in the regional office. Together, the regional office, the recommending congregation, and the candidate plan the service. The participation of the regional office in all Disciples ordinations symbolizes for those present the ties between ordained ministry and the work of ministry beyond the congregational level. The policies statement also recommends the presence and participation of some representative of the ecumenical church. This person's presence symbolizes the theological truth that all ordained ministry serves the whole church and is united with the whole ministry of Jesus Christ.

As such considerations indicate, ordination services among Disciples are designed to symbolize certain truths about ministry. This is most clearly illustrated, perhaps, at the culminating moment of the service. An ordination prayer invokes the Holy Spirit and seeks divine blessing for the ministry of the candidate. The prayer is accompanied by the biblical practice of the laying on of hands. This practice serves to signify the gift of the Spirit and also testifies to the church's endorsement of the candidate's ministry. In recognition that ministry is God-given, the candidate is ordained to the ministry of the whole church. Ordination, therefore, is not repeated should the candidate ever transfer to another denomination.

Disciples do not possess a strong history of theological reflection about the nature of ordination. This comes as no surprise since Disciples have always been so strongly insistent that there are no substantive distinctions between lay and clergy. Generally, Disciples have described ordination in functional terms: the minister is set apart, as the "Word to the Church on Ministry" recently stated it, "to fulfill tasks and purposes necessary for the health, vitality, and effectiveness of the church's corporate ministry." Yet in the years since 1960, this functional approach to the ordained ministry has been supplemented by a more theological reference to the "re-presentative" nature of ministry. Again, the 1985 "Word to the Church" from the Commission on Theology provides an example: "By ordaining people to particular ministries, the church designates them to re-present to the church its own identity and calling in Jesus Christ." This "re-presenting function," proclaimed the report, "is the defining characteristic of the ordained ministry."[40]

Barbara Brown Zikmund examined the differences between those traditions that consider ordained ministry as "empowerment" and those that consider it to be "embodiment." "Empowerment" traditions, like the Disciples, emphasize that the minister arises from the people, empowered by them, and, ultimately one hopes, by the grace of God, to perform certain functions of ministry. Other traditions, without denying the need for "empowerment" actions to demonstrate ministerial accountability to the congregation, emphasize an "embodiment" understanding of minis-

try. This understanding of ministry "recognizes that in the human community there have always been certain persons who are gifted religious
leaders." These individuals, whether the church empowers them or not,
believe they are called of God to ministry. The church, therefore, "is
called to recognize the gifts for ministry which they already embody."
Today's ecumenical movement, as it attempts to define its understanding
of ministry, seeks to maintain a "healthy balance" between the insights
of both "empowerment" and "embodiment."[41]

Since 1971, there have been several amendments added to the original Disciples statement on "the order of ministry." 1977 saw the addition
of a section pertaining to ministerial candidacy. In 1981, Disciples adopted
a general statement on the question of ministerial standing within the
denomination. This statement was occasioned, at least in part, by the
Jonestown tragedy. Jim Jones, who led over nine hundred people to their
deaths in a suicide ritual in Guyana, was an ordained Disciples minister.
If ministry affirms its continuity with the church in all times and places,
how might the church assure the faithfulness of its contemporary ministry
to the content of apostolic faith? The section on ministerial standing
attempted to address this question for Disciples. It defines ministerial
accountability and provides general criteria ministers must meet to continue their standing as Disciples ministers. In 1985, the General Assembly
added a section on ministerial relocation that clearly affirmed the rights
of congregations to call their own ministers, but provided policies by
which areas and regions may be more helpful to the process of relocation.

Though there were initial fears in some corners that regional offices
would exercise authority in the area of ordination arbitrarily, most of
those fears have disappeared. The system has worked fairly smoothly.
However, concern arose in a new way when the 1985 General Assembly received a document prepared by the Disciples Commission on Theology. The commission proposed that Disciples consider reconstituting
their two offices of ministry, licensed and ordained into three offices of
ministry, the ministry of service (deacon), the ministry of word and sacrament (pastor), and the ministry of oversight (bishop). All these offices
would be ordained, and would be subject to ordination policies and criteria.[42]

This Disciples proposal arose in response to the COCU recommendation that all denominations seek to recognize that the one order of
ordained ministry has three primary functions or offices, those of service, word and sacrament, and oversight. The COCU document concerned itself only with defining the ordained offices of the church. Congregational offices of ministry, like our current "deacon" and "elder" were
not addressed specifically, but the ministry of all lay persons by virtue of
their baptism is central to the COCU document. The Disciples proposal
presented to the General Assembly in 1985 did specifically affirm that

"the congregational offices of elder and deacon…have a valid place within the total ministry of the church Universal" and expressed the Disciples desire to contribute to the ecumenical understanding of ministry in this regard. The proposal also celebrated "the participation of such offices within the sacramental ministry of the church."[43]

The 1985 "Word to the Church on Ministry" did *not* propose that Disciples begin to call regional ministers "bishops." Instead, it rehearsed in a very general way the history of ministry among Disciples, and asked the denomination to consider recognizing that the three offices of ministry defined by COCU are already present in the current life and work of the denomination. Deacons, those who minister to both church and world, are active in our life as "fraternal workers" or as "Executive Directors of a Christian Home." Pastors, of course, work in the local congregation as ministers or as ministers of education. The ministry of oversight, the document affirmed, has been present for some time in Disciples life in the tasks of area and regional ministers.

The major concern expressed by some over this document rested in the question of ministries of "oversight," or, more precisely, over the use of the language of *episcope* ("bishop"—a word regularly used by Campbell to describe elders). Through the years following the Civil War, Disciples developed fairly active ministries of oversight without offering much theological or biblical rationale. The proposal set forth by the Commission on Theology has asked Disciples to think through more carefully the duties and responsibilities of the regional minister. There is no recommendation, and no expressed hope, that Disciples turn their "regional ministers" into "bishops," who will then be able to exercise authority in some hierarchical or imperial manner. The document did, however, express the concern that Disciples become more intentional in our understanding of regional ministers as those among us who "function collegially and exercise authority as that of a 'shepherd' or 'pastor to pastors.'"[44]

In 1988, at the 17th Plenary meeting of COCU, the nine member churches adopted a proposal indicating their desire to share their common life as "The Church of Christ Uniting." The document resulting from this plenary meeting explicitly indicated that no change in church polity among any of the member churches will be necessary to make "The Church of Christ Uniting" a reality. The plan of covenant communion approved in 1988 shifted away from the request that all nine churches adopt the three-fold ordering of ordained ministry and toward the recognition that each church already, in its own way, possesses an order of ministry of this design operating under different names. When the churches meet together, they will use the common language of deacons, presbyters, and bishops, but none of the churches will be expected to change the way it currently operates with respect to its ministers. "Uniformity among the several church polities is not essential to covenant communion," the document stated; rather "the mutual recognition of ordained ministries is a way of acknowledging both the headship of Christ over every ecclesial tradition and the freedom of the Spirit to work in and through these traditions however the Spirit wills." The standards for ministerial training and certification within each of the denominations, and the ways these churches call or appoint ministers will all remain unchanged by covenant communion and the reconciliation of ministries. But once the inaugurating liturgies are performed, after the nine churches have had the opportunity to act on the proposal, the ministries of those churches participating "may function, whenever invited, as a ministry to all." The expressed goal is the "reconciliation of ordained ministries" not the consolidation of ministries. The context for this liturgical "reconciliation of ordained ministries" will be accomplished in the preceding commitment between these churches to the "mutual recognition of members in one baptism, mutual recognition of churches, and mutual recognition of ministries." In 1995, the General Assembly, meeting in Pittsburgh, voted to commit itself to continuing in this "process of covenanting" as presented within the 1988 COCU document.[45]

## Conclusion

The discussions related to ministry no doubt will go on. Disciples, in their great diversity, have always been able to sustain a rousing discussion about almost any issue. No party to the discussion about ministry among Disciples favors hierarchical conceptions of ministry—not COCU, not the Disciples Commission on Theology, not the General Assembly, not the regional ministers, not the pastors, and not the lay people in the pews. Whatever conclusions may ultimately be reached, the discussion itself should remain collegial, serious, practical, theological, and forever grounded in the biblical (and early Disciples) notion of ministry as one arising from, and in service to, the whole people of God.

## Questions for Reflection and Discussion

1. As you look at the historical understanding of ministry among Disciples, what differences would you cite between the views of Barton Stone and Alexander Campbell?

2. Views of ministry among Disciples have proven to be quite adaptable to times and circumstances. What are the major shifts in the historical understanding of ministry among Disciples? What kinds of tensions have these shifts left in congregations of contemporary Disciples? What are the continuities between early Disciples and the present?

3. Talk about the role of culture in these changes. Do you regard adaptation of ministry to cultural developments as a strength or as a weakness, or both (provide reasons for your answer)?

4. What is the relationship, in your congregation, between the role of elders and the role of ministers around the table? What theological understandings support this relationship?

5. How does your congregation support, educate, and empower participants in lay ministry (for example, elders and deacons)?

## Notes

¹"Policies and Criteria for the Order of Ministry in the Christian Church (Disciples of Christ)," published by the Department of Ministry, the Division of Homeland Ministries, p. 1. See also paragraphs 89 and 90 of "The Design for the Christian Church (Disciples of Christ)."

²For church attendance figures, see Winthrop S. Hudson, *Religion in America: An Historical Account of the Development of American Religious Life.* (New York: Macmillan Publishing Company, Fourth Edition, 1987), p. 125f.

³D. Newell Williams, *Ministry Among Disciples: Past, Present, and Future* (St. Louis: Christian Board of Publication, published for Council on Christian Unity, 1985), pp. 7-10.

⁴*Christian Messenger* (April 1827): 139.

⁵*The Christian System*, p. 82.

⁶Robert Richardson, *Memoirs of Alexander Campbell* Volume II (Cincinnati: The Standard Publishing Company, 1868), p. 56.

⁷*The Christian Baptist* (August 1823): 9, and *The Christian Baptist* (October 1823): 18; see also articles pertaining to the Christian clergy in *Ibid.* (November 1823): 25f; *Ibid.* (December 1823): 29f; *Ibid.* (January 1824): 34; *Ibid.* (February 1824): 42f; see also the section entitled "The Christian Ministry," in *The Christian System*, pp. 77-85.

⁸"The Third Epistle of Peter, to the Preachers and Rulers of Congregations—A Looking Glass for the Clergy," *The Christian Baptist* (July 1825): 166-169.

⁹See W. Clark Gilpin, "Witness to the Deeds of God: Ministry in the Disciples Tradition," *Mid-Stream* (July 1987): 267-268.

¹⁰For Campbell's more mature view of the ministry, see *The Christian System*, pp. 77-85; see also the very good secondary interpretations of Campbell's view presented in Williams, *Ministry Among Disciples: Past, Present, and Future*, pp. 11-15; Barbara Brown Zikmund, "Alexander Campbell's View of Church and Ministry," in James M. Seale, ed., *Lectures in Honor of the Alexander Campbell Bicentennial, 1788-1988* (Nashville: Disciples of Christ Historical Society), pp. 167-182; William M. Smith, *Servants Without Hire: Emerging Concepts of the Christian Ministry in the Campbell-Stone Movement* (Nashville: Disciples of Christ Historical Society, 1968); and Robert L. Lemon, "Alexander Campbell's Doctrine of the Ministry," Th.D. dissertation (Pacific School of Religion, 1968).

¹¹McAllister and Tucker, *Journey in Faith*, p. 155.

¹²D. Duane Cummins, *The Disciples Colleges: A History* (St. Louis: Christian Board of Publication, 1987), p. xiv.

¹³Niebuhr, H. Richard, *Social Sources of Denominationalism*, pp. 165-199, for example.

¹⁴See David E. Harrell, *Quest for a Christian America: the Disciples of Christ and American Society to 1866* (Nashville: Disciples of Christ Historical Society, 1966); and *The Social Sources of Division in the Disciples of Christ, 1865-1900* (Atlanta and Athens, Ga.: Publishing Systems, Inc., 1973).

¹⁵McAllister and Tucker, *Journey in Faith*, p. 243.

[16] *The Christian System*, see especially pp. 77-85.

[17]These tensions are developed and explained by Barbara Brown Zikmund. The quotes within this paragraph are from her study, "Alexander Campbell's View of Church and Ministry," pp. 173-178.

[18]A.T. DeGroot, *Disciple Thought: A History* (Fort Worth, Tex.: By the author, Texas Christian University, 1965), p. 152f.

[19]See Hap Lyda, "A History of Black Christian Churches (Disciples of Christ) in the United States through 1899" (Ph.D. dissertation, Vanderbilt University, 1972), pp. 152-156; Lyda's work is referenced by Williams, *Ministry Among Disciples: Past, Present, and Future*, p. 31.

[20]Harrell, "The Sectional Origins of the Churches of Christ," *Journal of Southern History* (August 1964): 264; quoted in McAllister and Tucker, p. 252. C.J. Dull made the point about southern culture in his e-mail to me dated 14 April 1996.

[21]Much of what follows on these next few pages is dependent upon the work done by Williams in *Ministry Among Disciples: Past, Present, and Future*, pp. 17-20, and in "Elders as Assistant Ministers: A Call for Restructure of the Ministry in Congregations of the Christian Church (Disciples of Christ)," *Encounter* 48 (Winter 1987), pp. 93-103.

[22]On these points, see Williams, *Ministry Among Disciples*, pp. 18f.

[23]Williams, "Elders as Assistant Ministers," p. 97.

[24]See Williams, *Ministry Among Disciples*, p. 38.

[25]*The Christian System*, p. 82.

[26]Williams, *Ministry Among Disciples*, p. 32.

[27]See Mark A. Chaves, "The Changing Career Tracks of Elite Disciples Professionals," in Williams, ed., *A Case Study of Mainstream Protestantism: The Disciples' Relation to American Culture, 1880-1989*, pp. 343-358.

[28]I have a copy of this study in its unpublished and earlier form. It has since been published by the Disciples Historical Society; see Edwin L. Becker, *Yale Divinity School and the Disciples of Christ, 1872-1989* (Nashville: Disciples Historical Society, 1990).

[29]See Nathan Hatch, *The Democratization of American Christianity*, p. 78f.

[30]David A. Jones, "The Ordination of Women in the Christian Church: An Examination of the Debate, 1880-1893," *Encounter* 50 (Summer 1989): 199-217; Janet Riley, "The Ordination of Disciple Women: A Matter of Economy or Theology?" *Encounter* 50 (Summer 1989): 219-232. See also Martha Ann Williams, "'Shall the Sisters Speak?': Recovering Women's Story as Empowerment for Leadership in the Christian Church (Disciples of Christ)," (D.Min. dissertation, School of Theology at Claremont, 1988); Fred Arthur Bailey, "The Status of Women in the Disciples of Christ Movement, 1865-1900," (Ph.D. dissertation, The University of Tennessee, 1979).

[31]Riley, "The Ordination of Disciple Women," p. 219.

[32]"The COCU Consensus," p. 42.

[33]Osborn, *The Faith We Affirm*, p. 71.

[34]"The COCU Consensus," p. 40.

[35]*Ibid.*, p. 45.

[36]*Ibid.*, p. 44.

[37]*Ibid.*, p. 45f.

[38]See "Policies and Criteria for the Order of Ministry in the Christian Church (Disciples of Christ)." Copies of this document are usually available in the regional offices of the Christian Church (Disciples of Christ). See also Robert L. Friedly and D. Duane Cummins, *The Search for Identity: Disciples of Christ—The Restructure Years* (St. Louis: Christian Board of Publication, 1987), p. 103f.

[39]"The COCU Consensus," p. 40.

[40]See "A Word to the Church on Ministry," published in Williams, *Ministry Among Disciples*, pp. 46-56. See p. 47.

[41]Zikmund, "Alexander Campbell's View of Church and Ministry," pp. 180-181.

[42]See "A Word to the Church on Ministry," in Williams, *Ministry Among Disciples*, especially pp. 49-56.

[43]*Ibid.*, pp. 50-51.

[44]*Ibid.*, p. 55.

[45] See *Churches in Covenant Communion: The Church of Christ Uniting* (Princeton: Consultation on Church Union, 1989), particularly pp. 20-25; see also business item "No. 9519: Formal Action of the Christian Church (Disciples of Christ) In Response to *Churches in Covenant Communion: The Church of Christ Uniting*," in *Business Docket and Program: General Assembly of the Christian Church (Disciples of Christ) in Pittsburgh, Pennsylvania*, Oct. 20-24, 1995.

# 8

# FROM MISSIONS TO MISSION

*God has never, in any time or place, been without witness [see Acts 14:17]. One who is more fully known in Jesus Christ has been and is at work in the creation of community, the sharing of love, the seeking of freedom, the search for truth, the reactions of wonder and awe in the presence of nature's power and beauty and creativity, and the awareness of the worth of persons. Faith in God revealed in Jesus Christ produces a community empowered by the Holy Spirit to witness in word and deed to God's nature, (which may be described as righteous judgment, loving grace, and liberating power) and God's purpose (the redemption of all humanity, the full completion of the whole creation). The church is the community God calls into being and enables to engage in God's mission. It does not exist for itself alone but for the sake of the world.*

"General Principles & Policies"
of the Division of Overseas Ministries[1]

## Introduction

The twentieth century has brought enormous changes for what is today referred to as "mainline Protestantism." At home, here in America, this century has witnessed Protestantism's loss of its virtual monopoly on societal privilege. Prior to this century, Protestantism enjoyed unchallenged supremacy as the religious identification of choice among those who would hope to aspire to power and authority in the culture. Even though American Catholicism could lay claim to more members than any single Protestant denomination by 1850, personal identification with Catholicism usually meant the "kiss of death" for anyone aspiring to political or cultural authority.

By the 1960s, of course, all this had changed. John F. Kennedy successfully campaigned for the highest office in the land and became the

189

first non-Protestant president. His election served as a kind of symbol signifying that American Catholics finally possessed the full rights of American citizenship. One among them could even become president. (Before we congratulate ourselves on how far we have come, of course, we must admit that women, members of minority races, and aspiring candidates who are openly nonreligious still have ground to gain before the same could be said of them.) By 1960, Protestantism had become "the distinctive faith of a creative minority," surrounded by many other types of faith and non-faith. Religious pluralism had arrived in America and was here to stay.[2] Protestants would have to share their power and learn more and more just how to play out their rapidly developing minority status in American culture.

This change in Protestantism at home brought changes for the expressions of Protestantism abroad as well. This is especially true in the area now referred to as the "world mission" of the church. Protestants of earlier days were certain that God's work in the world could only be accomplished by Protestants, and most *American* Protestants were convinced it would best be accomplished by them. Some Protestants went even further and claimed God only worked through their own particular form of Protestantism. Mainline Protestant leadership in the twentieth century has developed a greater appreciation for the distinctive ways various Christian groups witness to the activity of God in the world. The pluralism of religious expression in the twentieth century has also occasioned a more general understanding that God's activity in the world is not limited to Christian expressions of it.

Such a recognition, however, has not lessened the continuing need for Christian commitment to global ministry. Nor has it lessened Christian responsibility to proclaim the gospel of Christ among the various peoples of the world. Yet the twentieth century has witnessed the passing of the era of the "foreign missionary movement." As the Disciples Division of Overseas Ministries (DOM) has put it, "the basic 'planting' of the church has been accomplished....An era of 'world mission' now exists in which the churches in each country and place in the world must engage in witness and service appropriate to that place."[3] What exactly do Disciples mean when they say that the "foreign missionary movement" is over and the era of "world mission" has taken its place?

Many members in local congregations are confused about the meaning of the current Disciples understanding of the "world mission" of the church. Slow as we have been in developing a theology of world mission, we have developed conscientious expressions of what we mean when we claim the church ought to be involved in the "world mission" of Christianity. Some Disciples long for the old "evangelism" and the passion many early missionaries felt for the urgent communication of the gospel to people in another place. Is this passion gone, or has it simply been transformed to find new ways of expression? What has changed, and why has it changed? What is the Disciples theology of world mission?

Disciples of Christ have not arrived at a theology of world mission overnight. During their history, Disciples have been through at least four different phases in their concern to be a church actively engaged in the missionary enterprise. Each of these phases is characterized by a different emphasis. The fact that Disciples have always been a diverse group means, of course, that each era contains people with dissenting opinions. Yet a dominant motif does seem to emerge in each period that helps to define theological development in this area of Disciples life.

## Phase I: Missionaries to the American Frontier, 1801–1874

Disciples of Christ membership grew nearly four times faster than the population of the United States after 1832 and during much of the nineteenth century. This rapid growth caused concern among some of the other Protestant denominations. Before the 1832 merger of the Stone and Campbell movements, many Presbyterian congregations had joined the Christian movement under Stone's leadership. The fact that the Reformers were successful in converting a good many Baptists over to their point of view contributed to the 1830 split between the Reformers and the Baptists. "Raccoon" John Smith, a former Baptist and one of the Disciples Reformers' earliest evangelists, liked to brag about his successes in evangelism. He once told his wife, Nancy, while reviewing the evangelistic work of a few months' time in 1828, that he had "baptized seven hundred sinners, and capsized fifteen hundred Baptists."[4] It is not hard to understand why Baptist leaders felt threatened by this new movement of Christians.

One of the edges of early evangelism for Disciples involved the active pursuit of converts from among other Christian groups. Since they believed that successful Christian unity depended upon a renewed dedication to restore "that simple original form of Christianity,"[5] early Disciples called members of other Christian denominations to the task. Before and after 1830, countless Baptists, and smaller numbers of Presbyterians, responded. In some cases, whole congregations came into the movement. Membership grew considerably. For that matter, so did ill will.

Disciples evangelism did, however, have another more traditional edge to it. The "Christians" from Barton Stone's movement, and the "Reformers" or "Disciples" of Alexander Campbell's movement, had always believed in the importance of evangelism—the preaching of the gospel to those who had not heard it. Prior to the uniting of the two movements, traveling evangelists from Stone's group spread their version of the gospel into the Middle West states of Illinois, Indiana, Iowa, and Missouri. When congregations associated with Campbell sought to employ an evangelist full-time in 1827, they chose Walter Scott. Scott brought theological consistency and organization to evangelistic efforts among the Reformers, and, later, to the combined efforts of the Campbell and Stone congregations. His success became the key to future growth and development among the united Disciples.

It took some time, however, for the churches merged in 1832 to develop a sense of what might be called "world mission." For the first fifteen years or so after the merger of their congregations, their world was the American frontier. They concentrated on the tasks at hand: sorting out the meaning of their new relationship with one another, urging other Christian groups to unite with them in their movement toward a restored church, and evangelizing among the non-Christians around them. The numerical growth, geographical expansion, and increasing organizational strength of the united church during these years is nothing short of impressive.

Beneath the move toward organization lay the desire to increase the effectiveness of evangelization. Slowly and cautiously, county associations began to appear in order to further evangelistic enterprises. Over a period of years, district and state organizations appeared. This evangelistic impulse, clearly requiring cooperation to make it work, finally led to the development of a national organization of Disciples.

As Disciples gained a sense of self-identity, they also gained an expanded sense of the task they faced. This awareness led to the meeting of the first national convention of the Disciples of Christ held in Cincinnati in October 1849. Though those who met discussed how to protect congregations from questionable ministers, and recommended the widespread organization of Sunday schools, the question of world evangelization came to dominate the meeting. Out of this meeting, Disciples of Christ came to address significantly for the first time the notion of the world mission of the church. They formed the American Christian Missionary Society (ACMS) and began to accept voluntary support for its work from ministers and churches.[6]

Unfortunately, this missionary organization had to contend with critics among Disciples who saw no scriptural precedent for a cooperative missionary organization. When, in 1863, the ACMS passed a resolution denouncing the "armed traitors" attempting to "overthrow" the government, the missionary society abandoned any semblance of neutrality and made even greater enemies among Disciples in the South.[7] Though it sent missionaries to Jerusalem, Jamaica, and Liberia, financial support for the work faltered and the mission work in these areas was quickly abandoned. The ACMS turned to home mission work and continued it throughout the Civil War period and beyond.

Those Disciples who fought these early cooperative endeavors began to think of themselves as a separate group, especially after the Civil War. By 1906, the federal census would recognize this developing group of Christians as a distinct group of congregations known as the Churches of Christ. In spite of these difficulties, however, all Disciples remained convinced of the need to be involved in the evangelization of the peoples of the world. From 1874 to 1900, the membership of Disciples congregations in America nearly tripled, from 400,000 to 1,120,000.[8] This increased membership brought more money and greater support for the cooperative endeavors in missions. At the beginning of this period, creative women provided renewed leadership in missions and their efforts produced a new day for Disciples.

## Phase II: Saving Souls in the World for the Kingdom, 1874–1928

During her devotions on a morning in April, 1874, Caroline Neville Pearre discovered a burning desire to lead women to assume significant leadership roles in support of foreign missions.[9] She began her work in her own church in Iowa City, Iowa, and within six months a new national organization, the Christian Woman's Board of Missions (CWBM), was formed to support missions. In order to do their part, Disciples men formed the Foreign Christian Missionary Society (FCMS) the next year.

Yet once again, the work progressed slowly. In the beginning the FCMS sent missionaries mostly to work among Christian peoples in the world, to witness to the union of all churches under the banner of the restorationism of the church. The CWBM did send missionaries to Jamaica to carry on the work begun earlier under the ACMS, but by 1881, neither of the new organizations had done much to further the cause of foreign missions in areas where there were no Christian witnesses. In the 1880s, members of these two organizations decided to become more intentional about communicating the gospel to those who had never heard it before. In 1882, the CWBM and the FCMS combined their resources and sent missionaries to India. Within the next few years, they sent missionaries to Japan, China, Panama, the Belgian Congo, and Cuba.

With these activities, the Disciples finally entered the arena of world missions to stay. Yet they did so without really discussing or thinking through the theological reasons for their involvement in foreign missions. They believed the "Great Commission" of Matthew 28:19–20 commanded Christians to go out into all the world and preach the gospel. Disciples tried to obey. The Christian responsibility meant the church should be involved in "saving souls." Saving souls would expand the membership of the kingdom of God, and these Christians could think of nothing more important. So, Disciples carried their gospel into remote areas of the world and attempted to do their part.

As to the meaning of the gospel they carried with them, Disciples took it for granted. They assumed they could preach Christ and people could accept Christ and that would be that. Little evidence indicates serious reflection about how their understandings of Christ and of the nature of the church might be colored by their own experiences as Americans. Nor did they seem to reflect about how portions of the gospel they preached might in fact be inappropriate for people who lived in different cultures and who had different experiences. At this point, Disciples were not very aware of the ways their culture had attached itself to the gospel they preached. Many Disciples assumed that when "savages" became "Christians," the end result would be that they would look like good, solid American citizens.[10]

For most of Disciples history, Disciples left unexplored the important theological questions related to world mission. Disciples of Christ did not begin to develop an adequate theology of mission until the 1950s.[11] Before that time, missionary leaders had not examined, for example, the nature of the "Word." Most Disciples simply asserted they should "spread the Word." It was something to be preached. They did not think about the possibility that the "Word" of God might be active apart from the Christian evangelistic preaching of it, and active in ways not readily understood by Christians in the West. Among Disciples, few seemed to recognize until much later that the incarnation itself (the fully divine/ fully human Christ in our midst) expresses the theological truth that God's activities in history are always inextricably attached to cultural, historical, and even finite forms. What implications might such a recognition have for world mission? These and other theological issues—the meaning of the gospel; the foundation, purpose, and hope of the church; the character of discipleship—remained unaddressed by leaders among Disciples missions until well into the 1950s and 1960s.

New approaches to world missions, however, were being developed by Disciples leaders as they faced the twentieth century. By the late 1890s, Archibald McLean had rejected the strict restorationism that had captivated much of Disciples mission life in the nineteenth century. Most restorationists refused to cooperate meaningfully with other Protestant groups, and some adherents refused even to recognize their legitimate status as Christians. McLean, on the other hand, through his world travels, moved joyfully into a fuller participation in the ecumenical movement.[12] In other words, McLean slowly came to adopt what might be referred to as a "moderate" or "modified" restorationism. Though he did not abandon the general presuppositions of restorationism, he began to modify the effect they had upon missions.

This more moderate restorationism among missionary leaders did not result from commitment to any theological affirmations that challenged the basic beliefs attached to restorationism in general; that development would occur among the next generation of Disciples. Instead, Archibald McLean and others like him merely came to the conclusion that the Methodists and the Presbyterians were well-meaning Christian people. They did not leave behind evidence that indicates they spent any time analyzing why these people should be regarded as Christian. They evidently did not think through what accepting members of other denominations as Christians might mean for the practice of the church at home or on the mission field. Instead, personal encounters with these other denominational types seems to have led these Disciples leaders to the conclusion that all denominations could share in a common task: world evangelization. Therefore, on mostly pragmatic grounds, McLean and a few other Disciples began to emphasize that Disciples really ought to cooperate with these other Christians in evangelizing the world. The task was too large to do by themselves.

The theological roots for this cooperative work could have been found in the writings and thought of Alexander Campbell. Campbell had always emphasized that the task of world evangelization belonged only to the church as a whole. Therefore, Christians, as members of *one* church, must cooperate with one another in the task of evangelism. His position on "cooperation" is clearly indicated in an essay he wrote for *The Millennial Harbinger* in 1838:

> With all this evidence before us, we must plead for cooperation among all the citizens of Messiah's kingdom, in whatever pertains to its enlargement, prosperity, and ultimate triumphs. We want cooperation. Some of our brethren are afraid of its power; others complain of its inefficiency. Still we go for cooperation; but it is the cooperation of Christians; not the cooperation of skeptics, deists, Jews and Christians, but the cooperation of Christians—practical whole-hearted Christians; not even a cooperation of churches; for in this sense of cooperation Christ has but one church. We go for the cooperation of all the members of that one church in whatever communities they may happen to be dispersed, and for their cooperation in heart and soul, in prayers, in contributions, in efforts, in toils, in struggles for the salvation of their fellow men at home and abroad.[13]

Based upon the theological principles that all Christians are "citizens of Messiah's kingdom" and "Christ has but one church," Campbell urged  Disciples churches to cooperate with one another in the task of world missions. His major interest involved his hope to get individual Disciples congregations to work with one another in tasks of ministry that went beyond those of the local congregation. His theological approach to the argument, however, had much wider implications. Since the church of Christ is one unified body composed of all citizens of the Kingdom, the mission of the church must express that unity.

Unfortunately, Disciples had difficulty implementing the practical side of Campbell's theological insight. Even though the modified restorationism of Archibald McLean and other church leaders in the late nineteenth century took a much more generous view of other denominations, it nonetheless maintained some very real vestiges of original restorationism. Disciples leaders were confident that their version of the gospel was better, even truer, than other Protestant or Roman Catholic versions of the gospel. They were more concerned, therefore, with finding efficient ways to spread their own gospel than they were with seeking a more complete understanding of how various members of the one church could act together in the expression of the same gospel message. As Joseph M. Smith, a leader in Disciples mission history, once put it, it reached the point among Disciples in general where many came to believe that "whatever [got] results must be the gospel."[14]

As these leaders pondered the question of greater efficiency, they decided to form a new missionary society, a united society to bring together various aspects of Disciples work in foreign missions. When the idea of a united missionary society emerged, articulate supporters emphasized the pragmatic advantages of such a society and specifically avoided doctrinal matters due to their fear that theological questions would only divide the congregations. The committee established to study the matter spoke of how unification would "reduce the number of our problems at home and abroad, increase our receipts, and add to our efficiency."[15] As is often the case in American denominations, "pragmatic concern" occupied the pulpit while "theological reflection" experienced grave difficulty even finding a seat in the congregation.

The United Christian Missionary Society (UCMS) emerged from these practical considerations in 1919. It combined the mission work of the FCMS, the CWBM, and the ACMS under one roof. The work of the Board of Church Extension, the National Benevolent Association, and the Board of Ministerial Relief were also brought under its supervision. The women of the CWBM had been the only group fairly successful at fund-raising. They brought to the merger the financial support that would make the UCMS a successful venture. These women were not particularly thrilled with the possibility that their leadership roles in the mission effort might be diminished by merging with organizations controlled by men. Yet they believed a more organized and cooperative effort would improve efficiency on the mission field. Without the background of their work and financial resources, it is doubtful that the Disciples mission efforts of the twentieth century could have succeeded quite as quickly.[16]

Traditional notions of evangelism lay at the heart of the founding of the UCMS. But the theological commitments still remained hazy. What are the biblical foundations for this gospel to be preached among other peoples? What is the substance of the gospel message? How might the gospel's significance be communicated to people of other cultures without violating the integrity of either its biblical foundations or its meaning? These questions were left unaddressed by Disciples during this period. As a result, the first ten years of the UCMS were dominated by the "open membership" controversy on the mission field.[17]

Due to Archibald McLean's leadership, Disciples began to recognize the value of cooperating with other denominational groups on foreign fields. In the early twentieth century, however, the Disciples' prevailing practice of believers' baptism by immersion kept the majority of Disciples from accepting unimmersed believers into church membership—required by a commitment to some form of restorationism for some, and by the commitment to a literal interpretation of the Bible by others. If followed to the letter, this obviously meant that Chinese Methodists and Chinese Presbyterians, for example, could not join Disciples churches without being rebaptized—even when they moved to areas of China where Disciples were the only mainline Protestants present. It also meant that there could be no free interchange of membership, pastors, or other church workers among the different Protestants working in these foreign areas.

In 1919, the same year the UCMS came into existence, two developing union movements caught the attention of Disciples missionaries in China. One was a national movement for unity under the direction of Presbyterian, Congregational, and London Missions. Leaders of this movement hoped that Disciples would make a formal statement on the mutual recognition of membership and become a part of the move toward unity. The other union movement had started in Nanking and consisted mostly of local goals shared by diverse congregations in that particular city. Its leaders wanted to unite all the evangelistic forces within the city under one banner, including the establishment of a union committee to oversee the complete and free interchange of memberships, pastors, and workers.[18]

Disciples missionaries were very excited about these possibilities, and they wrote the newly formed UCMS about the great potential for church unity that existed in China as a result of these movements. Many of the Disciples mission congregations already had accepted people of other denominational backgrounds into their fellowships. Few of the mission congregations actually maintained membership lists. Such things were not really needed on the mission field. Later, missionaries would use this fact to argue that they were not really practicing "open membership." Yet among the leadership in many of the Disciples mission congregations, it was not all that unusual that one would find a Chinese Christian who had never been immersed, but who had been baptized or sprinkled by Methodists or Presbyterians. The mission field context had led most, but not all, Disciples missionaries to abandon one of the remaining vestiges of restorationism, the connection between immersion and church membership. Though these missionaries remained convinced that immersion was the proper form, they were willing to accept as fellow Christians, and as fellow church members, those Christians whose baptisms took other forms.

When word of these developments reached home, many of the more conservative Disciples leaders began to attack the UCMS. Even before "open membership" became an issue, these conservatives had serious questions about the formation of a new united society. It seemed to them that such a society would only take responsibility for missions out of the hands of the local churches. Perhaps, more importantly, missions would be harder for local churches to control if a strong missionary society, viewed as out of touch with local churches by many of these conservatives, stood between the mission fields and the churches. The reports from China in 1919 only confirmed the deepest fears of these conservatives.

In the midst of this conflict, the UCMS leadership responded to missionaries on the field in ways that only increased missionary frustration. Leaders of the UCMS told missionaries on the field that they had to keep accurate membership lists, and that only those who had been immersed as believing adults could be counted on these lists. Everyone else could be welcomed in the congregation, though not as members, while, as Stephen J. Corey put it in 1923, relying upon his understanding of Acts 18:26, "they are being instructed in the way of the Lord more perfectly."[19] These leaders hoped that such instruction would lead to rebaptism by immersion.

In response to the UCMS directives, a few Disciples missionaries argued on behalf of the theological concept of the catholicity of the church. This concept recognizes that the church is, in its very nature, an inclusive community. When the awareness of God touches a human life, God calls that one into covenant with a human community characterized by faith and unlimited by either time or place. As Thomas Campbell said so well in his *Declaration and Address*: "The church of Christ upon earth is essentially, intentionally, and constitutionally one."[20] Its enduring witness through the ages serves as a signpost announcing to the world in all times and all places that God is at work reconciling human beings to one another and to God. To make distinctions between these persons would only contradict the nature of the church. Local congregations must be responsible to this larger framework of being church, and to those whose witness this broader notion of church includes, if they hope to fulfill the mission God gives to them in their own time and their own place.

Those missionaries who took this view heralded the dawning of a new day for Disciples. Missionaries like George Baird, Justin Brown, Guy and Pearl Taylor Sarvis, and Alvin and Margueritte Harmon Bro recognized the need for dialogue among Christians. They saw for themselves the destruction caused by Christians doubting the Christian standing of other Christians. They learned on the mission field that one could take oneself too seriously and miss out on the fullness of God's people. Though they represented the dawning of a new day for at least one aspect of the Disciples understanding of world mission, the complete dawning of that day remained in the future. The understanding exhibited by these missionaries proved a bit too progressive for leaders at home.

UCMS leaders, above all else, wanted to carry out the will of the constituency that supported them. Frederick Burnham, president of the UCMS from 1919 to 1929, illustrated how this served as a guiding principle for the organization when he wrote E. L. Thornberry of Kentucky that

> "[T]he United Christian Missionary Society does not attempt to deal in theological matters. It is a missionary society and carries on the enterprises which the brotherhood commits to its charge."[21]

As Burnham's comments illustrate, the society's leaders did not understand their task to be a theological one, leading the churches to more serious theological reflection about the nature of world mission; rather, the UCMS defined itself as an agency responsible to the will of the majority. Since American Disciples lived in a democracy, their congregations were to be democratic as well. This democratic principle received uncritical affirmation throughout the open membership controversy on the mission fields. The majority ruled, even when the majority had not taken any time to think about such things as world mission, church membership, or the meaning of the gospel from a theological perspective. The missionaries' experiences on the field led them to challenge this way of operating.

The practical considerations of financial support made it difficult to second-guess this general democratic principle. Any possibility of open membership on the mission fields, the leaders quickly learned, considerably threatened the financial stability of the UCMS coffers. Since the UCMS had only just begun its work when the open membership controversy flared up, the financial implications were hard to ignore. Without money, the evangelistic task would remain unaccomplished. Therefore, anything that threatened the support of the society struck at the very heart of what the society hoped to accomplish.

Both of these factors, the democratic principle and the pragmatic concern for financial support, led to another rather unfortunate development that assumed a bit more permanence due to the open membership controversy. Naturally, since the UCMS took its marching orders from the democratic majority who paid the bills, the mission churches, as well, had to take their directions from those who paid the bills. The extension of the democratic principle in this way led to American Christian control of churches thousands of miles away on the mission field. Indigenous leadership could not be effectively developed under these circumstances. This type of control from abroad served to reinforce an attitude of cultural superiority in mission work that greatly affected the work of mission churches through mid-century.

American Disciples in the early twentieth century, supported by a sense of their duty as caretakers of developments abroad, worked according to stereotypical characterizations of "heathen" and "pagan" peoples, language used in mission contexts to express a cultural superiority. They were not alone in this understanding; it was one they shared with most all other American Protestant denominations working in missions. Protestants showed little appreciation for non-Christian religions and exhibited a strong anti-Catholicism (it should be noted, however, that Catholicism during pre-Vatican II days was itself not blameless on the mission field). Christians in general confused their work of "Christianizing" people with much broader purposes that included "civilizing" them. Remnants of all these characteristics, stronger in some locations than in others, remained in Disciples missionary endeavors well into the 1950s.[22]

When, by 1928, both a United Church of Christ in China and a United Church of Christ in the Philippines had been launched successfully, the Disciples stood on the sidelines. Largely due to the pragmatic rather than theological response of the UCMS to the whole open membership question, organic union did not emerge on the mission field at all for Disciples until it became a coerced necessity brought on by the Axis powers during World War II. In this respect, actions during this phase of missions set back by decades Disciples contributions to the cause of unity on the mission fields in comparison to the contributions of other mainline traditions.

## Phase III: Building the Kingdom, 1928–1948

During this next period of Disciples life in missions, ecumenical contacts grew and matured. Disciples had, after all, been participants in the ecumenical movement in America from its very beginning. Even though Disciples did not consider themselves constituting a "denomination" in 1908, they were among the founding members of the Federal Council of the Churches of Christ in America that took shape during that year. This organization became American Protestantism's first major ecumenical success.

During these years, Disciples were especially influenced by occasional ecumenical gatherings of mainline Christian groups meeting to discuss the nature of world missions. Three Disciples, Stephen Corey, Samuel Inman, and E. K. Higdon, attended one of the earliest of these meetings, the Jerusalem meeting of the International Missionary Council in 1928. This particular meeting had an extraordinary impact upon Corey, who became acting president of the UCMS in 1929; he was officially installed in the office in 1930. Corey's travel diary for that conference includes the following notation: "Indigenous, self-governing, self-operating, self-supportive, the burning topic at Jerusalem. Shift from paternalism to partnership."[23] Though they tried to live up to the idealism expressed in Jerusalem for missions, Disciples were unable to accomplish this shift during the next twenty years. Instead their operations, though dedicated and characterized by good intentions, continued to reflect more paternalism than meaningful partnership.

On the other hand, theological developments did affect the Disciples approach to world missions during this period. Increased ecumenical contacts with other mainline Protestant theologians brought Disciples leaders under the influence of some aspects of mainline, as distinguished from conservative, theology. Surprisingly, however, few Disciples adopted neo-orthodoxy, the new theological emphasis on sin and human limits found in the theologies of Karl Barth and Reinhold Niebuhr. Rather, they found the Christocentric liberalism of the older generation more congenial. In fact, Disciples began to embrace Christocentric liberalism at about the time it began fading from the scene.

The theologians of Christocentric liberalism (or "evangelical liberalism") stressed human goodness rather than original sin. They emphasized an ever-present God of love without much mention of a God of wrath and punishment who stands above human history. These theologians also tended to share an optimistic belief that human actions would eventually overcome human need and lead to the establishment of the kingdom of God on earth. Above all, these thinkers featured Christ as the center of their theology by lifting up the relevance of his life as both model and source for the ethical and religious life of all humanity. For them, Christ-centered beliefs about reality were verified by the practical results of Christian experience.

Stephen J. Corey, president of the UCMS during the first ten years of this period, wrote two books addressing the missionary enterprise from this theological perspective. In one of them, he wrote that missions needed to develop the "Christian spirit" among people "so as to create a new society of the kingdom of God on earth."[24] He and other leaders among Disciples were convinced that Christianity offered the *only* solution to world problems. "Our task," Corey told the trustees of the UCMS in his final presidential address in 1938, "is to make Christ known in all his fullness and as the solution of every individual and human problem." "This," he continued, "is to build a kingdom of God on earth."[25] Or, as a 1937 UCMS pamphlet put it, "It is dawning on Christian leaders everywhere that it is Christ or chaos."[26]

The recognition that God might be active in areas of the world where Christianity had not been heard of, or that God's activity in the world might truly be contemplated by other religions, had not yet dawned on Disciples. As Christians entered non-Christian areas in ever-increasing numbers, the UCMS Board of Managers began to indicate an enthusiasm for mass conversions to Christianity, as particularly tended to take place in India. Mass conversions took place when some religious or political leader decided to follow Christianity and brought along all those who followed her or his leadership. The minutes from a 1936 Board of Managers meeting offer an example of the board's enthusiasm for the prospect of an impending mass conversion in India. "This movement has been greatly accelerated recently through the leadership of Dr. Ambedkar, an educated outcaste who urges his people to leave Hinduism and seek a religion that really offers some hope to them." The optimism of the board, however, was quickly deflated. Later in the year, the minutes grimly reported that Dr. Ambedkar and all his followers had become Sikhs instead of Christians.[27]

The earlier Disciples emphasis on individual salvation, or "soul-winning" as some called it, gave way during this period to a new and stronger concern with social reconstruction. Concern for evangelism did not disappear. It remained and, in some respects, flourished. Yet for the first time in Disciples mission work, concern about the need to construct a new society on the mission fields became prominent as an end in itself.

If you applied to be a missionary before 1928, you would find yourself answering questions such as "Have you had any experience in personal effort in bringing others to Christ? If yes, in what form of work, and with what success?" Related questions also appeared on the application: "Do you believe that personal effort to lead people to Christ is the paramount duty of every missionary? Do you propose to make such effort the chief feature of your missionary career, no matter what other duties are assigned to you?"[28] From these questions, it is clear that the UCMS, prior to 1928, considered personal evangelism to be the primary objective of the missionary task. Such a recognition does not mean, however, that the society ignored social work in these earlier years. Yet for Disciples, the establishment of hospitals, schools, agricultural projects, and other such social work served as yet another "means of the entree to the individual soul." At least that is how President Frederick Burnham expressed it.[29]

During this third period, the applications asked different types of questions that demonstrate the turn in thought taken during these years. Two of the first three questions on the revised application had to do with "educational, health and social services" rendered in the mission station. The fourth asked what the missionary should do "to further social justice and world order."[30] Concern for evangelism remained, but social reconstruction became more prominent. Without attention to theological rationale, evangelism and social reconstruction can end up serving ends unrelated to the gospel. Disciples were lax during these years when it came to thinking about and expressing the theological rationale behind their mission. Of course, theological rationale cannot stand alone either; it must be connected to practice if it is to serve the gospel. Disciples, like many American Christian groups, have had difficulty putting these two things together.

Don A. Pittman and Paul A. Williams have pointed out that Disciples today still have a split mind in regard to understanding the purpose of missions. Some Disciples emphasize the "homiletical" purpose, where the primary objective of missionaries must be to preach the good news in an effort to win souls for Christ and expand the membership of the kingdom of God. Other Disciples understand the primary purpose of missions to be "relational." Relational missionaries and their supporters emphasize service (*diakonia*) and fellowship (*koinonia*). They offer "compassionate service to others" and work to establish "human community." Those who follow the relational approach believe the missionary should live out the gospel and thereby contribute to the building of the kingdom of God. Homiletical Disciples accuse relational Disciples of compromising "the evangelical force" of the gospel. Relational Disciples accuse homiletical Disciples of becoming "so scrupulous in their concern with ancient form and correct order" that they have "lost touch with the Spirit in which all forms [are] grounded."[31]

Why did this tension emerge in Disciples history? As missionary leaders became more immersed in the ecumenical movement, and as they thought through the issues in missions more from the perspective of Christocentric liberalism than from the perspective of conservative restorationism, they adopted the more relational approach to world mission. At least for Disciples, there is not much evidence of this perspective becoming the dominant one until the middle of this third period. Even after it did become prominent, many people in the churches, and some missionaries on the mission fields, either never really understood or simply rejected the changing approach adopted by leadership. This fact resulted in a developing tension that has still not entirely subsided today.

Whatever theology missionary leaders offered during these years, however, came mostly from the perspective of Christocentric liberalism. Therefore, Disciples tended to emphasize human action over divine initiative. But, to be honest, Disciples have always exhibited this tendency. Since Disciples have their origins in this country, they have always tended to be rather American in their orientation. Americans are doers, succeeders, activists, and, above all, pragmatists. They believe that one gets what one works for; as my mother used to tell me repeatedly in my youth, you never get "somethin' for nothin'." The grace of God, undeserved and unmerited, is a foreign concept to most Americans. The same is true for most Disciples.

Even though Alexander Campbell regularly expressed his strong belief that God's grace could not be earned, that it depended upon no human action, he simultaneously asserted his belief that salvation resulted from a person's active and reasonable choice to believe the evidence of God's activities in history. If the person did not choose to believe, the person could not be saved. Campbell never really persuasively addressed the question of how this human "choice" should not count as a "human action" upon which salvation depended. Most Christians who make human choice a precondition for God's grace face the same theological dilemma.

When Christians concentrate on human action rather than divine initiative, they generally begin to become confident that their own human actions can bring in the kingdom of God. They begin to concentrate on methods of action, and the development of rituals, to aid their efforts. They begin to become convinced that if something works, it must be right. They begin to lose themselves in their own efforts and forget to seek the voice and direction of God. They become so concerned about their actions to build God's kingdom that they occasionally overlook the fact that, after all, it is God's kingdom and not their own. Though Disciples accomplished many great things in their mission work during this period, their efforts were tainted by some of these faults.

Disciples leadership shared many of the "social gospel" emphases set forth by Protestant theologians like Washington Gladden, Walter Rauschenbusch, and Josiah Strong. Though some theological expressions of the social gospel were set forth with a realistic appraisal of the human condition and its attendant limitations, many popular expressions of it became overly confident of what human beings could accomplish. With many other American Protestants who were influenced by these theologies—and, although with every good intention and with sincere devotion, without ever realizing what they were doing (for had they realized it, they most certainly would have reconsidered)—many Disciples ended up seeking to build a kingdom in their own likeness. Even though their efforts expressed a strong concern for the development of a new world order that would accept all people, these Christians nevertheless tended toward a parochial vision of Christianity and civilization that expressed itself in the language most familiar to them: the language of American civilization, of democracy, of anti-communism, and of anti-Catholicism.[32] This language made it hard for them to preach about a God who loves all persons truly *equally*, even the undemocratic peoples of the world, including the Communists, the Catholics, the "heathen" and the "pagan" the world over, and without any condition that any of these people be transformed or "civilized" before they could be the recipients of divine love. In an address before the General Board of the National Council of Churches in 1959, Virgil Sly, Chair of the UCMS Division of World Mission, announced the end of such views:

> We of the mission of the church must discover what it means to be Christian missionaries and what it means to establish the church in the midst of unprecedented tradition-smashing issues of change which may include our own tradition. Too much of our mission has been an attempt to reproduce the image of the church within its western setting. This cannot be in our time, if we are to be true to the ever changing needs of men to whom the message of "Good News" is to be given.[33]

## Phase IV: Responding to the Kingdom of God, 1948–present

This final phase in the development of a Disciples understanding of world mission began with a 1948 report from the Foreign Division of the UCMS delivered to the Board of Trustees. The document pointed out that the Society needed to make some decisions about what its stance on matters of Christian union in the mission field were going to be.[34] Within the next year, as Virgil Sly described it, "the situation became rather tense even within the administrative circles of the society when the Foreign Division insisted that something had to be done about our relationships to the United Church of Christ in Japan and in the Philippines."[35] Disciples congregations in these areas no longer had a separate identity. Their involvement in church unity, however, had not stemmed from a conscious decision to unify; instead, these churches were forced into unity.

In 1941, during the war, the Japanese required all Protestant churches in Japan and the Philippines to unite with all other Protestant churches. After the war, this military edict was lifted. The Disciples churches in Japan voted to remain connected to the union movement. Many of the Filipino churches also voted to remain a part of the unified work. When these churches took this action, many at home were concerned about how their organic union with other Protestant groups might affect their commitment to Disciples doctrines and practices. The document entitled "The Crisis in Foreign Missions" raised this question and urged the UCMS to take some action to address the critics.

As a result of this issue, Virgil Sly and Harry B. McCormick, president of the UCMS, took a 1950 fact-finding trip to Japan and the Philippines. When they returned, they reported to the International Convention of the Disciples of Christ that union in these areas was a fact. They also pointed out that the churches were participating in the union movement of their own free will. For the first time in UCMS history, Disciples leaders applied the principle of local autonomy (the right for a local church to govern itself) to mission field churches. The UCMS, argued Sly and McCormick, had no more right to tell these churches how they must conduct their affairs than it had the right to tell churches at home how they must act. These leaders offered no theological justification for extending the principle of local autonomy to these churches; it just seemed to be required by the circumstances.

Although this event led Disciples to recognize the importance of maintaining indigenous leadership on the mission field, it still had not occasioned any deeper theological understanding as to why the gospel they preached required such leadership. The majority of Disciples leaders in the 1950s did not demonstrate that they realized the difference between stressing the principle of "local autonomy" and stressing the principle of "indigenous leadership." As Disciples approached the restructure of the denomination in the years leading up to 1968, most leaders reached the conclusion that "autonomy" of the local church is tough to defend theologically. Individual congregations should resist the idea that their particular concerns are nobody else's business. They should also resist the idea that their particular business is nobody else's concern. No Christian congregation stands alone. Every Christian congregation is responsible to the entire body of Christ. That is why Disciples, in the *Design for the Christian Church (Disciples of Christ)*, adopted the notion that all local congregations are in "covenant" with one another. After formalizing this recognition in 1968, Disciples, as a gathered group, no longer defend the principle of local autonomy, though freedom in the congregation's sphere, understood within the notion of covenant, is protected and continues to this day.

The question of indigenous leadership in missions is related to this principle of congregational freedom. Congregational freedom does not mean that congregations are "autonomous." Rather, it means that congregations have the right to own property and, in dialogue with other congregations making up the body of Christ, to make decisions related to their particular expressions of ministry. Disciples emphasize the covenantal relationship shared by all their congregations. Therefore, decisions made locally should always be made in light of that relationship and under the emphasis of the Lordship of Christ. The recognition of indigenous leadership on the mission field means much the same thing. God's voice is heard in different cultures in differing ways. The good news remains the same, but theological insights arising from it often take on different accents. These differences only enrich the body of Christ and, when openly communicated and discussed, can serve to increase our understanding of the way God works in the midst of human history.

The family of Christ, the church, is made up of all the peoples of the world. This theological claim, like all others, has implications flowing from it. Families, if they are to be functional families, must communicate with one another according to principles of mutual respect and openness. Such communication ultimately serves to create stronger bonds of love between the differing peoples and cultures who make up the world's population. Before this can happen, Christians from different cultures must be willing to listen to one another, and, in contrast to the principle of "local autonomy," be equally responsible for, and accountable to, one another, even though strong disagreement on doctrinal and practical matters will likely never disappear. If large numbers of ordinary lay Christians from around the world became more adept at this skill, genuine hope for world peace might actually begin to blossom. Surely, the world mission of the church, rooted in theological claims, ought to include strategies that work toward this end.

Disciples delayed changing their stance on open membership until the early 1960s. In its "Strategy of Ecumenical Concerns," the Division of World Mission, while recognizing that mission congregations would only practice baptism by immersion, recommended that those congregations "participate in a plan of ecumenical membership." Such a plan placed members who were not baptized on a separate "ecumenical roll" and allowed for them to have "full fellowship with the church." The UCMS document concluded that such a policy was "not open membership" and "not closed membership."[36] Perhaps the document should have added that it was not full membership either.

As this ambiguity indicates, the theological justification for this change in recommended patterns of membership on the mission field remained weak. Pragmatic justification remained strong, as it did for those dealing with the open membership question at home. As families in the United States became more mobile, people who moved became less particular about maintaining their denominational status. They looked for congregations that felt comfortable more than congregations associated with particular denominations. Increasing numbers of non-Disciples visited Disciples congregations and decided to stay. Since the 1940s, Disciples churches in North America increasingly implemented open membership more on the merits of its practicality than as an inherent part of some comprehensive theological recognition.

However, during this period, Disciples missionary leaders did begin to engage in fairly serious theological discussions about the meaning of world mission. The major impetus to this new theological reflection grew out of the 1952 World Meeting of the International Missionary Council at Willengen, Germany. As delegates addressed their topic, "The Missionary Obligation of the Church," they came to recognize more completely the needs of the so-called "younger churches" on the mission fields. These younger churches were located in developing countries where revolutionaries struggled to overthrow Western colonialism. Many people in that revolutionary world viewed mission work as simply one more attribute of that colonialism. Chided by their own mission congregations at the conference, sponsoring Western churches pledged to move from an attitude of paternalism to one of partnership in their relationships with these younger churches. They hoped such an action might enable Christianity, untainted by Western powers, to remain a viable alternative for people in these countries. Willengen encouraged that any such changes be accompanied by renewed theological commitments as well.[37]

In response to the call of Willengen, the Foreign Division of the UCMS continued more seriously a study it had begun in 1950 after Sly and McCormick had returned from their trip to Japan and the Philippines. Out of this study, the Foreign Division produced a pamphlet entitled "The Strategy for World Missions." After undergoing several revisions over a three-year period, the final draft was approved in early 1955 representing official Disciples strategy for missions work.[38] Yet even this document did not involve a serious reconsideration of the theological nature of world missions. Rather, it represented a pick-and-choose method of excerpting sentences and parts of paragraphs from more comprehensive theological statements that had been prepared in ecumenical circles. Though the "Strategy" spoke a needed word on the changing nature of work on the mission fields, especially in its support for "younger churches," its very approach to the topic indicated that more serious theological analysis would have to wait.[39]

As the Foreign Division attempted to implement the policy recommendations of its new "Strategy of World Missions," it began to develop an increased awareness of its need to address more completely the theological task. As Virgil Sly put it in 1959, "The necessity of an adequate theology of missions must be faced." Mission leaders "need to know what we are trying to do, what we are trying to say, and what we are in mission for."[40] As a result of these considerations, and especially emerging from the impact of Willengen, the UCMS acted to rename its own "Division of Foreign Missions." In September of 1956, the new name for this aspect of UCMS work became the "Division of World Mission."

Why drop the final *s* on the word *Missions?* And why did the revised edition of the "Strategy" document also drop the *s* when it was published in early 1959 under the title of "The Strategy of World Mission"? According to Virgil Sly, it was the theological recognition that "the mission...is God's mission" that led to the change.[41] Willengen had emphasized these themes, and by 1956–1957, Disciples missionary leaders were taking them to heart. Disciples stopped thinking in terms of exporting "missions" work to foreign areas, and began to define their role as one of Christian witness and presence in the midst of the ongoing and ever-present "mission of God."

In 1958, long overdue but better late than never, the UCMS and the Council on Christian Unity cosponsored a Commission on the Theology of Mission. This commission did its work for over four and a half years. Composed primarily of seminary professors, missionary administrators, and missionaries, it met several times a year to hear and discuss papers prepared by members of the commission. Its stated purpose was "to seek a clearer grasp of the essential nature of the Christian mission" and "to help stimulate the brotherhood to deep levels of theological understanding of our knowledge of God and our urgent privilege to proclaim His love to the whole world."[42]

The commission clearly fulfilled the first portion of this charge, but also clearly failed to fulfill the second. Many commission members wrote first-rate essays addressing the theology of questions related to missions. Papers dealt with such topics as non-Christian religions, ecumenical membership, the gospel's relationship to Western culture, and the nature of the church—all from theological points of view. Other papers expressed particular theologies of evangelism, mission, and history. Yet the most theologically reflective of these working papers, along with others of course, collect dust in the archives of the Disciples Historical Society or in the mostly unread pages of journals resting on shelves in seminary or university libraries. How do church leaders develop theological awareness among lay people in the churches? Though the commission expressed great hopes to do something in this area, it never quite fulfilled them. The commission's work, however, did lay the groundwork for future reflection among Disciples leaders regarding the theology of world mission.

As Disciples moved into the 1960s, they began an earnest discussion concerning the nature of their church organization. This process eventually led to the development known as "Restructure," which culminated in 1968 with the adoption of the "Provisional Design." At this time, the governing board of the UCMS, under the leadership of Virgil Sly and, after Sly's retirement on October 1, Thomas J. Liggett, readily surrendered its considerable power and control in order to make way for the more responsible and accountable church polity developed by the process of restructure. In the restructured church, two new divisions were formed to oversee the work previously tended by the UCMS. Both divisions became directly accountable to the General Assembly of the Christian Church (Disciples of Christ). Disciples formed the Division of Homeland Ministries (DHM) to supervise work at home in North America. At the same time, they formed the Division of Overseas Ministry (DOM) to oversee, promote, and continue to develop Disciples work in other parts of the world.

Beginning in 1977, the Board of Directors of the DOM, under the leadership of President Robert Thomas, began once again to re-examine the Disciples understanding of world mission. After nearly four years of study and dialogue, including the study of earlier work done by the UCMS and the "Commission on the Theology of Mission," the DOM issued its "General Principles and Policies" statement. The General Assembly of the Disciples adopted this statement in Anaheim in 1981. This document currently guides Disciples efforts in global mission. Sandwiched between sections addressing "Historical Perspective" and "Policy Guidelines" is a section entitled "Theological Principles." In this section of the statement, Disciples, for the first time, self-consciously addressed the nature of their theological understanding of world mission. These six statements, taken from the DOM statement, indicate the developing Disciples theological reflection about mission.[43]

(1) **"God has never, in any time or place, been without witness. One who is more fully known in Jesus Christ has been and is at work in the creation of community, the sharing of love, the seeking of freedom, the search for truth, the reactions of wonder and awe in the presence of nature's power and beauty and creativity, and the awareness of the worth of persons."** This theological claim is based upon Acts 14:17. It offers the testimony that Christians should recognize that God is active in the world even where Christians have yet to set foot. Though the Christian community asserts its confidence in Christ as supreme revelation of God, it should also be willing to learn from other religious traditions and cultures whose members testify to the activity of God in their midst. Today's overseas staff enters global mission with a greater respect for the fact that the mission truly belongs to God. They recognize that God has already been at work among the people they serve, and they work to find a way to support this activity of God with their own Christian ministries.

(2) **"The church is the community God calls into being and enables to engage in God's mission."** What precisely is "God's mission"? Earlier in the text, the DOM document identifies the "purpose" of God as "the redemption of all humanity, the full completion of the whole creation." Called of God, the church "does not exist for itself alone but for the sake of the world." How does this church engage in God's mission? "At its best, the church proclaims the good news, nurtures the people of God, encourages worship, remembers and transmits the tradition, promotes social righteousness and justice, and exhibits the promise of the reign of God." The statement is relatively clear, therefore, about the work of the church. Whether engaged in world mission or working in a local neighborhood, the church witnesses to the reign of God in history. World mission is the task of the whole church, not just one specific part of the church. Therefore, the various manifestations of the church are

called to work together, rather than in competition with one another, in this task.

(3) **"This is not to say that the church is to be identified either with Christ or the Kingdom of God. The Kingdom in its fullness is solely the gift of God; any human achievement in history can only be approximate and relative to the ultimate goal—the promised new heaven and new earth. Yet this kingdom is the inspiration and constant challenge in all our struggles."** Here Disciples affirm that, even though the church is called to its task by God, it, nevertheless, must recognize its humanity. Though the church belongs to God, it is not a fully divine institution. Neither it nor its members constitute the kingdom of God. This theological affirmation keeps the church humble and enables its members to remember and confess the limitations placed upon all human actions. The kingdom remains the proper inspiration of the church's activities only so long as the church recognizes it as fully a divine gift dependent entirely upon the initiative and action of God.

(4) **"The church of Christ is one. All persons who confess faith in Christ are part of the one body. The divisions that historical, geographical, societal, theological and liturgical factors produce are limitations upon the proper functioning of the body. God wills that the church be one. That does not mean all alike, but rather a community capable of accepting with joy the enrichment of great diversity....Commitment to evangelism, mission, and justice is inseparable from a commitment to church union."** This theological principle serves as the foundation for the Disciples commitment to unity. When Disciples assert that the "church of Christ is one," they also assert their responsibility to work toward the natural expression of that unity. In the "Policy Guidelines" section of the text, the DOM statement indicates that "No church can afford to be disconnected from the churches in other places." Such "cross-cultural and cross national exchanges are critical for the church's witness to the universality of the gospel, and an important corrective for local and national limitations and perversions of the faith."

(5) **"Apart from accepting God's love, persons continue in sin, in estrangement and revolt against God. The declaration of God's forgiving grace in Jesus Christ calls forth a primary faith commitment....Confessing faith in Christ and being Christ's disciples makes persons more fully aware that they belong inescapably together in the fellowship and freedom of the Holy Spirit, and enables a witness to the ultimate hope for the world, the coming of the Kingdom."** The work of world mission ultimately rests in this theological affirmation of the saving power of God's love. Confessing

acceptance of that love enables persons to recognize themselves as members of the family of God. This "good news" is not something Christians have the option of keeping to themselves. As stated in the DOM text, "the uncommunicated gospel is a clear contradiction."

(6) **"God is the final source and author of all human justice and freedom. Christ calls the church to challenge all attempts to deprive persons of their humanity and to support all who suffer on behalf of justice and freedom, witnessing always to the Gospel's declaration of the uniqueness and value of all persons as children of God."** As it closes its theological principles section, the DOM statement clearly indicates that "mission implies the unity and integrity of social action and evangelism." Just as the gospel must be communicated, it must also be acted upon, and in some contexts, the only way to communicate the gospel is to act upon it. Since God seeks justice and freedom for all God's family, the church must engage itself in the struggle for a just social order. World mission, therefore, includes Christian advocacy on behalf of the poor, and the work of a church willing to "engage in the struggle to dethrone the destructive powers."

Disciples seemingly lack the will, the theology of church, and the structure "to engage in the struggle" very successfully. Some Disciples believe the recent restructure of the Division of Homeland Ministries, accomplished in 1991, illustrates this fact. DHM leadership quietly eliminated the Department of Church in Society. Though leaders at DHM intended by this action to direct their attention to more effective support for congregational involvement in social issues, they simultaneously removed an important and active witness to social justice from the life of the general manifestation of the church. Subservient to the question of how Disciples can express an authoritative gospel in any context, taken up in the next chapter, no other question faces present day Disciples with more urgency (and, perhaps, with more controversy) than the question of how (or, perhaps, whether) they intend to act on behalf of "the Gospel's declaration of the uniqueness and value of all persons as children of God." For Disciples to fulfill this responsibility, they will need to do so through the combined ministries of congregations, regions, and the general church.

## Conclusion

Disciples began their endeavor in world mission without much theological reflection. Yet they knew instinctively that they could not ignore the Christian call to ministry in the midst of the world's neediest people. They went to work, offered selfless service, and preached the only gospel they knew. The message of the good news came through, in spite of the fact that it was often unsophisticated, tainted with American culture, and usually expressed in paternalistic ways. People the world over were moved to respond to God and to understand their lives in relationship to the message of Christ. Their lives and the lives of those around them were transformed by this experience.

Yet the lives of the missionaries and the congregations supporting them were also transformed. The mission field taught its own lessons. Some congregations listened to those lessons earlier than others, but most mainline Protestant denominations eventually heard them. The missionary endeavor of the last two centuries has encouraged American Protestantism to reexamine the theological foundations of the gospel. This rebirth of critical theological awareness has enabled the church to recognize the need to distinguish gospel from culture. It has helped it to find a new prophetic voice that has been heard the world over. Most importantly, perhaps, the church's work in world mission has expanded the church's vision of how God is at work in the world. The church has an enlarged appreciation for both the wideness of God's mercy and the inclusive nature of God's family.

All these changes have affected the Disciples of Christ. In a relatively short time, the Disciples have come a long way. They have learned that instead of emphasizing their own human action to "expand" or "build" the kingdom of God, they should see their activity as a "response" to God's initiative to establish the kingdom of God in their midst. Their work in missions has led them to a more active engagement in church unity, one of their most important founding principles. Missionary work and accompanying ecumenical involvements have also strengthened commitment to the theological task. The Disciples expression of gospel is far more responsible today than it would have been had their nineteenth-century predecessors not dedicated themselves to the missionary task.

Though today's Disciples may find themselves critical of some aspects of yesterday's endeavors, they do recall the dedication and genuine sacrifice of those who traveled the missionary road before them. They also acknowledge the great debt the contemporary church owes to those ancestors who were driven by the missionary spirit. Not only have the errors of their ways taught important lessons, but the great successes of their limited endeavors also serve as a constant reminder that, ultimately, the work belongs to God, and God obviously blesses the effort when human beings offer their finite but dedicated service to its completion.

## Questions for Reflection and Discussion

1. Briefly describe the four different phases of the history of mission among Disciples by emphasizing for each the major focus and theological strengths and weaknesses.

2. Through much of our mission history, "Disciples were not aware of the ways their culture had attached itself to the gospel they preached." Can you name some examples of this phenomenon from your understanding of this history?

3. What implications for mission are represented in a theological reflection on the meaning of the incarnation of Jesus Christ (i.e., how should the church respond to the belief that "the incarnation itself [the fully divine/fully human Christ in our midst] expressed the theological truth that God's activities in history are always inextricably attached to cultural, historical, and even finite forms")?

4. Reflect on the mission of your congregation in light of the six principles taken from the DOM statement: In what ways are these six principles represented (or absent) in your own congregation's work in mission and evangelism? What other theological principles are either implicit or explicit in the way your congregation undertakes its work in these areas?

5. Make an attempt to write a mission statement (or revise a current one) for your congregation in light of what you have learned from this chapter.

## Notes

[1] *General Principles & Policies*, published by the Division of Overseas Ministries in the Christian Church (Disciples of Christ), p. 16.

[2] Martin E. Marty, "Protestantism Enters Third Phase," *The Christian Century* 78 (January 18, 1961): 72-75; Marty's defense of this new role of Protestantism as "creative minority" appears in his *The Search for a Usable Future* (New York: Harper & Row, 1969), especially pages 87-101.

[3] *General Principles & Policies*, p. 21.

[4] John A. Williams, *Life of Elder John Smith* (Cincinnati: R.W. Carroll and Company, 1871), p. 385.

[5] Thomas Campbell, *Declaration and Address*, p. 25.

[6] See McAllister and Tucker, *Journey in Faith*, p. 174f.

[7] The resolution's text is quoted in Harrell, *Quest for a Christian America*, p. 163; McAllister and Tucker have also reprinted a portion of the resolution, *Journey in Faith*, p. 206f. See also, Mark G. Toulouse, "Disciples and Social Transformation: Past," *Mid-Stream* 26 (July 1987): pp. 462f.

[8] McAllister and Tucker, *Journey in Faith*, p. 235.

[9] *Missionary Tidings* (August 1899): 102-103; quoted in McAllister and Tucker, *Journey in Faith*, p. 261.

[10] See, for example, the before and after pictures of one "savage" who became a "Christian" as printed in *The Missionary Intelligencer* 11 (February 1898): 33. In the picture labeled "savage," the man is without a shirt and has uncombed hair. In the picture labeled "Christian," the man is dressed in a black suit, white shirt, bow tie, and combed hair. The caption underneath the picture reads: "These pictures represent the same man. The first represents him before he heard the gospel; the second represents him after he had been justified and sanctified by the Lord Jesus, and by the Spirit of our God. These pictures speak for themselves." They do speak for them-

selves, but not quite in the way editors intended them to speak. The *World Call* magazine for Disciples also offers what it calls "Some Contrasts on Foreign Fields," pictures that depict Christians compared to non-Christians following much the same understanding of what Christians ought to look like. See *World Call* I (March 1919): 4-5.

[11]Joseph Smith makes this argument in his doctoral dissertation, "A Strategy of World Mission: The Theory and Practice of Mission as Seen in the Present World Mission Enterprise of the Disciples of Christ" (Th.D. dissertation, Union Theological Seminary, 1961).

[12]*Ibid.*, pp. 74-78, though Smith is overstating the case when he writes that there was "a clear abandonment of restorationism as defining either the goal or the method of Christian unity." Such an abandonment came sometime later, after the years represented by the life of Archibald McLean.

[13]*The Millennial Harbinger* (June 1838): 269.

[14]Smith, "A Strategy of World Mission," p. 114.

[15]Minutes of the Joint Convention called for organizing the UCMS, Cincinnati, 20 October 1919 (UCMS papers, The Disciples Historical Society, Nashville, Tennessee).

[16]Ironically, the women, who were responsible for bringing in the solid financial resources for the new organization, suffered the burden of an unfair salary structure as administrative staff, in comparison to that of men who held equal positions, clear through the 1950s. One interesting notation in the December 13, 1920, "Minutes of the Officers' Council Meeting" stated the following: "Miss Maus, Superintendent of our Young People's Division, and Miss Lewis, Superintendent of our Elementary Division are accepting their work with us on the new basis with reluctance, feeling that there has been some discrimination against them in fixing of the salary scale by the United Society of the workers here at headquarters." The UCMS also neglected to carry through its constitutional pledge to the women to move toward a 50/50 situation with regard to administrative positions; in fact, when women left their positions, they were often replaced by men (who were paid from the start more than the equally capable women they replaced had been paid after years of faithful service— as was the case when Cynthia Maus retired). On the positive side, the Board of Managers for the UCMS did maintain equal members of men and women from the beginning.

[17]The detailed story of these years is found in Mark G. Toulouse, "Pragmatic Concern and Theological Neglect: The UCMS and the Open Membership Controversy," in D. Newell Williams, ed., *A Case Study of Mainstream Protestantism: The Disciples' Relation to American Culture, 1880-1989*, pp. 194-235. What follows in paragraphs below is a very brief narrative based upon the detailed story related in "Pragmatic Concern and Theological Neglect."

[18]Details of these union movements are found in a letter from G.B. Baird to C.C. Morrison, 27 December 1919 (UCMS papers).

[19]Corey, "Statement Concerning the Report of the China Mission," p. 3 (UCMS papers).

[20]Campbell, *Declaration and Address*, p. 44.

[21]Burnham to Thornberry, 9 April 1928 (UCMS papers).

[22]All these elements (the democratic, pragmatic, financial, and stereotyping tendencies) are discussed and documented thoroughly in Toulouse, "Pragmatic Concern and Theological Neglect," pp. 213-228.

[23]Stephen Corey's Travel Diary for 1928 (UCMS papers). The "Laymen's Inquiry" into foreign missions took place in the years just following the Jerusalem Council. Published as *Re-Thinking Missions: A Laymen's Inquiry After One Hundred Years*, William E. Hocking, ed. (New York: Harpers, 1932). This study influenced

Disciples as it sought a more careful, critical selection of missionary candidates, a gradual transfer of responsibilities to Christian nationals, and the organization of administrative unity across ecumenical lines for missions at home. See Corey, "The Laymen's Foreign Missions Inquiry," *World Call* 15 (June 1933): 7f; and "Re-Thinking Missions," editorial, *World Call* 15 (January 1933): 3.

[24]Corey, *Missions Matching the Hour* (Nashville: Cokesbury, 1931), p. 107.

[25]Corey, "Executive Statement," 1938, p. 11 (UCMS papers). The 1940 UCMS handbook put it this way: "Thus the world missionary effort lives and gives life. It is building the kingdom of God even in this hour of world distress and hate." See *Handbook of the United Christian Missionary Society* (Indianapolis: UCMS, 1940). Other titles of books and pamphlets published directly by the UCMS during this period indicate this "building the kingdom" concept: see, for example, Jessie M. Trout, *Forward in Missions and Education: Disciples of Christ Help Build the Kingdom* (Indianapolis: UCMS, 1941); the pamphlet: *Twenty-Five Years of Kingdom Building Through the United Christian Missionary Society: 1919-1944* (Indianapolis: UCMS, 1944); Clement Manly Morton, *Kingdom Building in Puerto Rico: A Story of Fifty Years of Christian Service* (Indianapolis: UCMS, 1949).

[26]"Foreign Missions Day, March 7, 1937: Through Loyalty to Victory," p. 17.

[27]"Board of Managers Minutes," April 14, 1936 (UCMS papers); see also "Board of Managers Minutes," December 8, 1936.

[28]"Application for Appointment as Missionary," United Christian Missionary Society. The forms I looked at had been filled out by Nancy Adeline Fry in June 1920, Oswald Goulter in September 1921, and Grace Stevens Corpron in October 1922 (UCMS papers).

[29]Burnham, "The Thread That Ties the Work Together," *World Call* 8 (February 1926): 4-6.

[30]"Application for Missionary Service." The one I looked at had been filled in by Margaret Cherryhomes, June 17, 1946. Mrs. Cherryhomes was a graduate of Phillips University and a former secretary to G. Edwin Osborn, pastor of the University Place Christian Church in Enid, Oklahoma. She trained at Yale and was married in Marquand Chapel at Yale by Dr. Kenneth Scott Latourette, the great mission historian (UCMS papers).

[31]Don Pittman and Paul Williams, "Mission and Evangelism: Continuing Debates and Contemporary Interpretations," in Larry Bouchard and Dale Richesin, eds., *Interpreting Disciples* (Fort Worth: Texas Christian University Press, 1987), pp. 217-219. Pittman and Williams explain that this tension has been present from the beginning of Disciples history. As the next paragraph indicates, I believe the tension emerged primarily out of developments in this third period.

[32]Examples of some of these expressions are found in Toulouse, "Pragmatic Concern and Theological Neglect."

[33]Virgil Sly, "Mission and Change," address before the General Board of the National Council of Churches, December 2, 1959, Detroit, Michigan (UCMS papers).

[34]See "The Crisis in Foreign Missions: The Foreign Division Faces a Decision," 1948 (UCMS papers).

[35]Virgil Sly, "Christian Unity and World Missions," August 8, 1954, p. 24 (UCMS papers).

[36]"Strategy of Ecumenical Concerns," Division of World Mission, 1961 (UCMS papers).

[37]Virgil Sly attended the International Missionary Council, July 5-19, 1952, at Willingen, Germany. There were over two hundred participants from fifty countries.

[38]"Strategy of World Missions," (Indianapolis: Foreign Division of the United Christian Missionary Society, 1955).

[39]See Joseph Smith's analysis of the document in his dissertation, "A Strategy of World Mission," pp. 155-233.

[40]Sly, "Mission and Change," December 2, 1959, p. 7 (UCMS papers).

[41]"We are participants," said Sly, "in the mission of God." See Virgil Sly, "From Missions to Mission," in *The Christian Mission for Today: Five Addresses Presented to the Ninth Annual Assembly of the Division of Foreign Missions, NCC*, December 7-10, 1958 (New York: Division of Foreign Missions of the National Council of the Churches of Christ in the USA, 1958), p. 8.

[42]These original purposes were first stated in "Working Paper for a Study on the Theology of Missions," originally dated July 16, 1958, and attached as "Appendix II" to the "Minutes of Meeting, Commission on the Theology of Missions, October 18, 1958, Mark Twain Hotel, St. Louis, Mo." (UCMS papers).

[43]The following quotations are from the *General Principles & Policies*, published by the Division of Overseas Ministries in the Christian Church (Disciples of Christ).

# 9

# FROM CHURCHES TO CHURCH

*Within the whole family of God on earth, the church appears wherever believers in Jesus Christ are gathered in his name. Transcending all barriers within the human family such as race and culture, the church manifests itself in ordered communities of disciples bound together for worship, for fellowship and for service, and in varied structures for mission, witness and mutual discipline, and for the nurture and renewal of its members. The nature of the church, given by Christ, remains constant through the generations; yet in faithfulness to its mission it continues to adapt its structures to the needs and patterns of a changing world. All dominion in the church belongs to Jesus Christ, its Lord and head, and any exercise of authority in the church on earth stands under his judgment.*

The Design for the Christian Church
(Disciples of Christ)[1]

## Introduction

Major turning points are common within any movement's history. These points occur at those junctures where a movement finds itself charting a new course somewhere along the way in its march toward the future. Long-range planning simply cannot anticipate every contingency. Some combination of both circumstances and choices inevitably leads to the construction of new roads blazing off in the direction of uncharted territories. For individuals struggling to discover and maintain a newfound relationship with one another, these new roads promise shared experiences. They mark an exciting common search for the locations where the burgeoning community might appropriate some sense of its own corporate identity. Disciples, in their brief two-hundred-year history, have certainly experienced the geography of such unfamiliar landscapes more than once. Previous chapters detail some of these stories. Arguably, however, one of the most important turning points in Disciples life, in the direction of yet another unfamiliar landscape, has come in more recent years as Disciples decided to restructure the life of their common association with one another.

At the beginning of Disciples history, our ancestors found themselves clearing new trails on the American frontier, often heading off in directions they had not anticipated. Whether one talks about those "Christians" associated with Barton Stone or those "Disciples" who identified with Thomas and Alexander Campbell, the truth remains the same: neither group really intended to depart from the midst of the Presbyterians. In each case, members found themselves in settings where it seemed that leaving official Presbyterianism remained the only option open to them.

Stone's group quickly formed its own Presbyterian association. Campbell's group, on the other hand, after being rebuffed by the Presbyterian Synod of Pittsburg in 1810, discovered points of contact with the Baptists and decided to affiliate with them. These actions indicate an early willingness, even heartfelt desire, to continue traditional affiliations. But, in both cases, these alignments proved temporary. Stone's group dissolved its presbytery less than a year later and, even though Campbell's affiliation with Baptists lasted longer, it was ultimately short-lived as well.

From the time of the earliest splits with the Presbyterians, however, Stone, the Campbells, and those associated with them hoped to bring a new wholeness to historical church life. Human opinion, in their view, had successfully divided the church into various sects. Disciples wanted to reemphasize the church's dependence on God's word as the only source for authority in the church's life. This concern for the church's integrity has been a long-standing commitment in Disciples life.[2]

In response to the wild individualism of early American revivalism, Disciples arrived on the scene and stressed "the corporate context of the Christian life."[3] Where the revivalists claimed individual assurances of the presence of the Holy Spirit, the preaching of the early Disciples warned of the dangers of making private religious claims. Such claims, usually lacking in clear scriptural foundation, often became the very human opinions that divided the church.

Instead, Disciples believed that the church must rest only on the claims of the apostolic testimony found in scripture. In congregations related to such a church, individuals would find strength in the grace they experienced through their church life. Christians could best experience the presence and power of the Holy Spirit in the community's worship, and in its activities of baptism, the Lord's supper, and prayer. By emphasizing the scriptural priority of the church's life, the early Disciples hoped to counter the myriad of sectarian claims they found in congregational life on the American frontier. Such an attitude also helps to explain why both the Campbells and Stone, as well as their followers, had such difficulty accepting the fact that their own movement, after

1830, was beginning to show all the markings of turning into just another American denomination.

Though congregations associated with Stone set off on their own much earlier than those associated with the Campbells, it is the latter's separation from the Baptists that marks one of the movement's most important early turning points. Prior to that separation, Campbell's Disciples possessed a self-identity largely wrapped up in the notion of seeing themselves as a reforming movement of Christians with no formal organizational identity to call their own. Though they were "reformers," their organizational affiliations were among and with the Baptists.

These reformers, for various reasons,[4] separated from the Baptists around 1830. In order to maintain a high level of vitality and a close association with one another, these Christians and their reforming congregations began to recognize the need for some form of their own organizational structure. Over the course of the next few years, therefore, the "reforming *movement*" *within* other denominations became a "reforming *organization*" *alongside* other denominations. The effects of this unforeseen transition, not fully apprehended at the time, took early Disciples in directions they clearly had not originally intended to go.

As a reformer within an established denomination, Alexander Campbell could relish the role of harsh critic and play it to the hilt. His journal, *The Christian Baptist*, attacked abuses within Baptist life with impunity. After all, he was not responsible for the survival of the Baptist denomination; he had no vested interest in it whatsoever. If he had his wish, its demise would be but the first step in the movement to do away with all denominations. In their place, he would rather see a restored Christian community undivided by opinions of human origin. His perspective, however, changed considerably after the reforming congregations associated with him left the Baptist fold. Suddenly, he found himself largely responsible for encouraging the fragile witness of an increasing number of independent congregations. The harsh and critical tones of *The Christian Baptist* soon gave way to the more irenic and nurturing counterparts of his new journal, *The Millennial Harbinger*.

As Ronald E. Osborn's article in the panel of scholars collection indicates, anti-denominationalism is often found among those groups who believe their church is the one true church. These groups tend to be blind to the fact that their own existence has also contributed to the division of the church. Early Disciples had difficulty recognizing their own complicity in the sin of division in church life. Campbell and others were right: no scriptural basis for denominationalism exists in the New Testament. The Bible does not set forth a pattern for the development of any particular church structure. Yet, as Osborn pointed out nearly thirty years ago to Disciples of a previous generation, if the church is to have any relevance in history, it must have an existence as an institution in history, even though there is no clear blueprint in scripture as to how to design such an institution.[5]

The denomination in America, as tempted as it has always been to take itself far too seriously, represents one way the mission of the whole body of Christ has sought fulfillment. Its record of failures is certainly as long as its record of successes. Early Disciples told that part of the story very well. Yet the denomination has also powerfully re-presented the gospel story in history. Its success in these areas has been greatly furthered by the positive aspects of ecumenical cooperation during the twentieth century. The earliest Disciples did not live long enough to witness these developments for themselves.

Under denominational care and guidance, many women and men have experienced the call of God to enter ministry. Though denominations could still do better in this area, especially in cultivating wider support for the placement of women ministers, they have underwritten ministerial education and sponsored services of ordination on behalf of the whole church. At its best, especially in the ecumenical age, the American denomination has interpreted all aspects of its mission, including baptism, evangelism, and congregational worship, as a representative ministry performed on behalf of the whole church. At its worst, it has manipulated these acts, or other of its activities, to further its own selfish and parochial interests. H. Richard Niebuhr stated this dimension most bluntly: denominations, he wrote, "represent the accommodation of religion to the caste system" and "are emblems, therefore, of the victory of the world over the church, of the secularization of Christianity, of the church's sanction of that divisiveness which the church's gospel condemns."[6] The histories of most denominations include examples of both the best and worst dimensions of denominationalism.

Early Disciples anti-denominationalism grew out of their theological understanding that all denominations are necessarily fragmentary. They understood that all denominations are adversely affected by their surrounding history and culture. No one denomination could ever be considered as the whole church. In their own witness, one that often denied its own denominational identity, the Disciples hoped to point to that which existed beyond the many denominations. They sought to give witness to the gospel that carried all the way back to the time of Christ and the apostles. They sought to convey the truth that no institution in and of itself could ever capture the entire spirit of what it means to be the church.

When Thomas Campbell declared in 1809 that the "church of Christ upon earth is essentially, intentionally, and constitutionally one," he did not mean to say that any one institution in history could ever fully represent the essence and truth of that statement. Rather, he knew that the essential oneness of the church rested in Christ, not in history. He confessed the truth of the church's unity and purity by faith rather than by sight. That is why he and other Disciples in the later nineteenth century struggled valiantly to avoid the stigma of the denominational name, even as they found themselves seeking more effective structures to carry forth the mission of the church in history.

## Churches and Agencies

The nineteenth and early twentieth centuries proved to be the time when Disciples expanded their commitments to include financial support for the work of agencies operating outside the confines of the local congregations. The shift was gradual at first. Many Disciples accepted the changes only after being pulled along, feet dragging behind them. Others died without ever accepting the changes. Alexander Campbell, during his years with the Baptists, voiced opposition to most forms of cooperative enterprises. Before long, his opinion changed. Just after 1830, as he found himself concerned with the welfare of a growing number of congregations, Campbell wrote a series of essays on the topic of cooperation in which he stated that "a church can do what an individual disciple cannot, and so can a district of churches do what a single congregation cannot."[7]

Organization came slowly, but these autonomous Christian churches did develop consistent cooperation with one another. There were annual meetings in various regions of the country where congregations came together for worship and communication. Out of these annual meetings, there occasionally arose agreement between congregations to pool support and send out an evangelist to form new congregations. By 1840, some of the district cooperation had expanded in some areas to the state level. Indiana held the first statewide assembly in 1839. Barton Stone served as a preacher at the event. Kentucky, Virginia, Illinois, and Missouri were not far behind.

In 1842, Campbell wrote his most important article on church organization. The essay acted as a charter justifying cooperation and organizational development beyond the confines of the local congregation. Campbell argued that distributing Bibles, educating ministers, sending missionaries, and protecting congregations against fraud were all tasks demanding cooperation. "We can have no thorough cooperation," he wrote, "without a more ample, extensive, and thorough church organization."[8] Campbell followed this article with an interesting entry in the next year's *Millennial Harbinger*. Kenneth Teegarden, some years ago, first directed my attention to this fictional story Campbell composed about "the island of Guernsey" in order to demonstrate the necessity of cooperative church organization.

In this interesting story, Campbell told about a couple of evangelists who, over a period of five years, created six different congregations of

Christians on the island of Guernsey. These six congregations "constituted the whole church on the island of Guernsey; but as of yet they did not act as one church." Campbell described the difficulties these independent congregations encountered as they continued a separate existence. "Finally, to prevent the utter extinction of the churches of Guernsey, and to combine all the means and energies of all the brethren," the congregations met together and formed a cooperative association. Campbell provided details related to the formation of this "one body," complete with information about the appointment of "public officers...especially Evangelists, who are to be regarded as officers of the whole body." In closing his fictional story, Campbell offered the outline he set forth as "embracing much, if not every thing, that, in our judgment, is wanting to a complete and perfect organization." If there were "substantial objections" from any of the "brethren," Campbell stated he would be "happy" to receive them and that they would receive "a faithful, patient, and full consideration."[9]

Throughout the 1840s, many representatives of various congregations met to discuss the possibility of creating some form of national organization. Disciples journals kept the conversations alive through most of the decade. All the talk finally produced the first general convention of Disciples in 1849. One hundred fifty-six Christians, representing well over one hundred churches in eleven different states, gathered together at the Christian Church on Fourth and Walnut Streets in Cincinnati, Ohio.[10] The first session of the meeting elected Alexander Campbell, who was absent for some reason, president of the convention. Even though Campbell had earlier indicated his hope that the convention would provide a forum for specifically elected delegates, the gathering quickly recognized the voting status of all those present, whether they were elected by representative congregations or not. The first Disciples "mass meeting" was born.

The major organization spawned by this first mass meeting, of course, proved to be the American Christian Missionary Society (ACMS). The society, under the presidential leadership of Alexander Campbell, hoped to provide an avenue of participation for Disciples in the area of global evangelism. Membership in the society was entirely voluntary and dependent upon financial contributions. Between 1849 and 1967, the Disciples developed many such agencies, where cooperation between interested individuals resulted in a broadening of work beyond the local congregations. Since individuals made up the membership of these societies, their boards were independently controlled and the congregations had little to say about how they were run. In time, however, the governing of these agencies came under the limited supervision of the annual convention of the Disciples congregations.

Following 1849, the passing years witnessed an impressive record of cooperative endeavors among Disciples of Christ congregations. Most of these activities were carried out through this concept of the "associa- tion of interested individuals." Each year, these various societies reported to a mass meeting composed of many other interested individuals. Over the years, many leaders attempted to replace the mass meetings with some form of delegate representation. Mass meetings, they believed, could be dominated by the interests of whatever region hosted the gathering. Every time leaders attempted to shift toward a delegate model, most notably in a 1912 constitution, they ultimately failed due to congrega- tional fear that such a move would lead to too much general church authority.

Finally, in 1917, Frederick D. Kershner put together a compromise of sorts. He suggested a plan for two assemblies with mass voting in one and delegate representation in the other. The mass meeting continued to act as the final location for action on all matters of business. Yet business items were first sent to a new Committee on Recommendations, com- posed of equal delegate representation from the various areas of Dis- ciples work. The Kershner compromise also supported a new annual meeting to be called the International Convention of the Disciples of Christ. Though the compromise encountered some resistance, it worked reasonably well and led to a more effective and somewhat more repre- sentative annual gathering.[11]

The proliferation of national agencies and state societies, however, continued to cause problems. How were the relationships between them to be clarified? Who could help to negotiate areas where there existed a considerable degree of overlapping efforts? How could the congrega- tions respond effectively to numerous, and often persistent, calls for fi- nancial contributions? How could the congregations be kept aware of just how these agencies and societies operated? Could the work of these groups be trusted when the congregations had no effective say over how their programs were operated? These types of questions led to further attempts at consolidation in order to become more efficient and to de- sign clearer lines of accountability.

The United Christian Missionary Society (UCMS), formed in 1919, brought together the work of six different societies: the American Christian Missionary Society, the Christian Woman's Board of Missions, the Foreign Christian Missionary Society, the Board of Church Extension, the National Benevolent Association, and the Board of Ministerial Relief. In the next decade or so the last three of these societies became separate entities again (Pension Fund in 1928, NBA in 1933, and BCE in 1934). Even though the UCMS greatly simplified the structure of major Disciples agencies, it failed in its attempt to relieve the congregations from repetitive appeals for financial assistance. The development of Unified Promotion in 1934 finally helped to achieve this latter goal. Unified

Promotion brought much of the promotion of programs and most of the distribution of funds under one roof. In 1974, its work became the responsibility of the Church Finance Council. Today, congregational dollars given to Basic Mission Finance (BMF) help to support the distributed work of the church in all its areas. A new churchwide mission funding plan, associated with BMF, went into effect in 1996, designed to give more flexibility and control to congregations for the designation of their gifts to the work of the general church.

Currently, the trend among Disciples general and regional leadership is to give greater attention to serving congregational needs and offering supporting materials for congregational mission. This trend attempts to respond to the often-expressed congregational concern that the ministry of general and regional manifestations of church among Disciples have needed to connect more closely with the ministry of congregations. In many ways, this trend has highlighted for our day the important work of congregations in the ministry of the church. But other factors contribute to these trends as well. The post-denominational context of contemporary American religion, which has little respect for denominational institutions and "bureaucracies" (the word often used to describe them), and the reality of dwindling financial resources, have both contributed to our tendencies to emphasize the importance of congregational ministries. This preference for things local in the midst of a context where the competition for dollars is likely to increase means that Disciples will need to be deliberate and conscientious about support for the general manifestation of church if it is to survive into the next century. Today's pressures tempt us to fund local ministries, congregational and, perhaps, regional ministries (the things we can see) first and, only if anything is left afterwards, to send money on to ministries in other areas of the church's life.

Many Disciples prefer to stress local ministries over general ministries. But Disciples do possess a theology of church that might help in the counter-cultural endeavor to support the work of the church in its regional and general manifestations. Since restructure, Disciples have emphasized that regional and general manifestations, like congregations, are authentically "church." They do not simply serve the church (understood by some to be manifested only in congregations); rather, they are church (in the same way that congregation is the church). As church, they (regional and general manifestations) are neither more important nor less important than the church represented in its congregational form, but their ministries are eqaully deserving of Disciples support.

## The Restructure of the Church

By the time Disciples reached 165 years of age, they had gone through significant changes in their understanding of their self-identity. In their earliest years (1804–1830), they had seen themselves as a reforming movement within other denominations. Later (1830–1875), they continued their call for the denominations to abandon denominational identifications while, at the same time, they recognized the need for increasing structure and cooperative endeavors among their own congregations.

As one century gave way to another (1875–1919), they began to break out of their traditional isolationism in order to cooperate with other denominations in areas of social work and foreign missions, willing even to divide foreign areas of the work with those groups who baptized infants. During this period, they took on forms of denominationalism while many continued to insist their congregations did not constitute a denomination. The movement became known as "the Brotherhood." The name signaled Disciples belief that the fellowship of the church represented God's intention for the human family. But the name also provided a denominational handle of reference for members without alluding to definite denominational status. Increasing involvement in the ecumenical movement brought Disciples that status in practice, even though they studiously avoided it in name. Their 1908 founding membership in the Federal Council of Churches in America could be regarded in no other way.

They spent many of these later years (1919–1968) seeking more effective ways to fulfill their lifelong commitment to the mission of the church. From their first International Convention of the Disciples of Christ, held in 1919, to their first General Assembly of the Christian Church (Disciples of Christ), held in 1968, these Christians sought structural aids to enable them to be better stewards of both resources and talent. The effort known as "Restructure," accomplished by Disciples during the 1960s, finally brought Disciples to a new stage in church life.[12]

**Theological Foundations for Restructure**

The most pressing consideration urging restructure probably rested in the pragmatic need for it more than any particular theological demand for it. For years, even after the advent of the UCMS, the work of the national agencies and the state societies seemed hopelessly entangled. Conflicts over territory, financing, and program were constantly surfacing in some way or another. How could accountability be established for agencies, educational institutions, and congregations without resorting to ecclesiastical coercion? If congregations had no accountability to each other and no real responsibility for their agencies, meaningful ecumenical discussion with other Christian groups seemed impossible. Some attempt at restructuring Disciples life seemed inevitable.

Leaders could have pointed to that fact and addressed the question of restructure from a purely pragmatic perspective. They could have acted simply on the belief that better business practices would unravel the relationship agencies should have with one another and with the congregations whose funds helped to pay their bills. Instead, Disciples began to explore theological questions related to their heritage and mission.

Early on in the movement toward restructure, Willard Wickizer, the executive chair of the UCMS division of home missions, and Harlie L. Smith, the president of the Board of Higher Education, came upon the idea of gathering a group of Disciples pastors and theologians and charging them with the task of reexamining the beliefs and doctrines of the Disciples of Christ. By 1962, the year that the Commission on Brotherhood Restructure began meeting, these scholars had written forty essays examining most facets of Disciples belief.[13] Many of their conclusions had profound implications for the future of Disciples, but perhaps none had more importance at the time than their belief that the Disciples emphasis on congregational autonomy reflected life on the American frontier much more than it mirrored actual New Testament practices. This insight provided at least a starting point for the consideration of restructure.

The establishment of the Commission on Brotherhood Restructure resulted from the work of a committee appointed by the Disciples International Convention. When the committee, chaired by Wickizer, reported back to the 1960 Louisville International Convention, it suggested the appointment of a representative commission charged with the task of preparing a proposal for the restructuring of the church. The Los Angeles International Convention the next year elected 125 members to three-year terms. Granville Walker, pastor of University Christian Church in Fort Worth, Texas, was appointed the chair. A. Dale Fiers became the administrative secretary of the commission, serving until his election as executive secretary of the International Convention in 1964.[14]

As the commission contemplated its task, it came to recognize several important theological principles related to the nature of the church as bearing upon its work. First, the commission, in contemplating the biblical metaphors for the church, came to express concern for the church as the "Body of Christ." This meant that the church's dependence upon Christ must be recognized as of foremost importance. The church's unity is not dependent upon any structure or particular organization, but rather is an organic fact resting in the ministry of Jesus Christ. They referred to the church as a "Household of God." The phrase emphasized the fact that the church exists at God's initiative. Under God, in the covenant of love made clear in Christ, the people of the church belong to one another and are responsible one to another, and to the fulfillment of the mission of God in history.

The work of the commission recognized that God called the church, first of all, to be the "Servant of God." As Ronald E. Osborn put it, "The church is called by God to be God's people, bearing the servanthood of God's reconciliation in the world God created."[15] In their restructure efforts, Disciples attempted to recognize that their calling to the ministry of Jesus Christ was primary. Structural and organizational questions were only secondary and, they argued, must grow out of the church's concern for its call. Just as the apostolic church attended to structural matters in order to fulfill its mission more effectively (in the calling of the seven deacons, for example, or in the reflections of the Jerusalem Council pertaining to Paul's ministry), so must the church of today respond effectively to the challenges of its historical context.

During the process of restructure, many congregations and individuals expressed a concern that too much emphasis on structure would stifle the spiritual vitality of the church. Some believed that a concern for structure meant a concern for the mundane rather than the spiritual. Their argument attempted to separate the spiritual from the structural, as if the form of the church had nothing to do with its spirit. Osborn pointed out that "form and spirit" cannot be so easily separated.[16] Just as sin among Christians cannot be attributed only to the form of the human body, the sin in the church could not be solely attributed to its structural form. Members of the restructure commission tried hard to communicate their belief that concern for structures did not automatically translate into a loss of spiritual vitality. In fact, better structures might very well enliven the ministry of the church and aid the church in its concern for spiritual renewal.

The church is a divine creation. It is also inescapably and fully human. One cannot divide the spirit of the church from its body anymore than one could do that with Christ. A concern for the church's structural dimension could not be labeled as solely a concern for the human aspect of the church. Nor can a concern for the prayer life of the church, or any other aspect of the church's existence that might be designated as "spiritual," be considered as having nothing to do with the human aspect of the church. The spiritual and human dimensions of the church and its work are too intertwined for such an easy separation of the two.

As leaders among Disciples sought a new form for the church, they reminded themselves of the proper place for theology in considering church structure. Osborn set forth three theses: (1) No doctrine of the church could dictate the complete details of any particular pattern of church structure. This first thesis recognized the limits of theological reflection. (2) Every doctrine of the church contains some implications for church structure. The converse of this thesis is that every church structure illustrates certain theological doctrines behind it. (3) Because theology has its limits, practical questions of structure also enter into the picture. Where theology does not have anything particular to add, pragmatic questions need to be decided "on the basis of common sense and practical experience." On the one hand, the question of how many regions should make up the general body of the church might be purely pragmatic. On the other hand, the question of whether delegates of these regions ought to include women and men, lay and minister, and ethnic minorities might best be decided on theological grounds.[17]

Leaders supporting restructure also hoped congregations would come to accept the work of the general church as the legitimate and important work of the church as a whole. Under a system of complete and unlimited congregational autonomy it was hard to build credibility and acceptance for the work of the general church. Denominational leaders questioned theologically how any part of the body of Christ could be considered as completely autonomous. Each part of the body had to be responsible to every other part of the body. It was hard for some to imagine how the argument for complete autonomy would be able to serve the call of responsibility that accompanied such inherent and organic connections.

Restructure leaders hoped a newly established general church could challenge congregations to recognize their responsibility, not only to all the other Disciples congregations, but also to the larger Christian community as a whole. But this hope raised the specter of a general church that would hold authority over the congregations. Many Disciples feared this sort of development.

**The Question of Authority**

One of the major roadblocks to successful restructure rested in individual and congregational concerns centering on the question of authority. This critical question did not arise only among those who had refused to cooperate with the Disciples since the founding of the UCMS in 1919. Rather, it also surfaced among many loyal and fully cooperative members and congregations of the Disciples. This loyal opposition included a former president of the International Convention, Robert W. Burns, who also happened to be a member of the Restructure commission. Two Disciples professors, A. T. DeGroot of Brite and Frank N. Gardner of Drake, were counted among its number. Together, these and others presented an "Atlanta Declaration" vowing to protect "the present brotherhood as a free association of congregations."[18] W. E. Garrison held similar views even though he never formally associated with the Atlanta group.

The question over ecclesiastical authority obviously did not suddenly come from nowhere. It has remained an important question throughout Disciples life, and it has yet to be completely resolved. Richard Harrison argued in 1987 that a shift has taken place over the course of

Disciples history from a mostly personal authority to a largely institutionalized authority in the twentieth century. At the beginning of Disciples history, authority generally revolved around one or the other of the four founders: Barton W. Stone, Thomas and Alexander Campbell, and Walter Scott. Ministers and laity tended naturally to look to them for leadership, often approaching them seeking answers to their most difficult questions.

Authority, even before the first generation began passing from the scene, soon became associated with those who taught in Disciples colleges or who edited successful journals. Alexander Campbell, of course, did both. Perhaps due to his influence as teacher and editor, Disciples tended, toward the Civil War period and after, to look to its college administrators, teachers, or editors for leadership. Harrison pointed out that even this authority was more personal than institutional because the colleges and the journals were mostly privately owned.

The key to success for any movement, noted Harrison, demands the eventual institutionalization of the authority of the founders so that the earliest concerns of the movement will be enabled to live on with authority after the founders have died. Alexander Campbell's election as president of the American Christian Missionary Society in 1849 began this process of institutionalization. The process continued with the founding of the Christian Woman's Board of Missions (CWBM) in 1874. Caroline Neville Pearre, wife of a minister, like all other minister's wives, had no voice in the business sessions of the national meeting. So while the men met and discussed business, she and other women organized the CWBM in a separate meeting. Women, for the first time in Disciples life, assumed a slice of authority for themselves. From this time on, Disciples organizations were to have increasing authority in Disciples life. The men, not to be outdone, founded the Foreign Christian Missionary Society (FCMS) the next year.

Cultural factors contributed to this change in Disciples life. Disciples were spread out throughout the country by the end of the nineteenth century. They had outgrown a personal authority system. If their congregations were to be linked together in any significant way, there needed to be some way to draw them together. The organizations succeeded in doing that. Leaders of these institutions eventually acquired substantial informal authority as a by-product of their organization's importance to the life of the movement.[19]

When the six missionary and benevolent societies were combined in 1919 to form the UCMS, Disciples took another step toward a more formal institutional authority. At the same time, the UCMS and other agencies formed the new International Convention of the Disciples of Christ, which many viewed as the representative voice for Disciples of Christ in America and Canada. Through the International Convention, and particularly through the efforts of the UCMS, Disciples expanded their witness throughout the world.

Before the Depression hit in America, some 339 Disciples missionaries were on foreign fields. Over the years just before and after the Depression, Disciples performed an average of about 5,000 baptisms per year in foreign lands.[20] By the mid-1950s over 370 schools were established by missionary workers supported by Disciples churches. Further, many churches, social service centers, and hospitals all over the world owe their existence to the efforts of these selfless individuals somehow related to the UCMS and to the society's careful stewardship of very limited resources.

The UCMS possesses quite a distinguished history. No comprehensive description of its near-fifty-year existence has yet found its way into print. Perhaps the society's overwhelming accomplishments contribute to the elusive nature of its history. After all, whoever writes the history of the society will also have to address a half-century of Disciples work in foreign missions, home missions, Christian education, social welfare, church development, and church evangelism. Of course, one should not forget that the histories of the Pension Fund, the Board of Church Extension, the National Benevolent Association, and the Division of Higher Education also have points of intersection with the life of the UCMS.

The UCMS accomplished all its work without any formal delineation of its authority to act on behalf of all Disciples. As a society, it represented only those congregations and individuals who contributed to its work. Yet the informal authority the UCMS possessed in Disciples life far surpassed what anyone might have imagined at the time it began its work. The fifty-year existence of the UCMS arguably represents the most powerful and important factor in the development of Disciples church life in the entire history of the Christian Church (Disciples of Christ).

The UCMS even published its own journal beginning in 1919. *World Call* combined the editorial efforts of many previous journals, including the *Missionary Tidings*, the *Missionary Intelligencer*, the *American Home Missionary*, *Business in Christianity*, and the *Christian Philanthropist*. Since *World Call* went into the homes previously served by these journals, the first monthly issue began with a circulation of about sixty-five thousand strong. Through this journal and other efforts, the UCMS served as a major resource for educational and religious materials for Disciples churches everywhere. It stood behind the preparation of Sunday school materials and offered the official interpretation of Disciples work whenever such an interpretation was needed. Its staff spoke endlessly in Disciples churches on every topic imaginable.

At a time when Disciples congregations thought of themselves as independent churches only loosely related to one another, the UCMS provided the glue that held them together. One might even conclude that the work of the society actually laid the necessary groundwork for restructure. If there had been no UCMS, something like it would have had to be developed before any official restructuring of the church could have found general acceptance among Disciples churches. Over time, the work of the UCMS clearly demonstrated the usefulness of recognizing the denominational reality of Disciples existence. That contribution provided a key ingredient for accomplishing the relatively smooth transition into a restructured church life after 1968.

When the restructure process began, Disciples leaders had in mind the hope that the end result would be more congregational oversight of the church's agencies, not less. They believed that delegate conventions would give the congregations served by the agencies of the church more ability to participate in the governance of those agencies. Yet delegate conventions, many congregations feared, might, as representative assemblies, be able to speak with too much authority. Suspicion of the establishment of formal authority runs deep in Disciples tradition. Early Disciples are well known for their fear of authoritarianism in the church. Their only authority was that of the Bible. Restructure leaders hoped to find some way for the Disciples to speak with authority without being authoritarian. They believed that not all "authority" had to be expressed in "authoritarian" ways.

This brief narrative indicates that, though authority has always operated rather informally in Disciples tradition, Disciples have always had authoritative persons and institutions in its life. Odd as it may seem, as long as Disciples never tried to formalize authority, most of them have been content for it to operate in informal ways. This attitude has left the denomination nearly paralyzed in terms of its being able to offer reflective considerations of its theological position. Who has the right to express what Disciples believe about the nature of Christianity? Such an expression would require some formal location where such teaching could be hammered out and set forth for the Disciples as a whole to discuss, evaluate, and shape. For much of Disciples history, the anti-creedal dimension of Disciples life has prevented most generations from attempting any serious consideration of theological matters.

Disciples are still seeking ways to speak to each other and to others in the name of an authoritative gospel without practicing coercive forms of authority to go along with it. How does a tradition that respects the freedom of congregations speak with authority on important issues related to its expression of the Christian faith? The struggle to find an appropriate answer to this question continues. In 1983 the Disciples Commission on Theology presented a report to the General Assembly entitled "A Word to the Church on Authority." Admitting that restructure failed fully to "come to grips, pragmatically or theologically, with the issues related to authority in the church," the report cautioned that "a church which is unwilling to search for a common understanding of Christian authority will be controlled by biblicism, self-seeking individuals, or self-serving institutions." Yet the "Word to the Church on Authority" still offered no ultimate solution to the dilemma faced by Disciples.[21]

To speak with authority does not mean to speak from the top down. Among Disciples, local congregations, regions, and the general church all need to find ways to speak with authority to one another and to those in the whole community of the church beyond Disciples life. As Michael Kinnamon has pointed out, a church or a congregation speaks with authority when it attempts to interpret the meaning of its Christian faith in a way that will provide guidance for individual believers as they confront the challenges of the contemporary world.[22] How is that done in a tradition that is highly skeptical of authority of any kind?

Attempting to speak from a theological understanding, the 1983 "Word to the Church on Authority" emphasized that all genuine authority is consistent with the nature of God as revealed in Christ. The church must avoid the temptation to adopt cultural patterns of authority, where authority flows in hierarchical patterns. The crucified Christ reveals that authority is best regarded as sacrificial, arising out of the self-emptying servanthood that leads to the cross. Authority in the church, if it follows the pattern established by Christ, must be persuasive rather than coercive. Among Disciples, it must also be broadly participatory and widely dispersed throughout the life of the denomination.

Authority, as exercised in the Christian Church (Disciples of Christ), must be recognized for what it is: a human response to God's initiative. God acted in Christ and established the possibility for genuine community in the life of the church. As Disciples seek to exercise authority through the process of corporate decision-making, they must also seek a response consistent with their experience of God's initiative in Christ to meet the deepest needs of the human condition. Therefore, they must use scripture and tradition as guides for reasoning through these decisions. Because the church is one, any denomination seeking its own authoritative voice is responsible for seeking out the testimony of the church universal as well. For this reason, the "general" church structure among Disciples is more than just a service organization seeking to meet the needs of the congregations. It is also charged to hear the voice of the church universal and speak it to all aspects of Disciples church life, countering any parochial or provincial ideas that thrive there.

Disciples realize that authoritative teaching, even in the church, is subject to the foibles of human judgment. The church's judgment is sometimes flat wrong. For this reason, authority in the Disciples tradition must respect the claims of diversity. It is important that authoritative decisions made by Disciples respect, and even encourage, the voice of the minority. The will of God is not consistently synonymous with either a majority or minority vote.

In recent years, many Disciples ministers and lay people are coming to appreciate the idea of a teaching office (perhaps located in the office of the regional minister) that would encourage theological dialogue across all manifestations of church life among Disciples. Whatever form Disciples general teaching authority might take, it must always give proper attention to, rather than demean or ignore, the importance of the congregation as the most basic expression of the church in human history. Authority in the Disciples tradition must ultimately strengthen, rather than weaken, the ministry of the local congregations. When Disciples give more deliberate attention to their expression of the authority of the gospel, in both General Assembly and local congregation, they will also begin to understand better their identity as a Christian people.

Among Disciples, authoritative teaching remains informal. Whether it issues from congregations, regions, lay people, pastors, seminary professors, or general church administrators, it is often ignored, left unchallenged, or taken for granted. None of these responses are really beneficial for the spiritual maturity and vitality of the church as a whole. Growth is sure to take place for all concerned when the authoritative perspectives from any of these places or persons are more intentionally and formally brought into contact with the authoritative perspectives of the whole community of the church. As Disciples conscientiously seek the authority of the gospel, they will simultaneously arrive at a more confident witness against the false gods of this world.

## 1968: Disciples Celebrate Restructure

Even though Disciples leaders of the 1960s were unable to solve the authority issue once and for all, they were moderately successful in their effort to develop a more effective denominational institution. With Ronald E. Osborn at the microphone on September 26, 1968, Disciples coming together for their annual meeting in the Kansas City Municipal Auditorium voted overwhelmingly to accept the new *Provisional Design* recommended by the Commission on Restructure. Bill Guthrie, at the request of Osborn, led all those in attendance in the singing of the Doxology. This moment marks the first time Disciples corporately recognized, through their newly adopted *Design*, their own place as one denomination among others "within the universal body of Christ."[23]

The road traveled to arrive at that culminating moment had been a long one. Restructure required approval of two-thirds of all the states and the area associations related to Disciples of Christ. It also required two-thirds approval from each of the agencies, and from two-thirds of those delegates gathered at the General Assembly as well. Considering all factors, it is nothing short of amazing that the whole process of restructure, from conceiving the original idea to the final approval of the finished product in General Assembly, actually lasted only about six years.

The *Provisional Design* received its first public exposure in 1966 at the Dallas convention. (In 1975, Disciples dropped the "provisional" from the title when they decided they did not need a constitution and could live under the *Design* itself.) Though the Dallas assembly did not take any action on the document, it did vote to change future meetings of the general church into delegate assemblies. Each congregation would receive two voting representatives unless membership stood above 750, at which point delegate representation would be increased. Later, Disciples altered the *Design* so that congregations would receive, above the two delegates all congregations would receive, "one additional voting representative for each 500 participating members or major fraction thereof over the first 500."[24] The *Provisional Design*, as finally approved in 1968, called for the recognition, organization, and coordination of three manifestations of church life—local, regional, and general—among Disciples. The restructure committee purposely chose the word *manifestations* instead of the word *levels* to avoid any connotation of a hierarchy. The diagram below illustrates the relationship these manifestations have with one another. Any one of them might appear at the top of the diagram. There is no hierarchical arrangement intended in the division of the church into these three manifestations.

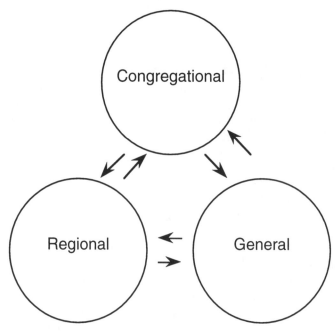

THE THREE MANIFESTATIONS

The General Assembly, as set forth by the *Design*, is composed of both a mass meeting and a representative body. It is held every other year, during the odd years. Voting is restricted to delegates from the congregations and the regions, to ordained and licensed ministers who have standing among Disciples, to General Board members, and to chief administrative officers of colleges, seminaries and general administrative units of the church. All other persons in the denomination are invited to attend and to take part in the discussion of issues as they are brought to the floor, but they are not able to vote.

The general manifestation includes a primary deliberative body known as the General Board. All issues scheduled to be discussed by the General Assembly are first studied and acted upon by the General Board. Though the final say on any given issue coming before the general manifestation of the church rests with the delegates of the General Assembly, the sheer number of both issues and people makes lengthy and deliberate debate impossible. Therefore, the General Board carefully studies each item and makes recommendations. The General Assembly, of course, is free to accept or reject those recommendations during its business sessions.

Besides restructuring Disciples life according to three manifestations of church, the actions taken by the denomination in 1968 also offered new opportunities to effect a new relationship between the largely white leadership structure and minorities within the church. Though Hispanic and Asian Disciples are considerably fewer in number than African-American Disciples, their growth among Disciples is impressive. The positive impact of their leadership among Disciples is increasingly evident throughout the life of the denomination. Hispanic Disciples formed a National Hispanic and Bilingual Fellowship in 1981 and have held several assemblies over the past decade.

African-American Disciples have a history of association that goes all the way back to the beginning of Disciples life. Their separate organizational life began in 1917 when Preston Taylor, a minister and funeral home director from Memphis, led black Disciples in founding the National Christian Missionary Convention. African Americans found it necessary to organize the separate, but cooperating, convention because they knew there were no possibilities of whites sharing leadership positions with them at that time or in their near future.

Until 1960, African-American Disciples had separate agencies and programs in almost every area of church life. At that time, most of these programs were brought under the general umbrella of the United Christian Missionary Society. Emmett Dickson became the director of church relations who coordinated most of the programs related to black Disciples. During 1969, after restructure, a merger was worked out between the National Christian Missionary Convention and the newly established Christian Church (Disciples of Christ). Finally in 1970, largely due to the leadership efforts of Raymond E. Brown, long-time officer of the Board of Church Extension, all business related to African-American Disciples was incorporated into the work of the General Assembly. At that time, these Disciples formed the National Convocation of the Christian Church, which has since operated by meeting every other year to discuss special concerns of African-American Disciples.

Perhaps the most important result of restructure rests in the new theology of church expressed by the change in structure. Adoption of the *Design* officially changed the Disciples notion of "church." For most of their history, Disciples had no clearly expressed theological understanding of the church. Rather, they viewed themselves as a collection of independent and autonomous congregations known by names like "First Christian Church," or "Second Church of Christ." When asked their name, they generally replied they were a part of the Christian Churches. Through the *Design*, Disciples expressed a much broader theology of church and of their own place within it. The accompanying change of corporate name from "Christian Churches (Disciples of Christ)" to "Christian Church (Disciples of Christ)" illustrates this broader notion of church.

The change from the plural to the singular is significant. When understood in the context of the denomination itself, the word *church* signifies the recognition that all congregations have covenanted with one another to form one church body, complete with acceptance of all the responsibilities implied by such a relationship. As paragraph 4 of the *Design* states it, "as a response to God's covenant, we commit ourselves to one another." When this covenant is understood in the context of the universal body of Christ (the church), the parenthetical "Disciples of Christ" signifies the recognition that Disciples do not constitute the whole church. Rather, they are but one partial and fragmentary expression of the church, longing for the time when all denominations within the church might somehow find more tangible ways to express the reality of the unity of the church universal.

Yet another illustration of the broader notion of church operating in the *Design*, is the recognition that the chief executive officer of the denomination is a minister. As the *Design* describes the primary function of that office, it is to provide "pastoral care and nurture" for the church. For that reason, Disciples chose to use the title "General Minister and President." This title gives primary emphasis to the recognition that the chief executive is first and foremost a *minister* for the general work of the church, and only secondarily one who *presides* over the general staff. By choosing this emphasis, Disciples demonstrated their growth beyond an earlier understanding of the work of the church as something done entirely by congregations.[25] Post-restructure Disciples finally affirmed what

Ronald E. Osborn had asserted in his 1964 lectures before the restructure commission:

> What then is the character of our corporate life? It is something more than a convention, far more than a policy of cooperation, far more than an association of churches. It is the church, as surely as any congregation is the church. It is not yet the whole church, but it is the church.[26]

Not all congregations were happy with this changing notion of "church." Restructure finally brought about a parting of the ways between Independents and Disciples. Ever since the formation of the UCMS in 1919, a significant number of churches had become known as "noncooperatives" or, eventually, as "independents." These churches, for most of the twentieth century, had refused to have much of anything to do with cooperative societies and national conventions because the New Testament did not appear to authorize any organization beyond that of the local congregation. Independent discontent might have helped to expose the fact that at least a part of the Disciples efforts in this area grew in Disciples soil fertilized by the long-standing desire among some Disciples to be counted among the mainstream of American Christianity. In other words, some believed the move was motivated as much by status-seeking efforts as it was by theological belief.[27]

During the years restructure became a reality, a significant number of congregations discontinued any formal identification with Disciples. Robert L. Friedly and D. Duane Cummins recently rehearsed the fact that, over the six-year period from 1967 to 1972, over thirty-five hundred congregations, with combined memberships of around three quarters of a million people, withdrew from the Disciples Year Book. These congregations are known today as the Christian Churches and Churches of Christ. Since these congregations normally had not contributed to the cooperative work of Disciples, their departure did not have a negative impact on the support for Disciples world causes. In fact, during the same period, giving for Disciples outreach increased by 1.3 million dollars.[28]

The new covenant relationship of the remaining Disciples congregations, approximately four thousand congregations numbering about one million members, stands in the tradition of the biblical covenant. Before restructure became a reality, Ronald Osborn described such a covenant by stating that it

> is intensely personal but never merely individual. Whoever binds [self] in covenant of faithfulness with God also binds [self] to God's people. It is that common covenant which makes the church. It is to a group of people what the good confession is to an individual. The

covenant is something that God initiates. We cannot make the covenant; we declare or acknowledge it and its consequences.[29]

Restructure accomplished a new way for Disciples to affirm a covenant with one another and with all those who confess Christ. The understanding of this covenant is perhaps best expressed through the "Preamble" to the *Design*. In the mid-1960s a special task force of the Commission on Brotherhood Restructure, chaired by W. Barnett Blakemore, studied various covenantal statements in order to see if it could come up with a general statement of belief that might describe the new relationship envisioned by the plans for restructure. The resulting statement eventually became known as the "Preamble" and today serves as the introduction to the *Design*. Many congregations print these words on their bulletins. Others frequently read them as a part of their liturgy in worship.

> As members of the Christian Church,
> We confess that Jesus is the Christ,
>> the Son of the living God,
>> and proclaim him Lord and Savior of the world.
> In Christ's name and by his grace
>> we accept our mission of witness
>> and service to all people.
> We rejoice in God,
>> maker of heaven and earth,
>> and in the covenant of love
>> which binds us to God and one another.
> Through baptism into Christ
>> we enter into newness of life
>> and are made one with the whole people of God.
> In the communion of the Holy Spirit
>> we are joined together in discipleship
>> and in obedience to Christ.
> At the table of the Lord
>> we celebrate with thanksgiving
>> the saving acts and presence of Christ.
> Within the universal church
>> we receive the gift of ministry
>> and the light of scripture.
> In the bonds of Christian faith
>> we yield ourselves to God
>> that we may serve the One
>> whose kingdom has no end.
> Blessing, glory and honor
>> be to God forever. Amen.[30]

Though no 170-word statement can do a complete job of expressing the nature of Disciples belief, this statement certainly provides a starting point. As Disciples continue (with biblical focus and historical understanding, with theological integrity and seriousness of purpose, with reason and experience) to assess their mission in the midst of an ever-changing world, they need most of all to remember they do not have all the answers, either in terms of theology, structure, or method. As sure as they feel they have arrived at some final resting point, they will be left behind, an irrelevant and powerless people unable to fulfill the mission God's timeless gospel has set for them in history.

## Questions for Reflection and Discussion

1. "When Thomas Campbell declared in 1809 that the 'church of Christ upon earth is essentially, intentionally, and constitutionally one,' he did not mean to say that any one institution in history could ever fully represent the essence and truth of that statement. Rather, he knew that the essential oneness of the church rested in Christ, not in history." Disciples, with this understanding, still hoped to realize a new wholeness for church life in America. How was this commitment affected by the shift from being a reforming movement within a traditional group to becoming a reforming organization alongside other groups (something none of the early Disciples or early Christians anticipated or initially wanted)? What are the strengths and weaknesses of denominational existence in America?

2. Though pragmatic considerations had much to do with the move toward restructure, what theological principles also laid the groundwork for restructure?

3. Reflect on the question of authority (after carefully reading that section of this chapter). How should authority operate in Disciples life? What is the relation of the general church structure to it? What is the relation of the congregational witness to it? Given your understanding of the need to present an authoritative gospel witness, how should the general offices, regional offices, and congregations relate to one another? Can you suggest ways Disciples can break out of their historical paralysis when it comes to being able to offer reflective considerations of theological positions that foster communication across all areas (congregational, regional, and general) of church life? What characterizes your own congregation's relationship to area, regional, and general manifestations of Disciples church life?

4. Consider the change of name, accomplished through restructure, from "Christian Churches (Disciples of Christ)" to "Christian Church (Disciples of Christ)." How does the concept of covenant come to fruition in this change, and what does that concept represent theologically over against the notion of the autonomy of local congregations?

## Notes

[1] *The Design for the Christian Church (Disciples of Christ)*, paragraph 2.

[2] See W. Clark Gilpin, "The Integrity of the Church: The Communal Theology of Disciples of Christ," in *Classic Themes of Disciples Theology*, pp. 29-48.

[3] *Ibid.*, p. 33.

[4] See Chapter 4 above.

[5] Ronald E. Osborn, "A Theology of Denominations and Principles for Brotherhood Restructure," in Wm. Barnett Blakemore, ed., *The Revival of the Churches*, Volume III, *The Renewal of Church: The Panel of Scholars Reports* (St. Louis: The Bethany Press, 1963), pp. 82-111.

[6] H. Richard Niebuhr, *Social Sources of Denominationalism*, p. 25.

[7] *The Millennial Harbinger* (May 1831), p. 237.

[8] *The Millennial Harbinger* (January 1842), p. 4.

[9] *The Millennial Harbinger* (February 1843), pp. 82-86.

[10] McAllister and Tucker, *Journey in Faith*, p. 175.

[11] *Ibid.*, pp. 340-342.

[12] Anthony L. Dunnavant wrote a first-rate dissertation that examines Restructure in light of what he referred to as the four "fundamental ideals" of the Disciples movement: restoration, union, liberty, and mission. See Dunnavant, "Restructure: Four Historical Ideals in the Campbell-Stone Movement and the Development of the Polity of the Christian Church (Disciples of Christ) (Ph.D. dissertation, Vanderbilt University, 1984). One might also take a look at Dunnavant, "The Search for Churchly Wholeness and the Voluntary-Associational Form in the Structural History of the Disciples of Christ," *Mid-Stream* 26 (July 1987): 408-418.

[13] See *The Renewal of Church: The Panel of Scholars Reports*, 3 Volumes (St. Louis: The Bethany Press, 1963) for the published essays from these years of study.

[14] See Robert L. Friedly and D. Duane Cummins, *The Search for Identity: Disciples of Christ and the Restructure Years*, pp. 29-41.

[15] Ronald E. Osborn, *Toward the Christian Church (Disciples of Christ): Intention, Essence, Constitution* (St. Louis: Christian Board of Publication, 1964), pp. 10, 12.

[16] *Ibid.*, p. 26-30.

[17] *Ibid.*, p. 8f.

[18] This sentence is quoted, in the midst of a discussion about opposition to restructure, in Robert L. Friedly and D. Duane Cummins, *The Search for Identity*, p. 62.

[19] This argument is made in Richard L. Harrison, Jr., "Places of Authority in the Disciples of Christ: An Historical Reflection," *Mid-Stream* 26 (July 1987): 317-323.

[20] These statistics are found among the UCMS papers. See for example, "Meeting the Crisis in the Missionary Benevolent Work of the Disciples of Christ: Carried on Through the United Christian Missionary Society"—a September 9, 1930 meeting discussing the severity of the Depression and its impact on missions (UCMS papers).

[21] "A Word to the Church on Authority," Appendix B, in William Baird, *What Is Our Authority* (St. Louis: published for Council on Christian Unity by Christian Board of Publication, 1983), p. 39.

[22] See Michael Kinnamon, "Authority: Reflections on the Future of the Disciples Tradition," *Mid-Stream* 26 (July 1987): 332-338.

[23] *The Design*, paragraph 3.

[24] *The Design*, paragraph 11a. At Tulsa, in 1991, Disciples rejected a resolution attempting to lower the figure from 500 participating members to 250 participating members; see Business item 9121 in *Business Docket and Program: In Remembrance of Me, General Assembly, Tulsa, October 25-30, 1991*, p. 317f.

[25] *The Design*, see especially paragraphs 4 and 40.

[26]Osborn, *Toward the Christian Church (Disciples of Christ): Intention, Essence, Constitution*, p. 54.

[27] Ronald Osborn, one of the theological proponents of restructure, discusses this aspect of the process in his essay, "The Irony of the Twentieth-Century Christian Church (Disciples of Christ): Making it to the Mainline Just at the Time of its Disestablishment," *Midstream* 28 (July 1989): 292-312.

[28]Friedly and Cummins, *The Search for Identity*, pp. 63-64.

[29]Quoted in *Ibid.*, p. 46.

[30]"Preamble" to *The Design*, paragraph 1.

# 10

# WHAT IS THE ROLE OF A DENOMINATION IN A POST-DENOMINATIONAL AGE?

*There's no chance of falling asleep during the sermon at First Lutheran church. There is no sermon. The Rev. John Kleist is trying a new way to draw people into the fold with an express 22 minute service that he says provides all the spirituality of the regular service in half the time. The shortened version eliminates sermon and sacrament, but retains most of the elements of a full-length service—statement of faith, apology for sins, prayer, interpretation of the weekly Bible reading and a song. Penny Bonawitz, after an express service with her two young children, called it a success with, "...that's just about the time the kids start acting up."*

"Sinfully Short and Sweet," published in the *Fort Worth Star-Telegram*, with a by-line from Greenwich, New Jersey, February 3, 1994, page 1.

## *Introduction*

This short news story illustrates rather graphically the difference between contemporary church and church life in America for most of the last two hundred years. Part of the ethos of American culture over the majority of those years was to attend, faithfully every Sunday, the church of your choice. Today more and more churches are having to resort to strange and new tactics in order just to get people to sit in their pews. What has happened?

Over the course of the nineteenth and twentieth centuries, denominations in America successfully built a new religious establishment in the context of religious liberty, a Protestant establishment, where it could be taken for granted that if you were American, successful, and possessed any real power in the society, you most likely were white, male,

245

and belonged to one of the Protestant denominations. As early as 1955, American sociologists and religious historians were beginning to notice that dramatic change was afoot. Religious sociologist Will Herberg pointed out that Catholicism and Judaism had joined the ranks of Protestantism as equal components of America's normative faith expressions.[1] By the end of the 1960s, it became clear to most observers that the fragmentation of Protestantism and the increased diversity of America's religions had led to a popular concern that public life in America find expression free of Protestant or even Christian associations. During these later decades, Americans have found themselves debating anew the foundation of their common life. Christianity in America, in all its forms, has spent the last four decades adjusting to this new and very different context. And for the mainline denominations, particularly, this context has led to a rapid decline in influence, numbers, and power within the society.

Ironically, as Ronald Osborn noted in 1989, Disciples of Christ officially joined the mainline "just at the time of its cultural disestablishment." With Restructure in 1968, Disciples claimed mainline denominational status. At least some of the Disciples ecumenical involvement during the early 1900s represented "in part a bid for recognition as an acknowledged unit in the Protestant cultural establishment." This bid for establishment status, argued Osborn, caused Disciples to abandon their effort to reach outsiders. The passion of their nineteenth-century witness diminished, and when this lack combined with an inherent aversion to theological reflection, Disciples easily fit into the malaise affecting most of the twentieth-century Protestant mainline churches.

As part of the Protestant establishment, Disciples hoped to rely on institutional loyalty to keep members in their churches. This establishment mentality led ministers to take their future in ministry for granted. Unfortunately for Disciples, they arrived at precisely the time "a rapid evaporation of denominational loyalty has occurred across the religious spectrum." The children of many mainline parents, and Disciples are not an exception here, end up in one of the new "nondenominational centers." Osborn quoted evangelical historian George Marsden: "It's like gasoline. Once you discover all gasoline is the same, brand loyalty disappears, and any station will do. Only octane matters, and the mainline Protestant churches do not sell high-octane religion."[2]

## *The Context of Post-Denominationalism*

Today, we live in a society where many are increasingly comfortable with using the description "post-denominational" to depict the American religious scene. The context defining the emergence of the post-denominational era is marked by at least three dimensions: Statistics Related to Church Life, Cultural Factors, and Mainline Factors.

**Statistics Related to Church Life**

The Protestant majority in general, in terms of expressed preference, has slipped from 67% in 1967 to 56% in 1991.[3] Catholic preference was 25% in both 1967 and 1991, though during the 1980s it climbed as high as 29% and has steadily declined since. Jewish preference has fallen from 3% to 2%. Other religious preferences have jumped from 3% to 6%, which testifies to the growth of Mormons, Jehovah's Witnesses, and other such groups. The other great gainer is "no religious preference." That category has grown the most dramatically of all categories since 1967; it has steadily climbed from 2% to 11%, a whopping 450% increase, and is still growing a percentage or two every year. This statistic provides fairly strong evidence of diminishing denominational loyalty.

Increasingly, many who have left traditional church life are today associating with other kinds of groups and counting that association as their primary "religious" activity. A 1992 study documents and describes how some Americans have found "substitute faiths" through their memberships in Common Cause, Sierra Club, or the nearest yoga, ballet, or martial arts classes. Others have found spirituality through various avenues enabling "self-awareness," whether through "Self-Realization Fellowships," self-help books, astrology, paranormal experiences, or the practice of witchcraft.[4]

Today's big eight denominations—The United Methodist Church (UMC), The Presbyterian Church (USA), The Christian Church (Disciples of Christ), The American Baptist Church (ABC), The United Church of Christ (UCC), The Evangelical Lutheran Church of America (ELCA), and the Southern Baptist Convention (SBC)—account for less than one-third of the white Protestant church attendance in America on any particular weekend.[5] Since this counts the SBC, it is clear that the vast majority of white Protestants are attending non-denominational congregations or congregations aligned with smaller Protestant denominations. If you subtract the SBC, not usually identified as a mainline denomination, you come up with some stunning figures related to church membership. In 1965, these seven mainline denominations had a combined membership of 29.48 million. By 1992, their total membership was 22.8 million, for a drop of about 22.7%. Of course, this drop in membership includes the schism between the Independent Christian Churches and the Disciples, numbering about 700,000.[6] If one discounts the 700,000 figure, the drop in membership for the mainline remains an impressive 20.3%.

Episcopalians, Methodists, and Presbyterians can expect nearly 50% of the children born in their churches to leave for good when they get older.[7] Between 1987 and 1988, the six mainline families—ELCA, CC (DOC), Episcopal, Presbyterian (USA), UCC, and UMC—counted a net loss of 194,000 members. This is the equivalent of "closing down a 530 member church every day of the year."[8]

In addition, a great deal of denominational switching is going on. Gallup information from 1991 indicates that about one adult in four (23%) has left the religion or denomination of the family's heritage.[9] Other information indicates that fully 33% of Americans have switched from one denomination to another. Among Disciples, it is rare to have less than 40–50% switchers in almost any gathered group. I have found the same to be true in my limited work with Presbyterians. Data from the late 1970s and early 1980s indicates that fully "45% of all Americans who had been raised Presbyterians now belonged to some other denomination or to no denomination at all." The same data revealed that approximately 40% of Methodists had switched as well.[10]

Fully 80% of Americans have attended religious services in a denomination other than their own. Wuthnow argued that "persons who grew up in a particular denomination are more likely to switch to a different denomination if they have been to college." About 20% of Americans switch at least twice, and 10% switch three times or more.[11] According to Gallup, "the smaller Protestant denominations frequently are the beneficiaries of these changes."[12]

Robert Bellah concluded in the fall of 1990 that "it is unrealistic to assume that Christians today will stay where they were brought up....Both the Protestant principle of voluntarism and the modern respect for autonomous decision make it natural for adults to choose their own religious affiliation."[13] Intermarriage has contributed to this phenomenon in about one out of four cases (24%). Relocation or convenience of location has caused only roughly 10% of the switches. Fourteen percent switched due to a stated preference for the beliefs of their new churches, while 7% said they were leaving because their previous church did not meet their beliefs or needs. Methodists lost 15% of the switchers; Roman Catholics lost 18% of the switchers.[14]

In some ways, church attendance figures have something to do with this whole question of denominational switching. Even though church attendance has remained virtually the same for nearly 45 years, there have been some changes. Protestant membership and attendance has swelled in evangelical and nondenominational churches. Neo-Pentecostals and Roman Catholics have also benefited.[15] These factors make the mainline decline all the more stark. The fact that church attendance figures remain basically the same, while attendance is drastically down in the mainline denominations, offers further evidence that there are shifting loyalties at work in American religion, and that the mainline is losing more than anyone else as a result of those shifts.

As one might expect, all the above factors have led to financial crisis for most of the mainline denominations. National denominational agencies are experiencing massive financial difficulties, especially among the mainline, though not entirely limited to the mainline (the Southern Baptist Convention, itself a denomination in an identity crisis, is experiencing problems for reasons other than a decline in membership). The Presbyterian Church (USA) recently slashed its budget by $7 million and 175 staff positions. The ELCA made up for a $14.8 million shortfall in 1988 by cutting both staff and spending; from 1989–1990, deficits continued to the tune of approximately $5.6 million. The Episcopalians have been forced to cut back. The UCC has experienced increased local giving, but decreased national giving.[16] The Disciples have cut staff and have restructured their Basic Mission Finance program.

Alongside these developments, there has been tremendous growth in parachurch agencies, non-denominational meta- and megachurches, paradenominational organizations, and congregations that hide their denominational name.[17] In *The Restructuring of American Religion*, Robert Wuthnow devoted a full chapter to the growth of "special purpose groups" since World War II. These groups include the conservative organizations of the "New Christian Right," organizations like the Moral Majority, Christian Voice, and the Religious Roundtable. But it also includes more evangelical groups like the Christian Legal Society, moderate-to-liberal groups like the Americans United for the Separation of Church and State, and more obscure groups like the Christian Chiropractors Association, the Fellowship of Christian Magicians, and the Fellowship of Christian Peace Officers.[18] Though special interest groups have no doubt contributed to the vitality of religious expression in America, they have also increasingly become competitors with the denominations for the participation and resources of the members they share in common.

The success of the megachurches (2,000 to 10,000 members) and metachurches (10,000 or more members) as nondenominational congregations also indicates American religion is entering a post-denominational era.[19] The most well-known of the nondenominational metachurches is the Willow Creek Community Church in South Barrington, Illinois. An evangelical church that stresses personal conversion, the infallible Bible, and the obligation of all believers to fulfill the Great Commission, Willow Creek has over 10,000 participating members. The congregation started in 1975 with approximately 125 people meeting in a rented movie theater. After conducting a targeted "customer survey," it has grown to one of the world's largest congregations in terms of attendance. Its minister, Bill Hybels, has built a building complex covering 130 acres that resembles a "neutral corporate setting" more than a church. Raised in the Christian Reformed Church, Hybels now sees his role in life as ministering to the 25–45-year-old white collar professionals.

Each church service usually includes some kind of dramatic presentation, "under the watchful eye of Willow Creek's full-time drama director." Weekend sermons are upbeat, soft-sell, and designed to help listeners to move toward accepting Christianity as a pathway to a more meaningful life. Weekend services are for the neophytes and potential Christians. According to Hybels, "You don't have to say anything, sing anything, sign anything, or give anything" to be a member. More serious members, however, return for "New Community" services on Wednesday and Thursday nights. These are the services meant to provide worship for the true believers, who are encouraged to tithe their incomes. This two-tier membership strategy has served the church well in terms of its growth. Up to 2,000 church leaders from across the nation flock to Willow Creek some three times a year in order to listen to Hybels describe "his seven-step program to bring non-churched Harrys and Marys full circle."[20]

Paradenominational organizations, groups possessing tight congregational connections without traditional denominational ties, are also thriving. Calvary Chapel of Costa Mesa, California, has cloned over 429 different congregations.[21] The Vineyard Christian Fellowship in Anaheim, offering a strict orthodoxy wed to charismatic "signs and wonders," has grown to 6,000 members and established a new network of over 500 Vineyard churches drawing over 100,000 followers, most of them denominational switchers or returnees from among the baby-boomers.[22] These movements indicate the power of "para" or "transdenominational" organizations today.

There are yet other powerful examples. A minister within The Presbyterian Church in America (PCA), the conservative Presbyterians, developed the new concept of the Perimeter Church. Though the congregations associated with this movement "stay within the heritage of the Presbyterian Church," they are associated with an umbrella movement called Perimeter Christian Ministries, Inc. It started with one congregation, the Perimeter Church of Greater Atlanta, and has since grown to numerous satellite congregations. The original goal was to establish one main congregation with perimeter locations throughout the city, "sort of like having a pizza parlor at every other freeway exit," joked the founding minister. Perimeter congregations have done away with the traditional feel of worship, though once a month on Sunday evenings, members of all the congregations are invited to meet at the headquarters church for a traditional communion service that follows traditional Presbyterian liturgy and uses hymnals brought out of the closet for the event.[23]

Marketing information also indicates that seekers don't appreciate denominational names. Increasingly, church growth experts are recommending that congregations wishing to grow should drop denominational names from their signs and should change their name if it indicates a particular denominational affiliation. The fastest-growing congregation in the ELCA is in Phoenix and is named the Community Church of Joy. The Shepherd Hills Church in Chatsworth, California, is a Southern Baptist Church. Other churches are not only spurning denominational names, but shunning the word "Church" as well. Consider the Capital Christian Center in Sacramento and the Crossroads Cathedral in Oklahoma City (both large Assemblies of God congregations). New Life Christian Fellowship is a nondenominationalist congregation in Biddeford, Maine. With seating for over 10,000 people, the Crenshaw Christian Center, a predominantly African-American charismatic congregation in Los Angeles, boasts a membership of over 16,000.[24] For some, obviously, hiding denominational affiliation, avoiding words like church and worship, and gathering in auditoriums without hymnbooks, liturgy, or anything that might recognizably be called a sermon has helped bring the people in the doors.

## Cultural Factors Contributing to a Post-Denominational Era

In addition to the statistical factors listed above, many cultural factors have contributed to the post-denominational context within which we live. Demographic factors have contributed to the decline of mainline Protestantism and denominational loyalty in the last few decades. The importance placed on mobility within the culture is one of the most obvious of factors. Americans have moved west and south, seeking the "good life." According to the 1990 census, the big metropolitan gainers have been coastal cities like Los Angeles and Seattle. The losing areas have been the rural areas found in Kentucky, North Dakota, the Midwest, and the areas around the Mississippi River delta. One in five Americans moves every year (most to Arizona, New Mexico, Florida, Georgia, Alaska, Hawaii, and California).[25]

Another major cultural factor is the increasing importance of immigration for religious trends in this country. According to Russell Chandler, nearly 40% of the increased population of the United States during the 1980s came from the 7 to 9 million immigrants who arrived from Asia, Latin America, and the Caribbean. In California, nearly 40% of the population is composed of various ethnic minorities. Some people are predicting that the new culturally disadvantaged class in America will be composed of those people who are able to converse in only one language.[26] White suburbanites need to become less ethnocentric and more sensitive to multicultural issues if they hope to succeed in the America of tomorrow. Churches will need to do the same. The struggles over the race and gender issues during the 1960s and 1970s have helped to produce a more inclusive and culturally diverse mainline witness in our day; perhaps the influx of immigration will help congregations incorporate that diversity into their memberships as well. A by-product of the immigration demographics is the decreasing importance of ancestry as an indicator of denominational classification. No longer are those of Latin-American heritage necessarily Catholic; neither are those of Scandinavian origin necessarily Lutheran or members of Free Churches.

Congregations face other cultural challenges today. In the fall of 1993, President Clinton told a group of religious leaders at a White House breakfast that they needed to read law professor Stephen Carter's new book, *The Culture of Disbelief.*[27] In the next few months, Carter's book received enough publicity to push it into sales figures that most authors only dream about. Carter's book speaks directly to some of the problems of the mainline. Civility in matters religious have sometimes led to not being able to speak meaningfully about the importance of religion. As James Wall commented in an editorial in the *Christian Century,*

> the tolerance and civility that are a priority for liberals soon led to a total retreat into secular language. Language, however, affects perspective. Keep quiet about God long enough, and succeeding generations will assume that out of sight and speech is out of mind.[28]

For many Americans, religion is a purely private matter. As the history of denominationalism in America indicates, this tendency was present even in the religious life of denominations immediately following the revolution. The passing of two centuries has tended to produce a social structure more supportive of a culture of disbelief than a culture of belief; today we live in a culture where faith is fully acceptable only where one does not take it too seriously. This cultural ethos has not tended to support denominational loyalty. Nor, ironically, has it helped to keep the doors open at churches where lowest common denominator faith is inculcated. When seriously regarded faith becomes expendable, church life evidently also becomes expendable.

American culture is also enamored with succeeding and with using technology to do it. It represents a culture where, as Southern Baptist minister Carlyle Marney once said in my hearing, "salvation by successing" is the norm.[29] The success ethic is strong and normative in American life. Robert Wuthnow has described American technology as the most important "legitimating myth" in our cultural life. "Though scarcely a religion," he wrote, "it presents itself with religious force, combining seemingly inevitable developments in the social infrastructure with belief in the unassailable sanctity of these developments." In short, technology "organizes and influences virtually every aspect of society." As a result, it affects everything we do.[30] In educational circles, technological disciplines are competing for scarce resources with the disciplines of the humanities and the arts, and they are dominating the struggle. In the words of one church growth expert, Americans today are "honking at our own taillights."[31]

The educational power television holds over our children, and over some adults as well, is, of course, only a small part of this problem. What happens to religion and church life when all the major values held dear by most Americans emerge from our cultural commitments to technology? How should the church respond to this cultural fact? Certainly, congregations that challenge cultural values with the values of the gospel will run the risk of alienating many potential members who make a handsome living representing the value of technology to the society. Is part of the success of megachurches due to their successful manipulation of technological resources? Certainly, the mainline has fallen behind in acceptable uses of technology, and it needs to do some catching up. But it also needs to heed the warning to the nation sounded by Wuthnow: "Given thoughtful guidance, technology can serve as a valuable tool; given license for its own excesses it can become an awesome master."[32]

The consumeristic characteristics engendered by a technological world have most certainly altered the personalities of the people the church hopes to reach today. Americans have a short attention span. We are a people most attracted to entertainment, glitter, and spectacle. We want to get the biggest bang we can for a buck. We are easily bored. And, frankly, traditional ways of doing church can be pretty boring. If the religious experiences in our worship services, supported by our consumer dollars, do not hold the value found elsewhere in our culture for the same amount of money, we will likely go elsewhere.

In metachurches of the seeker variety, wrote Lyle Schaller approvingly, "an increasing proportion of…expenditures now come from user fees rather than the offering plate."[33] How does this attitude correlate with a Christian understanding of the meaning of stewardship? Many Americans today approach stewardship with the idea that they are buying the services of their church. If their church does not meet their consumeristic needs, they will likely take their dollars elsewhere or not attend church at all. That fact has helped to diminish denominational loyalty considerably.

## Mainline Factors Contributing to a Post-Denominational Era

Church attendance reached a peak of 49% during the 1950s. Those were heady days for mainline Protestants. The 1950s cultural revival of religion is one of the most dominating features of the domestic situation in America during these years. Congress added the words "under God" to the pledge of allegiance and church attendance rose a full five percentage points. Corporations and civic organizations decided that providing outlets for prayer at work made good business sense. Church building boomed. Religious book sales soared. Television, the propaganda potential of which people were only beginning to realize, spread religious images far and wide, mostly at no cost to religious groups. Billy Graham's urban crusades were packed with people, and he became America's best-known religious figure for the next several decades.[34]

The 1950s revival, rather than benefiting Protestantism, actually served as the agent to usher in the post-denominational years of American religious life. The revival displaced more than revived mainline Protestantism. It fostered "an attitude toward religion" that had "become a religion itself." For the most part, the cultural revival presented a God who was "understandable and manageable,...an American jolly good fellow."[35] Religious historian Leonard Sweet described the 1950s as the "triumphant decade for the definition of church membership as going to church rather than being the church."[36]

The 1950s represented the time when the "bridge" between the mainline churches and the culture was most firmly established and widely traveled. While the bridge operated, "a vital synthesis of beliefs, values and national ideals existed, sustained by a cold war ideology and close links between civic society, national visions and self-understanding." In other words, the beliefs, values, and behavior patterns of mainline churches were "virtually indistinguishable from the culture." During the 1950s, church attendance in one of the mainline or evangelical churches was a natural part of life for any contributing and productive citizen in American culture.[37]

Then came the summer of 1965. Watts and escalation in Vietnam both appeared near the same time. Black power and the rise of Malcolm X proved to be profoundly disturbing to those who had hoped for easier solutions to racial difficulties. The tremendous diversity of Catholicism began to emerge. New religions, among them the Hare Krishna and the Jesus Cult, appeared. The drug culture surfaced from underground and went public. The appearance of the birth control pill opened the gateway of youth accessibility to the exploitation of their sexuality. The assassinations of Robert Kennedy and Martin Luther King, Jr., a few years later, added the exclamation point. In their response to many of these events, mainline Protestant leaders tore down the bridge that had existed between their congregations and the culture. Many of them protested against the Vietnam war, marched in civil rights demonstrations, and challenged traditional notions of human sexuality. These and other direct challenges to cultural values like patriotism altered forever the common spirituality most Americans had taken for granted before 1960. When the bridge between religion and culture fell into the waters of 1960s cultural discontent, so did the link between denominations and American life. In this respect, the mainline, through its ready affirmation of the right to criticize the culture in the name of the gospel, has contributed cheerfully to the creation of the post-denominational era.

A 1990 survey revealed that 89% of the nation's 500 fastest-growing Protestant churches were evangelical congregations.[38] Is the success of some of today's evangelical churches due to a 1990s reconstruction of the bridge between religion and culture? Or is it an indication of a revival of genuine religious expression? Tom Sine, an evangelical church leader, has quipped that "the Evangelical church is being co-opted slowly by the American dream—do it all and have it all—with a little Jesus overlay." James Davison Hunter, an evangelical sociologist of religion, recently wrote a book that warns evangelicals about trends that indicate accommodation with the world at the expense of key beliefs historically important to them. Russell Chandler pointed out that a recent study conducted by the Roper Organization indicated that the concerns of Sine and Hunter might be well founded. This study, concluded in 1990, showed that conversion makes little difference in the lives of today's born-again Christians. "In fact," reported Chandler, "the use of illegal drugs, driving while intoxicated, and marital infidelity all *increased* after the born-again experience." These results were precisely opposite to what the evangelicals funding the study had expected the study to show. Don Otis, vice-president of the organization that funded the study, concluded that "Accountability is lacking, confrontation is lacking, and we are 'marketing' salvation in such a way that discipleship is simply not occurring."[39] These studies are not cited to claim there is no legitimate growth in evangelical circles. Of course there is. But these evangelical studies do indicate the need for all Christians to be on guard against the powerful temptation to succumb to becoming little more than a mirror to the culture.

Did mainline political and social activity during the 1960s contribute to the loss of membership suffered by these churches in ensuing decades? This has been a popular explanation of mainline "decline." A recent study funded by Lilly, and conducted by three Presbyterian scholars, attempted to find the "real reason for decline." Drawing names from Presbyterian confirmation lists from churches in six states, the three scholars conducted "Gallup-style" interviews with over five hundred Presbyterians confirmed in the 1960s. Seventy-five percent of them had dropped out of church since their confirmations, usually around age 21, and about 50% of those have now returned to church. Fifty-two percent of the total interviewees attend church at least six times per year and consider themselves church members. Six percent are fundamentalists, 10% have joined other mainline denominations, 7% are members of Catholic, Baptist, or other churches outside the mainline, and 8% have severed their ties with the church altogether. Twenty-nine percent have remained Presbyterians, 19% occasionally attend church but are not members, and 21% describe themselves as religious, but neither belong to nor attend a church.

In interviews asking why these Presbyterians had left the church, the question of the church's political agenda appeared in only a very few answers. The interviews supported instead the conclusion that most of these baby boomers who grew up in the Presbyterian church were completely unaware of the programs and policies followed by denominational officials. Their understanding of church was mostly local and considered only the activities and life of the local congregations to which their memberships were attached. The problem of a liberal political agenda, at least for Presbyterians, does not seem to have contributed to mainline decline.[40] The greater problem for the mainline denomination seems to be its inability to communicate the agenda of the larger church to the various congregations and their members. Mainline leadership has historically found it difficult to connect controversial positions on social questions to clear theological and biblical rationale that are compelling for the laity.

In the massive study of Disciples in American culture, also funded by Lilly, editor Newell Williams argued that the study itself indicates the appearance of a vast gap between the theological views of the laity and those of the clergy. Were it not for the fact that Williams uses the general language of "liberal" and "conservative" to describe this gap, I would be inclined to agree with him. Certainly, a gap exists between these two groups in Disciples life. But the terms "liberal" and "conservative" are too relative to serve as accurate indicators of the definition of the gap. Such generalizations often lead to oversimplifications like the one Lyle Schaller offered concerning the rejection of Michael Kinnamon as general minister and president. Ignoring the fact that some 66% of those present voted for Kinnamon, Schaller described the rejection as evidence that the orthodox *majority* of the pews defeated the liberal minority of Disciples leaders. Further, Schaller's oversimplification ignores the fact that the vote for or against Kinnamon does not divide easily or accurately along liberal/conservative lines.[41]

The Presbyterian study funded by Lilly indicated that most of the baby boomers interviewed showed up as liberal on one issue and conservative on the next, frustrating any attempt to define a consistency of theological view that one could describe as either liberal or conservative. Some, for example, supported prayer in public schools while having no objection to ordaining avowed homosexuals.[42] Disciples laity and Disciples clergy are both so pragmatic in the expression of their theological views that a consistent theological system one could characterize as either liberal or conservative is probably rare.

Williams chided the leadership of Disciples for a "failure to identify a distinctively Christian standard for judging theological statements and moral action."[43] The gap between laity and clergy among Disciples, therefore, is probably similar to the gap that exists in most mainline churches, one that is based upon the conflict of cultures that exists between congregations and their denominational offices. The two cultures clash at many points, but neither culture could be accurately described as consistently either "conservative" or "liberal," though one is probably more liberal than the other. Ministerial leadership, in general, at all levels of mainline church life has demonstrated an inability to communicate effectively either a clear sense of mission or a compelling theological rationale for denominational activity. That failure has probably contributed to a loss of denominational loyalty among laypersons.

Robert Wuthnow mentioned that interseminary training has also diluted denominational ties. Even among Presbyterians, about 50% of seminarians to be ordained at any given time received their education outside the denomination's seminaries.[44] Most mainline denominational faculties hire ecumenical faculties today, though Lutherans and Presbyterians still favor heavy denominational majorities. In any case, ecumenical seminaries have probably led to an erosion of denominational loyalties at the grassroots level of the church.

Another side to the educational contribution to the demise of denominationalism rests with the demise of the denominational colleges. Most mainline colleges have become fairly well secularized. The education they offer might be better in some cases than that offered by large public universities, but it is rarely less secular.[45] Virginia Lieson Brereton's study of Disciples of Christ colleges concluded:

> By the late nineteenth century...many of them had grown weary of peculiarity. And such was the impact of the university, the power of the philanthropic foundations with their thousands of dollars, and the clout of the regional accrediting associations with their insistence on uniform standards, that most colleges began to resemble each other and the secular liberal arts colleges....The glaring reality of the twentieth-century history has been the effectiveness of the secular society and culture in shaping the educational agenda of the mainline churches. That act of shaping has made for an ambiguous legacy.[46]

In some ways, the role of twentieth-century ecumenism, and the failure of mainline leadership to communicate effectively with laypersons, has contributed to this post-denominational development. Ecumenical leaders have always hoped ecumenism would loosen denominational self-righteousness and enable new relationships to form between denominational groups, even perhaps relationships that would lead to mergers and the decline of denominational boundaries. To some extent, such goals have been successful. But, in other ways, the success of twentieth-century ecumenism has been more superficial than substantive, especially as those successes have only marginally reached the consciousness of the grass roots at congregational levels.

Perhaps the clearest way that the mainline has contributed to the post-denominational age has been through the inability of these ecumenical denominations to articulate a clear understanding of just what it is they believe. The Presbyterian study funded by Lilly once again is relevant here. The 500 interviews with confirmands from the 1960s indicated that most of them left the church because "religion itself had become low on the list of their personal priorities." Most of them represented the latitudinarian expression I characterized earlier. They appreciated tolerance above all other virtues. Most of them preferred Christianity to all other faiths, but mostly "because they were raised in that faith." The Presbyterian researchers found them "hard put to offer theological reasons why anyone should remain a Presbyterian, or even a Christian."[47]

This lowest common denominator kind of faith thrives in the mainline churches and among Disciples. It supports the basic virtues of an honest and moral human existence, but it possesses no real conviction out of which strong religious communities can emerge. Most baby boomers brought up in the mainline are simply unable to describe very accurately what it is they believe or exactly what it was their parents believed. This fact provides further evidence that the 1950s revival of mainline churches did not have much substance to it. The Presbyterian study shares the conclusion of the Disciples study that although "denominational leaders promoted ecumenism and dialogue…they did not devise or promote compelling new versions of a distinctively Christian faith."[48]

Though I do not endorse the details of William H. Willimon's agenda for the creation of the post-liberal church, I do agree that we mainliners (Disciples included) are sometimes "more concerned with how to live in a world where there is a plurality of truths—and with how to do so without killing each other—than we are with truth."[49] In our quest to speak a universal language, we have found it increasingly difficult to speak the language of faith. In many locations within the mainline house, the open-minded tolerance is really reflective of a nearly fundamentalist commitment to relativism, though most would not be comfortable with that kind of expression of it. Latitudinarianism, or lowest common denominator faith, never has been capable of inspiring great conviction. As Roof and McKinney expressed it, the mainline's major competition in the 1990s will not come from "the conservatives it has spurned but from the secularists it has spawned."[50] Part of the thesis of this book is that Disciples of Christ possess a rich tradition in Christian identity. The other part of this book's thesis is that we need to be more familiar with it than we are. Before turning to a summary of how that discussion relates to post-denominationalism, it is important to offer a brief review of other more popular strategies for living successfully in a post-denominational age.

## *Different Approaches: Role of the Denomination in a Post-Denominational Age*

### Popular Approaches

One popular approach taken these days is the "marketing" strategy. Church growth experts believe the answer to today's post-denominational crisis is to be found in learning how to market the church. In his book entitled *Marketing the Church: What They [the seminaries] Never Taught You About Church Growth*, already past its seventh printing, George Barna offers his prescription for the "organizational survival" of the church. "My contention," he writes, "based on careful study of data and the activities of American churches, is that the major problem plaguing the Church is its failure to embrace a marketing orientation in what has become a marketing-driven environment."[51]

Obviously, the church should not ignore the value of potential marketing strategies that might enable the church to be more effective in its evangelistic proclamation of the gospel. All congregations use some marketing techniques, for better or for worse. Marketing strategies are not in and of themselves a bad thing, but increasingly, megachurch congregations are *becoming* their marketing strategies. Os Guinness, well-known evangelical observer of the interaction between faith and culture, does not believe that the marketing assumptions and techniques utilized by megachurch congregations are neutral. The title of his new book makes his position clear: *Dining With the Devil: The Megachurch Movement Flirts With Modernity.*[52]

Another strategy is to establish new congregations catering specifically to "Seekers." Recent decades have introduced entirely new classifications of people to our common vocabulary—terms like YUPPIES (Young Urban Professionals); BUPPIES (Black urban professionals), DINKS (Dual income, no kids), and SITCOMS (single income, two children, outrageous mortgages).[53] The newest term, Seekers, seems to cover all these others under its umbrella of meaning.

My definition of "seeker" comes largely from the work of Wade Clark Roof.[54] He described four spiritual styles among the baby-boomers (born between 1946 and 1964): (1) The Loyalists: About one third of the boomers have never dropped out of church life. They were least touched by the cultural changes of their day. Participation in a congregation is a duty for them—these are the more conservative and somewhat traditional members of congregations who fall into the baby boomer age group. (2) The Returnees: About twenty-five percent of the boomers are those who dropped out of church in their younger years and are now returning. They see church-going more as something you do if it meets your needs. They want a "diverse menu of options" in their church life (athletic facilities, recovery programs, self-help programs of various types, etc.). Of these Roof says: "Even those returning to evangelical churches often look at faith in psychological terms, with a concern for inner meaning and self-fulfillment." (3) The Believers but Not Belongers: Twenty-eight percent of boomers have little or no contact with organized religion, but they consider themselves religious. They are mostly religious consumers when it comes to the institutional church; they will call on it for baptisms, weddings, and funerals. In the language of the Church of England, they attend church for events related to "hatching, matching, and dispatching." They tend to blend their Christian backgrounds with other ideologies, like astrology, reincarnation, popular psychology, and the like. (4) The Seekers: This is about nine percent of the boomers, who see themselves as spiritual more than religious, and involved in "high-energy personal quests." These New Age types are more concerned about self-fulfillment than almost anything else. In Roof's phrase, the seeker is one who believes "each person must follow his or her bliss wherever it leads." A fifth group is composed of about five percent who are neither religious nor spiritual.

All five of these groups are in some ways "Seekers." So, for many, the term "seeker" has come to describe the whole group of boomers. In some publicity Harper has published about Roof's book, the following blurb summarizes common characteristics of "seekers":

> Roof's research and analysis reveal a generation of diverse seekers who share surprising commonalities: they value experience over beliefs, distrust institutions and leaders, stress personal fulfillment over community, and are fluid in their allegiances.[55]

In general, seekers "resist commitment," possess "less company loyalty" than most groups, and are extraordinarily "skeptical of denominations."[56]

In light of these definitions, just what is a "seeker church"? Some of the congregations going by that name have become congregations shaped by how they can meet the needs of the seeker group. They provide a place where experience is valued over beliefs, where institutions and the claims of theological authorities (be they the claims of Christian tradition, or denominations, or contemporary ecumenical documents, or any other such thing that might challenge parochial or provincial claims of any particular congregational setting) are often carefully avoided or at least sanitized for painless consumption, where community is only important as it is an aid to fulfilling some aspect of the self. These kinds of congregations have become so widespread that even the comic pages have noticed. Last year, Trudeau's *Doonesbury* ran a series of strips spoofing "seeker churches." The "Little Church of Walden" grew out of an aerobics class and then added yoga and bingo before moving on to twelve-step programs, a soup kitchen, and cooking lessons.[57]

The media is giving these new-style churches considerable coverage, partly because they are such indicators of the current trends of popular culture. The brief quotation at the beginning of this chapter provides an illustration of this phenomenon. Lyle Schaller has encouraged the development of these new churches, but instead of "fast-food" style congregations, he recommends "full-service churches," congregations modeled after the full-service supermarket.

> Both recognize and affirm the need to draw people from a ten to thirty mile radius. Neither can survive with a walk-in neighborhood constituency. Both understand the need for a large parcel of land at a highly visible and convenient location with an abundance of off-street parking. Both accept the need to take advantage of contemporary marketing principles. Both recognize that their future lies in being responsive to the needs of their clientele. Both appeal to the two-car, two-income family as well as to adults without regard to marital status. Both are consistent with the strong "consumerism" of contemporary American society. Both operate on the assumption that the quality of their current performance, rather than inherited loyalties or brand-name allegiance or geographical proximity is what will cause this week's first-time visitors to return next week.[58]

Some congregations, like Willow Creek Community Church, have become very "full-service churches," with unbelievably rapid growth in membership. But at what costs?

UCC minister Anthony B. Robinson filed a "special correspondence" in the *Christian Century* after his visit to Willow Creek. Though he appreciated Willow Creek's masterful appeal to nonchurchgoers, he left feeling the worship experience had been mostly a private experience, with no real sense of community, even though the "auditorium" (preferred name for the worship center) was filled with thousands of people. Impressed by the massive programming at the church designed to bring healing to broken lives, programs that concentrated on offering "personal transformation," he left wondering what it might mean to have churches formed mostly around meeting the needs of one particular generation. He left questioning whether what had been offered that morning was truly "recognizable as the church" or whether the weekly services were "more entertainment than worship." He concluded:

> Nevertheless, established churches can learn something from Willow Creek's attractiveness to the unchurched. Is the distance between churched and unchurched widening? How can the distance be bridged—and are any churches interested in trying? Willow Creek's approach has been to maintain orthodox evangelical theology and

doctrine but to alter radically the format in which it is presented. And it seems that Willow Creek has accurately read the culture, or at least a significant slice of it. For people in a mass society, attending Willow Creek is like many other relatively anonymous activities, like going to a mall or sports event. Willow Creek may not, however, be a community with a common memory and identity that will persist through the generations.[59]

The trend in many seeker congregations is toward a "supply-side spirituality" where they work at selling the product of faith, and the job of ministers is to keep the people happy and the pews full. *Time* magazine published a lengthy article about seekers entitled "The Church Search." After pointing out that mainliners could learn from the way these new "houses of worship address real needs of people rather than purveying old abstractions, expectations and mannerisms," Richard Ostling concluded that "many of those who have rediscovered churchgoing may ultimately be shortchanged, however, if the focus of their faith seems subtly to shift from the glorification of God to the gratification of man."[60] Most of these seeker congregations do not make clear comparisons between what the customer wants and what the gospel presents as a picture of authentic human life.

Many of the seeker congregations have established very successful evangelism programs by incorporating many "twelve-step" programs as a part of their programming. Sunday school classrooms become meeting places for all manner of rehab meetings for people recovering from various types of addictions. Such programs have led some people to a strong faith in God, but many others have graduated from such programs to worship at what Russell Chandler called "Altars Anonymous." He described the trend as "Twelve Step Spirituality," a hybrid between popular psychology and personality-affirming religion where "faith in faith, not in God, may be the only substance at the bottom of the glass."[61]

In short, is the consumer mentality of the seeker congregations suited for a clear communication of the gospel, of the meaning of the Lordship of Christ and of the church as the body of Christ, of clarity about theological concepts like grace, Christian vocation, stewardship, or the "cost of discipleship," the radical transformation of perspective that is inherently a part of the "way of the cross"? Do seeker congregations connect their members to the whole story of the history of the church, the narrative that connects us to the blood of the martyrs and the sacrificial suffering of the saints? Though I am not willing to claim that traditional congregations have done a very good job in these areas either, I do not believe the seeker route is a viable path to lead us out of mainline malaise today. As Martin Marty quipped in a recent *Newsweek* article, "To give the whole store away to match what this year's market says the unchurched want is to have the people who know least about faith determine most about its expression."[62]

Do I think that the mainline should absolutely steer clear of the seekers? No, I don't mean that at all. Evangelization of the seekers should be a priority for any congregation. I simply do not want the seekers to redefine the meaning of Christian life, or church life, for the church. In his recent *Newsweek* essay about the mainline, Kenneth Woodward concluded with the following statement: "The mainline denominations may be dying because they lost their theological integrity. The only thing worse, perhaps, would be the rise of a new Protestant establishment that succeeds because it never had any."[63]

## Suggested Approaches

If these popular approaches are not particularly viable, what should Disciples and other mainline Protestants do in response to our post-denominational context? First, members of the mainline should affirm the disestablishment of Protestantism. It is a positive outcome of pluralism and has helped the mainline take intentional steps toward a more inclusive and globally aware church life. Mainline Protestantism is now situated on the fringes of American religious life. There is nothing inherently negative about that location. The power of culture over the church's life is minimized when the church no longer stands at the center of culture. But it does not necessarily follow that the power of the church's voice is minimized when it speaks from the fringes rather than the center. Dorothy Bass, a professor at Chicago Theological Seminary reminded a group of theological educators that "the most lively and faithful periods of the church's history have not been periods of establishment and ease."[64] Freed of its cultural attachments and temptations, the mainline church might be more able to concentrate on a renewal of what is most important to its future: the effort to gain a clearer sense of its own Christian identity. Ronald Osborn indicated that the affirmation of disestablishment may not come easily for Disciples of Christ:

> The increasing pluralism of American life necessitates our giving up the illusion that this is a Christian nation or that mainline Protestants are the acknowledged keeper of its soul....Such a thoroughgoing disavowal of prevailing assumptions may not come easily for Disciples, especially since the movement began with a hearty affirmation of American culture and a deliberate adoption, in the realm of expediency, of axioms and processes of the American political system. This sense of close affinity between faith and culture was doubtless a significant element in the early popular appeal of Disciples....Clarifying the distinction between the gospel and the American way of life is a prescription, not necessarily for rapid growth, but for the health of the Church.[65]

Second, Disciples need to concentrate on the task of renewing their Christian identity within the context of ecumenism. The pages of the *Disciple* magazine recently carried an interesting discussion about the current state of the denomination. Ronald Allen, from Christian Theological Seminary, declared Disciples to be "in the early stages of Code Blue." The patient, he concluded, is about to die. He argued that Disciples seemed to lack "a vivid sense of the presence of the living God." Michael Kinnamon, in an issue two months later, offered a second "medical" opinion. Instead of accepting Allen's prognosis of "Code Blue," Kinnamon argued that Disciples are in a period of "transition," a period that offers "a remarkable opportunity for new life." One sees the glass as mostly empty, the other sees it as mostly full. Yet both join one another in calling Disciples to a renewal of theological and spiritual awareness.[66] To have a lasting influence, as well as an immediate impact, worship and education within our congregations must reflect evidence of this renewal.

What does it mean to be Christian? What is distinctive about Christian identity? Disciples and other mainliners must wrestle with these questions and learn to articulate their answers intelligently and forthrightly. Mainline Protestants have had difficulty saying who they are. Disciples of Christ, in particular, must find a way to express their Christian identity. There are several ways Disciples could do so, not all of them equally appropriate. A recent essay by M. B. Handspicker, a professor of Pastoral Theology and Evangelism at Andover Newton, is helpful in thinking through the options. He offers four such options.[67]

(1) We can cloister ourselves into a carefully separated community and concentrate on the development of our own identity from that location of isolation. Though George Lindbeck, William Willimon, and Stanley Hauerwas are not at all sectarian when compared to the Amish, some of their advocacy for the development of the post-liberal church tends in a sectarian direction. The battle cry in this corner is "let the church be the church." The first task of the church is the formation of its own identity. It has no stake in this world other than to live faithfully according to its own vision, and to witness on behalf of that vision to others. The church should not have a social mission or participate in any efforts to transform the culture around it. Many Disciples will prefer this approach. This response reinforces the privatization of religious faith which has a long tradition in Disciples popular piety.[68] It also reinforces a two-kingdoms theory where the kingdom of God has nothing to do with the kingdom of the world, inherently denying the claim of God's redemption on all creation.

(2) Disciples could choose the dogmatist way. This is the way of the group known as Disciple Renewal, or currently as the Disciple Heritage Fellowship. Disciples could define their identity according to absolute categories generally conforming to a fundamentalist or strongly

conservative agenda and seek renewal that way. This position, however, rarely avoids idolatry due to its inability to allow for adjustment and self-critical reflection based on growth in grace concerning the meaning of God's gospel in our time.

Two somewhat ironic points need to be raised with respect to the claim of the Disciple Heritage Fellowship that Disciples have departed from the "true faith" of Disciples heritage because of their ecumenical attachments. First, the Disciple Renewal movement itself represents a departure from the Disciples tradition. Its particular espousal of biblical inerrancy is foreign to Disciples history, as is the rather obstreperous and sectarian manner in which this group has historically expressed itself about issues related to that viewpoint. Second, even though the Disciple Heritage Fellowship generally disapproves of the mainline ecumenical involvements pursued by the general church leadership in Disciples life, it represents, through its own actions and beliefs, its own form of ecumenism. The attitudes and doctrinal concerns of the group represent an ecumenical fundamentalism that crosses all denominational lines more precisely than they represent Disciples history and tradition.

(3) Disciples could simply embrace latitudinarianism, the lowest common denominator kind of faith. Christian identity would be a relative matter where tolerance would be the most important virtue. Yet this posture has been disempowering in the past and would likely be so in the future.

(4) Disciples could take the same route to Christian identity argued by Handspicker as the best path for mainline churches to take. He phrased it this way:

> We can take a nuanced and dialectical approach that sees the truth as a limit towards which we strive—where judgments of better or worse can (and must) be applied to the variety of theological positions but where the finitude and need for correction and enlargement of all positions is affirmed. This entails a willingness to argue for the truth of one's position, to give reasons why one holds it and holds it to be more adequate than any other position of which one is aware. It also entails openness to correction and a willingness to be as vulnerable to the arguments of another as you ask him or her to be vulnerable to yours.[69]

This position is not dogmatic, but does affirm that there are more and less acceptable versions of the meaning of Christian identity floating around out there and that it is a responsibility of the church to address those versions critically, with a view to determine what is more appropriate and what is less so in terms of its theological beliefs. This is an *ecumenical* endeavor. For that reason, it is especially suited to Disciples life. It seeks the discovery of apostolic faith in the company of the whole church. It speaks a faith born of conviction and one held accountable to both scripture and tradition. It argues for the truth it discovers but recognizes, in the spirit of the mainline tradition, that there were some good things to come out of the Enlightenment.

In other words, this position is unwilling to throw the liberal tradition out altogether. Instead, it affirms "the critical capacities that grew out of it," and is willing to "use those capacities in the service of truth," even in the search for the truth of Christian identity.[70] But the most important task remains one of claiming for ourselves a clear articulation of what we consider to be distinctive about being Christian and communicating that narrative through our congregations to one another and to our children and our children's children.

The effort to frame a contemporary Disciples understanding of Christian identity, accompanied by a comprehensive understanding of the mission of the church, still stands before Disciples as an unfinished task. My hope is that today's Disciples will choose this ecumenical approach to revitalize both their discovery and articulation of Christian identity. It better serves the long-standing Disciples commitment to a reasonable faith and an ecumenical heart than any of the other choices listed.

This ecumenical attempt to renew Christian identity is large enough to include an intentional renewal of denominational identity as well. Some might interpret an effort to recover an understanding of denominational heritage and tradition as an "anti-ecumenical" activity. I would argue instead that it should be regarded as a gift to ecumenism. When denominations come to the ecumenical table, they need to have something to say about Christian identity that is worth hearing. What from their heritage and tradition might enrich the whole church? If all of us in the mainline are unable to discuss the theological and historical insights we have uncovered through the study of our own particular denominational heritages, ecumenical discussions will represent more a pooling of ignorance than a quest for how the church today might embody apostolic faith for our time.

Martin E. Marty has described denominations as the place where traditions can survive.[71] I would stress also that the thoughtful and purposeful revival of the study of denominational history is one way of addressing the formation of Christian identity for any community of believers who live in an increasingly post-denominational age, perhaps one of the most important ways. There is a definite irony present here. Why is denominational identity important in an age that considers itself post-denominational? I can think of three reasons.

(1) In a post-denominational age, it is increasingly more difficult to find a place where people are forced to struggle over particular questions of faith in a context that provides a concern for Christian history, even if that history is merely denominational history. Christian identity

formed without taking history seriously, however short the historical look might be, is bound to be provincial, parochial, and culturally strait-jacketed. Denominations provide a relatively safe environment where people can grapple with beliefs that challenge the parochial life of the congregation. They can do this by providing an awareness of historical development that draws the congregation and the present denomination outside of themselves. The outcome of these studies brings insights leading to a broader notion of the meaning of Christian identity and fuller sense of the family of God that extends across time and place. Denominational history serves an antidote to the poison of the lowest common denominator kind of faith.

Most mainline denominations have an active church life in global environments as well as American locations. This revival of denominational history should also include learning how our denominational cousins in China, Latin America, the Ukraine, and other such locations view the nature of Christian life and work. Further, Disciples in southwest Texas, for example, ought also to attempt to understand how Hispanic Disciples in Texas, or Puerto-Rican and Haitian Disciples in New York City understand the nature of Christianity.[72] Such conscious attempts will strengthen our faith and challenge our parochial tendencies to understand the work of God in ways too tied to our own ethnic and cultural situations.

(2) The study of denominational history also leads people into an interest in the broader history of Christianity. It can lead to an expanded interest in the tradition of Christian faith and to a greater understanding of how other groups within the ecumenical church came to be who they are. This could lead to more congregational interest and involvement in the important ecumenical conversations about Christian identity that are taking place between mainline denominations.

(3) Contrary to the message of a recent cartoon in the *United Methodist Review*, the mainline churches do not face a fork in the road where they must choose denominational renewal or ecumenical ties.[73] Ironically, the ecumenical church needs a strong denominational witness more than ever before, but if it is to be helpful, it must be a witness that is fully responsive to the theological concerns of the whole church. It cannot be a self-righteous or dogmatic denominational pride in distinctiveness. Further, vital denominations could provide the much-needed bridge between the concerns of the congregation and the concerns of the wider ecumenical church. Though denominations have not done this task well in the past, perhaps a revitalization of denominational energy would enable different results.

Though Disciples have been active in mission, many of the successful mission activities of our congregations, and even of our denominational agencies, stand disconnected from an explicit theological understanding of Christian identity. Though we respond to the needs of the

268    *Joined in Discipleship*

poor, the hungry, the sick, and the homeless, how do we do so differently than many secular social agencies? How do we engage in our outreach effectively communicating that we do so as children of God? Do our congregations have a clear sense of the entirety of the church's responsibility of witness in the name of Christ to the whole inhabited earth? The mission of the church is only possible where Christian identity is affirmed and expressed. And it can only be accomplished through a recognition that the mission is God's, not our own. As Ronald Osborn put it, "A church which sees itself primarily as a fellowship of the like-minded or a support-group in time of need can expect little of the vitality of the apostolic community."[74]

As the new millennium approaches, Disciples are nearing their two-hundredth year. Good years are still ahead of them. But a post-denominational, some say "post-Christian," context means it must take seriously the intentional effort to maintain a Christian identity. Time may automatically improve wine, but it does nothing in and of itself for the growth, witness, or theological maturity of the church. For these areas to develop, lay and clergy together must continue to commit themselves to the effort. If the past and present story of faith among Disciples, the subject of these ten chapters, is any indication, one can be reasonably sure that future historians will someday extend this story of the Disciples of Christ. As contemporary Disciples struggle with the question "What does it mean to be Christian?" it is hoped their lives will inspire some historian in future years to write a new narrative describing emerging aspects of Disciples identity, and new turning points in both faithfulness and witness.

## *Questions for Reflection and Discussion*

1. What is post-denominationalism? How would you briefly describe the "signs of the times" that indicate we are living in a post-denominational age? How have these factors related to church life, culture, and mainline Protestantism affected the life of the church today?

2. When the text states that "the bridge between religion and culture fell into the waters of 1960s cultural discontent," what is meant? What does it mean that the mainline churches no longer act as an automatic link between religion and American culture? Are there positive implications for the church in the fact that this bridge no longer exists in the same way it once did? What value might there be in the mainline's recognition that it no longer stands at the center of the culture?

3. What is "lowest common denominator faith" and how has it acted as one of the most significant contributions the mainline denominations have made in helping to create a "post-denominational age"?

4. What are some of the more popular approaches taken by Christian churches today in order to respond to the post-denominational context in which they live? Describe the potential strengths and weaknesses you might attach to the strategy of meeting the challenges of post-denominationalism head-on by renewing Christian identity, which might include the attempt to seek an intentional renewal of denominational identity as well. What should be the relationship between a renewed denominational sense of identity and our historic Disciples commitment to ecumenism?

## Notes

[1] Will Herberg, *Protestant-Catholic-Jew* (Garden City, L.I.: Doubleday & Co., Inc., 1955).

[2] Osborn, "The Irony of the Twentieth-Century Christian Church (Disciples of Christ): Making it to the Mainline Just at the Time of its Disestablishment," *Midstream* 28 (July 1989): 293-312.

[3] These figures come from Robert Bezilla, ed., *Religion in America: 1992-1993* (Princeton: Princeton Religion Research Center, 1993), p. 40.

[4] See Russell Chandler, *Racing Toward 2001: The Forces Shaping America's Religious Future* (Grand Rapids and San Francisco: Zondervan Publishing House and Harper, 1992), pp. 191f.

[5] See Lyle E. Schaller, "What Happened to Denominations? A Diagnosis and a Prescription for Reform," *Church Management—The Clergy Journal* (October 1992): 44.

[6] One should also recognize that the figure of 1 million members in 1991, found in Kenneth L. Woodward, "Dead End for the Mainline?" *Newsweek* (August 9, 1993), pp. 46-48, is inflated. Currently Disciples are somewhere around 700,000 members.

[7] Richard N. Ostling, "The Church Search," *Time* (April 5, 1993): 46.

[8] Chandler, pp. 152-153. The figures of mainline membership are found on p. 153 of his book, with the 1992 figures gleaned from Woodward, "Dead End for the Mainline?" pp. 46-48.

[9] Robert Bezilla, ed., *Religion in America: 1992-1993*, pp. 38-39.

[10] See Robert Wuthnow, *Restructuring of American Religion: Society and Faith Since World War II* (Princeton, N.J.: Princeton University Press, 1988), p. 88.

[11] *Ibid.*, p. 89.

[12] Robert Bezilla, ed., *Religion in America: 1992-1993*, p. 38.

[13] Bellah, "Finding the Church: Post-Traditional Discipleship," *Christian Century* (November 14, 1990): 1061.

[14] Robert Bezilla, ed., *Religion in America: 1992-1993*, p. 38.

[15] *Ibid.*, pp. 39-40.

[16] See Kenneth L. Woodward, "Dead End for the Mainline?" Some of the ELCA figures come from Russell Chandler, *Racing Toward 2001*, p. 234.

[17] "Paradenomination" is Chandler's name for this phenomenon; see Chandler, p. 242.

[18] See Wuthnow, *Restructuring of American Religion*, pp. 100-131. James Davison Hunter also points to these parachurch organizations as evidence of the demise of the old Judeo-Christian cultural consensus. See Hunter, *Culture Wars: The Struggle to Define America* (New York: Basic Books, 1991).

[19] Chandler, p. 163.

# 270  *Joined in Discipleship*

²⁰See Chandler's extensive description of Willow Creek on pp. 246-255.

²¹Ostling, "The Church Search," p. 47.

²²See Chandler's extended discussion of this congregation's network on pp. 281-290.

²³Chandler, pp. 240-244.

²⁴Chandler, pp. 163, and 177-178.

²⁵Chandler raises the importance of the mobility factor and discusses the population trends on pp. 20-24.

²⁶Chandler, pp. 28-29.

²⁷Stephen L. Carter, *The Culture of Disbelief: How American Law and Politics Trivialize Religious Devotion* (New York: HarperCollins, Basic Books, 1993).

²⁸James Wall, "God as a Hobby," *Christian Century* (October 6, 1993): 923.

²⁹In the fall of 1974, in my first year in seminary, Carlyle Marney visited the seminary and I heard him describe Americans in this way; the phrase has stuck with me since that time.

³⁰Wuthnow, *The Restructuring of American Religion*, see chapter 11, pp. 268-296.

³¹Quoted in Chandler, p. 82.

³²Wuthnow, *Restructuring of American Religion*, p. 295.

³³These statements recommending the "full service church" come from the seventh chapter of Schaller, *The Seven-Day-a-Week Church* (Nashville: Abingdon Press, 1992), see pages 151 and 154. Chandler quotes a parishioner who makes the same observation, but from the negative perspective, noting that "stewards" have become "consumers" who "no longer return a portion of their incomes to God. They buy certain services—like a youth program or a place to have ceremonies—from the church." See Chandler, p. 221.

³⁴For a detailed study of the 1950s and 1960s, and the mainline response to the events of those decades, see Mark G. Toulouse, "*The Christian Century* and American Public Life: The Crucial Years, 1956-1968," in *New Dimensions in American Religious History*, edited by Jay P. Dolan and James P. Wind (Grand Rapids: William B. Eerdmans, 1993), pp. 44-82.

³⁵Martin E. Marty, *The New Shape of American Religion* (New York: Harper & Brothers, 1958), pp. 27-28, and 32.

³⁶Leonard I. Sweet, "The Modernization of Protestant Religion in America," in *Altered Landscapes: Christianity in America, 1935-1985*, ed. David W. Lotz (Grand Rapids: William B. Eerdmans, 1989), p. 24.

³⁷See Chandler, p. 154.

³⁸See Chandler, p. 159.

³⁹Sine's quote, the reference to Hunter's book *Evangelicalism, the Coming Generation*, and the Roper study are found in Chandler, pp. 165-166.

⁴⁰See Benton Johnson, Dean R. Hoge, and Donald A. Luidens, "Mainline Churches: The Real Reason for Decline," *First Things* (March 1993): 14-15.

⁴¹Lyle E. Schaller, "What Happened to Denominations? A Diagnosis and a Prescription for Reform," *Church Management—The Clergy Journal* (October 1992): 45-46.

⁴²Johnson, Hoge, and Luidens, "Mainline Churches," p. 15.

⁴³See Williams, "Why the Disciples Have Changed in Relation to Culture," in *A Case Study of Mainstream Protestantism: The Disciples' Relation to Culture, 1880-1989* (Grand Rapids and St. Louis: William B. Eerdmans Publishing Company and Chalice Press, 1991), p. 21.

⁴⁴Wuthnow, *Restructuring of American Religion*, p. 92.

⁴⁵Chandler discusses this phenomenon on pp. 108-109.

⁴⁶Brereton, "Disciples Higher Education in the Age of the University," in D. Newell Williams, ed., *A Case Study of Mainstream Protestantism: The Disciples' Rela-*

*tion to American Culture, 1880-1989* (Grand Rapids and St. Louis: William B. Eerdmans Publishing Company and Chalice Press, 1991), pp. 299-317; see especially p. 317.

[47]Johnson, Hoge, and Luidens, "Mainline Churches," pp. 15-16.

[48]*Ibid.*, pp. 16 and 18.

[49]William H. Willimon, "Answering Pilate: Truth and the Postliberal Church," *Christian Century* (January 28, 1987): 82.

[50]Quoted in Chandler, p. 157.

[51]Barna, *Marketing the Church* (Colorado Springs: NavPress, Seventh Printing, 1991), p. 23.

[52]Guinness, *Dining With the Devil* (Grand Rapids: Baker Book House, 1994).

[53]See Chandler, p. 15.

[54]HarperSanFrancisco, 1993.

[55]Harper's "Torchletter," March, 1993, p. 1.

[56]Ron Chaney, "'Seeker Services' Attract the Unchurched," *The Baptist Standard* (March 25, 1992): 12.

[57]A couple of these strips were reprinted to accompany Laura L. Nash's lengthy review of Roof's book, "A Generation of Seekers," that appeared as "Mallway to Heaven? Religious Choice Among the Baby Boomers," in *Christian Century* (January 5-12, 1994): 15-18.

[58]Schaller, *Seven-Day-A-Week Church*, p. 151.

[59]Anthony B. Robinson, "Learning from Willow Creek Church," *Christian Century* (January 23, 1991): 68-70.

[60]Ostling, "Church Search," p. 49. The term "supply-side spirituality" appears in this article on p. 48.

[61]Chandler, p. 196.

[62]Woodward, "Dead End for the Mainline?" p. 48.

[63]Woodward, p. 48.

[64]Quoted in Chandler, p. 157.

[65]Osborn, "The Irony," pp. 306-307.

[66]See Ronald J. Allen, "The Disciples: A Denomination in Code Blue," *The Disciple* (January 1994): 16-18; and Michael K. Kinnamon, "Code Blue: A Second Opinion," *The Disciple* (March 1994): 28-30.

[67]Handspicker, "Evangelizing Liberalism," *First Things* (October 1993): 35. I present them in a slightly different way than Handspicker does, but these are definitely the same options he addresses in his article.

[68]For a study of this dimension of Disciples heritage, see Mark G. Toulouse, "Disciples and Social Transformation: Past," *Midstream* (July 1987): 459-472.

[69]Handspicker, p. 36.

[70]*Ibid.*

[71] Martin E. Marty, "Foreword," *Joined in Discipleship: The Maturing of An American Religious Movement* (St. Louis: Chalice Press, 1992), p. xi.

[72]See Mark S. Massa, "Disciples in a Mission Land: The Christian Church in New York City," in Williams, ed., *A Case Study*, pp. 469-490. This essay would provide a good start.

[73]Stephen L. Swecker, "UMC's Ecumenical Ties Show Signs of Fraying," *The United Methodist Review* (October 8, 1993): p. 8. The cartoon, showing a man standing at a crossroads where street signs showed denominationalism going one way and ecumenism going the other, was drawn by Dani Aguila and carried the caption "Which way should the United Methodist Church go?"

[74]Osborn, "The Irony," p. 309.

# APPENDIX
## A STATEMENT OF FAITH AND IDENTITY FOR
## THE CHRISTIAN CHURCH (DISCIPLES OF CHRIST)

The following eight points represent my attempt to compose a statement of faith that expresses the theological identity and integrity of the Disciples of Christ. These points are drawn from my understanding of the history and tradition of the Disciples. Since Disciples are not a creedal people, we have never really expressed our faith according to traditional systematic theological categories (God, Christ, Holy Spirit, Human Beings, Sin, Salvation, Eschatology, etc.). The following expressions of faith have been developed from what I understand to be eight central features of Disciples life, both historically and in our present. I believe them to be broadly representative of a contemporary Disciples identity, though not without recognizing that one of the features of Disciples identity is diversity. No doubt, the reader will find sections within this faith statement with which she or he may not agree. I could set forth a statement representing the lowest common denominator of Disciples identity and faith, but such a statement would not say much. I believe it will be most healthy for the future of our church when we begin to dialogue about who we are, pushing ourselves to some sense of our identity. We do not have to agree in all particulars; in fact, it is part of our identity not only to tolerate differences, but to affirm our diversity wholeheartedly as a part of who we are.

1. **The Interpretation Principle:** Though we differ widely in our personal understandings of the Bible, we affirm the church's view of scripture as the major authoritative resource for Christian life and work. This authority rests in its testimony about the Lordship of Christ and its testimony concerning the revelation of God in Jesus Christ, the ultimate authority of Christian faith for us. We do not exalt the authority of the Bible above the authority of the act of God's revelation in Christ. In the biblical representations of God, the world, ourselves, our neighbors, we have discovered pictures disclosing the meaning of the gospel and of human existence.

273

We affirm the role of interpretation in our reading of the Bible, and the role of the Holy Spirit's guidance in the church's interpretation of scripture. We do not believe scripture should be approached haphazardly or flippantly. Interpretation should be a public process, guided by commonly affirmed principles of critical interpretation and informed by the ideas and understandings of the whole of Christianity. We do place a high value on freedom of interpretation for each and every Christian. We understand the Bible to be a human book as well as a divine book. Since God has no other avenue for the mediation of God's word to humanity except through some form of human agency, we understand the Bible itself to be a book affected by the limitations of the human condition. We do not believe the Bible is inerrant or infallible, but we do emphasize that the human testimony of the Bible is inspired by the Holy Spirit, and thereby meaningfully and authoritatively points us in the direction of what we mean when we talk about God or attempt to describe the truth of God's revelation in Jesus Christ.

2. **The Restoration Principle:** For early Disciples, the restoration idea represented the best path to divine authority, to the purity and simplicity of the original faith, a faith uncontaminated by either time or history. In seeking to restore the New Testament church, they actually sought the will of God for the church. They sought the voice of God in the midst of the human voices surrounding them.[1] Like those early Disciples, we still seek the will of God for the church of our time. We believe God is the Author and Sustainer of Creation. We recognize our total dependence on God's grace. Authority, for us, does not rest in human hands or human doctrines, but only in the revelation of God in Jesus Christ, the central fact of human history. For this reason, we assert the Lordship of Jesus Christ. Since we recognize the power of sin, we know we cannot properly be the "rulers" of our own lives. As Christians who believe all authority rests in God, we must affirm the limited nature of all human authorities, including our own. As Thomas Campbell put it, we do not believe in "the imposing of our private opinions upon each other as articles of faith or duty."[2] We confess that Christ is "Lord and Savior." Christ represents God faithfully for humanity, and it is through him that we, as Christians, understand the meaning of our redemption. We affirm God's forgiveness, in Jesus Christ, of our involvement in sin, and understand ourselves to stand before God as creatures being redeemed by grace.

3. **The Ecumenical Principle:** To quote Thomas Campbell, we believe "the church on earth is essentially, intentionally, and constitutionally one."[3] For us, the unity of the church does not arise out of human actions, but exists as the gift of God. Christian union is an essential attribute of the body of Christ. The task of the church is to live its life as a representation of this reality. In our theology, working toward an em-

bodiment of Christian unity is the task of the whole church and all its members. Denominations are partial and relative expressions of a Christian faith that can only be fully known in the unity of the church as a whole. Even our name reflects this belief. As Kenneth Teegarden has put it, "The generic first part, *Christian Church* points to our objective of unity; the distinguishing second part, *Disciples of Christ*, reminds us that we have not arrived."[4] Differences of opinion cannot nullify the Christian unity given by God. Disciples have argued that diversity is one of the great gifts God has given the church. We have been willing to grow in our own theological insights through our encounter with the theological reflections of others.

4. **The Eschatological Principle:** We believe our redemption in Christ points us to a future belonging to God. For this reason, we understand Christians to be shaped by a biblical vision of the kingdom of God. We believe God is acting in our history to save us. We stand as Christians in the midst of a time that is being redeemed. Human lives are being transformed by the love of God in Christ. Our evangelism rests in this truth of the gospel. As Christians, we seek to live "as if" the kingdom of God were an objective reality in our midst. We do not, however, define the church to be synonymous with the kingdom of God. The kingdom of God remains the proper inspiration of the church's activities only so long as the church recognizes it as a divine gift dependent upon the action of God. In other words, human action does not build the kingdom of God. We do believe that Christian action should (1) reflect our confidence that God holds the future, and (2) work toward society's realization of the justice promised within God's kingdom.

5a. **Sacraments: Baptism:** Our congregations accept the immersion of believers, the baptism of infants, and other generally accepted forms of baptism (sprinkling, pouring) to be representative of authentic baptism in the life of the one church of Jesus Christ. We do not believe in the appropriateness of rebaptizing those who have been baptized by these forms.[5] Though the majority of our congregations practice only the immersion of believers, they also accept those who were baptized as infants into church membership. We believe baptism is an active sign of God's grace toward us and a picture of our positive response to that grace. Because we view baptism as a central and formative act of the Christian life, we perform baptism as a public act in the midst of our worship. Baptism represents our adoption into the family of God and, through it, we are empowered by the Holy Spirit to turn our full attention to the ministry of God in all areas of personal and social life.

5b. **Sacraments: Lord's Supper:** We partake of the Lord's supper every Sunday morning in our worship together. We understand it to be

Christ's table, not ours. Therefore, we affirm the "open" table, inviting all those who confess Christ to share in communion with us. The Lord's supper is a central act of our worship. For us, the Lord's supper empha- sizes the divine action of God in the life, death, and resurrection of Jesus Christ. It is God who acts and it is we who receive. The Lord's supper dramatically demonstrates that God is acting in the midst of our gath- ered community of faith. Through the Holy Spirit, God acts in grace to convey the reality of divine forgiveness and acceptance to all human beings. Therefore, the Lord's supper participates in our proclamation that God forgives sinners. We believe the table calls us to respond to the grace of God and to act in ways consistent with our membership in the family of God. Therefore, the table strengthens our moral resolve to address the needs of the world. The Lord's supper not only reconciles us with our neighbors, it calls to our mind our active unity with all Chris- tians everywhere; it reminds us we are in covenant with God and with one another.

6. **Ministry:** We believe "the fundamental ministry" within the church "is that of Jesus Christ, whose servanthood, offered to God in behalf of humanity, defines and gives character to all ministry exercised in his name....by baptism all Christians are inducted into the corporate minis- try of God's people and by sharing in it fulfill their own callings as ser- vants of Christ."[6] Laypersons engage in the single ministry of God's church when they witness to the acts of God, participate in worship, seek justice in society, provide pastoral care, intercede for others, and share in the governance of their particular congregations and denominations. The Disciples tradition of using elders to offer the prayers at the table is a strong witness to the importance of the ministry of the laity in the life of our denomination. It also symbolizes our belief that all ministry arises from the laity.

Ordained ministry within the church expresses both the continuity and universality of the church's nature. We consider our ordained ministers to be part of the "order of ministry" through which Christian tradition has been transmitted from one generation to another through time. We do not consider our ministers to be a class distinctive from laypersons.

When ordained ministers and lay ministers fulfill ministerial roles in the world, they do not represent merely congregations or denominations. Rather, they serve as representatives of the one ministry of Jesus Christ in the world. We believe ministry should be performed with a view to preserve, not just a particular congregation or denomination, but the unity and health of all Christian churches. Ministry must also strive to represent the full range of meaning attached to the liberating and reconciling ministry modeled by Jesus Christ. Therefore, we believe that ministry is not limited merely to the church, but must also engage the world.

7. **Mission:** The mission of the church is to witness to the reign of God in history. We believe the Holy Spirit has been (and remains) at work, in all times and all places, reconciling human beings to one another and to God. Thus the mission of the church belongs to God, not to the church. The church does not exist for itself, but exists in order to witness to the mission of God for the sake of the world. Therefore, the church carries on the important work of evangelism. With the Bible (Acts 14:17), we offer testimony to the fact that God is active in the world even where Christians have yet to set foot. Though we assert our confidence in Christ as supreme revelation of God, we are willing to learn from other religious traditions and cultures whose members testify in their own ways to the activity of God in their midst. We further believe that the gospel must not only be communicated, but must be acted upon. Since God seeks justice and freedom for the whole human family, the church's involvement in mission also includes the struggle for a just social order.

8. **The Church:** We believe the church is the body of Christ; it belongs to God, not to its membership (laity and clergy), and must do what it can to discern the will of God if it hopes to fulfill its mission in the world. The mission of the church is characterized by its attempt to be God's faithful community in the world, through the avenues of worship, witness, and service. Though inspired and driven by a sincere commitment to divine purposes in history, the church can never completely escape its historical existence (its finite existence in history) or its humanity (its sinfulness). The church is at its best when it points beyond itself to the God to whom it belongs. We believe the church, by its very nature, is a changing institution. The life of the Holy Spirit within the church is permanent and dependable as it leads the church to express the gospel in changing times and changing ways. We do believe it is important to express our faith and the church's mission in the context of historical and faithful continuity with the whole Christian church, reaching back in time to the apostolic witness of the New Testament church.

Though our congregations are in full control of their property and resources, and we affirm the basic principle of congregational freedom, we understand all our congregations to be in covenant with one another. Even though we emphasize that congregations make their own decisions related to their particular expressions of ministry, we do not believe any congregation stands alone. Each Christian congregation is ultimately responsible to the entire body of Christ, the church. We believe decisions made locally should always be reached in light of that relationship, and with a conscious recognition that the congregation exists under the Lordship of Christ.

## Notes

[1]For a full treatment of the Restoration Principle in Disciples history and how it relates to this type of faith statement, see Chapter 3.

[2]Thomas Campbell, *Declaration and Address*, and Barton W. Stone and Others, *Last Will and Testament of the Springfield Presbytery*, with a brief Introduction by F. D. Kershner (St. Louis: Mission Messenger, 1978), p. 77.

[3]Campbell, *Declaration and Address*, p. 44.

[4]Kenneth Teegarden, *We Call Ourselves Disciples* (St. Louis: The Bethany Press, 1975), p. 36.

[5]See "Word to the Church on Baptism," published in Clark Williamson, *Baptism: Embodiment of the Gospel* (St. Louis: Christian Board of Publication, published for the Council on Christian Unity, 1989), pp. 46-60.

[6]*Policies and Criteria for the Order of Ministry in the Christian Church (Disciples of Christ)*, published by the Department of Ministry, the Division of Homeland Ministries, p. 1.

# INDEX

The index for this revised and expanded second edition has been prepared by Thomas J. Graca, the author's student assistant at Brite Divinity School, 1996-1997.